Reconstructing Karl Polanyi

Reconstructing Karl Polanyi

Excavation and Critique

Gareth Dale

www.plutobooks.com

First published 2016 by Pluto Press
345 Archway Road, London N6 5AA

www.plutobooks.com

British Library Cataloguing in Publication Data
A catalogue record for this book is available from the British Library

ISBN   978 0 7453 3519 3   Hardback
ISBN   978 0 7453 3518 6   Paperback
ISBN   978 1 7837 1791 0   PDF eBook
ISBN   978 1 7837 1793 4   Kindle eBook
ISBN   978 1 7837 1792 7   EPUB eBook

Typeset by Stanford DTP Services, Northampton, England
Simultaneously printed in the European Union and United States of America

Contents

In memory of Aaron Hess (1976–2015)

Acknowledgments

This book has benefitted from the kindness of many people. I am indebted to my interviewees, Kari Polanyi-Levitt and Anne Chapman; to Adam Fabry who translated the Hungarian materials; and to staff at several archives: the Karl Polanyi Archive (Montréal), the Michael Polanyi Papers (Chicago), the Polanyi Family Papers (Budapest), the SPSL archive (Oxford) and the Karl Polanyi Papers at Columbia University. In references, the archive's name is abbreviated, with numbers denoting container and folder respectively. One of my trips in connection with this research was funded by the Lippman-Miliband Trust, and grants for translating Polanyi's Hungarian writings were provided by the Nuffield Foundation and the Amiel-Melburn Trust. I would like to express my gratitude to all these bodies.

Presentations at universities, think tanks and literature festivals have helped me think through the subjects of this book. They include papers presented at several conferences – 'Intellectuals and the Great War' (University of Ghent), 'Historical Materialism' (London), 'Alternative Futures and Popular Protest' (Manchester Metropolitan University), 'Millennium' (LSE), 'Rethinking Social Democracy' (Swansea) and Karl Polanyi conferences (Istanbul and Montréal) – as well as guest lectures and keynotes at the Bath LitFest, the University of Sydney, the 'Res Publica' think tank (Oslo), the Kossuth Club (Budapest), the 'Market Society and the Alternatives' conference in Moscow (host: ЭКСПЕРТ magazine), the European University Institute (Florence), McGill University, Johns Hopkins University, Copenhagen Business School, Katholieke Universiteit Leuven, the New School of Social Research (funder: Rosa Luxemburg Stiftung), Université catholique de Louvain, the 'Re-Generation Europe' workshop in Berlin (funder: Stiftung Mercator), the 'Hungarian intellectuals in exile' symposium (organisers: IKGS and ELTE, Budapest), Vrie University (Amsterdam), Gyeongsang National University, University of Southampton, the Karl Polanyi Institute for Political Economy (Montréal), Korea University and RMIT University (Melbourne). I'm grateful to the participants at, and the organisers of, all these events.

As distant but vital inspirations, I'd like to thank my university teachers. They included, among others, Isabel Emmett, Tim Ingold, Rosemary Mellor, Paul Kelemen and Norman Geras in the social sciences, and Stephen Parker, Damian Grant and David Timms in the humanities.

While researching in the Michael Polanyi papers at Chicago, I was fortunate to stay with a brilliant and generous comrade and friend, Aaron Hess. As this book neared completion, Aaron met an untimely death, at the wheel of one of humanity's most treacherous inventions. It is dedicated to his memory.

Introduction

What accounts for the recent uptick in interest in the life and work of the Hungarian social theorist Karl Polanyi? At one level, it connects to the search for alternatives to neoliberal capitalism, an economic regime that resembles the 'self-regulating market' analysed in *The Great Transformation*. In that work, Polanyi skilfully untangles the threads of liberal-civilisational breakdown in the mid-twentieth century. Similar symptoms today of social and economic malaise, and ecological Armageddon, are surely another reason why he continues to attract an audience. Let me give an indicative snapshot. As I write, blowback from the 2003 Iraq War continues to fill the newsfeed. That attack, instigated by US neoconservatives in the hope of reversing their nation's hegemonic decline, and backed by social-liberal imperialists à la Tony Blair, served only to destabilise the Middle East, contributing to Saudi Arabia's assault on Yemen, the rise of Da'esh, and a new round of warmaking – this time in Syria and led by Russia, with an assortment of western and Gulf states muscling in too – which has generated the largest movement of refugees since the Second World War. NATO warships are patrolling the Aegean to deter Syrian refugees from entering Europe and to deposit them in Turkey; the European Union's member states are conspiring to trap refugees in crisis-wracked Greece; and in Greece itself, in Hungary and Germany and across Europe, fascist and far-right parties are on the march – scavenging not only on the ubiquitous spores of racism but more generally on the social fall-out from the Eurozone's permanent crisis and ordoliberal politics of 'austerity'. The odds, meanwhile, are shortening on further cycles of economic turmoil, as concerns mount over sluggish global trade and China's reduced growth rate. A whiff of 'fall of Rome' decadence hovers over Washington, as the contenders for presidential candidate of the quaintly named Grand Old Party debate their penis size on national television.

Divination of liberal-civilisational disintegration is hardly the monopoly of radicals. In the mainstream, complacent triumphalism of the Fukuyaman 'End of History' kind has been edged aside by anxious tones and darker predictions. A Brexit victory in the UK's June 2016 referendum may come to be seen as 'the moment when the west started to unravel', warns the *Financial Times*' chief economics commentator Martin Wolf as this book goes to press.[1] 'Is this the end of the West as we know it?', asks Polish-American journalist Anne Applebaum in the *Washington Post*. Her overarching fear is of Washington's imperial decline, but the monsters and black swans she conjures in the near term are the unpredictability and potential isolationism of a President Trump; the possibility that a Présidente Marine Le Pen could take France out of NATO and the EU; Britain's possible exit from the EU followed by copycat referendums in Hungary and beyond; and a social democrat, Jeremy Corbyn, leader of the Labour Party, entering Downing Street. Right now, Applebaum cautions, we may be 'two or three bad elections away from the end of NATO, the end of the European Union and maybe the end of the liberal world order'.[2]

Polanyi predicted that the collapse of liberal civilisation in world wars and the Great Depression would give way to a 'great transformation' away from market society and towards 'democratic socialism', and Polanyians in the current era have often repeated that prediction – or at least its 'away from' clause. And yet the neoliberal apparatus appears invincible. Onward it grinds, Terminator-like in its ability to re-assemble itself after each financial meltdown. When can respite be expected, and from where? Not, we presume, from traditional social-democratic organisations. Their decomposition continues, their accommodation with neoliberalism having become an inviolable tenet. In some cases the adaptation has been reluctant, as social democrats peddle 'austerity with a human face'. In others it proceeded with unseemly eagerness – most memorably in the case of Tony Blair, christened by the *Economist* magazine as 'the strangest Tory ever sold', already in his first year of office.[3] In consequence, established social democratic parties have faced challenges from the left: from the likes of Die Linke, Syriza and Podemos, or from internal upwellings, as in Corbyn's shock victory in Britain's Labour Party leadership election. These left-populist surges appear sporadic but they are not isolated, or without pattern. They have precursors – for example in Latin America, in the Zapatista movement and the presidencies of Hugo Chavez, Rafael Correa and Evo Morales. New blooms continue to appear, most recently in Bernie Sanders' unexpected popularity in the US Democratic primaries.

What do these developments signal for social democracy? Reflecting in 2015 on the rise of Syriza and Podemos, the economist Paul Mason predicted that 'a new form of social democracy is being born – and one moulded to a very different set of priorities to those that guided Labour and its socialist variants in the twentieth century'.[4] In the aftermath of Syriza's neoliberal turn, and its tergiversation in the face of the Greek electorate's όχι (no) to austerity, Mason's prediction appears hasty. More importantly, it is oblivious to the history of social democratic organisations. In their early phases, they – including 'Labour and its socialist variants' – invariably possessed outsider status, offered bracingly radical programmes and 'very different priorities' to the established political vehicles of the lower orders, but sooner or later they clipped their revolutionary wings and assumed a seat at high table. It is a social-democratic dialectic that was pursued by old-style European parties but also by most of the recent left-populist formations. They invariably follow what Robert Brenner refers to as 'a characteristic paradox': their rise has, on the one hand, 'depended upon tumultuous mass working-class struggles, the same struggles which have provided the muscle to win major reforms'. On the other hand, 'to the extent that social democracy has been able to consolidate itself organizationally, its core representatives' (trade union officials, parliamentary politicians, leaderships of the organisations of the oppressed) 'have invariably sought to implement policies reflecting their own distinctive social positions and interests' – specifically, to maintain a secure place for themselves and their organisations, a goal that requires accommodation with institutions of capitalist power. As a result, they tend to relinquish socialism as a goal, and to contain and crush working-class upsurges – the very risings that had brought social democracy into being. The upshot is that such parties systematically undermine the basis for their continuing existence.[5]

If recent decades on the global scale witnessed relatively few sustained mass movements (compare the 2010s to the early 1910s, 1918–23, the mid-1940s or the 1960s–70s) and, correlatively, a tendency to social-dem-ocratic atrophy, there have been some dazzling exceptions. Latin America's left leaders drew their energy from remarkable popular insurgencies: Chavez from the *caracazo* and Morales from the Cochabamba 'water war', the nationwide 'gas war', and other indigenous and *campesino* mobilisations, while Podemos in Spain gained its strength from the *indignados* movement. These sites of struggle have witnessed creative engagements between social movements and leftist parties, including attempts to construct non-state (or para-state) communal power structures. Upon entering government, left parties have endeavoured to make existence more habitable for the poor and have made resounding interventions into global political debate. But they have tended to return to recognisably social-democratic tracks, adapting to the priorities of global and local capital and slotting their cadre into the hierarchical structures of the existing state.

Although in some respects similar to traditional social democratic parties, the new left formations are not facsimiles. They tend to be less closely tied to trade unions, and, arguably, more open to previously non-incorporated constituencies – indigenous communities in Latin America, for example. For some of them, in addition, social democracy's 'third position' features prominently. By this I refer to mutualist (or 'utopian') socialism – the attempt to create islands of socialism within capitalist society, for example in the production of goods and services by workers' cooperatives, or credit unions and other worker-owned institutions of financial intermediation. Although, Owenism notwithstanding, mutualism was relatively peripheral in Britain's socialist tradition, it did receive vocal support among the Fabians and was for decades at the heart of French socialism, and the 'liberal socialism' of Eduard Bernstein and Franz Oppenheimer – in whose book on 'cooperative settlements' the young Polanyi expressed a burning interest.[6] Now more commonly tagged the 'solidarity economy', mutualist socialism overlaps more closely with Proudhonism than do social democracy's more familiar strands of union organisation and party politics.

I mention these phenomena because, were he alive today, Polanyi would surely be searching for a left-populist alternative to mainstream social democracy, or for the means by which to reinvent social democracy or to turn it toward the mutualist 'third position'. He has been described by Tariq Ali, rightly I think, as 'the most gifted of the social democratic theorists', but his social democracy was not of the orthodox kind.[7] His daughter Kari Polanyi-Levitt characterises his socialism as 'neither that of traditional European social democracy, nor that of centralised communist planning' but more of 'the populist, syndicalist, quasi-anarchist, and corporativist' variety.[8]

THE 'HARD' AND THE 'SOFT' POLANYI

This book covers a range of topics but its central thread concerns Polanyi's relationship with socialist politics and ideas. What bands of the social-democratic spectrum do his writings reflect? On this, there is no shortage of paradoxes. Some read *The Great Transformation* as a liberal treatise, others as a Communist Manifesto. Its concept of the 'double movement', referring to the extension of market control over human livelihoods and the 'protective counter-movement' that arises in response, has been described as a 'metaphor for class struggle', and, conversely, as a metaphor for cross-class coalitions, with the counter-movement envisaged as uniting otherwise antagonistic social groups: workers with employers for 'protection' from foreign capital, and peasants with the landed aristocracy in opposition to the importation of cheap foodstuffs.[9]

Polanyi's socialism has been the subject of an ongoing controversy.[10] To simplify a little, it is a debate with two sides. One constructs a 'soft' Karl Polanyi (to borrow Iván Szelényi's term), the other a 'hard' one.[11] The former is positioned in the social-democratic mainstream, for which the only goal that is both realistic and desirable is a regulated form of capitalism. For him, the market must remain the dominant coordinating mechanism in modern economies, albeit complemented by redistributive and socially protective institutions. Interpreted 'softly', Polanyi frames the double movement as a self-equilibrating mechanism: at its least-regulated extreme, the market economy breeds institutional inefficiencies, social anomie and ethical debility, but a natural balance arises in the form of social protectionism. Taking the idea of balance to the limit, Sylvia Walby plugs Polanyi's critique of market self-regulation into a cybernetic model of social self-regulation: the double movement commences with a harmful tendency to commercialism which then, by tickling 'civil society' into launching a healthy response, delivers 'a better balance of economy and society', with 'society restored to equilibrium' thanks to a beneficent and effective 'negative feedback loop'.[12]

In the 'soft' interpretation, then, Polanyi's counter-movement is explained in a distinctive way. In response to depredatory tendencies of *laissez-faire* capitalism, in particular the instability of the business cycle and mass unemployment, social forces struggled to socialise and regulate the conditions of investment. Their success led to a recognition that the self-regulating market needs to be supplemented with (not supplanted by) extra-market institutional arrangements, including fiscal policy and social security systems, which serve simultaneously to stabilise capitalism and to safeguard its vitality. For some, the emphasis is on what the neo-Polanyian sociologists Andrew Schrank and Josh Whitford describe as 'the pendular swing at the heart of Polanyi's *Great Transformation*.' The ebb and flow of laissez-faire and privatisation, on one hand, and social protection, on the other, they argue, represents 'the principal source of dynamism in capitalist society' – it 'brings to life' the capitalist system.[13] Others emphasise the tendency for free-market capitalism to submit to its social democratic nemesis. Polanyi's double movement, in this reading, reached its apotheosis in the postwar decades, during which Keynesian and Fordist political-economic regimes enabled politics to restrain the excesses of the market, ensuring that the state was relegitimated as the regulator of the economy and guarantor of a reasonable degree of social equality. Under the Bretton Woods regime, also known as 'embedded liberalism', states were able to play a muscular role in mediating between the national and international economy. Through regulation, including legislation and collective bargaining over the terms and remuneration of labour, the market economy was to a substantial extent 're-embedded'. With capital obliged to behave within a framework in which the state and trade unions also had a significant say, social progress ensued. Polanyi should therefore be read, in Jürgen Habermas's words, as the herald of 'the Bretton Woods system, which set up the framework for the more or less successful social welfare state policy' that most OECD countries followed in the embedded-liberal age.[14] Arguably, Germany was in the vanguard. Its 'social market economy' has been singled out by the Polanyian theorist (and leading light of 'Blue Labour') Lord Glasman, as 'close to the Polanyian ideal'.[15]

Polanyi's 'hard' alter ego is quite a different creature. A red-blooded socialist for whom the market could not remain and should never be the dominant mechanism of economic coordination, he advocated a mixed economy governed by redistributive mechanisms. According to his wife,

Ilona Duczynska, he had always avoided limiting himself 'to a special field like "reform of capitalism", [and] in his heart of hearts he thought jolly little even of the welfare state proper (there was a marked distaste for Sweden, for instance) on the grounds that no new society was emerging'.[16] The double movement, Polanyi-Levitt, maintains, was not intended to be understood as 'an in-built repair operation', an automatic self-correcting mechanism that simply moderates the excesses of market capitalism. It contains, instead, profoundly critical implications, theorising as it does the 'existential contradiction between the requirements of a capitalist market economy for unlimited expansion and the requirements of people to live in mutually supportive relations in society'. Her father was and remained a socialist, and refused to believe that capitalism could be viable in the long term, due to its disembedding tendencies.[17] The 'disembedding' thesis of the hard Polanyi contains a radical, even Marxian, tale: of the market economy coming to dominate 'society', bringing forth a sorcerer's-apprentice world of untrammelled market forces which, although human creations, lie beyond conscious human control. The case that Polanyi argued, in Timothy David Clark's paraphrase, is 'for the radical supersession of capitalism itself'.[18]

Hannes Lacher, similarly, denies that social policy, or Keynesian or Fordist modifications to the market economy, represent a Polanyian 're-embedding' of economy in society. Re-embedding signifies nothing less than the complete subjugation of economic life to democratic control and the full decommodification of land, labour and money. Welfare systems may create non-commodified zones of society but under capitalist conditions they are necessary to the constitution of labour-power as a commodity.[19] Neither labour market regulation nor restrictions on capital mobility in the postwar era, Lacher argues, represented even the partial fulfilment of Polanyi's vision of an embedded economy, and the welfare state itself 'must be seen as the negation of all that Polanyi hoped and wrote for'.[20] For, state regulation and protectionism form an integral part of the pathogenesis of market society. Welfare institutions are not a *break from* but a *support structure for* an economic system based upon commodified labour power, with social policy acting to incorporate the working classes into the wage-labour relation and the state. Protectionism, Jan Drahokoupil concurs, figures in *Great Transformation* as 'part of the market pathology': it impairs the market's self-regulation and dislocates economic life.[21]

Of the two interpretations, the 'soft' Polanyi enjoys a greater following but less textual support. Much evidence casts doubt on the supposition that Polanyi believed the market should prevail as the dominant mechanism of economic integration, and there emphatically is no 'pendular swing' at the heart of Polanyi's *Great Transformation*. Polanyi failed to anticipate that state intervention could contribute to the long-term stabilisation of market society; he was not a champion of 'embedded liberalism' or, as this book shows, of Keynesian economics, but was committed to the replacement of capitalism by a socialist order. *Pace* Habermas, he was a trenchant critic of the Bretton Woods system and, *pace* Glasman, he did not regard Germany's social market economy as exemplary. (We may recall that the term social market economy, and to a considerable degree its reality too, was of ordoliberal manufacture.[22]) Indeed, Polanyi paid no particular heed to postwar Germany – in marked contrast to the Soviet Union, which he genuinely did see as admirable and pioneering in certain respects.

This does not mean that the 'hard' interpretation faces no difficulties. Although Polanyi's 'soft' interpreters may be misguided in postulating a pendular swing between marketisation and protectionism, Polanyi does tend to dichotomise these two moments and to neglect the ways in which protectionist means may be deployed to capitalist ends. For all the radicalism of his views, particularly as they appear in the present age, his beliefs that the inequity and iniquities of modern society can largely be overcome through institutional reform, that islands of socialism – not merely as consciousness, spirit and organisations but as actual established institutions – can be securely planted within capitalist society, and that social democratic governments (such as Attlee's) are desirous and capable of implementing a socialist transformation, were all of a piece with the social democratic credo, as was Polanyi's belief that 'actually existing democracy' in the political sphere provided the platform on which a socialist democracy could be constructed.

WHYS AND WHEREFORES OF PROTECTION

Polanyi is best known as a theorist of the market economy. It is conventional to divide market theories into two types. One, neoclassical economics, conceives of the market system as self-sustaining and self-regulating, of market actors as rational agents, and supply and demand as independent, abstract forces. The other, gathering sociologists, anthropologists and heterodox economists, views markets as socially constructed institutions and 'supply' and 'demand' as fields of social struggle. In essence, Polanyi belongs in the latter camp. He is known for his theorisation of the part played by ideas and political forces in constituting the market system and he regarded the idea of a self-regulating market system as absurd. However, he also retained elements of the neoclassical position that he had adopted when young.[23] The resulting tension in his thought found expression in several ways. One was his assumption that the neoclassical method is applicable to market societies but not to non-market societies. A second was his thesis that the aspiration to construct the self-regulating market was utopian and therefore doomed to fail. In this belief, he retains the neoclassical conception of the self-regulating market, but refigured as utopia, or ideology: a zone beyond the reach of policy. The third, relatedly, was his belief – shared with Austrians such as Ludwig von Mises and with many neoclassical economists – that protectionism impairs the functioning of markets, reinforcing monopolies, rendering prices (including wages) inflexible and catalysing escalating rounds of government intervention. Thus, Polanyi's explanation of the social catastrophes that accompanied the Industrial Revolution was that 'protective action conflicted fatally with the self-regulation of the [market] system', and his explanation of the disintegration of liberal civilisation in the early twentieth century was that the protective measures that societies adopted in order not to be 'annihilated by the action of the self-regulating market' mortally impaired the functioning of the economic system.[24] The relationship between the market economy and protectionism, he argued, sharpened into a clash in the twentieth century due to the rise of political democracy. He was alert to the thesis, expounded for example by Walter Lippmann, that demands for universal suffrage were part of the protectionist movement, but he developed it in a very distinctive way, as this book will show.[25]

What was Polanyi's general approach to 'protection'? In *The Great Transformation* it is broadly left-Romantic. Traditional economic organisation, medieval towns, rural culture, nature and human beings, are all protected from the market system with its commodifying imperative. Protection is invoked, frequently, as applying to 'society' and 'nature'; sometimes it is aligned with paternalistic anti-industrialism; and in one or two places capitalist corporations are included as institutions that require protection from the market. As regards agency, *The Great Transformation* portrays the protective movement as, normally, initiated by political elites and the state (protecting citizens from market externalities and foreign competition), flanked by labour-movement organisations, churches and landlords. Polanyi's analysis of protection is historically and spatially differentiated. He posits protective measures as having been essential to society and to the natural environment in the nineteenth century, but also to the functioning of the market system – examples include 'tariffs, factory laws, and an active colonial policy'. From the 1880s, these were 'prerequisites of a stable external currency', and only when they were in place could 'the methods of market economy be safely introduced'. Whereas in Europe, states were able to 'protect themselves against the backwash of international free trade', the 'politically unorganized colonial peoples could not'. As a result, peoples in the 'exotic and semicolonial regions' were subjected to 'unspeakable suffering', and their anti-imperialist revolts should be seen as the attempt 'to achieve the political status necessary to shelter themselves from the social dislocations caused by European trade policies'.[26]

Who, one might ask, do protectionist policies protect? The line between protection and protection racket is not always easy to discern. By way of illustration, consider one 'exotic region': the British-occupied Gold Coast (now Ghana). Its major export crop was cocoa, for which colonial administrators, during the Second World War and under the postwar Attlee government, operated a state-controlled marketing scheme. They informed the growers that the scheme, with its administered price for cocoa, was designed to protect them from market volatility. Polanyi regarded interventionist measures such as this as signs of a global shift away from 'market society'. Yet the pressure to introduce this one had come from the European cocoa corporations, motivated by an interest in predicable profit-making, and from His Majesty's Government, motivated by interests in funding the war effort and in warding off the social protest (with its inevitable anti-colonial sting) that price fluctuations could spark. The Colonial Office's justification of the scheme carried an almost Polanyian ring. In the absence of state intervention, it warned, 'the working of the price system may ... operate at the cost of dangerous social strains'.[27] But who creamed the best of the deal? Without question, the corporations and the UK Treasury, for prices were set at the lowest levels that could be achieved without serious risk of social unrest. Following their success on the Gold Coast, marketing boards mushroomed across the post-colonial world, supported by Keynesian and developmental-étatiste economists and by governments of all colours. While the boards' actions were invariably justified in terms of price stabilisation and the avoidance of social strain, the net material effect was to depress agricultural incomes, redistributing resources from peasants to corporations and the state. By setting prices below average world levels they imposed what was in effect a tax on agricultural communities, in the interests of industrial capital accumulation.[28]

The moral of the tale is not only that protectionist policies serve particular interests (and never 'society' in the abstract) but also that partial decommodification can operate, sometimes very effectively, in the interests of capital accumulation – and thereby reinforce commodifying logics over the long run. An example discussed in Chapter 5 of this book is central banking and fiat money, institutions that in Polanyi's view developed in order to protect 'the community as a whole' from the deflationary pressures associated with commodity money but which, according to critics, serve an altogether different purpose.[29] Another example is the Soviet system (discussed in Chapter 4). Although it appeared as an island of decommodification in a world of encroaching capitalism, its material base was a process of proletarianisation that accelerated the commodification of labour in particular and the 'economisation' of society in general.[30]

RECONSTRUCTING POLANYI

Why has Karl Polanyi been subject to divergent interpretations? Aside from the obvious (that interpretive battles inevitably flare over the work of significant figures; that his work spanned decades, during which his outlook evolved), three factors present themselves. One is that the critical literature focuses upon a few English-language publications written in the 1940s and 1950s, with little awareness of Polanyi's *oeuvre* in the round, with its innumerable texts penned in several languages between 1907 and 1964. Secondly, significant scope exists for misinterpretation, as a result of a lack of familiarity with the contours and context of Polanyi's thought, not least the Central European political and intellectual environment in which his outlook was anchored and the interwar debates that inspired the writing of *The Great Transformation*. Thirdly, Polanyi was not an especially systematic thinker. He possessed a penchant – boldly innovative to his admirers, eclectic to his detractors – for splicing together ideas from contrasting intellectual traditions. Adding mud to the waters was his tendency, as one of his followers has put it, 'to be inconsistent in his definition of key concepts' and to 'contradict himself in the same work'. (His writing, she adds – rather harshly – 'is abstract, often to the point of incoherence and incomprehensibility'.[31]) There is some semantic slippage, for example, in Polanyi's usage of the pivotal concepts 'market economy' and 'market society'. He refers to the 'first phase of Industrial Civilisation' in which 'a separate and distinct "economic sphere" in society' existed, 'controlled by a system of markets', but he elsewhere construes market society as a chimera, an 'inherent impossibility', the market economy as 'more of an ideology than an actual fact', and the institutional separation of spheres as an analytical construct that in practice 'did never quite hold'.[32]

On all three points, scope exists for Polanyi to be 'reconstructed,' for his ideas to be re-presented with attention to their historical and discursive context and drawing on a much broader range of sources. I have begun these tasks in other publications and intend to complete them in this book. Chapter 1 surveys Polanyi's reflections on social-scientific method, including his fascination with positivist social science, his quest for an ethically oriented sociology, and his attraction to 'liberal,' 'guild' and 'Christian' strands of socialist thought. Chapter 2 analyses Polanyi's engagement with a fourth socialist strand: Marxism. It probes some shortcomings in his critique, identifies two sub-species of Marxian thought to which he was drawn, Austro-Marxism and Eduard Bernstein's 'revisionism', and finds in them a form of determinism: a conviction in democratic-socialist progress.

Democracy itself is the subject of Chapter 3, together with the related (and at present hotly debated[33]) question of its relationship with the capitalist economy. Polanyi was an ardent advocate of democracy – in the form that he describes as 'the transformation of souls' rather than 'the artificial kneading of the electorate'[34] – and was concerned that its advance, at one time facilitated by capitalism, was entering conflict with it. He was of course far from alone in advocating the thesis that capitalism and democracy exist in irreconcilable tension, and Chapter 3 assesses his writings on the topic in juxtaposition with those of a galaxy of other thinkers. 'Capitalism', in Polanyi's rendition of the argument, 'cannot hold out against democracy and the advance towards socialism', and yet the victory of socialism, or at least the triumph of 'society' over 'economy', could conceivably be implemented by non-democratic means.[35] We are witnessing, he declared in 1943, 'a development under which the economic system ceases to lay down the law to society and the primacy of society over that system is secured', a process that could be implemented under a wide assortment of political regimes, including the 'democratic and aristocratic, constitutionalist and authoritarian'.[36] In his day, the apparent alternative to capitalism was Soviet Russia, a state which in his view was socialist and tendentially democratic. Polanyi's understanding of the paradoxes of the Soviet system forms the subject of Chapter 4.

Polanyi's thesis on the incompatibility of democracy and market economy is a leitmotif of *The Great Transformation*, but that book roams widely, taking in its era's fundamental political-economic controversies – concerning socialism, capitalism, corporatism, planning, mass society and totalitarianism. In Chapter 5 I reconstruct and critically parse Polanyi's engagement with these debates. *The Great Transformation* contains, if *sotto voce*, Polanyi's case for a democratic socialist society, organised within the nation state. But what sort of world order could accommodate that arrangement? This is the subject of Chapter 6. It introduces Polanyi's case for a regionalised world order, and remarks upon the conundrum that he showed negligible interest in the great regional adventure of the age: European integration. Polanyi's European lacuna, the same chapter details, has been more than compensated for by his followers. Yet here we encounter another puzzle: among them, despite kindred theoretical foundations, strikingly discordant conclusions are reached. From Europe the focus then shifts to the United States. Chapter 7 tackles Polanyi's response to America's totalitarian turn, examines commonalities between Talcott Parsons' explanation of the red scare and Polanyi's diagnosis of 'social strains' and assays the nature and extent of his Aesopian adaptations to McCarthyism.

To an eye-catching degree, the transformation of the social sciences in 1950s America was driven by Polanyi's colleagues at Columbia University. Their achievements included the construction of the pluralist paradigm in political science, which I interrogate in Chapter 7, and the seminal work of radical archaeologists and anthropologists, which, godfathered in part by Polanyi, forms the subject of Chapter 8. The 1950s also saw the first forays by the economist Douglass North, whose later (1977) paper on 'The Challenge of Karl Polanyi' inaugurated a new research programme for economic history: the New Institutional Economic History (NIEH).[37] The NIEH aimed to supplant the 'old institutionalism' of Polanyi and his ilk by showing institutions to be amenable to analysis by the (suitably tweaked) tools of neoclassical theory, and also to overcome the impasse that had been reached in the debate between 'primitivists' and 'modernists' on the character of ancient economies. The NIEH is widely thought to have succeeded in the first aim, but how convincing is the result? And what of the second aim? Chapter 9, co-authored with Matthijs Krul, analyses these questions, with ancient Greece selected as a case study. These final chapters explore Polanyi's research on the economic life of antiquity, which stands as arguably his most impressive achievement.

1

Reconstructing Sociology

Karl Polanyi belonged to an extraordinary generation.[1] The city of his childhood, Budapest, was a magnet for thousands of 'migrant workers, professionals, and intellectuals from all quarters of the kingdom of Hungary and beyond' in the words of historian Tibor Frank. It was a crucible in which myriad social norms, values and behaviours could interact, their fusions and frictions detonating 'an unparalleled outburst of creativity, a veritable explosion of productive energies'.[2] Intellectually, the atmosphere was conducive to the experimental spirit – and this was especially pronounced among Jewish *Bildungsbürger*. In the late nine-teenth-century Habsburg Empire the Jewish bourgeoisie was thriving. It had benefited from civic emancipation, and federative arrangements afforded some degree of protection. Yet anti-semitic discrimination and prejudice was growing, as Habsburg society buckled under the pressure of the 'social' and 'national' questions.

Austro-Hungarian Jews found themselves ironically situated, Ernest Gellner has remarked. The Habsburg Empire was an authoritarian dynasty, steeped in the 'dogmatic ideology of the Counter-Reformation', and yet, 'under the stimulus of ethnic, chauvinistic centrifugal agitation' it found its 'most eager defenders amongst individualist liberals, recruited in considerable part from an erstwhile pariah group and standing *outside* the faith with which the state was once so deeply identified'.[3] On the whole, they identified with Whiggish *Gesellschaft* rather than Romantic *Gemeinschaft,* or, in Gellner's terms, with the individualistic-universalistic horn of the 'Habsburg Dilemma' – a conception of knowledge as the work of solitary, Crusoe-like individuals, busily constructing the world out of its accumulations of quotidian atoms – rather than with the contrasting claus-trophilic vision: of human thought construed as a communally motivated quest for 'meaning' within a fixed framework that exalts the particular in its decreed 'organic' place within the enveloping totality.[4]

In its standard depiction, the politics of the Habsburg Dilemma pitted liberals, on the side of Enlightenment universalism, against conservative ethno-nationalism. But one should not forget the appeal that romanticism, with its exaltation of life, love and spontaneity, could exert upon left-liberal radicals. For all the elegance of Gellner's ideal types, the reality was unkempt. By way of illustration, consider the case of Endre Ady, the brilliant poet of the Budapest counterculture, a writer of love lyrics and a 'romantic patriot'. One might not expect a saintly Bohemian bard to pen paeans to the sciences, and yet he did exactly that. He eulogised sociology as 'the most important and most modern science'. A new 'humane and luminous world,' he crooned, 'is driven ever higher by the eternal law of causality: by the only truth, that of natural science'.[5]

If Ady was Polanyi's muse, his mentor was Oscar Jaszi.[6] Founder and chair of the Sociological Society, Jaszi's journal, *The Twentieth Century*, helped to spark an intellectual awakening following its foundation in 1900, was read by an influential section of Hungary's academic and commercial elites, and was the outlet for Polanyi's first published articles. Following the departure of its conservative wing after 1905, the Sociological Society engaged closely with the labour movement, and hosted discussions on the merits, and applicability to Hungarian conditions, of Fabian socialism, syndicalism, anarchism, Austro-Marxism and Millerandism.[7] Its purpose was to wage battle for modernity and against clerical obscurantism and traditionalism; its weapons were natural science and positivist social science. Recalling the period some years later, Jaszi describes his mindset in these terms: 'We believed in the invincible strength of truth; in the weakness of the debauched "ancien regime"; and above all, in the importance of spreading our noble, simple, and clear principles among our fellow men.' He and his fellows were 'rationalist knights' waging 'proud, solitary' warfare against the fortresses of reaction.[8] In Jaszi's memoirs we find the familiar Enlightenment motifs of progress, truth, rationality and utilitarianism. Yet the intellectual discipline that appeared to bear the most invigorating promise was not philosophy or political economy but sociology.

As in Europe more widely, fin-de-siècle Hungary experienced a vogue for sociology, the dominant positivist incarnation of which defined society in organicist and functionalist terms as a system determined by specific laws that functioned to promote cohesion and differentiation through successive evolutionary stages. To Ady, Jaszi and company, sociology appeared the inheritor of Enlightenment philosophy, and in a sense it was. Unusually strong bonds of intellectual comradeship and personal amity linked, for example, the *philosophes* of progress Condorcet and Turgot with the founding fathers of sociology, Henri de Saint-Simon and Auguste Comte. All four were devotees of the idea of progress; they exalted scientists and philosophers as its vanguard caste. Saint-Simon's achievement was to fuse the idea of progress with those of industrial society and socialism. Through the inauguration of the machine age, coupled with a 'socialism' characterised by technocratic administration and the rationalist eradication of avarice from the human soul, Progress would achieve its telos.[9] Saint-Simon's disciple, Comte, elaborated the positivist current in philosophical and sociological terms, and before long it had gained a critical, even revolutionary, aura as a movement that pitted the belief in science and reason against absolutism and organised religion. Comte's theories represented the sociological appropriation of the Enlightenment notion that human behaviour is rationally comprehensible and predictable according to natural laws, and, as for the Enlightenment reformers, the practical message of the new sociological positivism was that social conditions could and should be re-engineered such that human beings would at last be free to act according to Reason. The radical liberals around Jaszi greeted positivism in precisely these terms: it provided unassailably rational support to the cause of progress.

For some years, around the 1900s, the idol of the Budapest counter-culture was Herbert Spencer. The enthusiasm of radicals for this Victorian sociologist may seem surprising. A utilitarian, and supporter of *laissez-faire* economics, Spencer distrusted parliamentary government due to its propensity to enact redistributive social policy. Several decades later, Polanyi was to pass withering judgment on Spencer: he had enunciated 'the crudest views on economics and economic policy ever uttered by a scholar',[10] preached 'dehumanization' and 'amoral economysticism' and was an influential source of that most fateful error of modern thought: the axiom that the workings of economic systems should be understood as the consequence of material motives.[11] In 'swallowing Bentham', Spencer had become a 'swollen monster', and worse was to follow: his methodological individualism gained a new and even more fanatical lease of life thanks to the equally swollen and monstrous Friedrich von Hayek.[12] Nonetheless, Spencer offered Hungary's radicals a reassurance that history was on their side: that, just as life evolves to higher states of sophistication, human society progresses from crude 'militant' formations toward bourgeois individualism and excellence.

Hungary's educational establishment refused to grant positivism any space whatsoever. In its insistence that human institutions, including religious faith itself, should not be granted uncritical loyalty but should accord with the principles of Reason, its logic was patently subversive. Officials at the University of Budapest were alarmed by the thesis of Polanyi's university teacher, Gyula Pikler, that no law or social institution possessed absolute validity. As human beings become aware of new needs, Pikler argued, new institutions have to be created to satisfy them. To conservatives, this smelled of relativism. Alarmed, they launched a campaign of vilification. Conservative students attacked Pikler's lectures for their 'atheism' and 'cosmopolitanism'. A countermovement in defence of Pikler was organised, which in 1907 issued into the Galilei Circle – of which Polanyi was the founder. At one of its inaugural meetings he delivered a lecture on the epistemology of another positivist, but one of a distinctly non-Spencerian kind: Ernst Mach.

THE EMANCIPATORY PROMISE OF EMPIRIO-CRITICISM

For Budapest's liberal radicals, the uncomfortable aspect of Spencerian thought was its evolutionary determinism. It seemed to devalue human agency, and sat uncomfortably with their commitment to moral regeneration. In a sense, the tension between determinism and ethical idealism expresses the old antinomy of Enlightenment philosophy: on one hand, human consciousness is understood as freely self-determining, and progress occurs through the triumph of reason over ignorance, with a privileged role accorded to ideas and education; on the other, consciousness is a reflection of external, objective realities. The problem was felt keenly by Polanyi and his peers, due to the intense promise with which rationalist scientism, romantic aestheticism and socialist militancy were simultaneously invested – in the same historical conjuncture and often by the same individuals. It was addressed head on by Polanyi's friend Georg Lukacs in his early writings, and, later, by Michael Polanyi in his philosophy of 'personal knowledge'. As for Karl, he wrestled long and hard with the tension between the ethic of 'individual responsibility' and recognition of what he called the 'reality of society'. Throughout his life, but especially in the 1910s and 1920s, his philosophical and political reflections revolved around puzzles concerning the role of the individual in 'complex society', positivism and its discontents, and how to navigate between the shoals of determinism and voluntarism. His initial reaction against the 'objective' positivism of Spencer (and, in his idiosyncratic interpretation, Karl Marx) was manifested in an enthusiasm for a different species of positivism, that of Ernst Mach.

It is difficult to exaggerate Mach's importance for the intellectual life of early twentieth-century Central Europe. He inspired natural scientists (Einstein), novelists (Hofmannsthal, Musil), anthropologists (Malinowski, Lowie), legal theorists (Kelsen), social scientists (Franz Oppenheimer) and philosophers (Wittgenstein, William James, Bertrand Russell). The Vienna Circle was known as the 'Ernst Mach Society'. Mach was admired on the political right – he was, for example, Hayek's first intellectual enthusiasm – but, being an atheist and a supporter of educational and social reforms, not to mention a friend of the prominent social democrat Viktor Adler and his son Friedrich, his popularity was greater on the left. Polanyi attended Mach's seminars at the Vienna Law School, lectured frequently on Mach during the years before the outbreak of the First World War, and translated and introduced the first three chapters of Mach's *Die Analyse der Empfindungen*. He considered Mach the most important thinker of the age, adding, with customary hyperbole, that 'every positive idea in Europe today is related to his work'.[13]

Mach's importance lay in challenging the Newtonian model of a mechanistic universe, and the Newtonian concept of 'absolute space'. Scientific concepts such as 'ether', 'molecules' and 'atoms', he held, are fictions. They may facilitate the recording of observations but they belong to the realm of metaphysics. Atoms cannot be observed but are, 'like all substances, aspects of thought' – and whenever Mach heard mention of them by 'believers' in atoms he would quip 'Have you seen one?'[14] Physical objects, he maintained, do not exist as things in themselves but as perceptual phenomena or sensory stimuli; they are pure data, whose existence is to be considered anterior to any arbitrary distinction between mental and physical categories of phenomena. Thus, in Mach's 'physiological psychology', there is no epistemic difference between the statements 'this wooden support is firm' and 'Mr. A is excited'.[15] An empiricist, Mach argued that knowledge, if it is to have truth content, must derive from the positive affirmation of hypotheses through scientific procedures that draw upon sensory data. According to his principle of 'mental economy', science is the most convenient summary of experimental observations, an economical arrangement of 'connections', an adaptation of thoughts to facts.[16] An anti-realist, he denied that inquiry into the reality of the universe – its existence independent of our observations – possessed any legitimate meaning. So-called natural laws are nothing but creations of the human mind constructed for the purpose of apprehending complex sensory data.

If set against Polanyi's later outlook, his youthful enthusiasm for Mach seems peculiar, for several reasons. First, Mach opposed religion and metaphysics, both of which Polanyi was to embrace. Religion, Polanyi came to believe, 'has to shoulder the gigantic tasks' of the age, 'for which, if at all, there can be a solution only with its help'.[17] He also made his peace with metaphysics, maintaining that human consciousness itself is metaphysical in its very structure, in reflection of our 'recognition of the inevitability of the alternatives confronting us in society'.[18] Secondly, Mach's scepticist phenomenalism evinced 'a dangerous kinship with solipsism',[19] and was, as such, conducive to political quietism. Thirdly, Mach exemplified the individualistic-universalistic horn of the 'Habsburg Dilemma'. He stimulated the development of methodological individualism; his epistemology presupposed an atomistic ontology, and a sociology that conceives of people as passive sensors of given facts. His insistence that statements about values, unlike those about facts, cannot be verified – that the cognitive claims of metaphysics, morality, aesthetics and politics amount to nothing – expressed what Alisdair Macintyre has termed the 'emotivist' approach to ethics: the belief that moral statements express only the subjective attitudes of their speaker.[20] And however one may characterise Polanyi's moral philosophy, it was anything but emotivist.

Why, then, did Mach electrify Budapest's radicals, and Polanyi in particular? One reason is that he was a prominent physicist, to which some cachet surely attached. The industrialisation of science in the late nineteenth century had made it a pervasive force in everyday life, and at the century's close the enthusiasm for physics approached fever pitch, not least in Austria-Hungary. More importantly, this was the age of subjectivism. In their different ways, its stand-out thinkers – Freud, Weber, Croce, Lukacs and Wittgenstein, as well as Bergson, Dilthey, Gramsci, Mannheim, Mosca and Spengler – were all striving to comprehend the newly recognised disparity between external reality and the internal subjective appreciation of it. Their generation had come to believe that Enlightenment conceptions of a rationally ordered external reality were inadequate, that human consciousness was the critical mediator between individuals and society, and that the nature of reality did not appear in a coherent form but had to be approached through the deployment of conventional fictions. All this contributed to a revival of idealist thinking, albeit one that contradicted traditional clerical dogma – the eternal character of spiritual values, and so on.

In a series of articles written in his twenties, Polanyi expatiated on Machian philosophy. He was much taken with Mach's thoughts on 'function', with his insistence upon the interdependence of subject and object (that the scientist's vantage point influences her findings), and with his critique of metaphysics. By liberating science from the illusions of metaphysics, Mach had cleared the way for rational human intervention in history. In essence, the appeal to Polanyi of Mach's empirio-criticism was that it rejected the prevailing deterministic materialism but not the scientific attitude that, Polanyi believed, remained an indispensable tool with which to simultaneously counter traditional conservatism and justify rational social engineering. In Mach he found assistance in formulating a metaphysics-free critique of the rigid application of scientific determinism to social processes, and also, as Chris Hann has put it, in developing that 'distinctive concept of individual responsibility which was to remain central to his value system'.[21]

THE SATANIC SCIENCE OF SOCIOLOGY

In 1912, according to an autobiographical digest prepared by Polanyi some decades later, he 'discarded Naturalism and started on a line of dynamic idealism'. This brought him to reject 'the claims of sociology, science and statistics to determine what was right or wrong in politics' and to embrace instead the principle of 'individual action as against the current theory of sociological determinism'.[22] Mach's influence on Polanyi's philosophy declined, while that of others grew, notably the Catholic publicist G. K.

Chesterton and the Christian anarchist Leo Tolstoy. The appeal of Tolstoy to Budapest radicals was succinctly summarised by Lukacs: his philosophy charted a path out of a world stamped by utilitarian individualism, with its 'anarchy, despair and godlessness'.[23] Tolstoy advocated an ecumenical engagement with religious texts, above all the Sermon on the Mount; he preached pacifism, love and moral regeneration, and railed against technological civilisation and the private property system. Pacifism and the denigration of private property apart, Polanyi shared these dispositions.

Initially, Polanyi's criticism of positivism, naturalism and determinism was based on 'pragmatic, ethical, … psychological and philosophical grounds',[24] but in 1918–19 a rapid shift occurred. His thought took a mystical and religious turn. The war, he believed, had raised a mirror to humankind, revealing its moral disintegration. To describe and explain what he could see in that mirror was to become his project over the next two decades.

Polanyi's contribution to meeting the challenge to civilisation posed by the war proceeded along two tracks. The first was intellectual: to bring ethics back into contemporary social science, and to challenge the widespread assumption that ethics and politics are determined by the 'objective', external environment. The second was spiritual and political: to inspire a renaissance of Christianity and socialism by conjoining the two movements. Although Polanyi was never an affiliated or observant practitioner, what he prized in religion in general and Christianity in particular is that it creates a framework that sanctions the emergence of a communal order based on the self-consciousness of individuals. Viewed in historical perspective this was a 'revolutionary mission', and in New Testament revelation in particular it had acquired a 'socialist flavour'.[25]

Spurred by his conversion to Christianity, Polanyi's understanding of sociology underwent a further, rapid shift. In speeches and a series of articles he railed against 'objectivist' sociology. Against the prevailing determinism, he countered that individuals must adjust the laws of economics and history and not be adjusted to them, that the wellspring of action is the inner life and the impetus for social change comes from the individual's moral stance. Society rises to higher 'spiritual levels,' he intoned, 'not in accordance with material interests but in disregard of them; and human faith and self-sacrifice bear us aloft not by the downward-bearing gravitational force of material interests but by force of the hallowed laws of the spirit which defy them!'[26] It was Marxism in particular that drew Polanyi's ire, principally for its postulation of the determination of 'being' by 'consciousness', but he presents its shortcomings as symptoms of a wider flaw within social-scientific thought, from Ricardo and Malthus through Comte (the 'Pope of a satanic science he called sociology'[27]) and Spencer up to the present. That flaw – and here we find a continuity with his previous Machian outlook – consisted in the attempt to make general-isations about society that rely upon hypostasised categories such as class interests, *raison d'état* and social forces. This was the approach of the 'old sociology' – Comte's 'social physics', Spencer's social biology and Marx's historical materialism. Common to them all is the attempt to derive the meaning of life from science, with the substitution of statistical tables for the voice of conscience, and the assumption that society is law-governed, with Liberty itself nothing but the rationalised submission of the individual to pseudo-natural laws.[28]

In this volatile phase in his formation, Polanyi's distaste for the intrusion of scientific thinking into policymaking and sociological theory knew no bounds. 'Social kabbalistics' is the term with which he described sociology, for it represents 'little more than a forced application of scientific knowledge upon the social existence of the people'. Today, he added, 'we are no closer to being able to make predictions in history than we were ten thousand years ago'.[29] The prophecies 'of the oracles and of astrology, of the kabbala and chiromancy' were 'modest enterprises by comparison with the gigantic obscurantism of this science of the human future'. But sociology's scientism, its ordurous naturalism, was not merely risible. It was dangerous. The idea that human behaviour is determined by sociological laws denies our true freedom and licenses a form of delusion – and in this could be found the taproot of the wars, revolutions and struggles that his generation was suffering.[30]

This was not, however, grounds for the outright defenestration of sociology. In these same years, 1919–21, Polanyi had come to identify as a Christian socialist, defining his worldview as based on 'the ultimate validity of the law of Christian ethics'.[31] Correlatively, he believed 'that there was no necessary connection between socialism and the philosophy usually associated with it ... and that its political possibility rested not on scientific but on religious grounds', and added that 'true socialism' should be 'established firmly on a religious basis'.[32] As for sociology, it had lost its way but could be founded anew, shorn of all positivist pretension. It should be reborn as an ethically directed discipline, 'identical ... with Christian Socialism'. Its purpose should not be to derive the meaning of life from science but to discover the causes of social phenomena *within individuals*. It should be premised on an understanding that beliefs translate into action, altering – and, indeed, bringing into being – external social reality, in the process rendering the distinction between being and consciousness irrelevant. In discovering the causes of social phenomena within ourselves, society would cease to possess its beguilingly but misleadingly 'objective', 'external' appearance. The decisive question for the new sociology would not be how we *do* behave but how we *should* behave. What made this project sociology rather than ethics is that its avowed purpose was the socialisation of ethics, the aim being to expand the awareness of moral agents of the repercussions of their behaviour upon society as a whole. The ultimate aim of the new discipline would be to enhance our experience of the unity between the autonomous individual and human society. ('And I shall experience the greatest deeds of humanity as I experience my own gestures. My heart will beat in every heart, my soul in every breath.'[33])

To what extent was Polanyi's promotion of a new sociology original? For several decades, sociology had been undergoing a 'normative turn'. In part as a counter to historical materialism, it had begun to intrude into areas previously cornered by theology and normative philosophy, with close attention to questions of values and moral beliefs. Polanyi's *verstehende* approach is more radically subjectivist than, say, Weber's, but is not an altogether different species, and if one brackets out his rejection of positivism, the sociology to which he aspired bore a distinct resemblance to that of two sociological giants to whom I shall shortly turn, after first discussing a partiality that they shared with Polanyi: the 'liberal' and 'guild' varieties of socialism.

FROM LIBERAL TO GUILD SOCIALISM

By the early 1920s, Polanyi had come to hold that politics exists in 'believing' and 'unbelieving' forms. The latter, which subdivides into reactionary and Marxist wings, assumes that political goals can be achieved without individual change. It is pessimistic in its assumption that human nature is unchangeable. 'Believing politics', by contrast, cannot conceive of any significant social advance without the advancement and elevation of individuals. It places its faith in the changeability of people – at least of their mentalité, if not 'human nature' itself – and recognises that without a transformation of souls no institution can guarantee the long-term achievement of social goals. In strategy, it focuses not on social structures but on what can realistically be changed within individuals: their views and judgments, their ideas and ideals. The techniques appropriate for this are *Bildung*, rational instruction and schooling, and persuasion – by force of ideas and by moral example.[34]

The socialist movement, Polanyi maintained, divided along the belief/unbelief faultline, with liberal socialism belonging to the former. Liberal socialism represented the meeting point of liberalism, socialism and anarchism. Its progenitors and proponents, in Polanyi's conspectus, form a motley pantheon, including economic liberals (Turgot, Adam Smith) and protectionists (Henry Charles Carey), Social Darwinists (Herbert Spencer) and their opponents (Eugen Dühring), socialists (Otto Bauer, the Fabians, and the revisionist Marxist Eduard Bernstein), anarchists (Proudhon, Kropotkin) and the sociologist Franz Oppenheimer (who had studied with Adolf Wagner and Gustav Schmoller, on whom more below). Its most prominent Hungarian exponent was Jaszi. He tossed Henry George into the mix, as well as 'British Guild Socialism, which builds upon good sense, education and moral discipline'.[35]

For many years Polanyi identified as a liberal socialist, but in the aftermath of the war he began to rethink the social effects of market economy, turned against economic liberalism and embraced guild socialism.[36] Guild socialism had been forged in the fires of the 1910s: the Great Unrest (1910–14), and the shop stewards' movements, workers' councils and mass strikes of 1916–19. It was the product of the Fabian vessel – accustomed to placid Victorian conditions – entering the choppy waters of the 1910s. Within the Fabian milieu, groups with a more radical mindset emerged: impassioned, utopian and fiercely democratic. Against the backdrop of the Great Unrest, some, such as Harold Laski and Douglas Cole, chafed against Fabianism's authoritarianism and utilitarianism and its partiality to bureaucracy and the wage system. They broke away in 1915 to form the National Guilds League. Although guild socialism was small in scale (at its height, members of the National Guilds League numbered around five hundred, concentrated in London and academia), its reach extended into the union movement, inspiring rank-and-file militants and influencing officials' thinking on workers' control.

For Polanyi, the appeal of guild socialism rested on three features: its rejection of the idea that labour is a commodity;[37] its advocacy of workers' control over production, with industrial self-government seen as indispensable to enabling working people to cultivate the desire to serve their community and develop higher moral characters, and, thirdly, 'functional theory'. Functional theory derived from the philosophy of John Ruskin. For Ruskin, 'organic society' evolves from the cooperative relationships of its constitutive elements. Cooperation represents the law of life, while 'anarchy and competition' represent 'the laws of death'.[38] The market system belonged in the latter category: in essence, it is a congeries of exchange transactions that reflect the degraded tastes of consumers and the deplorable habits of producers who cultivate and profit from those tastes. For guild socialists, a functional society would enable individuals to fulfil their function, and therewith serve the common good. Its institutions would grow from the needs of individuals: the economy from material needs; religion, education, artistic and scientific institutions from citizens' cultural needs; and the guilds – for which inspiration came from Owenite small-scale producer communities and from the medieval guilds – from workers' commonality. The state would grow from citizens' need for justice. It would be merely one functional organisation *inter pares,* cooperating with but not commanding the others.

In 1922 Polanyi thought that guild socialism was becoming a reality in Britain, but that same year saw its collapse, due to a withdrawal of state funding and a dip in labour militancy. The unions, reeling from defeat, forsook the pursuit of 'encroaching control'. The same processes that witnessed the decimation of the guilds and the thwarting of hopes in encroaching workers' control brought political questions of capitalist power and the nature of the state into focus. The Labour and Communist parties, which in their divergent ways responded politically to these questions, found themselves in the ascendant. Guild socialism divided. Broad streams flowed each way to the reformist and revolutionary left, while a much smaller distributary snaked its way to fascism.[39]

GUILD SOCIOLOGIES

Guild socialism was not only central to Polanyi's politics of the early 1920s; it also smoothed his rapprochement with sociology. Two garlanded sociologists of the age were Émile Durkheim and Ferdinand Tönnies. Both developed their thinking on the economic constitution of society in dialogue with, and divergence from, the political economists of the German Historical School (GHS), a group that included Schmoller, Wagner, and Albert Schäffle as well as two authors whose work Polanyi read avidly in the interwar period: Karl Bücher and Dühring. They developed a distinctive approach to economics characterised by institutionalism, an inductive historicist methodology, and a research programme that sought to elaborate a comparative history of economic institutions and identify a typology of the social conditions relating to these in different economic orders. It emphasised the entanglement of the economy in other spheres of life, notably cultural and religious practices. In understanding market behaviour, for example, Schmoller's starting point was not 'formal calculation based on the magnitudes of supply and demand, but the psychic interaction of a number of people'.[40] This primal community 'is an order of life which has grown out of these harmonious psychological foundations and become an objective fact, it is the common ethos, as the Greeks called the moral and spiritual community crystallized in custom and law, which influences all human behaviour, hence including the economic'.[41]

The GHS scholars were Smithians to the extent that they theorised capitalism as an essentially harmonious order based on the co-operative division of labour. Unlike Smith, however, they advocated a powerful economic role for the state. The modern 'national economy', in Polanyi's paraphrase of Bücher, was a recent invention: it is 'integrated through national markets, themselves largely creations of the state, a development that had never occurred before'.[42] Alongside economic integration they accorded the state a guiding role in ensuring social cohesion. Troubled by the pace of social change and the potential for workers' revolt, they appropriated elements of conservative-romantic and social-democratic critiques of *laissez-faire* economic policy: it provided an unsuitable institutional framework for the enhancement of national power and prosperity, and encouraged egotistical economic behaviour and social atomisation, aggravating tensions between the business class and workers. A deregulated market economy spawns a 'casino speculation mentality', warned Schmoller in words that would not seem out of place today. It threatened to break loose from its cultural context, undermining all integrative values and creating anomie, criminality, egotistic individualism and an insecure underclass.[43] All higher civilisations had collapsed as a consequence of uprisings by the lower orders catalysed by 'excessively strained social antagonisms'. As prophylactic he prescribed institutional reform, comprising welfare measures, state regulation of the economy and a humanistic educational policy. In this way the state would be charged with translating the normative premises of social justice into a new institutional framework in order to recreate community, resolving the conflict between workers and the other classes such that the former could be 'reintegrated harmoniously into the social and political organism'.[44] Schmoller positioned this institutional approach to the question of social harmony within a theory of economic development. 'As civilisation advances,' he proposed, 'the state and the national economy diverge more and more the one from the other, each a separate circle with its own organs; and yet this separation must again constantly make way for a unifying guidance, a growing interaction, a harmonious joint-movement.' That 'unifying guidance', the chief coordinating function, must be assumed by the state. To that extent the prescription was liberal-étatiste social policy, on Bismarckian lines. Yet he also accorded importance to a range of organisations that could play a role parallel to the guilds of the medieval age: trade unions, trade corporations and employers' organisations.[45] In such ways, intervention by the state and civil-society associations could repair the social damage wreaked by the separation of politics and economics. This was an outlook with clear affinities to Polanyi's, particularly in his later years when he conceived of the state as an organ for the self-regulation of society as a whole.[46]

In the 1880s, with the GHS in its heyday, Durkheim studied in Berlin, Marburg and Leipzig. He familiarised himself with the GHS, and appreciated its critique of Manchester economics for taking no account of social context and only acknowledging 'individuals … who exchange their products'.[47] He applauded Schmoller's *Grundriss* (a 'complete sociology seen from an economic point of view'[48]) and admired in particular his 'historical and relativistic' approach to economic life.[49] Finding inspiration in the work of Schmoller, Schäffle and Wagner, he grappled with the apparent contradiction in industrial society between economic growth and moral decay, and aspired to develop a historically grounded ethical theory that explains human institutions 'in terms of their moral possibilities to further human potentiality'.[50] With Schmoller et al., he wrestled with the question of how a sense of community can crystallise out of the molecules of individual self-interest and conscience.[51] One of the institutional keys to revitalising a communitarian morality, in his view, was the development of a corporative economy, with an updated system of the medieval corporations and guilds. His guild socialism was not of the deepest red. (One contemporary dismissed it as a 'capitalistic flirtation' with the 'least revolutionary' face of guild socialism.[52]) Nor did his writings exert a forceful influence on Polanyi. Nonetheless, Polanyi's very earliest published writings discuss the French sociologist, and he studied him, again, in the 1920s.[53] More importantly, Durkheim represented one variant of a current within sociology that drew Polanyi back to re-engage with that discipline, a current that sought to explore and explain the construction (and disintegration) of society's moral unity, emphasised the role of institutions in enabling (and disabling) that project, and identified guild socialism as the most promising means to that end.

Of greater influence on Polanyi was Ferdinand Tönnies. If Polanyi's notes from the interwar period can be taken as a guide, he studied the German sociologist more closely than any other author, with the possible exceptions of Marx, Dühring and Joseph Schumpeter. His daughter confirms that he 'engaged intensively with Tönnies', who was 'certainly of importance in the formation of my father's confection of ideas'.[54] More than Durkheim, Tönnies was a sociological ally of the GHS, with which he shared a dual critique of 'Manchester liberalism' and Marxism, both of which he held to be irredeemably disfigured by an economic-determinist methodology. He was a student and friend of Wagner, but unlike Wagner and the conservative wing of German historicism he steered to the political left. He gave support to various movements of liberation against the remains of feudalism, was frozen out of the German academy due to his support for a dockworkers' strike, and in the 1930s was reduced to impecuniosity as a result of his opposition to Hitler's regime. He advocated welfare and regulatory state collectivism and economic democracy, was close to the right wing of the German SPD (which he joined in 1930), respected many of Marx's teachings – and as such acted as an important conduit between the Marxist and institutionalist traditions in Central Europe – and aspired to the supersession of capitalist *Gesellschaft* by a global socialist *Gesellschaft* that would incorporate *Gemeinschaft*-style elements.[55] He fostered 'communitarian' institutions, such as workers' educational associations and cooperatives, and joined the German branch of the Ethical Culture movement.[56] And he harboured sympathy for

Guild Socialism. As he wrote in 1922, he was thrilled to hear 'the call for "Community"' growing 'louder and louder, very often with explicit or (as in the case of British guild socialism) tacit reference to [his] book'[57] and was peeved to note that it had not been cited in the bible of British guild socialism, Douglas Cole's *Social Theory*.[58]

Tönnies is best remembered, ironically, as sociology's forgotten founding father. (A Google search on 'neo-Marxist' yields 241,000 entries, an order of magnitude ahead of 'neo-Weberian' with 25,000, and 'neo-Durkheimian' with 10,000. For 'neo-Tönniesian': a single entry.) Yet his influence has been more pervasive than this void in the ether would imply. *Community and Society* in particular exerted a profound impact upon social theory, especially in Central Europe. In that work Tönnies famously contrasts the ideal types *Gemeinschaft* and *Gesellschaft*, the former denoting the society of the peasant: an 'organic' and 'natural' social habitat in which actions are rooted in *a priori* communal unity and manifest the will and spirit of that unity even when performed by an individual. The latter refers to the world of the merchant: a realm of inauthentic experience in which individuals exist in a permanent condition of separation from others. He describes *Gesellschaft* as 'abstract', 'artificial' and 'fictitious'; in a later work he dubs it a 'fictitious totality'.[59] Characterised as it is by the sharp separation of social spheres, the common values that enable group behaviour to function are not rooted in custom and governed by face-to-face relations but must be deliberately fashioned with the aid of abstract systems. In particular, the creation of contracts requires the momentary and artificial construction of a common will. On the labour market,

> labour is bought and paid for as if it represented merely future services to be consumed in the performance itself. The fiction underlying this is that the [manufacturer, capitalist or joint stock company] is the real author and producer and hires workers only as helpers. This fiction gains in verisimilitude the more the conditions of co-operation and later the implements of production become, as it were, alive and capable of carrying out automatic imitation of human craft and skill through their cleverly planned construction.

Labour power, it follows, is 'a purely fictitious, unnatural commodity created by human will'. Tönnies gives pride of place to labour as the fictitious commodity that defines *Gesellschaft*, but extends the same analysis to land (which 'cannot be made or fabricated') and to money (which, being held by people who have not produced it themselves, is 'a purely abstract commodity'). He perceived that what he termed the 'great transformation' from *Gemeinschaft* to *Gesellschaft* was irreversible and tragic and yet believed that, thanks to the waxing influence of the working classes, a new communal era would yet dawn. For him, the road thereto was not signposted class struggle but moral enlightenment and political reform.[60]

In several respects, Tönnies' thinking was akin to that of Owen, and Polanyi explicitly noted the likeness.[61] For example, Owen wrote of the supply-demand market mechanism as an 'artificial law' – artificial because 'the principle of individual gain' prevails over and exists 'in opposition to the well-being of society'.[62] In the summary of his biographer, Douglas Cole, Owen's approach was 'what we should call nowadays a sort of benevolent State Socialism, to be achieved by authority working from above. But it differed materially from the State Socialism of later days in its insistence on the necessity for the greatest possible measure of local devolution and autonomy'.[63]

With the caveats that ideas develop dialogically, with continuous interaction with previous traditions, and that several concepts which Polanyi valued in Tönnies' output resembled those of Owen, it is possible to identify a number of Tönniesian elements in Polanyi's social theory. With the German sociologist he saw *Gesellschaft* as a two-class society, a division that had become, in terms of the needs of society, redundant and the retention of which 'therefore, turns into a denial of community'.[64] With Tönnies, he criticised economic reductionism, conceived as including 'Manchester liberalism' and Marxism alike, and viewed the institutional separation of polity and economy as 'artificial.' (For example, he argued that 'the market system' had, in the early twentieth century, 'succumbed to its artificiality'.[65]) The most striking similarity, however, lay in the theory of 'fictitious commodities' (and its corollary, the 'dis/embedded economy') that Polanyi elaborated in the interwar period. 'The Fascist Virus', for example, argues that for labour to be bought or sold a contract must be formed that sanctions

> the transfer of the invisible and immaterial commodity labour from the seller to the buyer. It is only by means of such a construction that the term commodity can be made to apply to labour. However, legal fictions are mere instruments of thought which by themselves do not affect the actual world. The invidious element which changed the course of civilization lay in the human implications of that fiction. For if labour is to be handled as a commodity then the vast majority of human society, or rather of its adult males, must be put at the disposal of the market on which that fictitious commodity is being bartered.[66]

Essentially the same Tönniesian idea underlies the central premise of *The Great Transformation*: the commodification of land, labour and money poses a mortal threat to nature, human beings and business respectively, inevitably generating grievances, resistance and, consequently, the imperative of protection. The protective counter-movement is *Gemeinschaft*, characterised by social unity, while the self-regulating market is the economy of socially fissiparous *Gesellschaft*. Human beings and nature, according to this argument, are either not produced at all (like land) or, if so, not for sale (like labour); as such they are not genuine commodities at all, but the fiction of their being so produced was to become the organizing principle of nineteenth-century society. Because labour is inseparable from the human beings of which society consists, and land is their natural habitat, their insertion as fictitious commodities into the market mechanism brought the subjugation of 'the substance of society itself to the laws of the market'. Whereas previous economies had been 'embedded in social relations', in the market system economic behaviour becomes 'disembedded' from the social fabric: society becomes 'an accessory of the economic system', and, given that the vital ingredients of human social life, labour and land, are commodified in a market economy, such an economy 'can exist only in a market society'.[67]

'Embeddedness' is a contested, not to say contradictory, concept. Some suppose that the contradictions in Polanyi's usage reflect a theoretical clash between Marxist and non-Marxist frameworks, as his thought shifted from the former to the latter. In fact, the same contradictions were already evident in Tönnies' sociology. In particular, the *Gemeinschaft-Gesellschaft* couplet can be interpreted in two quite different ways. First, it can be taken to refer to different types of society – one based on contract and interest, the other on status, feeling and custom. Tönnies used it to describe historical transitions in Europe in two periods: from the Roman republic to the Roman Empire, and from feudalism to capitalism.[68] If read in this way it encounters a series of difficulties. On one hand, as Kurtuluş Gemici has noted,

> historical research shows that the common acceptance of ancient societies as status societies is ill-founded and rather mythical; it discards evidence indicating that even friendship or familial relations could have been contractual in the ancient world. On the other hand, comparative empirical examination of social entities at different levels of economic development presents a picture that is considerably more complex than the hypothesized movement from community to society as industrialization and capitalism develop.[69]

Secondly, Tönnies' dichotomy can be applied to customary and contractual relations that exist symbiotically in every society. He himself used the dyad in this way: as an 'ideal type' (a structural-analytical concept for the purposes of comparison), such that one finds elements of both *Gesellschaft and Gemeinschaft* in any given social order. Similarly, in the interpretation of the philosopher (and saint) Edith Stein, the social relationships characteristic of *Gesellschaft*,

> need to be informed and sustained by relationships characteristic of *Gemeinschaft*. Individuals come together in the forms of association characteristic of *Gesellschaft* for their own purposes, treating other individuals as instruments for the achievement of the purposes of the association. But nonetheless, they bring with them to these new relationships habits of living together with others that do not allow them to treat others *only* as such instruments. And in the course of their working together with others further sympathies are engendered that motivate the treatment of those others in ways characteristic of *Gemeinschaft* rather than *Gesellschaft*.

No association, she concludes, 'no matter how well organized, no matter how faultless a social mechanism, could continue to function, if it were no more than the norms and values of *Gesellschaft* require it to be'.[70]

Just as for Tönnies' analogous concepts, Polanyi's 'embeddedness' can be understood either as a methodological axiom that holds that *all* economic behaviour is enmeshed in non-economic institutions or as a theoretical proposition that refers to differences in the degree of that 'enmeshment',[71] and, as in Tönnies, there is slippage between the two usages – Polanyi was quite capable of confusing the use of embeddedness as historical description and as ideal type. Consider, for example, this passage: 'In a pure exchange economy, in utopian capitalism, in Ferdinand Tönnies' *Gesellschaft*, nothing but contract matters; its content is the cash nexus: payment for labour power. In the *Gemeinschaft*, of the future and of the past, it is status that counts.'[72] Similarly, in *Great Transformation*, the disembedded economy is understood both as a descriptive empirical term and as an ideal type. In this, the Polanyian ambiguity is directly analogous to its Tönniesian predecessor. The tensions within Polanyi's 'embeddedness' are inherent in the Tönniesian matrix on which he draws.

CONCLUSION

What stands out from this survey of the young Karl Polanyi's intellectual journey is its volatility. The sharp twists and turns doubtless tell a story of youth and insatiable curiosity, but they also carry imprints of the sociopolitical conjuncture. The first quarter of the twentieth century witnessed scientific breakthroughs, the acme of modernism, an obscenely gory war, and social and political upheaval across the region. The previous quarter century had been scarcely less tumultuous, with an accelerated expansion of capitalist production relations, urbanisation, the second industrial revolution and a spectacularly rapid deployment of science and technology to the production process and beyond. Intellectually, the age experienced a series of explosive conflicts. In the philosophy of history, Whiggish meliorism clashed with Spenglerian pessimism, and utilitarianism came under fire from Romantic and Niezschean directions. In Nietzsche's own work, motifs of the heroic individual jostled with those of cultural rejuvenation through a Dionysian, myth-inspired melting of individuals into the collective. Theorising the role of individual and collective was itself another tension – in Germany in particular, where the *Bildungsbürgertum* cleaved to a vision of society geared to the cultivation of 'renaissance' individuals, a perspective that clashed with the processes of atomisation and individualisation that were being limned in their different ways by Tönnies, Weber and Simmel. In economic theory, the Austrians championed deductivism and atomistic individualism while German 'historicists' rallied to holistic inductivism. A related battle within the social sciences flared between positivism and its enemies, notably neo-Kantian and hermeneutic approaches.

The last of these is one instance of a wider tension between what Terry Eagleton has termed the 'search for ever more formalized models of social explanation, from structural linguistics and psychoanalysis to Wittgenstein's *Tractatus* and the Husserlian *eidos*', and 'an anxious turning back to "the things themselves"', exemplified in that 'romantic pursuit of the irreducibly "lived"' characteristic of German *Lebensphilosophie*.[73] Against encroaching capitalism, against *Gesellschaft* with its levelling of rank and tradition and its disrupting of 'organic' social ties, the Romantics defended qualitative and intuitive forms of life and thought. Their revolt included a questioning of forms of rationality associated with the physical sciences, above all mechanical materialism and 'objective positivism'. On its left wing the thrust was anti-capitalist, extolling qualitative values as opposed to exchange values, with a deep revulsion towards capitalism's calculating rationalistic ethos.

The vortex of many of these debates was Germany but Vienna was a storm centre too, as was Budapest. Liberalism, with 'science', 'law' and 'positivism' on its banners, appeared to herald social justice and egalitarianism but as the future swiftly arrived those promises withered. The liberal faith that social progress would arrive courtesy of capitalist development crumbled, as did the liberal consensus on the benefits of international trade. A still-insecure bourgeoisie confronted mass movements demanding political intervention in social and economic life. On the political right, nationalists agitated against immigration and against oppressed nations' demands for political equality; and anti-Liberal sentiment among peasants alloyed with anti-democratic and anti-socialist reaction among the nobility and petit bourgeoisie to forge a conservative anti-semitic coalition. On the left, opposition to the new ills of commodification and exploitation coalesced around the trade unions and the Social Democratic Party.

Politically, Hungarian liberalism entered the twentieth century in crisis and divided. Its mainstream compromised with the nobility and the Church, while its more principled outliers – including the Budapest counterculture to which Jaszi, Pikler, Polanyi and the Galilei Circle belonged – regrouped as a 'radical bourgeois' current, unrepentant in its hostility to 'clericalism', and in partial sympathy with social democracy. Most of these thinkers, in their different ways, adopted the Galilei creed, which has been elegantly described by Adam Tolnay as 'a highly intellectualized desire to devise a moral basis for social organization at a time of profound spiritual crisis'.[74] Many of them were of Jewish heritage and, having experienced oppressive division at first hand, saw the unification of their fragmented society as an imperious necessity. Lukacs' diagnosis centred on the social atomisation effected by capitalist social relations, for Mannheim it was the separate spheres – economy, politics, religion – into which society had splintered, and for Karl Polanyi it was the separation of economy from society. Social progress, and the flourishing of individual responsibility and community – of *Gesellschaft* alongside *Gemeinschaft* – depended upon its repair.

That repair work, he believed in the 1920s, would best be undertaken under guild-socialist leadership, and he propagandised on behalf of that movement and its conception of functional society. This latter should not be conflated with the *normative functionalism* advocated by Durkheim, which conceives of society as 'a moral and ultimately a religious entity whose intrinsic feature is a set of commonly held values and beliefs'.[75] However, Polanyi did, as it happens, hold to a variant of normative functionalism, and he believed that it dovetailed with functional theory. The social vision that he was elaborating was based upon 'the belief that *because* a basic harmony exists between the functions of life, a fundamental harmony *must* exist between the functions of social organisations, which are built upon the functions of the individual'.[76] For a society to function harmoniously, 'moral unity' is indispensable, and this in turn rests upon 'the ultimate personal convictions of its members about the significance of human life in society, that is, in plain English, upon an underlying unity of a religious kind'.[77] Patently, this thesis belongs within the folds of consensus sociology. Nonetheless, Polanyi as a theorist resists a too easy identification with consensus sociologists such as Durkheim or Talcott Parsons. Whereas for Parsons 'human life is essentially one and no concretely possible degree of functional differentiation can destroy its unity',[78] for Polanyi social differentiation does not necessarily contribute to functional social harmony. Specifically, the market system can indeed destroy social unity, in particular when the institutional cleavage between economics and politics maps onto the battle between the major social classes – as I discuss in Chapter 3.

The intellectual journey through which Polanyi arrived at Tönniesian sociology passed through enthusiasms for a diverse group of thinkers and movements: Mach and Chesterton, Tolstoy and Dühring, guild socialism and functional theory. In most cases, after his youthful interest had dimmed he did not revisit his early passions, and neither did he devote systematic scrutiny to their work. To this rule there was one exception: his ongoing reappraisal of the work of Marx.

The Marxist Orbit:
Polanyi's Double Movement

'I started life,' Polanyi wrote shortly before the Second World War, not entirely without hyperbole, 'as a socialist and referred all my hopes and fears to this ideal.'[1] In his teens he belonged to a socialist student group and avidly read Marxist literature. In his words, he was 'brought up' in Marxian socialism;[2] it was 'the intellectual medium of the socialist student movement.'[3] But in his twenties he grew increasingly critical, especially of Marxism's avatar in Hungary, the Social Democratic Party. In his thirties he moved to Vienna, where he 'became a socialist again, more strongly convinced than ever.'[4] There, his relationship to Marxism underwent what might be called a 'double movement', beginning with a salvo of vituperative attacks that soon subsided, giving way to a sympathetic engagement with Austro-Marxism. In his forties, he was a critical but loyal friend to orthodox Communism, and his enthusiasm for Marx was rekindled by the publication of the Landshut-Mayer edition of Marx' early writings. The final two decades of his life saw his interest in Marxism wane, even as his attachment to Marx's early works remained undimmed.

There is thus no shortage of material with which to spin Polanyi's relationship to Marxism in different directions. In the 1960s and 1970s his most zealous disciple, George Dalton, resisted all suggestions that the master's approach was anything but sovereign and *sui generis*. Polanyi was dedicated to the reform of capitalism, a project that would receive vital intellectual stimulus and guidance with the creation of a new 'substantivist' school of economics. Substantivism and Marxism were warring camps; to reconcile or conflate them was to slur the originality and independence of the former.[5] A second position is associated with Fred Block and Margaret Somers. For them, Polanyi embraced a Hegelian form of Marxism in the 1930s and *The Great Transformation* was first sketched upon a recognisably Marxist canvas. The actual writing of the book, however, coincided with his shift away from Marxism, a turn that, while never quite effacing its imprint in his thought, did enable the development of a genuinely original research programme.[6] I examine this case below. A third interpretation emphasises the overlap between the Marxian and Polanyian traditions. Like Polanyi, Marx and Engels discussed at length the threats to nature and to human society posed by the market system. They held that progress in capitalist agriculture is achieved through robbing the labourer and the soil, that the commodification of land marked the final stage in the transformation of human beings into 'an object of huckstering', and that the worker in a market economy 'sinks to the level of a commodity and becomes indeed the most wretched of commodities'.[7] Other Marxian concepts and methods that have clear Polanyian analogues include the analysis of the institutional separation of politics and economics as an artefact of market capitalism, the use of anthropological materials to defamiliarise capitalist social relations, the debunking of the 'market mentality', and the arguments given to justify the case for socialism: historically, with reference to the crisis tendencies of capitalist society, and anthropologically, with reference to the human being's ability to cooperate with others in directing nature's resources to the satisfaction of human needs and wants. Both traditions protest the determination of human lives by impersonal market forces and share a set of basic criticisms of capitalism: that it is unjust, anarchic and an impediment to the further development of human freedom.[8] Both define human beings as fundamentally social, with the corollary that economic behaviour cannot be meaningfully studied as if it were isolated from society. Both identify labour(-power) and land as peculiar commodities, the value of which are determined to an extraordinary degree by political and cultural factors. Both invite us to consider the effects on economic thought of the particular mode of economic organisation that arose in recent centuries, criticising the 'economistic fallacy' that identifies 'the economy' with its market form and regards pre-modern societies as underdeveloped forms of capitalism, the belief in the existence of a trans-historical economic rationality and the concomitant lack of conceptual tools that would permit the recognition of different economic systems. Both scorn the quest for a universally applicable economic theory, insisting that the conditions conducive to market behaviour (notably commodification) and to capitalism in particular (crucially, the generalised commodification of labour-power) are anything but transhistorical universals. And both agree upon a further set of charges against orthodox economics: that in its equation of market behaviour with rational choice the concept of the market expands to occupy the entire panorama of social action and loses all determinacy, and that the discursive constitution of the individual as *private* individual is a historically specific phenomenon, one that rests upon a mode of economic relations in which the co-ordination of cooperative labour occurs through the alienated form of the market exchange of its products.

A pioneer of the third interpretation was Rhoda Halperin, an anthropologist who studied at Bennington College with one of Polanyi's closest collaborators, Harry Pearson. In her reading, Polanyi's project amounted to an interpretation and development of Marx's, as much as or more than a departure from it.[9] Both 'Karls' worked within 'an evolutionary framework; they both placed transformations in economic processes at the centre of their analyses; and they both emphasised that these transformations involved changes in the institutional arrangements organising economic processes'.[10] Like Dalton, she was a substantivist anthropologist, but while he perceived the advance of Marxist anthropology in the 1970s and 1980s as a threat, she saw it as a potential ally in the contests against formalist economic anthropology and the New Institutionalist Economics.[11] If she imagined a marriage between the two traditions, however, it was to be squarely under the sign of Polanyian institutionalism.[12]

A more recent case that highlights Marx-Polanyi affinities has been advanced by Michael Burawoy. For him, Polanyi figures as a Marxist theorist, albeit one whose eye was not trained on production or exploitation. If synthesised with Gramsci's theses on hegemony, a 'sociological Marxism' results. It, in contrast to the classical Marxist emphasis upon class struggle, focuses on 'the coordination of class interests through compromises and alliances'. With this move, Marxism is divested of its core theses and reconstructed as an essentially Polanyian research programme.[13]

Not long after Burawoy's thesis appeared its antithesis was published by Gáspár Miklós Tamás. For the Hungarian philosopher, socialist endeavour may be usefully parted into two principal traditions. One was founded by Marx. For him, capitalism 'is history'. It will meet its quietus by way of the self-abolition of one of its fundamental classes. In Tamás's reading, Marx implied that the moral motive for such a self-abolition 'is the intolerable, abject condition of the proletariat'. Hence, his socialism is historicist, with human emancipation its telos. The other, of which Polanyi is the archetypal representative, was inaugurated by Rousseau. In his theodicy, capitalism is 'evil'. Rousseauian socialism is moralistic. Its agenda: the replacement of a complex, hierarchical society with a simple, 'natural' order of 'the people', limned in angelic colours as 'a purely egalitarian and culturally self-sustaining, closed community'.[14]

In Tamás's account, it was Rousseauian philosophy, frequently channelled by Marxists, that underpinned mainstream socialist ideas in the twentieth century. It spoke to the labour movement's need to defend its organisations and constituency and to the associated tendency to extol the moral superiority of those who fought its corner. The material base of Rousseauian socialism consisted in the 'counter-power' of working-class organisations (trade unions, parties, newspapers, choirs and so on) as well as its own autonomous political superstructure, 'from "reformist" social democracy to revolutionary anarcho-syndicalism, a whole separate world where the bourgeoisie's writ did not run'. The marriage of Rousseauian and Marxian socialism resulted from 'the special interests of this established counter-power'. What Tamás calls 'the truth about class' is that two contradictory objectives informed the proletariat. One was 'to defeat its antagonist and to abolish itself as a class'. The other was to preserve its own social values, habitus and above all its institutions – the practice of social democracy, which replaced the goal of 'emancipation with equality, Marx with Rousseau'.[15] Its historical project demanded the uprooting of the power of aristocracy and clergy – the elimination of 'caste' or 'estate', such that the Third Estate became the Nation – but not the abolition of 'class'.

In the rest of this chapter I explore this terrain, contextualising and reconstructing Polanyi's relationship to Marxist theory.

REVISIONISM AND ORTHODOXY IN HUNGARIAN MARXISM

In the 1900s, with Polanyi in his teens, Marxism was enjoying one of its periodic great debates. The orthodox philosophy of Second International Marxism exhibited a rigid determinism, alloyed to a crude materialism and a contemplative epistemology. The role of free will was downplayed, in the manner of eighteenth-century materialists such as Helvetius. History was envisaged as an extension of natural evolution, a journey onward and upward from hydrogen clouds via organic life to human society, which, propelled onward by technological innovation, would be shepherded by social democracy toward its ultimate telos: the socialist state. Karl Kautsky, to take the classic example, portrayed history as an evolutionary process with a pre-determined outcome. 'The capitalist social system has run its course,' he thundered;

> its dissolution is now only a question of time. Irresistible economic forces lead with the certainty of doom to the shipwreck of capitalist production. The substitution of a new social order for the existing one is no longer simply desirable, it has become inevitable.[16]

Kautsky did pay tribute to the role of human will, but less as a conscious creative factor in history than as a quasi-vitalist 'will to live' that undergirds the material economic process.[17] He was prone to technological determinism – as when, in a letter to Polanyi's cousin Ervin Szabó, he identified technology as the most active and 'revolutionary' of historical forces in comparison with which other factors are 'conservative and passive, becoming revolutionary only occasionally, under the impact of changed technology'.[18] With class struggle relegated to the status of History's executor, his outlook spoke to the needs and experiences of party and union officials, for whom the preservation of the apparatus had become an end in itself – even as, paradoxically, the role of the party continued to figure in Kautsky's thought as the tool through which to elevate working-class consciousness from spontaneous militancy to a revolutionary awareness of its hegemonic destiny.

Kautsky's determinism did not, Alan Shandro has pointed out, entail fatalism, a philosophy of passive submission to the inevitable. Determinism breeds inaction only if one believes 'that one knows that the actions one might take will have no significant or positive effect. It is often the case, however, that there is no way of achieving this kind of knowledge other than by acting'.[19] That said, even Kautsky's defenders concede that his optimistic, 'ever-upwards' style of deterministic argumentation tended to justify strategic inaction. It is a mentality that Jules Townshend has neatly captured as 'pessimism of the will, optimism of the intellect'.[20]

Little is known of Polanyi's attitude to Kautsky before 1922, but in that year he published a review of *Die proletarische Revolution und ihr Programm*. It praises Kautsky's critique of Bolshevik Russia but the overall tenor is disparaging. It takes the SPD leader to task for exaggerating the scientific nature of Marxism, for presenting Marxism as a movement that values economic rather than moral purposes, and for his theories of exploitation, the concentration of capital and the immiserisation of the proletariat. Kautsky had failed to understand the import of new forms of democracy that were developing spontaneously within the labour movement and displayed 'a flabbergasting lack of comprehension towards the forms and future possibilities of the cooperative idea and movement'. The roots of this myopia were philosophical: Kautsky's materialism, and his failure to place socialism upon an ethical foundation. To comprehend the new tendencies of socialist democracy he would have to 'liberate himself from his amoralist prejudices and construct his worldview upon the active force of socialism's moral ideals'.[21] All of Polanyi's criticisms betray an unmistakeable resemblance to those levelled against the Second International orthodoxy a generation earlier, by Bernstein.

Arraigning Marxism for its alleged reduction of ethics to economy, Bernstein sought an alternative account of the moral basis of socialism. He found inspiration in the German Historical School (notably Dühring), and in neo-Kantian philosophy – above all Kant's invocation of duty. In this endeavour he found support from Ramsay MacDonald and other Fabians whom he befriended during his British exile.[22] It was during his London years that his critique of Marxism gained shape – and the 'Revisionist Controversy' of German social democracy arguably began in Britain in 1896, when Bernstein, an apostle of the civilising effects of bourgeois culture, debated colonialism with the revolutionary socialist (and anti-colonialist) Belfort Bax.[23] Three years later, Bernstein's *Evolutionary Socialism* made its explosive appearance, assailing a host of positions that had become ingrained among Marxists. It proposed that, thanks to the inevitable development of society's productive forces, contemporary bourgeois society was – quite unlike all previous civilisations – teeming with ideas that were not strongly determined by natural or economic forces. This had sharply expanded the scope of ethics as an independent determining factor of social evolution. Secondly, it theorised the state in pluralist terms, as an essentially autonomous body that supervises the common affairs of individuals.[24] This thesis dovetailed with Bernstein's marginalist, subjective-psychological value theory, and with his conception of class not as a relationship of irreconcilable struggle rooted in the ownership (and lack of) of means of production but as a spectrum of inequalities in privilege and income.[25] In turn, the disavowal of a connection between class structure and social structure permitted the project of evolutionary socialism to be conceived of as the product of a discrete 'political' sphere in which the general will of the citizenry found democratic expression in parliament.[26] Whereas for Kautsky, democracy meant the suppression of government by one class and its replacement by another, for Bernstein it represented the dissolution of class rule *tout court* and its replacement by 'political majorities constructed around programmes and objectives, and hopefully around the ethical ideal of socialism, not around the interests of classes'.[27] Capitalism, for Bernstein, did not tend to produce class polarisation but, instead, ameliorated social division through its fostering of a robust middle layer. If the position of workers was intolerable, this was due to the uncertainty of their existence in a volatile environment and not to an inherently capitalist tendency to social polarisation or so-called law of immiserisation.

In general, Bernstein sought to distance himself from economic determinism and from 'iron laws' of evolution, but in this he did not always succeed. With the Fabians, he believed that Reason, flanked by the 'Spirit of Progress' and the steady expansion of the labour movement and the cooperative mentality, would carry the day.[28] With Kautsky, he was convinced that the supplanting of capitalism by socialism is inevitable. (Indeed, its certainty stares at us from 'the grave-stones of our dead'.[29]) The molecular evolution of everyday social-movement and political practice that he celebrated was of a piece with Kautsky's 'strategy of attrition' – the 'patient accumulation of forces through preliminary skirmishes until enough strength had been gathered for a final, victorious confrontation'.[30] In the words of his biographer, Bernstein's evolutionary optimism could sound 'deterministic and dogmatic'; for, having been marinated for many years in the 'liberal-Victorian' solutions of the Fabians, he had become convinced that 'modernity was "inexorably" moving toward increasing social complexity and nobler forms of 'socialist culture'.[31]

Whereas Kautsky held that capitalism was laying the foundations for socialism, which *would* come about through the achievement of state power via social-democratic majorities in parliament, for Bernstein it was *actually* mutating into socialism by way of the extension of democracy. He thought that he could see, inherent in liberalism, an 'evolutionary logic toward democracy', a logic that would *naturally* progress onward to socialism.[32] The route to greater working-class influence lay not along the low road of class struggle but via the high road of joint campaigns with the 'progressive' bourgeoisie for an expanded franchise. The labour movement should seek allies above all in the milieu of 'bourgeois radicalism', for its enemy was neither capitalism nor the capitalist state and still less the bourgeoisie 'but the small group of private interests which stubbornly refused to see the light of reason and social justice' by resisting the expansion of democracy.[33] Universal suffrage, he averred, is the aspect of democracy that 'must draw the other parts after it as a magnet attracts to itself the scattered portions of iron'.[34] An iron law indeed.

In Hungary, Bernstein was a prominent influence on both of the political milieux that mattered to the young Polanyi: the 'bourgeois radicals' around Bernstein's close friend, Jaszi, and also the Social-Democratic Party. The Hungarian SDP was broadly Marxist in its theoretical commitments but in practice it inclined to revisionism.[35] It placed the struggle for universal suffrage at the centre of its programme, alongside '*Sozialpolitik*' – the corporatist reformism that had been pioneered by the Historical School and was later adopted by Bernstein's revisionist camp. While supporting the SDP, Bernstein simultaneously encouraged Jaszi to establish a 'radical bourgeois party'.[36] It was unveiled in June 1914, with Jaszi and Polanyi installed at its headquarters.

Polanyi was close to Jaszi, but he had his own outlook, and one difference with his mentor was that he was not so dismissive, or at least not consistently dismissive, of the third alternative in the debate that Bernstein had ignited. In Germany this third current was most closely identified with Rosa Luxemburg and in Russia with Lenin and Trotsky. They were later to be joined by the likes of Gramsci, Karl Korsch and Georg Lukacs, practitioners of what Althusser later referred to as the 'revolutionary humanist and historicist' current of Marxism.[37] Philosophically, these individuals challenged the determinism and mechanical materialism of the orthodoxy.[38] Consciousness for them involved a subject-object relationship that could not be reduced to the status of an epiphenomenon of objective reality; ideas participate in the constitution of knowledge and individuals' purposes in cognising are inextricably bound up with their life and labour. Their philosophy of history did not posit a pre-set endpoint that can be predicted with scientific certainty but envisioned the human future as a range of possibilities (summarised by Luxemburg as 'socialism or barbarism'), its outcome not predetermined by economic development but radically open to conscious human intervention. Politically, the Luxemburg-Lenin camp was noted for its critique of the conservatism of Second

International social democracy and its emphasis upon the involvement of socialists in mass movements. Against Kautsky and Bernstein they championed the mass strike as a means of unifying economic and political interests of the proletariat and advocated a revolutionary rupture with the capitalist order – the 'self-abolition of class', in the terms discussed above.[39]

The most philosophically involved of the third group was Lukacs, whose *History and Class Consciousness* Polanyi studied in depth.[40] Lukacs' book engages with the 'ethical socialism' of Bernstein and Otto Bauer, contending that it represented the flip side of 'economic fatalism'. The lacuna in the philosophy of ethical socialism is the category of 'totality'. In its absence, theory and practice cannot be comprehended as a unity, and the stance of the observer is necessarily contemplative and fatalistic. Her environment, her social milieu, appears as

> the servant of a brutal and senseless fate which is eternally alien [and] can only be understood by means of a theory which postulates 'eternal laws of nature'. […] Within such a world only two possible modes of action commend themselves and they are both apparent rather than real ways of actively changing the world. Firstly, there is the exploitation for particular human ends of the fatalistically accepted and immutable laws. […] Secondly, there is action directed wholly inwards. This is the attempt to change the world at its only remaining free point, namely man himself (ethics).

If, instead, theory and practice are considered in their unity, the 'ethics' of the proletariat is seen to be class consciousness. It represents the point at which the 'economic necessity' of the workers' struggle 'changes dialectically into freedom'.[41]

After the Great War, Lukacs became Hungary's most prominent Marxist theorist, but he received that baton from Polanyi's cousin, Szabó. In 1900s and 1910s Hungary, Szabó was the figure who most closely resembled Luxemburg – although his relationship to the Social Democratic mainstream was even frostier than hers and his syndicalist leanings somewhat stronger. If he had a motto, it was 'the liberation of the working class can only be achieved by the working class itself'. The Second International parties, in his analysis, had abandoned this fundamental Marxist tenet in favour of Lassallean statism (the idea that the Party will bring about the new order through the power of the state). He railed against the distortions to which historical materialism had become subject. Its deterministic predictions of an inevitable socialist transformation implied that 'even if we should not budge an inch, the economic conditions will automatically bring about socialism'. This was a travesty of historical materialism. In neglecting the role of the individual in the development of society it had departed dramatically from the ideas of Marx and Engels.[42]

The Marxism that Szabó developed was no naïve, Canutian voluntarism. He accounts for the rise of the socialist movement as the product of struggle between the 'two great opposing camps' of contemporary class society, the preconditions of which were created by the rise of a new mode of production based upon 'the machine'. However, when individuals' actions are 'consonant with the general direction of social progress' they supply the indispensable creative factor in effecting social change. The subjects of the historical process, he argued citing the *narodnik* Piotr Lavrov, are the bearers of ideas; 'that is, human beings who select their ends and act intentionally'.[43] Rather like Sorel, he espoused an ascetic, heroic morality, radically opposed to 'capitalist hedonism and the crude materialism of the bourgeoisie'. He also cultivated strong links to Russian populism. In the description of his personal friend and political opponent, Jaszi,

> he was intimately attached to the peasants and the village. He was instinctively aware of the morbid and corrupt nature of the big city; and in his thought, or at least in his subconscious feelings, the countryside occupied a much greater role than it did for most socialists of urban origin.[44]

By 1907, Szabó's syndicalist current within Hungarian social democracy had been effectively isolated, and he thenceforth devoted his energies to smaller movements, including a Tolstoyan anarchist group.[45] Yet his influence, even after his death in 1918, burned bright. Lukacs later recalled him as 'the only one of the Hungarian thinkers of the day' to whom he was 'seriously indebted',[46] and Polanyi's admiration for him was boundless.

MARXISM CRITIQUED

Of the three strands under discussion above, Polanyi was for many years closest to Bernstein's but during his years in Vienna he grew increasingly appreciative of a fourth: Austro-Marxism. The historical context was marked by mass revolts and political polarisation. Rolling waves of political strikes and anti-war demonstrations had spread via Budapest to Germany, culminating in the mutiny of the Austro-Hungarian navy and the establishment of soviet republics in Bavaria and Hungary. A few months before his arrival, the first general election in the new Austrian republic had taken place, in which the Social Democratic Party gained 41 per cent of the overall vote and an absolute majority in Vienna. Polanyi was war weary and barely able to relate to the tumult. Instead, he devoted himself to the study of economics and Christian sociology. He was growing impatient with the Tolstoyan philosophy of inner contemplation and individual moral rectitude that had captivated him for some years, and began to criticise it for failing to appreciate the interdependence of individual and society. He also threw himself into a critique of Marxism, singling out what he regarded (inexplicably) as its 'utilitarian ethics', alongside its 'materialist conception of history, positivist epistemology [and] determinist philosophy' as well as 'the Labour Theory of Value, and the economic programmes seemingly based upon it'.[47]

At the heart of his critique lay two conjoined claims: Marxist philosophy reductively holds consciousness to be determined by social being, and it sees the world 'from the outside', with human society thought to follow laws as rigorous as those of the natural sciences.[48] For example, the law of the development of the productive forces (a term which Polanyi reductively takes to mean 'machines') leads inevitably to capitalism's collapse and proletarian dictatorship.[49] Marxism's theory of 'stages' of labour-historical development (slavery, serfdom, wage labour) represented 'the greatest single obstacle to the understanding of economic history'. These assertions formed the core of his critique of Marxism throughout his life. The labour movement in general and Marxism in particular, he argued, had arisen within liberal society and were thoroughly infected by its economic determinism.[50] He likened 'Marxist inevitability' to 'laissez-faire inevitability': both, if in different ways, were products of economic determinism, and both proclaim 'the inevitability of the loss of our freedoms, unless we resign ourselves to the status quo, changelessness and certain destruction'. Marx himself, Polanyi averred, tended to see political processes – including even revolutions – as the servants of 'historical necessity' rather than the acts of living people, with history relegated to a 'function of the instruments of production'.[51] He failed to see that social structures are constructed entirely from beliefs and values. Consider class struggle. It occurs only to the extent that individuals are aware of and believe in its existence; or capitalist competition: it is no simple material mechanism but rests on 'customs and beliefs'. Or take the political sphere: it is only when people *believe* in revolution that it breaks out. ('When nobody believes in the state, it has already ceased to exist'.[52]) In its repudiation of moral freedom, Marxism's belief in the inevitability of socialism is corrosive, as is its faith in collective action. Social change, Polanyi argued, comes from the inner lives of individuals; the masses, by contrast, 'can have no true belief'. Their typical motive for action is 'material self-interest, and the likely means of achieving it will be by exerting their own physical force'.[53]

Polanyi also found fault with Marx and Engels' theories of the state and economic value. On the first of these, he faulted what he saw as their theorisation of the state as an armature for capitalist economy and society, with its strategic corollary that progressive change requires its dismantling through revolution. Polanyi's preferred tradition, initiated by Saint-Simon and continued by Dühring and Franz Oppenheimer, explains the origins of the state in terms of 'conquest', a phase that had been transcended through democratisation – an institutional revolution that had tamed state power, subjecting it to regulation in the interests of the 'common people' through their control of parliament.[54] As regards value theory, Polanyi found it unconvincing. Even when his orbit around Marxism reached its periapsis he remained adamant that its 'politically dynamic elements' are 'entirely independent' of value theory.[55] His critique commences with a rejection of the utility of Marx's distinction between labour and labour power.[56] On this basis, he presents Marx's theory as nothing but the final croak of a long tradition that posits the value of a good to be objectively determined by the labour embodied within it, which Polanyi dubs 'the Locke-Ricardo-Marxian labour theory of value'.[57] The theory was already 'bourgeois' in its origin with Locke and Petty; it was elaborated by Smith before achieving its acme with Ricardo.[58] Like Ricardo, Marx conceived of labour metaphysically, as an 'invisible abstraction', such that value and price are explicable in terms of elements intrinsic to commodities – notably the number of working hours expended in their production.[59] Marx, as ventriloquised by Polanyi, 'accepted the Ricardian analysis as valid [and], having accepted Ricardian economics, he turned it into an argument against capitalist society. This was the meaning of *Das Kapital*'.[60]

Little, if any, of Polanyi's critique of Marx and Engels was original. On most points, it hewed closely to arguments advanced earlier by Dühring, Tönnies, Simmel and Bernstein, the shortcomings of which are well known.[61] Nobody doubts that Marx and Engels inhaled the positivism of their age, but the suggestion that it became an addiction is myopic – the notion that their philosophy was at its core positivist, teleological and deterministic has been repeatedly refuted.[62] In one of their earliest works, Marx and Engels make the point without any shade of ambiguity:

> *History* does *nothing*, it 'possesses *no* immense wealth', it 'wages *no* battles'. It is *man*, real, living man, who does all that, who possesses and fights; 'history' is not, as it were, a person apart, using man as a means to achieve *its own* aims; history is *nothing but* the activity of man pursuing his aims.[63]

There is, of course, a tension in Marx and Engels' work between determinism and its antitheses. Engels' Introduction to Marx's *Class Struggles in France* – its bowdlerisation by the editors notwithstanding – did contain passages suggesting that the victory of social democracy is as inevitable 'as a natural process'.[64] And Marx, famously, referred to a 'law' of the development of the productive forces. But the supposedly derivative theory of the evolution of modes of production was never posited as a script to which future history must conform.[65] At times Marx seems to 'posit a *teleological* projection of working-class organization and consciousness leading to ultimate proletarian victory' but elsewhere he presents historical development 'in term of *alternatives*'.[66] He did speak of the 'law' of capital accumulation, but his writings, from *Poverty of Philosophy* to *Theories of Surplus Value,* abound with criticisms of those who would make laws of economic relations, and he explicitly attacked political economy for having metamorphosed capital accumulation into 'a pretended law of nature'.[67] He treated capitalism not as an 'economic' sphere reducible to the market but as a historically specific set of social relations that take the appearance of separate 'economic' and 'political' forms. 'Never in Marx,' Lucio Colletti underscores, 'do we find economic categories that are purely economic categories. All his concepts, on the contrary, are both economic and sociological.'[68] On the whole, as Colin Barker observes, the Marxian opus makes more sense when read as a 'non-teleological theory', one that treats human activity rather than some extra-human force – such as 'history' – as the essential determinant of social transformation.[69]

Equally misplaced is Polanyi's contention that Marx portrayed human behaviour as directed by base materialistic motives, determined by economic forces and saturated with grubby economic calculation. Marx's thesis was, on the contrary, as David Harvey points out, 'that it is the capitalist mode of production which forces such rationality upon us *against* all of the evidence as to what human beings are really all about'. Far from being a practitioner of economic determinism, 'it was precisely Marx's point that the realm of freedom begins where the realm of necessity ends and that it is only through struggle, political and personal, that we can achieve the command over our social and physical existence which will yield us that freedom'.[70] The notion that being determines consciousness does not diminish the role of ideals. Rather, it suggests that certain forms of consciousness are not trans-historical but only become attainable after 'new material conditions emerged of which people could then become conscious'.[71]

As regards Marx's theory of the state, Polanyi's critique contained little of substance. Its core contention was briskly controverted by Eugene Genovese in his review of Polanyi's *Dahomey and the Slave Trade*:

> For Polanyi state-building is a secular force within the economic organization and is not derivative from it. There would be nothing to quarrel about here, and indeed the proposition is far less original than the tone of the discussion suggests, did he not insist that his viewpoint refutes the Marxian theory of state formation. It may refute

vulgar-Marxism and economic determinism, but it presents no special difficulties for the Marxian theory of the state.[72]

In Polanyi's critique of Marxian value theory, similarly egregious flaws can be found. These are suggestive in what they reveal of his broader theoretical framework. His assumption that Marx had simply appropriated Ricardo's theory is a particularly wretched misreading – one that he shared with Dühring, Tönnies, Cole and Keynes.[73] Ricardo's theory, following Locke and Smith, views value through the eyes of the property owner. This is especially visible in Locke. The object of his value theory was not labouring human beings but what Locke construes as the productivity of property.[74] Following suit, Smith posited labour as the measure of exchange value, such that the value of a commodity is equal to the quantity of labour that its owner can command.[75] Labour, for Smith, is the labour-time of the individual, it is the *measure* of value but only one among its several *sources*. For Ricardo, likewise, labour is understood as the individual's labour time, as crystallised in the products of her labour.[76] He takes as givens the existence of exchange, prices and commodities, and his theory of value is sorely lacking in conceptual precision. (At times he even conflates value with exchange value.[77]) For Locke, Smith and Ricardo, the concept of value is introduced as a yardstick; its magnitude is of interest but not its form, such that value plays no critical role in their theory of capitalism.[78] For Marx, by contrast, labour and value are understood historically, as assuming different forms in different societies. His labour theory of value is a historically specific, critical inquiry; its guiding question is why, in capitalism, social labour becomes the source of exchange value. Generalising from the perspective of social labour, he conceives labour as the basis and connective tissue of human society, and the substance of value ('socially necessary labour time').[79] For him, the concept of value is subordinate to that of the commodity. The 'two sides' of the commodity, in the case of labour power, explain the source of surplus value: labour power is human creativity for sale, capable of generating more value than it requires for its own (re)production. This proposition marked a fundamental departure from Ricardo; indeed, it was among the handful of theses for which Marx claimed originality.[80] ('All the more remarkable,' quips the philosopher Scott Meikle, that the differences between Marx and Ricardo are so rarely heeded.[81])

Marx's value theory, in short, is not a stand-alone thesis but is folded into a multifaceted, critical analysis of political economy and capitalist society,[82] a framework that integrates the theory of capital as self-expanding value that accumulates through the exploitation of wage labour (with ancillary 'laws' of capital accumulation) together with a critique of classical political economy for its neglect of the social form of capitalist production and concomitant naturalisation of capitalist relations, as well as critiques of alienation, social atomisation and utilitarian self-interest. Taken together, these are understood as integral elements of an economy based on generalised commodity production, in which private property commands the commodities produced by labour while the labourers receive the value of their labour power. Thus, alienation and exploitation are understood as two sides of the same coin: in capitalist conditions, labour produces the worker's capacities as commodities, and capital as capital; the estrangement of the worker from herself, from other workers, their products, and nature, are all effected through a process of class exploitation.

MARXISM WINNOWED

In the early 1920s, Polanyi's attitude to Marxism was at its frostiest but it rapidly thawed. This was in large part due to his experience of Red Vienna, in particular the transformation of working-class political culture over which the Austro-Marxist SDAP presided. From this experience he took three crucial lessons: that a rapid transformation in the values of the mass of the population is possible, that such change is not internally generated but requires a radical restructuring of social conditions, and that the achievement of political power by a socialist workers' movement encourages a flourishing of Christian values.[83] He found himself warming to Austro-Marxism, which repudiated economic reductionism in theory while pursuing a deterministic reformism in practice. He re-engaged with Marx's writings, finding them to be 'essentially concordant with Christian philosophy', and communist theory to be 'deeply indebted to Christianity, to the substance of its moral aims'.[84]

The Marxian insights that spoke to Polanyi were the theories of alienation and commodity fetishism. This is apparent in his writings of the mid-1920s, for example 'On Liberty' which, following Marx and Lukacs, proposes that in capitalism the decisive economic relationships are created behind the backs of human actors, with the exercise of power over their fellows assuming the appearance of rule by 'capital' and 'prices': a fateful mirage that under existing social relations can be transcended only through the human mind as 'a theoretical insight of sociology' pending its transcendence in practice – 'the task of socialism'.[85] Polanyi's appreciation of Marxian sociology deepened in the 1930s, following his reading of newly published early writings of Marx (no mere 'wild oats' over which Marx had later repented but instead 'the general human basis' for all his work).[86] In its philosophy, he now argued, Marxism was progressive, undogmatic, and 'essentially revolutionary'.[87]

Leaning heavily upon Marx, Polanyi elaborated a critique of the capitalist social order as (i) governed by abstract economic forces, with a private property system that ensures the domination of living labour by past labour in the form of capital;[88] (ii) organised through markets, which isolate human beings from one another and dissociate moral considerations from economic behaviour, with 'greed and self-seeking' enshrined as the 'only rational attitude allowed by circumstances';[89] (iii) reliant upon a labour market that constructs human beings as commodities, opening the way to their 'abuse' on a scale capable of destroying the 'fabric of society';[90] and (iv) generative of mystified social relations, a bewitched world in which cognisance of the impact of our economic actions becomes impossibly difficult, thereby hobbling the capacity to undertake moral reflection and judgment. Marx's dialectic of modernity also found a strong echo in Polanyi: that industrial society experiences the development of a complex division of labour that expands societal interdependence but in the process engenders 'a new and tragic form of self-estrangement', suffered above all by the proletariat – a class that is celebrated by Polanyi not principally for its power but for its status as the universally oppressed class which, in Christ-like suffering, personifies the promise of redemption.[91]

For the first half of the interwar period, Polanyi's 'double movement' vis-à-vis Marx saw him embrace the theories of alienation and commodity fetishism without altering his rejection of the labour theory of value. In his reading of *Capital* – at least of Volume 1 (he did not read the others 'or if he did, showed no interest in them') – he agreed with Marx's critique of the *command* of private property over labour but not with the idea that that relationship should be viewed simultaneously as enforcing the extraction of surplus value.[92] One might say that he wished to separate the sociological wheat in *Capital* from the economic chaff. He 'sociologises' the commodity fetishism section – reworking it, with infusions from Tönnies and anthropology, as the 'disembedding' of economy from society – while condemning the rest of the work, with extravagant disregard for its argument, as 'Ricardian economics'.[93] But the misreading of the 'economic' element of *Capital* is entwined with – subsidiary to and symptomatic of – the attempt to abstract a sociology from Marx's critique of political economy. As Hüseyin Özel points out, Polanyi championed Marx's theory of commodity fetishism while rejecting the labour theory of value. Marx's theory of commodity fetishism, Özel adds, describes the process through which individuals become 'the personification of reified social relations'. In this respect, marginalist value theory is itself a symptom of commodity fetishism: it is the expression in economic theory of the 'reduction of the individual to *homo oeconomicus*'.[94]

It is paradoxical, then, that in parallel with his elaboration of a Marx-influenced sociology of capitalism Polanyi immersed himself in marginalist economic theory (as interpreted in their different ways by Eugen Böhm-Bawerk and Schumpeter). For Polanyi, as for Alfred Marshall and others, marginalism possessed not only a scientific but also a manifestly ethical edge, in that it places human decision-making at its centre, in contrast to the 'mechanistic' and 'objective' value theory of Locke-Ricardo-Marx. However, this had come at a price: a mechanistic theory of human decision-making, with economics geared to technical ends rather than to critical inquiry. In his attempt to sociologically square the economic circle, Polanyi found inspiration in the work of Oppenheimer and Emil Lederer, whose research focused on the economics-sociology divide. Oppenheimer proposed that because human behaviour is never reducible to economic action, economics must be complemented by sociology, or should even become its subdiscipline.[95] Fundamental economic laws may be universally applicable, as marginalist economics proposes, but social structures and normative cultures vary greatly across space and time and so too does the behaviour of economic actors. For example, in a market society, but only in such a society, individuals are obliged to behave in ways that approximate to the *homo oeconomicus* model. Lederer, a liberal socialist, had initially found Marxian value theory persuasive but rejected it in favour of marginalism. His *Grundzüge der Oekonomischen Theorie*, which Polanyi studied in the early 1920s, advocates that economic behaviour be understood as a meaningful, historicised totality.[96] Polanyi's own position combined marginalist value theory as applied to capitalist economies with a historicist critique of the transhistorical assumptions and pretensions of marginalist theory. Insofar as he held a 'pure economic theory' he conceived of it as referring to the realm of 'choice induced by scarcity of means'.[97] He appears, moreover, to have endorsed the position that economics is a science that studies universal laws, in that it deals not 'with raw materials, labour or production as such, but with the act of choice'.[98] However, his political economy, as it evolved in his Vienna years, was increasingly characterised by a set of radically historicist tenets: that the quest for a formal, rule-governed economic theory is futile, that economic behaviour is determined by social norms and conventions which change fundamentally over time, and that economic analysis must be grounded in empirical inquiry.

For all his earlier anathema toward sociology, Polanyi's critique of capitalism, in the 1920s, relied heavily on theories and concepts provided by that discipline. His endeavour manifested the disciplinary divide between sociology and economics that had consolidated in the final quarter of the previous century, with economics tasked with the scientific analysis of price movements within the economy (which Polanyi conceived in the Oppenheimerian manner as a 'purely economic' system) while sociology was tasked with the cultural-historical interpretation and critique of economic behaviour – the drawing of ethically appropriate boundaries around the market, defining which commodities are 'natural' and which are not, and advocacy of the re-embedding of 'economy' in 'society'. It is in this context that Polanyi's conception of the commodity should be understood. For him, commodities are things to be bought and sold at the market – much as in mainstream economics except that, with a Tönniesian twist, he makes a moral distinction between natural and fictitious commodities. This, the ethical critique of certain types of commodification (notably of labour), underpins his sociological critique of the boundaries of 'the economy' and an understanding of social resistance as the response to the suffering engendered by the creation of fictitious commodities. For Marx, by contrast, the commodity is theorised in social-relational terms: a good or service is a commodity by dint of its insertion within social processes of labour and exchange. The contradiction at its centre – between the commodity's use value and exchange value – provides the genetic code of capitalist society. In Marx's schema, labour-power is simultaneously a commodity like any other, its value determined by the socially necessary labour that goes into its (re)production, and it is unique, as the creator of value – and thereby of a surplus that takes the form of capital, an alien power. This idea underpins Marx's theories of exploitation, capital accumulation and alienation (of humans from their 'species being' and from nature; of workers from one another and from their products). Marx's *Capital,* a critique of political economy, attacks above all its neglect of the *social form* of capitalist production, which was the basis of the economists' naturalisation of capitalist relations. It construes the market system as based on a class relationship and generative of tendencies both toward polarisation between property owners and the proletariat and to economic crisis, as the revolutionising of the productive forces generates conditions that are inconsistent with the further self-expansion of capital, a tension that surfaces in crises of overaccumulation. Correlatively, Marx's theory of social movements identifies the working class as the wellspring of resistance, given the conjunction of its latent economic power with its experience of oppression. If *Capital* can be said to contain a sociology at all, it is inextricably bound up with its value theory. To extract Marx's theses on alienation and commodity fetishism as a separate 'sociology' is to render them static.

There are of course alternative readings of the distinction between Marxian and Polanyian theory. Fred Block, to give a notable example, suggests that Polanyi embraced a Hegelian form of Marxism in the 1930s when he conceived *The Great Transformation* but then, as he commenced writing in 1941, he was in the process of exiting the Marxist orbit and the concepts he introduced, such as 'fictitious commodities', the 'double movement' and the 'embedded economy', were not Marxist. The resulting incompatibility of theoretical frameworks explains the conceptual tensions at play in *The Great Transformation*, in particular with regard to 'embeddedness'. In an initial Marxian formulation Polanyi implies that the advent of the market society served to disembed the economy, with the pursuit of individual gain elevated to the organising principle of economic life. Yet a purely self-regulating market system, he came to see, is a utopia. As such, it cannot be truly disembedded. When Polanyi started 'to elaborate the moment of contradiction in his argument', in Block's construal, he gave the concept of embeddedness 'a new and unanticipated meaning'. He demonstrated that 'for most of the history of market society, the strength of protection effectively reembeds the economy' and, correlatively, that 'effectively functioning market societies must maintain some threshold level of embeddedness or else risk social and economic disaster'. Evidently a tension between the two meanings exists. On one hand, 'the reembedding of the market economy is normal and necessary for it to achieve any degree of functionality', on the other, there is 'the more Marxist argument that the protective countermovement weakens the ability of market self-regulation to function so as to produce crises of growing intensity'. The former challenges 'a core presumption of both market liberals and Marxists', for both traditions 'are built on the idea that there is an analytically autonomous economy that is subject to its own internal logic'.[99] (Neoliberalism and Marxism are alike, Block and Margaret Somers opine, in prioritising 'the economy as the central organizing force in society'. They both 'disdain' state power, imagining that 'it is possible to escape from governance and political constraint'.[100]) In conclusion, Block suggests that 'Polanyi glimpsed the idea of the always embedded market economy, but he was not able to give that idea a name or develop it theoretically because it represented too great a divergence from his initial theoretical starting point'. The 'always embedded' thesis is Polanyi's original contribution, and the one that offers the greatest heuristic potential.[101]

How persuasive is Block's account? There is no doubt that in the interwar period Polanyi was close to Marxist movements and ideas. Where Block errs is in his exaggeration of the degree to which the 'always embedded' notion – the idea that economic behaviour is always already woven into legal, political, customary and religious fabrics – is original to Polanyi. Leaving the ancients to one side, it was taken for granted by Adam Smith, whose *Moral Sentiments,* as Don Robotham remarks, 'argued that the extension of market relations brings with it not only utilitarian attitudes and self-seeking relationships, but also the broader sympathies of society, civic culture and humanity they help to create'.[102] It was a core concern for the GHS and nineteenth-century sociologists in their explorations of the market economy's institutional preconditions, and it formed the explicit theoretical thrust of *Der Güterverkehr in der Urgesellschaft,* by the economic anthropologist Bódog Somló (1909), Polanyi's doctoral supervisor – which electrified him when he stumbled across it in 1948. The idea that economic behaviour cannot be studied as if it is isolated from society was elementary for Marx, too. In the *Grundrisse* he cautions that the simplest economic category, e.g. exchange value, presupposes population, moreover a population producing in specific relations; as well as a certain kind of family, or commune, or state, etc. It can never exist other than as an abstract, one-sided relation within an already given, concrete, living whole.[103]

Pace Block, the Marxist tradition is not 'built on the idea that there is an analytically autonomous economy that is subject to its own internal logic' – unless, that is, 'analytically' refers merely to analysis of 'the economy' within a broader understanding of its role within the social totality, and if it does, Polanyi stands equally accused. Marxists recognise that the self-regulating market is politically engineered. It is 'a form of State "regulation", introduced and maintained by legislative and coercive means', as Antonio Gramsci put it, anticipating Polanyi. It is 'a deliberate policy, conscious of its own ends, and not the spontaneous, automatic expression of economic facts. Consequently, laissez-faire liberalism is a political programme designed to change ... a state's ruling personnel, and to change the economic program of the state itself – in other words the distribution of the national income'.[104] *Pace* Block and Somers, Marxism does not prioritise 'the economy' over the state, as society's 'central organizing force'. Quite the reverse. Moreover, Block and Somers' coupling of neoliberalism and Marxism relies upon an idiosyncratic understanding of the former. To suggest that neoliberalism is 'disdainful' of state power is to confuse its libertarian fringe with the neoliberal mainstream, as any serious survey or exegesis of neoliberal theory will confirm.[105]

An alternative interpretation of the Polanyi-Marx distinction has been offered by Maria Szecsi (Polanyi's niece), Kari Polanyi-Levitt and Marguerite Mendell. For Szecsi, whereas Marx took as his subject 'the capitalist process of production and exploitation as producer of mass misery', Polanyi emphasised 'the market mechanism as producer of social dislocation'.[106] Similarly, Polanyi-Levitt and Mendell propose that whereas Marx developed his argument 'to prove exploitation in the process of production, Polanyi placed at the center of his critique of capitalism the capitalist market mechanism as the source of self-estrangement and social dislocation'. Polanyi's thesis that in capitalism the economy is 'disembedded' from society, they add, flows from its tendency to market expansion 'as distinct from its exploitative character'. His critique is that capitalism creates unfreedom, in the sense that interpersonal economic relations are impenetrable and opaque, appearing as mechanical responses to impersonal, 'objective' market forces.[107]

In their presentations of the Marx–Polanyi distinction, Szecsi, Polanyi-Levitt and Mendell misrepresent Marxian theory in suggesting that it downplays processes of commodification and social dislocation such that these can be meaningfully counterposed to production and exploitation. This is to recapitulate Polanyi's own approach to *Capital*, which, as discussed above, cleaves its critique of capitalism into a sociology and an economics. In effect, Polanyi 'sociologised' *Capital* by extracting its heart, the theory of commodity fetishism, while discarding the remaining body as 'Ricardian economics'. In contrast to Marx, the weight of explanation in Polanyi's writings falls upon patterns of 'economic integration' and rarely, if ever, upon the exercise of control over productive property and the systematic relationships of inclusion and exclusion that flow from it. Hence, where for Marx generalised commodity exchange and large-scale proletarianisation are two sides of the same coin, *The Great Transformation* roots the socio-cultural corrosion of nineteenth-century capitalism not in the commodification of labour-power and nature *and* exploitation and domination, but solely in the former.

If it is misleading to identify Marx as a theorist of exploitation in contrast to Polanyi as theorist of commodification and alienation, how might their differences more accurately be defined? One could do worse than begin with anthropology. For both thinkers, *homo* is fundamentally *socialis,* but if, for Marx, humankind's sociality evolves out of its interaction with the natural environment through labour, with labour forming the material connective tissue of human society, Polanyi privileges the creation of moral community. Their approach to understanding socio-economic structures and dynamics differs accordingly. For Polanyi, the focus is upon the shuttling of goods and services between individuals and other centres of appropriation. The basic term of reference is the mechanism of economic integration (that is, the economic prerequisite of community), and to this corresponds a method of analysis: to describe the manner in which trade, money and markets are institutionalised within societies dominated by one or other mechanism. Hence the emphasis in accounting for the rise of market society (in nineteenth-century Britain) is on the institutionalisation of market exchange, which 'disembeds' economy from society. For Marx and Engels, the focus, in class-divided societies, is upon the framework of social relations through which the transfer of goods and services is organised over sustained periods from one social group to another. How is a surplus produced, who controls its distribution, by means of what institutional arrangements and to what ends? On the origins of capitalism, relatedly, their attention is on the forcible uprooting of peasantries from the land, which, coupled with colonial appropriations and the accumulation of capital in mercantile hands, created the conditions in which a capitalist economic system could emerge.[108]

A second point of comparison concerns the subordination of morality to utilitarian self-interest. Polanyi and Marx/Engels both tackle this aspect of market society but they do so along different routes. For Polanyi, the problem derives from the egotistic mentality, understood as a product of laissez-faire liberalism, social atomisation, and the subsumption of 'society' under 'economy'. For Marx and Engels, social atomisation and the egotistic mentality are understood as consequences of processes of exploitation and alienation that are rooted ultimately not in laissez-faire liberalism but in the diremption between private property and the proletariat. For them, the axial opposition within capitalist society is not economics versus politics but capital versus labour, and the defining problem is not the commodification of money, land and labour but its consequence: the systematic subordination of human activity to capital.

What of Marx and Polanyi's theories of politics? For the former, the state in capitalist society is an institution that is based on, and polices, the divisions within civil society even as it affects to transcend them; it is an instrument of oppression through which the ruling class organises its own interests and those of civil society. Revolution is necessary to dismantle the state and to empower citizens, thereby enabling, initially, a plebeian active democracy – as in the Paris Commune – and, ultimately, a society whose rules and institutions are comprehensively and radically democratic. For Polanyi, the modern state is conceived not primarily as a means of political oppression or instrument of bourgeois rule but in the mainstream sense: as the institution through which a community of citizens fashions itself as a collective subject with a common will, as an instrument for the self-regulation of society, and even as 'the guarantor of freedom in a complex society'.[109] For him, modern democracy is inherently social democratic. This is because, as discussed in Chapter 3, parliament provides the deliberative arena through which 'the common people' exercise control over the state.[110]

CONCLUSION

This chapter has mapped the watershed occupied by Marxian and Polanyian social theory, tracing the common contours and the ridgelines of divergence. Polanyi, it has argued, elaborated a Tönniesian understanding of the commodity that was quite unlike Marx's. This entailed a rejection, as Burawoy has put it, of the 'idea of capitalism, with its imperatives for accumulation and new sources of profit'.[111] Lacking theories of capitalism and the commodity form, the meaning he gave to the process of decommodification that a socialist transition would entail remained nebulous. With a sufficiently commodious definition of decommodification, many 'actually existing market economies' can be categorised as decommodified mixed economies, and whether 'decommodification' entails the abolition of the wage labour system altogether or merely socio-political measures to ensure workers' full incorporation as citizens into the body politic is unclear. As Mike Haynes and Rumy Husan observe, this underlay Polanyi's misreading of corporatist trends within mid-twentieth-century capitalism as harbingers of its demise.[112]

Nevertheless, in Polanyi's youth there were two currents of Marxist thought and practice that engaged him deeply: Bernstein's 'revision' and Austro-Marxism. With their assimilation of ideas from Rousseau, Tönnies and guild socialism these were congenial to his outlook. Paradoxically, given Polanyi's antipathy to determinism, both currents bore the imprint of nineteenth-century determinist sociology: the notion that the twin revolutions of modernity – industrial and democratic – would, via an expanding working class and the introduction of universal suffrage, guide human civilisation inexorably toward a condition of freedom and rationality (in their idiom: socialism). Translated into Austro-Marxist practice, this philosophy decreed that patient organisation and education, rather than active mobilisation, was the order of the day. For example, Max Adler's repudiation of economic determinism and mechanical materialism, and his elevation of the autonomous role for ethics and the decisive role played by human consciousness in effecting social change, were directly plugged into an argument that foresaw progress towards socialism as evolving by way of Party-led mass education.[113] This strategy, as Ilona Duczynska argued in *Workers in Arms* (discussed in Chapter 3), ultimately led SDAP leaders to perform a similar (although less egregious) refusal to mobilise mass action of which their German comrades stood accused during Hitler's rise to power. The Austro-Marxists' theoretical recognition of the decisive part played by conscious human activity in history did not inspire them to mobilise against fascism but instead sanctioned policies that literally and figuratively disarmed the working class.

In some accounts, Polanyi's embrace of deterministic philosophy stemmed from his attraction to Marxism, but as this chapter shows, matters are not so simple. Of the four currents that dominated Marxist philosophy, Polanyi rejected the most rigidly deterministic – Kautskyan social democracy – but also the one that explicitly and systematically sought to transcend the voluntarism–determinism antinomy: that of Lukacs. In the 1920s Polanyi was strongly attracted to Austro-Marxism, and in particular to the Cole-inspired 'functional theory' of Bauer. Its imprint can be seen in the functionalist arguments in *The Great Transformation*. In the 1930s, Polanyi found inspiration in Marx's early writings, and warmed to the communist orthodoxy of that decade, concurring with its forecast that, in his words, 'an abrupt transition … to Socialism is almost inevitable'.[114] What would be the central mechanism of socialist transition? In Polanyi's understanding, it is the conflict between capital and the demos.

3

Capital versus the Demos

The 'Politics 101' thesis on the relationship between capitalism and democracy is straightforward: the former facilitates, or generates, the latter.[1] A market economy with private property in the means of production fosters an open civil society conducive to the flourishing of individual liberties and a pluralist and competitive political arena. Others propose that the connection, such as it is, is indirect. So, for modernisation theories of democratisation, a market economy not only tends to complexity, and as such is less amenable to state direction, but also encourages economic growth. Higher living standards and education foster trust and competence among the wider citizenry; trade and tourism expand, inspiring openness to the world, including to the infectious idea of democracy; social mobility catalyses a shift in balance of individual identities from the ascribed to the achieved; education and rationalisation foster secularism; and, last but not least, middling layers of businesspeople and professionals burgeon, creating a buffer between the ruling and the toiling classes which, by tempering and mediating class conflict, engenders a moderate political climate in which democratic institutions can thrive. There is, thirdly, a dialectical ('structuralist') account. It holds that the development of capitalist relations creates democratic pressures by weakening traditional landowning classes (which rely upon labour-repressive relations of production), strengthening the working class, and enabling states to subordinate the military caste to civil government. Through a democratic *List der Vernunft*, capitalism inadvertently brings forth an organised demos, which, in the struggle against it, brings capitalist democracy into being. In theory, capitalist-democratisation should be an ongoing process.

Over the last three decades or so, market norms and practices have spread, and markets have intruded into areas of life previously governed by non-market techniques. Meanwhile, the relative decline of landowning classes and the peasantry, as compared to the urban middle classes and working class, has continued. We should therefore be living, one would suppose, in an era of ongoing and triumphant democratisation. And in a sense we are. Democratic transitions have rippled through southern Europe in the 1970s, South America and Eastern Europe in the 1980s, and parts of Africa and Asia too. Yet the same period has also witnessed anxiety, often voiced by the same people who champion the market system as the fount of democracy, that the former is under threat from 'too much' of the latter. In political theory, Fareed Zakaria warned of democracy's 'illiberal' tendencies: when elected governments mistake their popular legitimacy for absolute sovereignty, they extend and centralise their power, undermining the fundamental rights to property and liberty that liberals hold dear.[2] In economics, ordoliberal and public choice theorists warned of the dangers to profitability posed by democratic politics. Markets, they argue, function correctly when strictly insulated from democratic influence. Within the state, zones of governmental authority and policymaking, particularly in the realms of economics and finance, should be shielded from the purview of elected officials, restricting the tools that had once been available for social-democratic reform. 'The economy must be depoliticised!', as the *Financial Times* advised the Arab world during its ill-starred spring.[3] Some liberal economists have gone further, commending the economic benefits delivered by anti-democratic institutions. 'The Chinese are our teachers now!' was the lesson drawn from the 'Great Recession' of 2008 by the *Independent's* economics editor, Hamish McRae. Learning from China, liberal states should drive down the influence of democracy on fiscal matters and on welfare. Put bluntly, he concluded, 'the Chinese authorities, unencumbered by democratic pressures, have been much better at managing public finances than any Western democracy'.[4]

The victory and attenuation of democracy in the neoliberal age has been thematised by social movements – as in the *indignados'* war cry ¡Democracia Real!, envisioning a 'movement democracy' antithetical to its parliamentary simulacrum, the formal democratic system run by *la casta*. On the far left, actually existing democracy is viewed sceptically: at best, a watery ersatz for the real thing, or, even, a political canopy to justify and protect ever uglier forms of capitalism. It has been analysed and dissected by critics in their legions. Some speak of 'low-intensity democracy' or a 'new constitutionalism' – the constitutional and legal innovations that increasingly circumscribe the regulatory authority of states, in the interests of the corporate sector.[5] Democracy since the end of the Cold War, in the dialectic of Nigerian political theorist Claude Ake, appears 'triumphant and unassailable, its universalization only a matter of time' yet its global triumph has only been permitted 'because it has been trivialized to the point that it is no longer threatening to power elites.'[6] Wendy Brown has catalogued the 'undoing' of democracy, and gazes into the void that it has become: 'an empty signifier to which any and all can attach their dreams and hopes'.[7] Perhaps, she hazards, capitalism 'has finally reduced democracy to a "brand", that late modern twist on commodity fetishism which wholly severs a product's saleable image from its content'.[8] Alain Badiou and Slavoj Žižek, while retaining the traditional connection between the socialist movement and democratic norms and practices (*isonomia*, majority rule, freedom of discussion and assembly, mass participation and so on), have critiqued the perversion of democracy in the discourse and practices of mainstream politics: its fetishisation, its elevation into an Absolute – a fig leaf for liberal capitalism.[9]

In the political centre, attention has been directed less to neoliberalism than to economic globalisation. Once upon a time, according to the globalisation story, the world was partitioned into discrete national economies presided over by states that generally acted in the citizens' interests, but with economic internationalisation and financial deregulation, markets increasingly usurped command of the political sphere. The space of democratic politics narrowed, with decision-making dominated by unelected financial institutions. A version of this narrative was proposed by David Held and his 'cosmopolitan democrat' co-thinkers. More polemical variations were issued by social democrat politicians, notably the former Labour Party minister, David Blunkett. In a 2012 pamphlet, Blunkett identified the conflict between markets and democracy as the contradiction that defines the conjuncture. 'Political democracy was and remains the counterweight to the market,' he intoned, and the financial turmoil of recent years has 'made this more relevant than ever. ... The unseen and unaccountable hand of the global financial markets can make or break governments in devastating fashion.' Blunkett equates 'the market' with 'globalisation' and democracy with the local – with identity and belonging, participation and engagement in the political process.[10] His pamphlet concludes with an appeal to the political left to 'put a shot of electricity back in the political system and find new ways of re-engaging people with government'. Governments can only balance the debilitating force of bond markets if they have behind them an active electorate: an 'engaged political democracy has to be the countervailing force against the unfettered market'.[11] (Curiously, Blunkett makes no reference to the fact that the governments in which he served worshipped at the altar of that same unfettered market, nor saw fit to consider whether the neoliberal deification of markets may have contributed to the undermining of the electorate's 'engagement'.) Lest his readers conclude that markets ought to be more tightly regulated, or even progressively replaced by other mechanisms of distribution, he urges acceptance of the fact 'that the market is a reality, that the power of finance is here to stay, [and] that globalisation cannot be wished away by dreamers setting up tents in the heart of the City of London'.[12] Thus, in Blunkett's hands, the thesis on the conflict between democracy and the market enjoins acquiescence to 'the power of finance', with democracy restricted to pleas for a more 'engaged' civil society, and with the scope of democratic engagement drawn tight: it includes canvassing for the Labour Party but prohibits radical aspirations of the sort that gathered under the banner of Occupy.

For mainstream social democracy today, capitalism cannot be challenged. What can be done is to encourage civic and electoral engagement (Blunkett) and to advocate the democratisation of existing institutions, especially at the international level (Held). Polanyi's era knew similar debates, but its left social democracy possessed a more vigorous sense that capitalism represents the antithesis of democracy. 'The issue in a capitalist democracy resolves itself into this,' thundered Nye Bevan in the 1940s: 'either poverty will use democracy to win the struggle against property, or property, in fear of poverty, will destroy democracy.' The function of parliamentary democracy 'is to expose wealth-privilege to the attack of the people. It is a sword pointed at the heart of property-power. The arena where the issues are joined is Parliament.'[13] Declamations such as these contained a polemical edge, but there was more to them than that. They were expressions of a longstanding and elaborate social-democratic thesis. It had arisen in the nineteenth century but achieved its full form in the interwar period, an exceptional historical conjuncture that witnessed the disciplining of national economies by international capital collide with a democratic moment, the rise of universal suffrage. One product of that collision was a distinctive thesis on the relationship between capitalism and democracy in the interwar period. The rest of this chapter explores its origins, evolution and morphology, with a focus on Polanyi's contribution, and traces its influence within left-liberal and social-democratic thought through the latter part of the twentieth century.

WORLDWIDE WEBBS: THE 'IRRESISTIBLE PROGRESS OF DEMOCRACY'

Polanyi's thinking on democracy and capitalism developed within a particular historical conjuncture and as an attempt to explain it. Prior to the twentieth century, democracy had been held in mistrust and contempt. For property-owners and elites it posed a threat to property and to their rule. It gives power to the poor and ignorant, constituting them as an organised 'party' and enabling them to get their horny hands on the levers of government, which would inevitably lead to social deterioration, as they tear into the carefully tended boundaries of class and rank. In an unpublished essay, 'The Fascist Virus', Polanyi diagnosed 'the old hostility of capitalism to popular government. Their incompatibility was recognised by capitalists and employers from the first', as well as by theorists from all points on the political compass. (He mentions Edmund Burke and Robert Owen, both of whom 'opposed the extension of the franchise to the masses'.) In the Chartist decade, the argument was honed. The Liberal peer John Russell held that universal suffrage would be a gamble too far, given that British society is so 'very complicated', with its property 'very unequally divided'. His colleague on the lordly Liberal benches, Thomas Babington

Macaulay, submitted that because 'civilization rests on the security of property, this principle follows: that we never can without absolute danger, entrust the superior government of this country to any class which would, to a moral certainty, commit great and systematic inroads on the security of property'.[14] Liberal political theorists – commencing, arguably, with the American Revolution[15] – began to recognise the inevitable approach of some form of democratic rule but even the most enlightened of them remained gravely concerned. Tocqueville regarded democracy as a comparatively just system but liable to spiritual degradation because it enables the majority to impose their base prejudices on all. John Stuart Mill supported various elements of democratic government but shared Tocqueville's trepidation toward democracy *qua* collective will formation. Unless the influence of the masses over policymakers and officials were carefully restricted, it would inevitably endanger the sovereign liberal principle: individual liberty.

The age of Tocqueville and Mill saw the start of a sea change in elite attitudes to democracy. With the consolidation of capitalism, the division between a public (state) sector and the private (family and economy) sharpened, such that the democratisation of the former posed a less immediate threat to power relations in the latter. The principle of legal equality and its associated norms (the levelling of the status order, the rise of individualism) were conducive to a pervasive societal democratisation: mentalities of subjecthood and deference yielded imperceptibly to those of citizenship and equality. Governments bargained with legislatures for the authorisation to tax and with citizens over the delivery of taxes. Together with revolutions in transport, communications, media and literacy, all this contributed to the mobilisation of populations. Social movements and political parties gained a new form, and placed demands upon government. 'Political entrepreneurs' discovered they could promote their proposals by organising public displays of popular support.[16] Social movements broadened the range of participants in public politics and integrated previously segmented trust networks into the public sphere. Gradually, more and more of the elite came to see that the political system would have to adjust to the new reality. 'Might it not be better,' they reflected, 'to bow to the inevitable' and accept democracy in its limited representative form, 'as a framework within which as much as possible of the traditional structure of power and values' could be preserved?[17] After all, when the franchise was extended by an increment, property, commerce and hierarchy all survived intact. Perhaps they would survive its further extension? Conversely, would not the persistence of a liberal-autocratic constitution pose a greater threat to 'property and civilisation' in the long run?

Throughout Europe, the mainstay of the democratisation movement was social democracy. It combined political engagement for a broadening of the suffrage with a conviction that societal democratisation was inevitable. This Tocquevillian belief was ardently held by members of the Fabian Society, such as George Bernard Shaw – whose dramaturgical and political repertoire Polanyi admiringly surveyed in his very first published essay. The Fabian goal was to further the course of social progress through replacing the prevailing acquisitive and materialistic value system – which had thrived in the *laissez-faire* jungle of nineteenth-century Britain – with spiritual and collectivist ones. Its credo was a Social Darwinist determinism according to which social life, guided by the political elite, tends toward rational – which in modern conditions meant collective – organisational forms. It was felicitous that the trajectories of political and economic progress were converging toward a socialist future. Socialism, as Sidney Webb put it, was 'the inevitable outcome of Democracy and the Industrial Revolution'.[18] Its inevitability, he and Beatrice mused, was unmistakeable in the early twentieth century when 'every nation of advanced industrialism' found itself 'increasingly driven to measures of Socialist character'.[19] Shaw, similarly, maintained – citing Tocqueville – that 'the main stream which has borne European society towards Socialism during the past 100 years is the irresistible progress of Democracy'.[20] Socialism, in this prospectus, represented a common step toward the synthesising of 'human purpose'. It signalled, in H. G. Wells' phrase, the 'awakening of a collective conscious-ness in humanity, a collective will and a collective mind out of which finer individualities may arise'.[21]

Fabianism was 'permeationist' and pedagogical. Permeationism refers to the strategy of infiltrating the structures of power in order to tilt the capitalist system towards its inevitable self-collectivisation.[22] In tactical terms, it can also denote the Fabian practice of joining an assortment of social and political organisations, persuading their members to adopt anonymously presented Fabian positions, and then resigning when it appeared more advantageous to peddle their policy prescriptions elsewhere.[23] For Fabians, moral suasion and social-scientific education were the levers of social change. In Beatrice Webb's words, they believed 'that any reasonable man or woman could be moralized into supporting reforms, and educated by social science into choosing those which were most likely to come to the desired result'.[24] Perhaps fittingly for a grouping that took its name from a Roman dictator, the Fabian perspective on democracy was patrician. Social progress would come through 'the consent of the populace, exercising peaceful, orderly, legal power through democratic electoral institutions'.[25] For this, the democratic machinery that existed in nineteenth-century Britain was eminently serviceable, even if some progressive tweaks were necessary. In 1896, Shaw declared himself content with the basic framework of British democracy, with the exceptions of the House of Lords, the system of remunerating MPs and, most importantly, the exclusion of the working classes.[26] Granting the vote to workers would result in a government 'responsive, and responsible, to a majority of the population'. But if democracy ought to be *extended to* the working classes it must not be *dominated by* them. Democracy represented a means of distributing authority equitably and 'preventing the monopoly of authority by any individual or class', with neither employers *nor the employed* able to monopolise political power.[27] It would ensure, moreover, the election of qualified and responsible administrators. Sidney Webb, like his mentor John Stuart Mill, believed that the advance of collectivism was first and foremost a civil-service task, with at best an ancillary role for grassroots democratic initiative.[28] He deemed particularly objectionable 'the prospect of a candidate winning an election because of personal popularity rather than administrative or leadership prowess', and proposed a system whereby individuals interested in competing for office 'would be required to successfully complete an examination – thereby meeting an objective standard for overall fitness'.[29] The citizenry would then select from the list of approved candidates.

In short, the Fabian route to socialism proceeded through gradual democratic reform, guided by enlightened mandarins. When it arrived, the socialist order – in the imaginaries of leading Fabians – would be more Platonic than democratic. This was certainly the case for Annie Besant. 'A democratic Socialism, controlled by majority votes, guided by numbers,' she argued, 'can never succeed; a truly aristocratic Socialism, controlled by duty, guided by wisdom, is the next step upwards in civilization.'[30] Likewise, Wells' vision of a socialist society was more elitist than democratic. 'More than that,' Margaret Cole adds, it was 'highly Malthusian, quasi-imperialist, and racialist'.[31]

The Fabian prospectus was notoriously elitist but it did make room for one roundly radical tenet. The principal conduit through which democratic norms and practices would irrigate civil society were the labour organisations. 'Industrial democracy', in the lexicon of the time. This radicalism, however, was tightly circumscribed. In *Industrial Democracy*, the Webbs spell out their antipathy to direct forms of democracy. These lead either to 'inefficiency and disintegration' or – and here they anticipate Robert Michels' iron law of oligarchy – to the 'uncontrolled dominance of a personal dictator or an expert bureaucracy'.[32] Their preference in respect of industrial democracy was instead 'the typically modern form of democracy' in which government is in the hands of freely elected representatives of the people. It would yoke popular consent to administrative efficiency, with elected representatives appointing 'an executive committee under whose direction the permanent official staff performs its work'.[33]

The Fabians were 'the least internationally conscious of any radical group', in Cole's judgment, but they exerted considerable influence abroad.

In the early twentieth century Wells was all the rage in Germany and was the most widely discussed English writer in Hungary.[34] In Austria, the social-democratic leaders Bauer and Karl Renner closely tracked the progress of Fabianism and its guild-socialist offshoot. Bauer was especially drawn to the work of Douglas Cole while Renner sought to find 'an equilibrium between the positions of Cole on the one hand and Sidney and Beatrice Webb on the other'.[35] As for Polanyi, he was a devotee of Wells and Shaw and an attentive reader of the Webbs. He applauded in particular the Webbs' schema for the institutional embedding of industrial democracy: a state with two parliaments, 'a political parliament in the narrow sense' and 'a social parliament' responsible for economic affairs, redistribution, education, science, culture and 'the hygiene of the race'.[36] Generally speaking, however, he found less inspiration in orthodox Fabianism than in guild socialism – as discussed in Chapter 1.

If the Webbs regarded themselves as followers of Mill, guild socialists were closer to romantic and revolutionary socialist traditions. They looked to the likes of Jean-Jacques Rousseau and William Morris, were less inclined to elitism than were mainstream Fabians, and liked to speak of the 'common man', with its resonances that linked peasants, artisans and workers with 'the common good' and indeed the 'House of Commons'. This was Polanyi's language too. 'The common sense of the common man,' he declared, is 'the actual and factual basis of politics in a democracy'.[37] 'It is a simple fact,' he averred in 'Common Man's Masterplan',

> that the way of life of democracy was not developed by so-called educated people nor was it practiced by them ... but it was practiced by communities of simple people like those of the History of the Apostles, or the Quaker communities, pioneering villages of the early frontier or the pilgrim fathers on board the Mayflower. [...] The truth is that common human experience is at the back of democracy, and where that experience includes tolerance, patience with the views of dissenting minorities, there democracy itself will be tolerant and not enforce more uniformity than necessary to give effect to the decisions of the majority.[38]

Another of the Fabians' Central European admirers was Bernstein. His conception of democracy was closer to Mill and the Fabians than to the Cole-Rousseau lineage. For Bernstein, democracy must be of the parliamentary-representative species, with a 'permanent and professional' bureaucracy.[39] He did not doubt the capacity of liberal-democratic institutions 'to accommodate the interests of the working class'.[40] With Mill and the Fabians, he saw parliamentary democracy as an educational and moral institution, a 'university of compromise' through which different social classes learn to cooperate.[41] He envisaged the advance of socialism as a process of piecemeal legislative initiatives, necessitating support 'from as many quarters of society as possible for as many legislative reforms as possible', with the party playing the role of broker among interest groups and with a crucial role for its advisors and other experts, skilled as they are at finessing the complex decisions that can unite disparate interests on instrumental grounds.[42] Like the Fabians, he equated the discrete economic reforms achieved under capitalism with the '"organic growth" [*Hineinwachsen*] of a socialist alternative'.[43] More vehemently than they, however, he championed democracy. It figures in his theory not merely as a form of government but as the method and goal of socialism. His *Evolutionary Socialism* borrows from the Webbs in proposing that the 'trade unions are indispensable organs' of industrial democracy, but he came closer to identifying socialism with democracy *tout court*. For, democracy's *principle* of equal rights ensures the 'absence of class government' (such that political privilege belongs to 'the whole community' rather than a particular class); its *strategy*, acquired in 'the high school of compromise', represents 'the alternative to a violent revolution'; and its *political philosophy* is confident and optimistic: although the vote may once have appeared merely as the right to choose among different 'butchers', as the working class expands in size and education it evolves into 'the implement by which to transform the representatives of the people from masters into real servants of the people'. Social democracy ought therefore to establish itself 'unreservedly on the theory of democracy'.[44]

In relation to socialism, democracy, in Bernstein's assessment, is simultaneously 'the means of attaining socialism' and its form of realisation.[45] However, as Stephen Eric Bronner remarks, 'the connection between ends and means' upon which Bernstein insisted was not remotely as tight as he liked to suppose. His chain of explanation relied upon the surreptitious introduction of 'a notion of progress that, while standing beyond empirical verification, remained as optimistic and linear as that of any orthodox Marxist'.[46] Bernstein did not simply conceive of the winning of a democratic republic as a means of strengthening socialist forces but held that it would *necessarily* lead to the decentralisation of power and to socialist democratic structures. Like Bernstein, Polanyi saw democracy as a way of life, and essentially synonymous with socialism. A socialist transformation of society, he held, cannot occur 'by means of political democracy and socialisation alone. It is democracy combined with the cooperative spirit that leads to socialism'.[47]

THE BLOCKED ROAD TO DEMOCRATIC SOCIALISM

With regard to theorising the clash between capitalism and democracy, the germinal moment occurred in the aftermath of the Great War. The postwar

years witnessed three developments that catalysed a profound reconstitu-
tion of socialist political thought and practice. One was systemic crisis:
the cataclysm of war, followed by an acute economic recession. To many,
it appeared that the established political-economic system had reached its
endpoint. It had, the Webbs declared in 1920, 'demonstrably broken down'.
Across 'the civilised world', capitalism had,

> at least among the young generation that is growing up, lost its moral
> authority. Whole nations have avowedly rejected it as the basis of their
> social and economic structure; and, in all countries of advanced indus-
> trialism, great masses of people are increasingly refusing to accept it as
> a permanent institution.[48]

The second was the triumph of parliamentary democracy. Universal
suffrage was introduced across much of Europe – for example in Hungary
and Poland (1918); Germany, Sweden and the Netherlands (1919). The
third was the revival of the idea of councils' democracy – a form of
constituted power that promised to overturn class divisions and re-unify
society's political and economic spheres. Already glimpsed in Paris in
1871 and again in Russia in 1905, it then, following the 1917 revolutions in
Russia, made appearances in Hungary and Bavaria. Workers' and soldiers'
councils arose in Austria, too, where Polanyi lived from 1919.

In a 1922 article entitled 'The Rebirth of Democracy', Polanyi addressed
the concern of leftists that established elites had captured and tamed
democracy. They could point to the plebiscitary use of universal suffrage
by Napoleon III in France, or to 'the covert rule of corporations' in the
USA and conclude 'despondently that the achievement of political
democracy, rather than serving those oppressed and excluded by society
in their fight for social and cultural equality, seemed only to shore up the
power of the ruling classes'. However, Polanyi responded, they should take
heart. 'Historical progress driven by genuine ideals cannot be derailed
for long ... The idea of democracy is being reborn, with redoubled
potency, in the minds of the masses, and no power will be able to halt its
victorious march.'[49]

Polanyi's confidence in the forward march of democracy referred
above all to events in two countries. One, Britain, had recently beheld
'the triumphant entry of the Labour Party onto the stage of the world's
oldest Parliament, girdled by its thousand traditions'.[50] Under Ramsay
Macdonald, Labour was 'using the weapon of old-fashioned democracy
as an iron hammer, banging at the gates of world reaction'.[51] Polanyi was
effusive in his praise of Macdonald's 'proletarian government' of 1924, and
especially of the Labour leader's determination to hitch his party 'to the
Liberal wagon'.[52] Under Macdonald, he believed, Labour's working-class

roots were weakening somewhat but this would enable it all the more vigorously to champion socialism 'in the name of conscientious idealism'.[53]

Britain was home to a clutch of labour-movement intellectuals on whose ideas Polanyi drew when elaborating his thesis on capitalism and democracy, notably Cole, Laski, Richard Tawney and John Macmurray.[54] In Laski's view, because capitalism and democracy are essentially incompatible, Britain 'has to face the issue of whether it will adjust its economic and social constitution to the political democracy upon which its legislative constitution depends', as democracy increasingly becomes the instrument of working-class policies.[55] In other words, the institutions of capitalist democracy, 'being built on inescapable contradictions, issue inevitably into revolution'.[56] Of greater importance to Polanyi was Tawney's *Equality* (1931). Polanyi was on friendly terms with Tawney and hugely appreciated *Equality*. He singled out a passage that posits a common culture as prerequisite for a functioning democracy. 'What a community requires,' wrote the Labour sage, in a passage that Polanyi typed out and filed, 'is a common culture, because, without it, it is not a community at all.' Yet a common culture,

> cannot be created merely by desiring it. It rests upon economic foundations. It is incompatible with the existence of too violent a contrast between the economic standards and educational opportunities of different classes, for such a contrast has as its result, not a common culture, but servility or resentment, on the one hand, and patronage or arrogance, on the other. It involves, in short, a large measure of economic equality – not necessarily, indeed, in respect of the pecuniary incomes of individuals, but of environment, of habits of life, of access to education and the means of civilization, of security and independence, and of the social consideration which equality in these matters usually carries with it.

Tawney was reluctant to define democracy as *either* a method of government *or* a social arrangement more or less synonymous with socialism,[57] but, he argued forcefully, if it were institutionalised merely as the former 'and nothing more, instead of being, as it should be, not only a form of government, but a type of society, and a manner of life which is in harmony with that type', it would remain precarious.[58] To make it a 'type of society', he added, required 'the resolute elimination of all forms of special privilege' and the conversion 'of economic power, now often an irresponsible tyrant, into a servant of society, working within clearly defined limits and accountable for its actions to a public authority'.[59] In short, political democracy was unstable so long as it coexisted with class divisions, or at least with 'extreme economic inequality', for this left democracy vulnerable to the magnates of industry and finance; hence democracy needed to be extended into the economy.[60] If democracy does not 'extend its authority from the political to the economic system', he wrote in 1939, 'it will cease to exist, save in form, as a political institution'.[61] The vehicle for this economic-democratising agenda was the Labour Party. Its socialism represented 'a conscious, systematic and unflagging effort to use the weapons forged in the victorious struggle for political democracy to end the capitalist dictatorship in which democracy finds everywhere its most insidious and relentless foe'.[62]

Even more than Britain, Polanyi's attention was pinned on Austria. In 1919 the prospect existed, in Duczynska's words, of Austria becoming 'the bridge between the two Councils' Republics: the Bavarian and the Hungarian'.[63] Still in 1920, the social democrat Julius Braunthal could opine that 'the Austrian working class has had the ability ever since November 1918 to establish its own power, the dictatorship of councils, at any time it wishes'.[64] Braunthal's comrade and leader, Otto Bauer, thought likewise: the workers' and soldiers' councils could have assumed power if they wished.

On this assessment Bauer and Duczynska concurred, but their evaluations were worlds apart. For Duczynska, social democracy had missed an opportunity to effect revolutionary social change. Its attempt to construct a workers' state from parliamentary ingredients, and by patiently constructing its Viennese fortress, failed. Its leaders gambled on gradualism. Bauer, for example, possessed enormous respect among socialists 'due to his brilliant mind, power of persuasion, and sterling integrity', and yet, at each moment of decision, he 'was incapable of action'. Although sometimes likened to Hamlet, Bauer 'never acted' (unlike Shakespeare's protagonist, who ultimately avenged his father's death by dispatching Claudius).[65] Bauer's gradualism was sanctioned by a deterministic conception of social progress that shrouded the actions of social democracy's opponents, 'as well as its own inactions, with the magical mantle of "historical necessity"'.[66] He believed that a balance of class forces had been achieved (on which more below) and that momentum would tip further toward social democracy, but it controlled only the capital and its province while the Christian Socials and Pan-Germans retained command of the nation. Critically, the means of production remained in bourgeois hands. Increasingly, the political right took the initiative. A milestone was the workers' uprising of 1927, during which the SDAP leadership refused to lead. (In a farcical moment, Bauer hid from a delegation of electrical workers who had arrived at SDAP headquarters to solicit orders to shut down the power plants.[67]) The resulting demoralisation ensured that armed struggle, when it eventually arrived, was unlikely to win. 'The people everywhere feel despondent, beaten flat, due to our continuous retreats', as the militia leader Theodor Körner put it to Bauer.[68]

How did Bauer perceive these same developments? He subscribed to the social-democratic belief that parliament, when it includes social-democratic representatives, no longer simply serves bourgeois interests.[69] But he went further. For him, democracy was not just a mechanism that would assist in the advance of socialism; rather, socialism was 'only a more extended system of the same thing, democracy'.[70] Accordingly, his – and the SDAP leadership's – goal was to consolidate the SDAP's position within a parliamentary-democratic framework, understood as a sufficient precondition for a socialist transformation that would ensue later, 'in the context of well-ordered social relations'. Had this task been attempted by a 'purely bourgeois government', Raimund Loew argues, it would have failed within days, but the SDAP succeeded in deterring the masses from what Bauer referred to as 'revolutionary adventures'.[71] Bauer penned article upon article and spoke at meeting after meeting in order to ensure a less-adventurous outcome – and with signal success.[72] (Arguably, he was, more than anyone, responsible for averting socialist revolution in Austria.[73]) As the revolutionary tide ebbed, the councils were deprived of their status as organs for the democratic control of society as a whole, and were confined instead 'to a principally economic field of action'. Incrementally, they were deprived of their remaining functions, before eventual incorporation into the social-democratic militia, the *Schutzbund*.[74]

Parliamentary democracy, in Bauer's conception, could serve as a tool of class power, but which class would wield it depended upon 'the level of development of factors of social power', above all the numbers and class consciousness of workers. Because capitalist development propelled the proletariat towards becoming a majority of the population, it automatically generated the preconditions for that class to assume control of the democratic state. That moment had not yet arrived. Vienna was undergoing a socialist transition, but if a socialist-voting working class prevailed there it could only be an outpost within the republic as a whole, and this rendered a frontal assault on capitalist power inconceivable. If in the capital and in Austria's industrial belt 'all actual power was in the hands of the proletariat', in the form of SDAP municipal government and 'functional democracy' in unions and workplaces, in the country as a whole social democracy could not triumph, for it was balanced by the 'clerical peasantry' and by the bourgeoisie, which prevailed in the parliamentary arena. If in normal circumstances states were the instruments of domination of one class by another, in 1918–20 Austria, where equilibrium between the classes obtained, that no longer applied.[75] The bourgeoisie had relinquished some political and legal privileges but retained its hold on the economy. This resulted in a hybrid of bourgeois and proletarian power, of political and functional democracy. 'The conflicting classes hold each other in equilibrium,' Bauer concluded, and this necessitated compromise.[76] In the 1930s, Bauer developed this 'equilibrium' thesis into an explanation of fascism: its rise was the outcome of a stalemate of class forces that resulted from democratisation, with workers using the vote to demand concessions and capitalists reacting to the ensuing profits squeeze by fostering fascism.

As for Polanyi, he developed his perspective contemporaneously with, and partly inspired by, Bauer. Polanyi's analysis was folded into a historical-philosophical thesis on freedom, social integration and the separation of the political and economic spheres. Two tendencies, he held, are at work within modern history: one to freedom, the other to social unity. Their conjoint telos consisted in the extension of democracy into the economy, a prospect that, however, was 'prevented by the class structure of society due to the capitalist system'.[77] For, the counter-movement that had arisen in reaction against the *laissez-faire* regime was tightly bound up with democratisation: the economically dispossessed classes used their new-won vote to demand protection from market forces. In a sense, the expansion of the market system had summoned 'widespread reactions and helped to create a strong popular demand for political influence of the masses', but 'the use of the power so gained was greatly restricted by the nature of the market mechanism'.[78] The result, Polanyi argued, was social impasse. Workers, armed with trade unions and political representation, defended themselves against the depredations of the market by electing parties to parliament that 'continuously interfered with the working of the market mechanism'.[79] This prevented market forces from functioning properly, and their beneficiaries, above all 'the captains of industry', reacted by seeking either to subordinate democracy to their interests or to abolish it.[80] A 'delicate balance' between 'liberal economics and popular government' was achieved, but at the expense of 'the elasticity of the economic system'.[81] (In this, we see Polanyi rehearsing the 'Austrian' credo: social protection impairs the functioning of the market.) Within governments, the interests of capital controlled monetary policy while the voice of voters, via parliament, influenced fiscal policy.[82]

In fleshing out this argument, Polanyi's eye was trained on the political events of the day, viewed through a social-democratic lens. To recap: capitalist development expanded the working masses; their instincts are socialist; ergo, capitalism leads via democracy to socialism. Polanyi's thesis accords a crucial function to the social-democratic parties. They had played a prominent role in re-organising the states of Central Europe following the war, and 'had saved society from anarchy and organised a democratic community on the ruins of the old. No wonder that they set their imprint on the constitution of the new states, their social legislation, their factory laws and general welfare administration'. In Germany a former saddler's apprentice, Friedrich Ebert, became head of state, while

Vienna was transformed 'into a world famous metropolis of a fine working class culture'. The mechanism that 'maintained the working class in power was universal suffrage and representative government. In short, it was democracy'.[83] This posed a challenge to capitalist elites, whose every effort to restore the prewar system was countered by workers and peasants, their grievances and demands now strengthened by their institutionalised political voice.[84] In turn, this decreased the flexibility of the price system and the elasticity of markets, with the consequence that the assumptions that had underpinned the gold standard – that national economies adjust, and that governments would willingly enforce this – no longer held.

Stymied in the attempt to restore a liberal world economy, economic elites sought 'to eliminate working class influence on policy', using 'market panic' and the threat of capital flight to lever Labour governments out of office: in Belgium (1926), France (1926) and Britain (1931), and then again in France in 1936, when 'the capitalists' utilised the gold standard 'as an instrument of class war' against the elected Popular Front government.[85] Where economic elites still felt threatened by democracy they pressed for its outright abolition, a tendency that reached its acme with the elevation of fascist governments to power. Here, again, Polanyi drew attention to the threat of capital flight, in particular with reference to Prussia where a dem- ocratically elected social democratic government 'capitulated to the mere threat of unconstitutional violence on the part of Herr von Papen', whose technocratic government was committed to austerity – and this, famously, aided the rise of Nazism.[86]

Polanyi's conclusion was that democracy was not a natural accessory of capitalism, as some supposed. Rather, the two systems were, at least in the contemporary conjuncture, irreconcilably antagonistic.[87] Their incompat- ibility led inevitably to an impasse, manifested in the interwar cataclysm. As capitalism entered a crisis-ridden period following the war, workers and peasants, empowered by the vote, demanded that parliamentary parties shield them from the worst effects. This prevented markets from clearing, intensifying the crisis. At that moment a sharp alternative was posed: society would be integrated either through political power 'under the leadership of the working class' and in the form of a real 'democracy; i.e. economic socialism', or under the leadership of the propertied classes in the form of a recharged capitalism, purged, with fascist assistance, of all democratic elements.[88]

RETREAT AND REVIVAL OF A THESIS

The idea that capitalism and democracy are incompatible systems was a significant component of leftist discourse in the interwar period. Socialists and radicals such as Bauer, Laski and Polanyi took it for granted that a conflict existed between capitalism and democracy. They did not see capitalist principles and institutions (the divisions of private property; the inequality of rewards; allocation according to monetary resources) as merely antithetical to democracy (with its principles of collective decision-making, political community and equal citizenship) but as incompatible with it. This thesis, however, was rarely subjected to careful scrutiny. Its proponents used it in different ways – sometimes absolutely and apodictically, sometimes with caveats. Polanyi was well aware that democracy in rural Austria was stuck on a muddy track, that 'democracy in a peasant country could only take the form of peasant democracy'. But this provincial peculiarity, although real and bothersome, would not disrupt the grand trend. (In Austria, the road to 'democracy travels through the free and organic manifestations of peasant conservatism'.[89]) He was aware, too, that elites were learning to live with parliamentary democracy. 'A democracy restricted to the merely political field,' he warned, 'is bound to *degenerate*. Its parties become a nuisance because they absorb the civic energies of the people and divert them to useless purposes.'[90] However, he refrained from working through the tensions between such considerations and his thesis that democracy and capitalism exist in irreconcilable antagonism.

As outlined above, the conditions sustaining the 'capitalism versus democracy' thesis in the interwar period were the simultaneous advance of parliamentary democratic government and the ascendance of social-demo-cratic parties that placed their faith in the incremental extension of political democracy into the social and economic spheres. The same conditions that favoured the institutionalisation of formal liberal democracy would also, it appeared, support the progress of radical, social democracy. The political mobilisation of subordinate classes nourished reformist political movements and social democratic parties; these tended to favour egalitarian policies, which, in turn, enabled wider layers to participate in the political process, contributing to a further deepening of democracy. A virtuous circle, it fostered the illusion that a historical law was at work that would probably, even inevitably, lead to a socialist society. If in the 1930s that faith was sorely tested, the thesis in other respects gained renewed credence from the evidence of capitalism's dysfunctionality and decline; and the rise of fascism could be explained as a pathological symptom of democracy's stalled momentum.

Over subsequent decades, all these conditions were overturned. Liberal states fought a war 'for democracy', and although it was followed by major social upheavals, no fundamental ideological challenge to managerial control emerged as it had after the previous war.[91] There followed a cold war that pitted liberal-democratic powers against their communist enemies. For all the reforms of Roosevelt, Attlee and their confrères, they left intact the entrenched power of business elites whose systemic goal remained the accumulation of capital. In this conjuncture the belief that democracy is *impossible without* capitalism became a commonplace. In political theory, elitist conceptions of democracy à la Mosca, Weber and Schumpeter – democracy as a set of procedural political rules, not a 'type of society' – became hegemonic.[92] Capitalism re-stabilised and entered a period of unprecedented growth, with welfare expansion and steady rises in average incomes. Democracy, it appeared to social democrats, was being deployed to successfully tame capitalism.

Whereas in its interwar heyday the 'capitalism vs democracy' thesis had functioned simultaneously as an explanatory social-scientific tool and as a rallying cry for a political current (left social democracy), when the conditions of its emergence dissolved away, it too faded from the scene. But it did not vanish altogether. Attentive observers of British politics were reminded of this during the 'Great Recession' when Labour Party leader Ed Miliband remarked that his 'father [Ralph Miliband] would probably have said [the crisis] is about a conflict between democracy and capitalism'.[93] This surmise by Miliband Jr. is not inaccurate. Capitalist democracy, according to Miliband Sr., 'is a contradiction in terms, for it encapsulates two opposed systems'.[94] At face value this sounds similar to Polanyi, who regarded political democracy as an aspect of the political system while capitalism belongs to the economic.[95] At other times, however, Miliband was closer to the Marxist tradition, for which capitalism is not an 'economic' system counterposed to a separate system of democracy but an ensemble of social relations that assumes the appearance of separate 'economic' and 'political' spheres, such that 'exploitation takes the form of exchange [while] dictatorship tends to take the form of democracy', to borrow an aphorism from Stanley Moore.[96] Miliband certainly sympathised with a number of Marxian critiques of democracy: that it is not only an instrument by which the working class can press its demands but also an apparatus through which to divert, fragment and contain pressure from below; that democracy in capitalist society is suborned and constrained by the owners of the means of production (including communications), by 'the market' and by the state machinery itself; that it is therefore, 'whatever its context, undemocratic' and democratic procedures in capitalist regimes 'are a simulacrum of democracy, utterly vitiated by the context in which they function'.[97] He was, moreover, sharply critical of interwar advocates of the 'capitalism versus democracy' thesis for their assumption – patently absurd, he quipped – that the Labour Party would steer Britain inevitably toward a revolution in its economic constitution.[98]

On the whole, the conditions of the postwar boom were not conducive to reflection on the incompatibility between capitalism and democracy. On the left, the more typical subject was the tensions and strains among society's institutional subsystems. Here, the classic text was Jürgen Habermas' *Legitimation Crisis* of 1973. Habermas was interested in the new grammar of crisis attendant upon the expanded role of states. States found themselves equipped to engineer a 'class compromise': to smooth the volatility of the business cycle and to mediate between capital's interest in maximising exchange value and 'the generalizable interests, oriented to use values, of various population groups'. Although perfectly compatible with capitalist principles of economic order, formal democracy posed the state with the problem of 'facing use-value oriented demands' while simultaneously securing mass acquiescence to the overarching system of power.[99] Insofar as the political system took responsibility for economic management, however, economic crises tended to translate into problems of political order and legitimacy.

In truth, talk of 'class compromise' and the overcoming of the contradictions of capitalism crises was exaggerated. The power of business elites remained intact, the contradictions erupted again shortly soon after publication of *Legitimation Crisis*,[100] and the former responded to the latter by pressing for rafts of reforms that later became known as neoliberalism. The neoliberal ascendancy witnessed, simultaneously, the roll-back of social-democratic gains in Europe, the elevation of the thesis on the correspondence of markets and democracy into imperial doctrine under Ronald Reagan and Bill Clinton, and the 'second wave' of democratisation across southern and eastern Europe and South America. For social democrats, the confluence of democratisation and neoliberalisation appeared paradoxical. They had traditionally assumed, not without reason, 'that the same social and historical conditions that promoted formal democracy – in particular, a shift in the class balance of power in civil society favouring subordinate classes – would also advance the cause of greater social and economic equality'.[101] Even in the worst case scenario, this should yield a self-correcting system, in which voters, facing widening inequality, demand redistributive policies, thereby ensuring that egregious inequality is a temporary affliction.[102] In the best case, a virtuous circle would result: the votes of the poor would yield redistributive social policies; these would enable more citizens to participate in the political process; in turn, higher levels of political mobilisation would see rising support for social democratic policies, contributing to a flourishing and deepening of democracy. As late as the 1980s, political theorists could propose that the history of capitalism since the introduction of universal suffrage be read as the story of the 'progressive decline of the unchecked power of the capitalist class' in response to the social consequences of democratisation – the extension of equality of opportunity to the labouring masses and the elimination of structural poverty.[103] Instead, the 1980s saw the global spread of formal democracy alongside strong tendencies *away* from economic democracy and egalitarianism. Hopes in a virtuous social-democratic circle faded. Instead, a vicious circle arose: inegalitarian policies marginalised and demobilised the poor, and cowed labour movements. Moral panics over the threat of excluded groups were deployed to justify the erosion of civil rights. As the gap between rich and poor widened, the former 'revolted', as Christopher Lasch put it, by retreating further from the public sphere.[104] All of this contributed to a widespread unease, and to a sense, discussed above, that the universalisation of democracy was accompanied by its trivialisation.[105]

The trivialisation of democracy in neoliberal times served as backdrop to the trivialisation of the 'democracy vs capitalism' thesis, exemplified by Blunkett's manifesto discussed above, with its insipid pleading for civic and electoral engagement. But the same period has also witnessed its most brilliant reinvention, by German sociologist Wolfgang Streeck. In a raft of articles and a book, *Buying Time: The Delayed Crisis of Democratic Capitalism*, Streeck folded theses on the new constitutionalism, 'low-intensity democracy' and the corruption of the public sphere into an original and penetrating theory of *capitalist-democratic* crisis. This was reminiscent of the social democracy of Polanyi's day, not only in its sophistication but in its argument that contradictions between capitalism and democracy (in Streeck's phrase, 'the highly limited compatibility of capitalism with democracy') have spawned a concatenation of crisis tendencies that appears set to bring capitalism to its knees.[106]

Fittingly perhaps, in that he studied at the Goethe University in Frankfurt when Habermas taught there, Streeck theorises capitalist crisis as a combined product of economic destabilisation and political delegitimation. But whereas Habermas, writing at the end of an étatiste era, accentuated the ability of states to determine social relations, Streeck's eye is on the limits of political engineering. Capitalism possesses a 'specific directionality': markets possess a tendency to expand.[107] Like incoming waves around a sandcastle, they circumvent whatever institutional structures have been erected to keep them in check. In addition, Frankfurt School theorists erred in their depiction of capitalism as 'a technocratic wealth-producing machine'. It is better apprehended as 'a site of class struggle from above, with highly class-conscious and profit-conscious capitalists'.[108] Like Polanyi, Streeck interprets capitalist economic crises as investment strikes undertaken by owners of productive resources in response to the penetration of democratic politics 'into their exclusive domain' and other restrictions upon their ability to exploit their market power to the utmost. He applies this analysis to the Great Recession and the ensuing uprush in public debt: these manifest 'the ongoing, inherently conflictual transformation of the social formation we call "democratic capitalism"'. By democratic capitalism he refers to 'a political economy ruled by two conflicting principles, or regimes, of resource allocation: one operating according to marginal productivity ... and the other based on social need or entitlement, as certified by the collective choices of democratic politics'. Thus understood, democracy is 'a regime which, in the name of its citizens, deploys public authority to modify the distribution of economic goods resulting from market forces'. Under a democratic-capitalist regime, governments should, in theory, align these principles, but in practice they tend to

> neglect one in favour of the other, until they are punished by the consequences: governments that fail to attend to democratic claims for protection and redistribution risk losing their majority, while those that disregard the claims for compensation from the owners of productive resources, as expressed in the language of marginal productivity, cause economic dysfunctions that will become increasingly unsustainable and thereby also undermine political support.

Exemplifying the latter was wage growth and welfare expansion during the *trente glorieuses*, which provoked a crisis of capital's confidence. This culminated in the 1970s in a reluctance to invest and a growing 'discontent on the part of "capital" with democracy and its associated obligations'. The 'normal condition of democratic capitalism' resumed – a condition governed by 'an endemic conflict between capitalist markets and democratic politics'.[109] Capital's revanche took the form of neoliberalism, centred on securing greater protection of the market economy from democratic interference. (In Streeck's phrase, the 'de-democratisation of capitalism through the dis-economisation of democracy'.) This assuaged the owners of capital but at the cost of renewed legitimation crisis – for the legitimacy of postwar democratic capitalism had come to rest on the premise 'that states had a capacity to intervene in markets and correct their outcomes in the interest of citizens' and that they would act to extend some of the benefits of capitalism to those without capital, ensuring 'steady growth, sound money and a modicum of social equity'.[110]

The rise of the neoliberal regime, in Streeck's analysis, led to, or at least exacerbated, three processes of degeneration. One was of the public sphere. As corporatist and social-democratic traditions of collective will formation found themselves subordinated to the logic of market choice, politics became individualised and 'de-contextualized'. The public sphere was beset by corrosive tendencies, communities fissured and fragmented, and political acts came to resemble 'acts of consumption, or of hedonistic individual utility maximization'.[111] A second, operative primarily in richer countries, was the secular decline in the rate of economic growth and its replacement by 'illusions of growth'. Here too, the process commenced in the 1970s. The need for states to simultaneously shrink (as demanded by capital) and to maintain legitimacy, responding to the interests of voters whose expectations were governed by victories notched during the long postwar, could not be squared. Processes of displacement resulted – in a sense, to 'buy time' – from 'the inflation of the 1970s, through the public debt of the 1980s, to the private debt of the 1990s and early 2000s'. The Great Recession revealed these strategies to have been at best short-term fixes, at worst, dangerous illusions. Thirdly and relatedly, globalisation and neoliberalism weakened the demos and strengthened the power of markets. 'Since investor confidence is more important now than voter confidence, the ongoing takeover of power by the confidants of capital is seen by centre left and right alike not as a problem, but as the solution.'[112] This last process, Streeck shows, is exemplified in the European Union, which graphically illustrates the impasse that democratic capitalism has reached. His prognosis is further decay. 'Disorganized capitalism is disorganizing not only itself but its opposition as well, depriving it of the capacity either to defeat capitalism or to rescue it. For capitalism to end, then, it must provide for its own destruction' – a process that is ubiquitously visible today.[113]

The early-twentieth century social-democratic thesis of 'capitalism versus democracy' has been reinvented by Streeck, but with a difference. The reinvention consists in his conception of capitalism and democracy as intertwined but rivalrous systems and his forecast of capitalism's self-destruction. The difference is that Streeck possesses little, if any, faith in the forward march of democratisation or the inevitable dawning of socialism. His analysis is original and refined, but it faces two difficulties. One lies in the presumption that democratic-capitalist society is governed by two regimes of resource allocation, one of which is determined by profitability and marginal productivity, the other by social need, protection and redistribution. The latter regime is sustained by a particular mechanism: where political parties fail to attend to popular social demands they risk losing power. But even if we allow that such a mechanism exists, it is powerfully overdetermined by the other regime. For example, during the *trente glorieuses* when profits were buoyant, political parties of whatever stripe were able to preside over welfare expansion. During the leaner years since the 1970s, the opposite applies. The other difficulty concerns Streeck's ambiguous use of 'democracy'. Take for instance the claim that capitalist crisis is occasioned by owners of productive resources undertaking an investment strike 'in response to the penetration of democratic politics'. If this refers loosely to organised pressure 'from below', is 'democracy' anything other than a euphemism for 'the lower orders', with 'democracy versus capitalism' a stand-in for class struggle? Or does it refer strictly to jurisdictions with liberal-democratic political systems? If so, why do economic crisis dynamics in democratic and non-democratic capitalist societies so plainly resemble one another? Consider Streeck's claim that soaring public indebtedness following the Great Recession 'reflected the fact that no democratic state dared to impose on its society another economic crisis of the dimension of the Great Depression of the 1930s', and that this attested to political power being 'deployed to make future resources available for securing present social peace'.[114] This purported demonstration of the 'capitalism vs democracy' thesis applies equally to capitalist non-democracies – for example, China.

CONCLUSION

In this chapter I have surveyed the fortunes of the social-democratic thesis on the incompatibility of capitalism and democracy. Polanyi's version was at once typical of the genre and uniquely his own. Its ingredients included a keen awareness of the antipathy to democracy espoused by traditional liberal elites, in Austria-Hungary and in Britain (exemplified by Lords Russell and Macaulay); the belief, most explicitly in 'Rebirth of Democracy', that capitalism had not successfully 'tamed' democracy; a liberal-pluralist assumption that the institutional systems of politics and economics are founded upon altogether different bases; and a set of Fabian (Bernsteinian) postulates: the state is a neutral force, a site of justice (in contrast to the market, which allocates resources but cannot dispense justice); liberal democracy is fundamentally democratic in the political sphere; and socialism is in essence 'the retention of the democratic political system'[115] plus, crucially, the socialisation of industry and the extension of democracy within the economic sphere; the democratisation of the economic sphere is a certainty, as a consequence of the expansion of the suffrage to include the working class (ergo, socialism is the inevitable inheritor of the world-historical trend toward democratisation); and, finally, social-democratic parties represent working-class interests and are unambiguously committed to the socialist transformation of society.

Distinctive in Polanyi's understanding of liberal democracy is that it rests on his critique of the separation of the spheres. Freedom in the 'liberal age' is illusory, he believed, for it denies the 'underlying unity of society': liberty is restricted to 'the possibility of acting "freely" in the political sphere', with the industrial sphere – where the organisation of production 'necessarily implies acting under orders, and the great mass of the people act under the orders of a small group of owners' – totally excluded. Every worker knows 'how much coercion he undergoes in his daily life as a producer that cannot be remedied by the use of his vote at general elections'.[116] Polanyi's critique of the sporadic and atomised character of the parliamentary-democratic process, however, is muted. It exists implicitly in his schema for industrial democracy, which would afford a *continuous* and *collective* process of debate and information flow through workers' organisations such as trade unions and co-operatives.[117] He regarded continuous-collective democratic forms as suited to the industrial sphere, and a punctuated-individual arrangement more appropriate for the political sphere.

If developed in a Fabian direction, Polanyi's guild-socialist schema, despite his critique of the separation of politics and economics, ultimately replicates a traditional social-democratic demarcation between parliamentary politics (in which parties compete for votes) and industrial democracy (in which workers organise collectively). In this, the idea of industrial democracy is confined to a strengthening of union power and an expansion of workers' cooperatives. But the idea of industrial democracy contains revolutionary germs too: the critique of parliamentary democracy, advocacy of new forms of 'bottom-up' democracy in industry and other 'non-political' spheres, and recognition that such advances are blocked by the established relations of capitalist power. Did Polanyi develop his argument in this direction? Certainly, he subscribed to the full gamut of criticisms of liberal democracy advanced by the left social democracy of his era: capitalism forbids democratisation in the workplace, keeping workers disempowered in this fundamental quotidian realm; it exalts the private sphere at the cost of the public, privileging the consumer over the citizen and undermining social cohesion; it generates social inequality, and alienation of the have-nots; and, by underpinning a divide between economics and politics, with democracy only applying to a section of the former and economic decision-making left to market forces, it surrenders a vital sphere of collective self-determination to the anarchic play of private choice and to powerful and unaccountable organisations, ensuring that advantage is systematically tilted in favour of the wealthy and that the power of the economic elite is kept intact. However, he maintained, nothing in the constitution of liberal democracy prevented it from becoming 'an instrument of working class policies'.[118] He retained a confidence that, in spite of their lobbying advantages, economic elites could not systematically prevent the interests of the masses from being genuinely represented in parliament, and that the same historical conditions that had enabled the development of formal democracy – the growth in education and mobilisation of the subordinate classes – would also advance the cause of social and economic equality, loosening the lock on political power enjoyed by the propertied classes. Alongside Bernstein, Bauer, Lederer, John Strachey and others, he held that in western democracies the trends in the political and economic fields were moving in opposed directions. As trade unions grow in strength and the suffrage is extended, political power shifts into the hands of the working classes even as economic power concentrates in giant industrial and financial institutions. In this perspective, 'actually existing democracy' in the political sphere provides the platform upon which a socialist democracy can be constructed. It need not undergo a fundamental transformation but simply requires extending into the economic sphere.[119]

Polanyi shared the critiques of representative democracy neither of Rousseauians – that it is the alienation by citizens, through elections, of their capacity to make political decisions[120] – nor of Marxists. Marx's writings contain flashes of an optimistic faith, similar to Polanyi's, in the potential of universal suffrage to enable the exploited classes to gain 'possession of political power', assisting them in the quest to overthrow bourgeois society.[121] Like Polanyi, he sees democratic capitalism as inherently unstable, and envisages universal suffrage as an important 'school of development' *en route* to socialism.[122] But his critique of representative democracy goes further. The divide between politics and civil society, for Marx, entails not only an atomised civil society (comprising citizens in their 'sensuous, individual, *immediate* existence') but also, correspondingly, a political sphere that constitutes the citizen as 'only abstract, artificial man, man as an allegorical, juridical person'.[123] The sphere of citizenship, of universal rights and equality before the law, manifests the levelling tendencies of capitalism, but while equality is elevated to a principle in the sphere of formal rights and law it is denied in the broader social and economic spheres. Norms of equality provide the scaffolding for the institutions of representative democracy but they mask entrenched socio-economic power relations – and these do not hold sway in civil society alone, but sustain the state itself as a bureaucracy-controlled apparatus.

The idea that capitalism and democracy exist as separate systems, from a Marxist perspective, is a reified reflection of the institutional separation of economy and polity, which is itself, ultimately, an institutional effect of capitalist relations. To adopt Jason Moore's terminology, capitalism's underlying principle of motion is the logic of value accumulation, operating through processes of exploitation (of paid labour) and appropriation (of unpaid labour, and nature).[124] That exploitation occurs via wage labour facilitates the structural division between polity and economy, expressed in the institutional differentiation of private and public power. The latter, Nancy Fraser suggests, is in a sense a 'background condition' on which capital accumulation depends. As such it is 'part and parcel of capitalist society, historically co-constituted in tandem with its economy' and marked by its interdependence with it.[125] That steep hierarchy in the economic sphere coexists with formal equality in the political sphere has allowed bourgeois interests to prevail in the structuring of political representation: in the restraints placed upon representation (the exclusion of the proletariat, women, slaves, racialised minorities, etc.), and in the power of the bureaucracy, civil service and military. Such measures enabled the landowning and capitalist classes, *pace* Polanyi, to tame democracy, to learn to live with it, 'to regulate the suffrage' in their interests.[126] This thesis – that political democracy is shaped by capitalism – should not be read through a reductive or functionalist lens. Democracy is a particular institution, formed by capitalist society but not reducible to it, and how the line is drawn between economy and polity 'varies historically, according to the regime of accumulation'. Capitalism's institutional divisions 'become foci of conflict, as actors mobilize to challenge or defend the established boundaries separating economy from polity, production from reproduction, human from non-human nature'.[127] If capitalism exhibits a totalising drive, it also continuously runs up against constraints and opposition, not simply between 'economy' and 'democracy' but within each institutional field.

In distinguishing between Polanyi's theory of democracy and that of Marx, my intention is not to query the radicalism of Polanyi's position. A common approach to Polanyi dresses him in the uniform of mainstream social democracy. 'Polanyi teaches us that periods of prosperity and rising living standards were a direct result of democratic gains', it is assumed (without textual support) by some.[128] He is casually presented as a theorist of the *democratic capitalist* mixed economy. In fact, as this chapter shows, his thesis on capitalism and democracy concerned not their symbiosis but their clash: democratic demands *undermined* capitalism; the rise of democracy led to a socio-economic stalemate that culminated in the Great Depression, and it, in turn, stimulated a recrudescence of the old Whig hostility to democracy, in the form of fascism. Whereas fascism sought to sacrifice democracy, the path of democracy must lie, Polanyi argued, 'with a change in the property system', from capitalism to socialism.[129] Democracy, however, was hardly flourishing in the land of 'actually existing socialism'. It is to Polanyi's attempt to resolve this paradox that we now turn.

4

Democratic Tyranny: The Soviet Union

In a letter of 1943, in rebuttal of what he felt to be an accusation by his zealously anti-communist friend, Jaszi, Polanyi stated that although he had 'always hoped that Russia will provide one of the real solutions of the problem of industrial civilisation' he had *never* referred to himself as a 'Christian Communist'. Nor had it ever occurred to him 'to be a Communist and even less to be a "fellow traveller"'. Nor even had he 'ever done anything to deserve the Communists' approval'.[1] If these asseverations were not lies, they curve the truth asymptotically toward falsehood. Polanyi's repudiation of fellow-travelling may have been accurate in the letter, but not in the spirit.

Had the same lines been penned at the time of Jaszi's departure to the USA in 1925 their letter and spirit would have been aligned. In the 1920s Polanyi's attitudes towards Bolshevism ranged from intent curiosity to outright hostility. On the international left, Soviet communism in the age of Lenin was viewed more or less warmly, but essentially as a member of the socialist family and not as a vanguardist-terrorist Other. Polanyi was not a cold warrior *avant la lettre*. By way of illustration, in an article detailing the crimes perpetrated by Lloyd George he includes, alongside his counter-revolutionary interventions in Ireland and Egypt, the despatch of a 'pointless and criminal expedition force against Soviet Russia'.[2] His stance was occasionally sympathetic but usually sternly critical. He could caricature Bolshevism as a movement dedicated to the 'overcoming of the individual's personal life' and the construction of a 'system of unbounded centralism and state power', and he accused the Bolsheviks of promising peace, internationalism, democracy and socialism but delivering their antitheses: war, nationalism, dictatorship and 'a decaying and impotent but economically unaltered capitalism'.[3] But in the following decade his attitude altered – to such an extent that he felt able to confide to Aurel Kolnai that 'the Revolution is not, after all, Oscar Jaszi; the Revolution is Lenin'.[4] He did not join a communist party, yet his criticisms in the 1930s were comradely in nature, or merely abstract and technical. For example, against communists who grounded their case for the inevitability of socialism upon 'economic necessity' he countered that its inevitability is in fact based upon 'spiritual necessity'.[5] Their party would achieve greater success if it sought to 'arouse the force of latent Christianity in the people'.[6]

If Polanyi's turnaround on communism, considered as a movement, is puzzling enough, more perplexing is his dogged defence of Stalin's regime. Was he not an 'ethical socialist' who set his compass by the ideals of individual freedom, humanism and democracy? Did he not maintain that 'Socialism is democratic or it is nothing', and that 'democratic control of industry *is* Socialism'? One would presume from such statements that he figured among Stalin's most implacable critics. In fact, as the Soviet Union evolved from the chaotic but relatively free post-revolutionary period to the conservative authoritarianism of the 1930s his hostility evaporated. In the early 1930s he cast a sceptical eye over developments in Russia, particularly in respect of the tautness of the Five-Year-Plans and the 'appalling privations' that resulted for workers. He argued that an economy without a mechanism for calculating profit was 'impossible' and that Russia would evolve into a 'free-trade territory'.[7] Nonetheless, he took out a subscription to 'USSR in Construction', a monthly propaganda periodical set up by Maxim Gorky, and by the middle of the decade he had become 'a staunch supporter' of Stalin's Russia, which he came to celebrate as the living proof that the exploitation of labour could be abolished and that socialism could be established 'in one country, under the dictatorship of a working class party'.[8] None of Stalin's detractors, he fingerwagged, could be regarded as 'a true Socialist'.[9]

Most students of Polanyi neglect this aspect of his political profile and see no need to offer an explanation. A salutary exception is Mohammad Nafissi. Polanyi supported Stalin's project, Nafissi suggests, because in the 1930s his belief system was in flux: freedom was becoming a residual concern, 'normatively as well as historically and conceptually'.[10] For this claim, evidence can be found. In the 1930s Polanyi's outlook certainly was shifting. His antipathy to market society was becoming more impassioned and he placed greater emphasis on the ideal of social integration, a process that could proceed under the sign of politics (as in the New Deal or Stalin's Russia) or under the sign of economics (as in fascism). However, this represented an alteration in his definition of freedom and not its marginalisation. In the early 1920s Polanyi had promoted a theory of socio-economic development that held that freedom, in the form of libertarian socialism, represents the ultimate outcome of the forward march of political democracy, economic growth and the market economy. At this time, Soviet communism had evoked his hostility because it sought to erect obstacles to the development of democracy and economic liberalism, and because it created confusion among progressives by identifying socialism with anti-market policies. In later decades, *pace* Nafissi, freedom remained his watchword and the normative centre of his theory of development, but its meaning evolved. Citing Mill's 'On Liberty', he insisted that whether trade was conducted by private businesses or by states is 'not an issue of liberty'.[11] The vanguard of freedom, he argued in the 1930s, was socialism. It embodied a cluster of emancipatory historical trends: toward democracy, and the replacement of market mechanisms by planning and institutional fragmentation by social integration.

In this prospectus, socialism and communism figured as two wings of a common project – the unification of society, including industry, under the aegis of politics – the 'true enemy' of which was fascism, seen as synonymous with 'the control *of* government *by* industry'.[12] The 'communism contra socialism dichotomy'. Polanyi argued, was refuted by the fact that fascism, 'the only serious non-socialist movement of our age, is not willing to make any difference between those who merely want to nationalise the means of production and those half-crazy men (if they really exist) who want to eliminate the market'.[13] There were differences between the two movements. Socialists placed greater emphasis on the democratisation of economic life. Communists supported dictatorship, but, in contrast to fascists, as a transitional means not a permanent end.[14] This is why Polanyi could be equivocal about the democratic credentials of Stalin's Russia, and noted certain similarities with fascist regimes – economic planning, the regulation of income, the cartelisation of industry and disregard for the value of individual liberty[15] – while nonetheless celebrating it as living proof that 'the state can be an instrument of emancipation',[16] a regime that joined together 'social and national' purposes and pioneered the world-historical trend toward planning and social integration.[17] Stalin's Russia was the very chariot of freedom.

In his youth, Polanyi had been fleetingly attracted to anarchism and varieties of socialism 'from below', but in the bearpit of Russia's socialist factions he backed those who maintained that socialism could only be achieved following a lengthy stage of capitalism against those who supposed that a global socialist transformation could begin on Russian soil, and his post-1917 trajectory was via guild socialism toward social democracy, a comparatively patrician current that in several respects – notably its advocacy of nationalism and state-led social engineering – resembled the new edition of communism that was emerging in late 1920s Russia. For Polanyi, socialism was defined by two principal claims. One was for workers' control of production. This would have precluded him from defining Stalin's Russia as socialist were it not for his propensity to conflate the labour movement with what he held to be its political organisations. Thus, he justified his acceptance of the CPSU as a representative of Russian labour by the assumption that it was devoted to the 'democratic control of industry'.[18] The other claim was that a socialist economy is by definition geared to 'the maximum development of the means of production' combined with a socially just distribution of the product.[19] In Russia, the Five-Year Plans were visibly producing 'the enrichment' of

Soviet territory,[20] and, with some creative accounting and a willingness to disbelieve journalistic reports of gaping class divisions, the 'just distribution' criterion appeared to be met too. Consequently, Polanyi could marvel at the achievements of Soviet Russia, including industrialisation and collectivisation. Although these led to 'severe suffering for the masses', he justified this in terms of the putative intention – to ameliorate poverty – and the 'spectacular' and 'admirable growth rate' that they enabled. They had, he maintained, proved 'the possibility of socialist economics on a large scale', and, paradoxical though this sounds, had also demonstrated the unassailable truth of marginalist economics.[21] The evidence was there for the world to see: 'Russia, which ten years ago was of no account as an industrialised country, ranks now amongst the very first. Socialism has been established in one country.'[22] Though temporarily restricted to one country, Stalin's regime cast a bright light on the future of humanity as a whole.

STALIN'S REVOLUTION

In the 1930s Polanyi's political views converged with those of official communism and he volubly favoured Stalin's faction over Trotsky's. But his wish was for a 'third way' between western social democracy and Soviet Russia, and his analysis of the latter was not one that any devoted Communist Party member could have shared: whether his understanding of the Soviet economy as undergoing a business cycle comparable to that of market economies,[23] or his rejection of the claim that Stalin was overseeing a continuation of the Leninist project, or his estimation of Trotsky as Russia's most admirable revolutionary leader after Stalin and Lenin.[24] In Polanyi's view, Trotsky's theory of permanent revolution 'fitted the facts', for what had begun as a 'middle-class revolution' in 1917 had to be carried forward by the working class in order to 'safeguard the newly won democracy' and avert the threat of Tsarist counter-revolution 'and the unspeakable cruelties' with which it would have avenged itself upon the forces of revolution. Having once taken the lead, Russia's workers 'were left, through developments in the world situation, the choice between socialism and fascism'.[25]

Polanyi was an astute analyst of the Soviet system as it underwent reconstruction in the late 1920s. He believed that what he termed Stalin's 'Second Revolution' of 1928–30 marked a sharp rupture with the past, and he regarded Uncle Joe as a 'great innovator' because his theory of

'socialism in one country' amounted to the attempt to make Russia into an industrial country by her own means, without foreign loans and without the help of other countries. In Marxist theory as it was traditionally understood this was not possible, for [it] meant the adjustment of political to economic reality. Stalin's policy was the reversal of this and [...] almost the whole of the old Party refused to follow [his] line.[26]

Equally, however, he maintained that the new system was not consciously crafted but arose through an unforeseen lurch, when the aims of the *nomenklatura* linked to Stalin – industrialisation and state-building – confronted a series of interconnected crises. One of these was the war scare that ignited in 1927 when Britain broke off relations with Moscow and which, Polanyi perceptively observed, had 'created a new global conjuncture'.[27] The war scare was exploited politically, with invocations of an external threat deployed wholesale as a pretext to justify internal repression: against peasants resisting requisitioning and collectivisation, against labour unrest and against internal party opposition. Myths were concocted in order to threaten and cajole, to turn the population against the enemy within: the 'kulak menace', the 'saboteur in foreign pay', the 'right-wing appeaser', the 'Trotskyist', and the sundry stock miscreants and evildoers of the Stalinist imaginary. Meanwhile, the panic buying and hoarding that the war scare provoked exacerbated food shortages that were in any case approaching crisis proportions as government procurements of grain dwindled. By the end of the year the country was sliding into severe economic crisis. Peasants faced increased taxation and forcible requisitioning of grain. Wages and benefits slumped and social conflict grew. Policymakers reacted with short-term expedients, notably the arbitrarily enforced procurements of grain in 1927–28 – which only encouraged the *muzhik* to sow less. In 1929, crisis rippled through all sectors of the economy and prompted policymakers to respond with a *Flucht nach vorn*: ratcheting industrialisation targets upward and imposing state ownership and continual operational control over agriculture. Within a matter of years, a traditional agricultural arrangement consisting largely of petty production was subordinated to a single landlord. This was no feudal fusion of economics and politics; it was the sundering of peasants and their means of production into absolute property, on one hand, and a proletariat, on the other. No longer did the state need to batten upon the peasantry as pre-modern landlords had done. Rather, it inserted itself between the means of production and the agricultural labour force, declaring itself owner of the former. The peasantry, meanwhile, was thrust *en masse* onto the labour market or into the Gulag.

Polanyi's account of the Second Revolution emphasises the international economic climate. The onset of the Great Depression hit agricultural produce first, adversely affecting Russia's trade balance precisely when its demand for industrial imports was soaring. There was, he argued, little option other than autarky. With demand for Soviet exports falling, the ability to import manufactures weakened, forcing an even more rapid industrialisation drive. The foreign trade crisis made the acceleration of industrialisation and agricultural collectivisation imperative, such that one might even say that the Second Revolution was 'forced upon' Russia by the 'failure' of the international system and the western market economy. The geopolitical failure to which he alludes is the aforementioned war scare which, in his view, necessitated a Soviet arms drive and an expansion of heavy industry regardless of its economic rationality. By failure of the western market economy he is thinking chiefly of the decline in world prices of foodstuffs, which helped to push the government toward comparatively autarkic industrialisation and forced collectivisation. It can therefore be assumed, he concluded, 'that international conditions formed an appreciable factor in the decision to resolve the interventionist dilemma by means of the Five Year Plans'. This would not be the first time that 'war and crisis have decisively accelerated the industrialization of a remote, undeveloped territory'.[28]

As Russia's social fabric was shredded in the years around 1929, social struggles erupted, and it was in the concatenation of repressive moves that flowed from their crushing, coupled with the perceived imperative to industrialise and re-arm, that the distinctive structures of Stalinist rule took shape. The conflictual aspects of the industrialisation and collectivisation process are downplayed in Polanyi's narrative, but he did display an acute awareness that the shift to 'Socialism in One Country' in Russia represented a break with the revolutionary communism that had characterised the first years of the Communist International, a rupture on such a scale, indeed, that the suppression, exile or persecution of its proponents would be indispensable if the new strategy was to succeed. Despite his approval of the campaign to marginalise and rout Stalin's opponents, a campaign that culminated in the Show Trials, and despite his belief in the juridical legitimacy of the Trials themselves, he was adamant that they were no ordinary purge, no routine rotation of personnel in order to discipline bureaucracies, but should be understood instead with reference to the intensity of the breach with previous practice that Stalin's dictatorship represented.[29]

GOD SAVE SOVIET RUSSIA!

Polanyi's rapprochement with communism drew upon his observation of unfolding events in Russia, but other factors played a part. They included the global economic and geopolitical conjuncture, and his involvement in a Christian Left group in Britain, many of whose members were convinced supporters of the Soviet Union. Political realignments were also involved. In response to the crisis and the rightward shift of the Labour Party, leftists in the Independent Labour Party broke away, while others remained as a vocal and visible left wing within the official party. For the first time in the Labour Party's history the notion that a parliamentary majority might not suffice to ensure a socialist transformation gained a hearing.[30] Radicals gathered in the Socialist League, an organisation with which Polanyi sympathised.[31] The Communist Party, meanwhile, was shifting to the right and seeking allies. Ex-Labour leftists who had found homes in the Socialist League, such as Harold Laski, reappraised the CP as a valuable ally in the fight against fascism, both domestically and in Spain, where at last its advance was meeting armed resistance.[32] A 'unity manifesto' calling for closer collaboration between social democrats and communists was drawn up in 1937, signed by Laski and Cole.

Socialist League supporters such as Laski were, on the whole, positively inclined toward Stalin's Russia. In this they were hardly in an isolated position. In the mid-1930s, mainstream opinion in the west was not monotonically hostile to the Soviet Union. In 1933 Washington had recognised its sovereignty and before long accorded it most-favoured-nation treatment as a trading partner. Many a western ambassador and politician held Stalin in high regard, and in 1936 the *New Statesman* could observe that 'even amongst Conservatives' the old hostility toward the Soviet Union was vanishing. At a time when swathes of liberal and conservative opinion advocated state interventionism, Soviet-style planning exerted a broad appeal. For many western intellectuals, the Great Depression represented the 'shipwreck of Western assumptions and values', as Lewis Coser put it, including freedom and democracy. Western democracies appeared feeble in their response to the great threats of the age: mass unemployment, and fascism in Southern and Central Europe. In contrast to their decadence, not to mention the bombs raining on Guernica, the red star shone bright. Many western progressives, disappointed by the decline and decadence of liberal civilisation, were open to the Soviet alternative, with its bullish confidence in human rationality and its utopian prospectus of a 'planned and ordered society under the aegis of an enlightened elite that ruled in the interests of the population as a whole'.[33]

In its strategy and policies, international communism turned sharply to the right in the mid-1930s – precisely the period in which Polanyi was most favourable towards it. Once Stalin's group, rallying around the slogan of 'socialism in one country', had routed the 'old bolshevism' in the 1920s it turned its attention to calling communist parties elsewhere to heel. Moscow began to play the diplomatic game according to the rules that had been normalised and perfected over the course of the nineteenth century. The coordinates that now guided its foreign policy were formed by the Triple Entente (alliance with Britain and France) and Rapallo (alliance with Germany), complemented by rapprochement with the League of Nations. Rebellions and uprisings elsewhere threatened these arrangements and were opposed and in some cases suppressed by communist parties (notoriously in Catalonia). Communist parties were encouraged to subordinate themselves to bourgeois-nationalist movements (such as China's Guomindang) and to align the socialist quest with existing nation-state structures. In Britain, communists found themselves adapting to quite new experiences and symbols: singing 'God save the King' alongside the 'Internationale', with the Union Jack and the Red Flag 'sociably intertwined'.[34] The new strategy, with communist goals curbed in the interests of collaboration with social-democratic and liberal forces, was known as the Popular Front. Against its critics, campaigns were launched, with 'Anti-Trotskyism' the rallying cry. In the motherland these were backed by state power, culminating in the Show Trials.

Comintern policy in the 1930s was seen by some as a stage in its decline from revolutionary movement to instrument of Russian foreign policy and of the bureaucracy which directed it. A distinguished early advocate of this view was an acquaintance of Ilona and Karl, the former communist functionary Franz Borkenau. But Polanyi would have no truck with such talk, for a Russia 'that had committed her resources to the long-term job of industrialization could no longer afford to engage in a revolutionary foreign policy'. It had no choice but to adopt a foreign policy which, 'like that of any other country, is primarily determined by self-interest'.[35] Moscow's new approach was exemplified by its attempts to strengthen the League of Nations and by the revised strategy of the Comintern, the 'moderation' of which had become 'a main factor of world politics'.[36] In 1935, he communicated to his brother his new-found optimism 'with regard to the international situation': the communists were moving 'rapidly towards a democratic front', and if 'Russia will be able to grow strong enough in time to take over the leadership of the democratic states against the fascist states ... then there is still hope'.[37] Outside Russia, the old revolutionary programme that directed communists to pit their efforts first and foremost against their own nation state and its ruling class had to yield. The overriding imperative now had to be to 'put the international issue first and say "save Soviet Russia"'.[38]

In justifying his support for Stalin's dictatorship, Polanyi found additional assistance in reflection upon the dynamics of bourgeois revolution. History, he believed, pointed toward democratisation. The trend had been thrust forward by great revolutions the democratic consequences of which are not immediately apparent. Drawing an analogy between the process and destiny of the Russian revolution and three previous revolutions, the English, American and French, Polanyi noted several differences. The English revolution was libertarian, with no room for equality; the French was egalitarian, with less emphasis on individual liberty; and the American struck a balance between égalité and liberté. For its part, Russia's revolution centred upon 'the forms of the daily life of the working people' and therewith emphasised the ideal of 'fraternity rather than liberty and equality'. However, the inspiration behind them all was the same: the desire for self-determination. With the partial exception of the American, in each revolution, absolutist political rule legitimated in terms of divine right was overthrown and replaced by popular sovereignty in a process that included phases of protracted civil war and dictatorial government. A settled new regime, based on the rule of law, emerged only after the establishment of a new constitutional settlement (England: 1688; France: 1830), with democracy evolving only in later decades and centuries. At any period before that, 'freedom would have meant freedom for the counter-revolution to restore its lost power'. In Russia this final phase had not yet been reached.[39] None of the four revolutions could realise its potential immediately. In each, clashes of interests were dangerously exacerbated by ideological conflict, and these fused with geopolitical threats: to revolutionary England by Catholic France, to revolutionary America by colonial England, to revolutionary France by Royalist England, to revolutionary Russia by the capitalist west. If the regime of religious tolerance that was the ultimate outcome of the dictatorship of 'that greatest of all Englishmen', Oliver Cromwell, had been inaugurated at once, the result would have been 'an immediate victory of an intolerant religion over the state, or chaos'. Either way, 'England would soon have fallen under the sway of the European counter-reformation and the cause of religious tolerance would have been buried for many generations'.[40]

The lessons for Russia were clear. Its domestic conflicts were 'being complicated by the injection of ideological elements' from abroad.[41] To defend the achievements of 1917 against Tsarist counterrevolution and foreign intervention, the expropriation of the banking system and the bulk of manufacturing industry was unavoidable, as was the roll-back of democracy. But once a literate population came into being, pressures to democratisation would build, and Polanyi was willing to interpret the flimsiest straws in the wind as the herald of its imminent arrival.[42] One such straw was Stalin's 'right turn' of 1934.[43] In the following year Polanyi declared that 'the tendency towards Democracy' in Russia had become 'clearly discernible'.[44] His faith in Soviet democratisation was strengthened further in 1936, with the passing of a new constitution that guaranteed – on paper – free and secret elections as well as freedoms of assembly, press, and religion.[45]

MORAL TRIALS

Polanyi's astonishing credulity towards the promises of the 1936 Constitution was soon surpassed by his swallowing of all the claims by

Soviet prosecutors in the mid-1930s Moscow Show Trials. He believed
the accused Bolshevik leaders to have been guilty of conspiracy against
Stalin, intended to deliver Soviet Russia into the hands of its enemies.
The 'old Bolsheviks' in the dock had been rightly convicted of 'one of the
greatest political conspiracies ever engineered by an ideological faction
of former revolutionaries in league with a foreign power'. Such was the
strength of his feeling that he took to crowing over the confessions of
Nikolai Bukharin and his fellow conspirators. Practically the entire former
Bolshevik leadership had 'opposed Stalin's realist departure' of 'socialism
in one country' and, 'when the Party decided against them, joined hands
under the leadership of Trotsky in a conspiracy of unprecedented scope
and recklessness.' They formed alliances with 'German and Japanese
imperialism', with which they planned to terrorise the Russian people and
organise the sabotage of socialism in Russia. And why? All in the name of
the world revolution which Stalin, they claim, had betrayed. The accused,
he continued – without an iota of evidence other than their 'confessions,'
which he thought bore witness to their 'moral collapse' – planned to
assassinate Stalin and would have endangered the lives of 'millions and
millions of people' had the authorities not unmasked them in time.[46] 'It is
impossible,' he thundered,

> to read the Verbatim Report of the Third trial without being convinced
> of the almost literal truth of the accusations and at the same time not to
> feel that perhaps the most gigantic criminal conspiracy in the history of
> the world has been brought to justice.[47]

The Trials did not simply expose to the world the depth of divisions
within the CPSU. (In Polanyi's précis, that Stalin's course 'was unacceptable
to the great majority of the *Old Guard*'.[48]) They revealed something much
grander: 'that the ethical standards of a great Revolution are far in advance
of any our present world can conceive.'[49] With such elevated judgments in
mind, Polanyi had no difficulty in dismissing those who harboured doubts
about legal process at the Moscow trials as 'sentimental intellectuals' or
those who refused to equate Stalin's Russia with socialism as 'traitors'.[50]

In this stance, Polanyi diverged from many of his comrades on the
social-democratic left, for whom the Trials prompted a re-evalua-
tion of their support for the Soviet Union.[51] It was also an attitude that
exacerbated his differences with his brother, Michael. The Polanyi brothers
were temperamentally quite different – the elder one was 'outgoing, open,
exuberant, accessible, and always cheerful',[52] in contrast with Michael, who
was rather 'British' and restrained – but they were exceptionally close.
In the 1930s, however, their relationship was plagued by disagreements,
in respect especially of the Soviet Union. Michael was, after Khristian

Rakovsky, the first major thinker to propose that the Stalinist economy was not centrally planned at all. On this issue the brothers' disagreement was vehement. For example, after Michael's *USSR Economics* appeared, Karl wrote him 'I am still completely baffled by the almost complete lack of human meaning and significance of your booklet'.[53] The argument acquired an emotive tremor when it turned to the treatment of their own niece, Eva, who lived in Russia at the time, and whose husband had become acquainted with Bukharin during his brief period of rehabilitation in the mid-1930s. Eva was arrested and charged with belonging to a subversive group that intended to assassinate Stalin. Allegedly, she had been assigned to pull the trigger.[54] Under duress, and facing the prospect of being left to rot in prison without trial, she eventually signed a confession and then, Michael reported to Karl, 'she tried to commit suicide but failed'. Eva's story occasioned acrimony between the brothers. Michael felt 'deeply indignant' over Karl's defence of the Soviet judicial system,[55] while Karl maintained that Eva herself had insisted that the Soviet Public Prosecutor was obliged to act lawfully, applying 'all the so-called guarantees of a fair hearing'. He had been surprised to hear this, but interpreted it as a positive sign 'that under a dictatorship changes are sometimes very swift'.[56]

FROM DEVOTION TO DEFEAT

In the interwar period a substantial body of social-democratic opinion, including most famously the Webbs, spurned the Soviet Union when it bore the promise of workers' emancipation in the immediate post-revolutionary period but came round to its support in the thirties, just as the regime's despotic turn was achieving full throttle in the Moscow trials.[57] In this period, the Soviet Union's corporatist-étatisté aspects attracted western intellectuals, but the threat of Nazism, and the Comintern's 'Popular Front' strategy, were influential too. Certainly, that decade saw Polanyi's enthusiasm for Soviet Russia reach its peak. This helps to explain the comparatively optimistic flavour of *The Great Transformation*. Whereas Victor Serge could in 1939 survey the destruction of hope, by fascism and Stalinism, and announce that 'Midnight in the Century' had been reached, Polanyi, armed with optimism of the intellect and faith in the Kremlin, remained comparatively upbeat. In a letter of 1943 to his brother, Michael, he harked back to the apocalyptic predictions they had shared in 1914:

> The Apocalypse was *not* imminent as we thought. Our world is still going to live and thrive for a very long time to come. [...] We believed too much in the goody-goody rationalism and Fabianism of Wells,[58] who was convinced that if mankind takes *one* wrong step it would infallibly lose its way.[59]

Over the course of the 1940s, Polanyi's pro-Soviet sentiments cooled somewhat but he continued to regard Moscow's influence on world affairs as overwhelmingly positive – even compared to the USA. There, the prestige of big business remained disturbingly high, as could be witnessed in its pinnacle of social reform, the New Deal, which was a programme designed not 'to supersede private enterprise, but on the contrary to save it from monopoly and modernize its working. It was this outlook,' Polanyi lamented, that 'made the American people instinctively hostile to the USSR', for here was 'a great block of planned economy which would have to go or be isolated if the world should be made safe for liberal capitalism.' Washington's market fundamentalism, moreover, threatened to stymie any movement, in Britain or elsewhere, towards 'planned capitalism, or regionalist currency, or a European, i.e. a regional, cooperation with Russia'.[60]

As in the previous decade, the threat of fascism continued to feature prominently in Polanyi's justification of Soviet behaviour. In a letter of June 1945 he warned of 'the terrible danger of a Nazi-led European counter-revolution finishing off Western civilization'. If the western powers were to force Moscow 'to accept a hostile government in Warsaw', similar regimes would unquestionably follow 'in Helsinki, Bucharest, Budapest, Sophia and Belgrade, not to mention Athens and Ankara', and this would pave the way for a pan-European 'Nazi-generalled onslaught of the old ruling classes' in the shape of aggressive nationalism and agrarian counterrevolution. The Nazis, the same letter explains,

> rightly judge that leadership in the social landslide directed against the Second French Revolution – that which is conducted by the USSR in Eastern Europe at present – must fall to them. This will exalt them to a preeminent role in the organizing of Europe as a whole. If Hitler in 1933 was potentially dangerous, how very much more dangerous are his Nazis today with the certainty of European chaos and international dissention to underpin their ambitions and to serve as a ladder for their rise to dominance!

In view of the Nazi threat it was imperative that the wartime alliance be reconstituted. The western powers would have to reach out to Russia – and if they did, if London and Washington extended tolerance towards Moscow's policies within its security sphere, it would respond with a gentle approach to its occupied territories. They should therefore applaud its 'sensational bid for the setting up of a free democratic Germany' and follow up with cooperative acts.[61] For, 'if the Russians have no reason to fear the Western states they will be less inclined to intervene' in their Eastern European buffer zone, 'and the same applies in reverse: that is why peaceful cooperation among the three great powers is vital'. Instead, the west's stance was belligerent, and this, in Polanyi's view, gave Moscow little choice but to build its buffer zone into a glacis.[62]

In the 1950s, the spectre of recrudescent fascism having melted away, Polanyi's scepticism toward the Soviet experience grew. His tone remained generally supportive. Soviet Russia had 'refuted the economic axioms of the West with the solid mass of her practical achievements'; it remained 'what I consistently maintained it was, the repository of the meanings of Western civilisation'; and it represented a step beyond 'the morally indifferent market; one step towards the conscious human control of everyday life'.[63] However, he criticised Moscow's activities on a range of fronts. On the conduct of international trade, for example, he came to accept one of his brother's criticisms: 'the Russians' have adopted a 'very conservative' approach, and 'are absolutely self-regarding when it comes to "business"'. (Much like the Americans, added Karl.[64]) In the intellectual realm, he increasingly regarded Soviet-sphere economics and economic history as 'a joke', and repeatedly drew attention to the 'unexpected similarity between Soviet Marxian and American sociology, a conservatism which ignores the very possibility of history continuing into our own times' in a sociologically meaningful sense. Soviet Marxism was 'barren', due in part to the philosophical initiative of the early Marx having been 'buried' by Stalin ('as it had been before by Kautsky, Bernstein, Jaures and Otto Bauer').[65]

Polanyi raised these criticisms in the years following Khrushchev's denunciation of Stalin, and in the same period he reversed his earlier appreciation of Stalin's regime and behaviour. In a letter to his friend Erich Fromm he described Stalinism as a 'mind-blackout caused by fascism'.[66] In a comment on *Dr Zhivago* he criticised Pasternak for having failed to draw attention to 'the Stalinian Inferno, the mountainous horror of unspeakable crime' to which Russia had fallen victim.[67] And in his *Diary of an Anti-Marxist* he went so far as to describe Stalin as 'a cunning madman' whose 'mass-murderous blows' had ensured that 'socialism's first stage of fiery devotion' would end in defeat. For Russia to experience 'moral sanity and recuperation', he now believed, the 'rehabilitation of Trotsky' was indispensable.[68]

In his final years, then, Polanyi's view of the Soviet Union was characterised by ambivalence. He continued to hold out hope for its democratisation and to regard it as a leader of the worldwide socialist movement. However, whereas in his 1943 letter to Jaszi he described it as representing 'one of the real solutions of the problem of industrial civilisation', in subsequent decades he came to see it as, also, a symptom of that same pathology. 'Industrial civilization,' he wrote Fromm, is the problem. Socialist revolution was a 'catastrophic social initiative of extrication'. The Soviet command economy, he argued elsewhere, contributed to a type of 'conformism' that was fundamentally the same as that associated with market capitalism, for both societies represented forms of the same underlying 'technological civilisation'. The world, he lamented in 1961, had polarised between 'inhuman fascism and inhuman Stalinism', with withering consequences for 'our inner life'. The political conclusion to be drawn was that one should keep one's distance from Soviet East and capitalist west alike. The world, he wrote his friend György Heltai, had become divided between 'secret Russian influence' and 'secret American money'. Whoever speaks today 'must first give assurances of his moral independence from these two influences'.[69]

DEMOCRATIC TYRANTS AND WAR ECONOMIES

Throughout his life, Polanyi maintained an ambiguous relationship to communism. (In György Litvan's phrase: 'sharp criticism of the communists coupled with a magnetic attraction to the movement'.[70]) He looked to Communist Russia for leadership and inspiration, and, while never visiting the country, took a keen interest in Soviet affairs. His support for the Soviet regime was strongest during the 1930s and early 1940s, and rather weaker during the 1950s. In the latter decade, however, his Russian interests intersected with his historiographical work on ancient civilisations. In particular, his study of ancient Athens (discussed in Chapter 9) reminded him of the manner in which the ground for the rise of democracy had been laid by tyranny. Where the Athenian tyrants seized power they did so by virtue of popular backing, and 'the *tyrannis* was mostly a strong regime of the common people'.[71] The rule of the greatest of the tyrants, Peisistratus, may have been obtained irregularly but it was exercised constitutionally and in the interests of the masses. His reforms, notably the institution of a system of local justices in the *demes* and the fostering of the popular cult of Dionysus (a democratic god, plying wine to rich and poor alike), strengthened accountable power at the local level, eroded relations of dependency between the middling and aristocratic layers, reduced the power of the old aristocratic families, hastened the dissolution of traditional hierarchy and encouraged the rise of a new type of citizen-community.[72] Tyranny formed a necessary prelude to democracy, a lesson that Polanyi kept in mind when pondering the future direction of the Soviet Union.

A similar observation applies to Polanyi's reflections on the *economic* aspects of ancient and archaic empires. Those that he found particularly admirable, such as Classical Athens, the various states of Sumer, Ptolemaic Egypt and the Kingdom of Dahomey, all exhibited forms of economic dirigisme that, as in the case of the Soviet Union, were forged from the exigencies of coping with the pressures of a threatening security environment. They all depended upon a combination of martial and command-economic prowess. In his books, essays and unpublished notes on these civilisations he tended to downplay the degree to which economic étatisme was bound up with an apparatus of control over exploited groups and to emphasise instead the tendency of economic 'redistribution' – his term for coordination through appropriational movements toward and away from a centre, organised through custom, law or central administration – to cement the constitution of community. 'What, as in some native African kingdoms, may often appear to the Western eye as despotic taxation or ruthless exploitation of subjects,' he argues in *The Livelihood of Man*, 'is more often merely a phase in [the] redistributive process.' A few pages later he proposes that 'redistribution strengthens internal communal ties', thanks to individuals' 'self-identification with power and authority' and their 'enjoyment of equal rights of status and standing', all of which 'invigorate the societal emotions and bind the community closer'.[73]

Polanyi's concept of redistribution was later adopted by his compatriots György Konrád and Iván Szelényi as a core concept on which their diagnosis of the nature and dynamic of Soviet-type societies was constructed.[74] Following their lead, a broader current of Polanyi-influenced theorising of Soviet societies arose, comprising such scholars as Michael Burawoy and Linda Fuller.[75] Although Polanyi himself did not present a systematic theorisation of Soviet-type societies and published nothing comprehensive on Soviet socio-economic structures, Polanyian (or at least Polanyiesque) theories of the Soviet Union were developed by others. They adopted concepts that he had, *prima facie,* elaborated for application to other civilisations in different historical epochs, but always with the Soviet Union at the back of his mind.

Reconstructing
The Great Transformation

The Great Transformation, Polanyi's masterwork, was born in the Great War.[1] The edifice of liberal civilisation had collapsed. For social theorists, Polanyi argued, the ensuing crisis demanded the design of a new 'image of society'. His attempt to fashion such an image was informed initially by guild socialism and Austrian social democracy, but the vision faced a growing menace from fascism. It was his attempt to comprehend that threat that led to the initial drafts of *The Great Transformation.* The book's animating motive brought together its author's abhorrence of market society and his loathing of fascism – or, more precisely, his belief that the two evils were systemically connected. By 1939, Polanyi had drafted all of its central theses,[2] and a year later he communicated to his friend Jacob Marschak the form that his vision now took: 'the urgent thing today is to produce a simple and clear i.e. rational picture of a regulated market-system in a plastic society i.e. in a society which can attain its self-organisation by political means'.[3] The book was published in New York in 1944 and, with an expanded final chapter, in London the following year.

For some decades, *The Great Transformation* remained a book for connoisseurs but since the 1980s it has become a bible of leftist critique. In this chapter I shall not attempt a comprehensive exposition of its argument. Rather, I begin by reconstructing its major theses in the form that Polanyi developed them in lectures and unpublished texts in the 1930s and early 1940s. I then contextualise his argument via a survey of the contemporary literature that was grappling with the questions on which his book was to focus: the collapse of liberal civilisation, the nature of market society and the interwar crisis, the trends towards corporatism and totalitarianism, and the meaning of freedom in the modern era. Finally, I look at controversies that continue to surround *The Great Transformation,* and what they reveal of Polanyi's political outlook.

THE THESIS: A RECONSTRUCTION

In essence, the thesis that Polanyi developed during the 1930s was that his generation's sufferings – world war, fascism and the Great Depression

– were not discrete but constituted a single cataclysmic field, the root of which lay in the utopian liberal attempt, in Britain initially, to construct a self-regulating market system. The attempt was utopian in the simple sense long ago noted by Adam Smith – that to expect Britain to convert fully to a free trade regime was 'as absurd as to expect that an Oceana or Utopia should be established in it' – but also in a deeper and more critical sense: if economic liberalism ever takes hold of society's material life in its entirety, social collapse will surely follow.[4] The core agenda of economic liberalism was defined by David Ricardo as the commodity treatment of land, labour and money. A liberal market society, as Polanyi reinterpreted the case, requires that all factors of production are highly responsive to the forces of supply and demand. But the commodification of land, labour and money was based upon a 'fiction', because they are not, like commodities proper, produced for sale.[5] 'Land has not been produced at all, and as for men, well' – he wrote in one of his drier moments – 'they are produced for a variety of motives'.[6] Of the three, labour occupies a privileged position in his framework. It was not until early nineteenth-century Britain that capitalism (or 'liberal capitalism' or the 'market economy' – Polanyi uses the terms interchangeably) was born. For it depended upon a labour market that threatens the unemployed with the sanction of hunger, and this only truly came into being in 1834.[7]

Drawing upon evidence from the ethnographers Raymond Firth and Bronisław Malinowski, whose studies of Pacific island societies portrayed economic behaviour overdetermined by non-economic values and institutions, and 'archaic' civilisations (discussed in chapters 8 and 9), Polanyi contrasted their 'embedded' economies with nineteenth-century market liberalism. It had disembedded the economy, disintegrating society 'into separate economic, political, 'religious and other spheres'. The economic system had come to dominate to such a degree that all other social relations became its 'by-product'. Economic life, subordinated to the self-regulating market, became debased, with the motivational bases of economic behaviour reduced to the fear of hunger (for workers) and greed for profit (entrepreneurs).[8] In this 'market society', economic-determinist ideas appeared to make sense. They reflected a truth of the prevailing system: that there now existed 'a separate economic sphere to the requirements of which the 'rest' of society must conform'.[9]

In several ways, the market economy destabilised society and undermined its unity. It delinked economics from religion. It promoted a thoroughgoing rationalisation of human relationships and a 'vastly increased interdependence of regions, functions, etc.'. And the whole system suffered the convulsions of a volatile trade cycle. In short, it subjected 'man and his natural habitat to the working of a blind mechanism running in its own grooves and following its own laws'.[10] Of course, this did not go unchallenged. Whereas Ricardo had postulated that if the state seeks to intrude arbitrarily into the market mechanism spontaneous social forces will resist, Polanyi proposed the reverse. The imposition of 'unrestricted' market competition upon society spontaneously provokes a protective response, or 'countermovement,' expressed in some countries through a 'vast extension of government functions' (including social legislation, and subsidies to industry and agriculture) and in others through 'Trade Unions, Cooperatives, the Churches'. Indeed, nineteenth-century history was 'dominated by the reaction of society as a whole to the new growth in its midst'.[11]

Initially, by ameliorating the damaging effects of the market system the countermovement facilitated its continuation. The history of the nineteenth century, as Polanyi read it, 'is the coming of economic liberalism' and its 'inevitable' transformation into 'regulated capitalism'.[12] A delicate balance between the principles of laissez faire and state intervention was manifested in the new, regulated capitalism, but it was too rigid to survive indefinitely. It was 'bound to prove incompatible with a system of world economics based on economic liberalism'.[13] In the long run, the contradiction between market economy and 'society' (or 'countermovement') could not be sustained, and disruptive tensions accumulated. On one hand, protective measures such as tariff policies and trade union practices 'were the only means to save society from destruction through the blind action of the market-mechanism'. On the other, these same measures 'were directly responsible for the aggravation of slumps and the restriction of trade'.[14] Polanyi subscribed to the pre-Keynesian tenets that interference with markets causes them to malfunction, that higher wages lead to lower investment, and that stronger labour movements diminish the recuperative powers of capitalism. Regulated capitalism, with its ossified price system and inelastic markets, was inherently unstable. Its economic contradictions spilled out onto the political stage as states strove to influence foreign trade. Formerly distinct and separate, the spheres of state and industry 'began to interpenetrate', but because their new integration was partial and therefore 'false', it resulted in 'strains' which, originating in the 'incomplete self-regulation of industry', then 'spread into politics' where they acted as an 'irresponsible force'.[15] Strains in the domestic sphere – which for Polanyi revealed the perverse effects of government intervention and, simultaneously, the clash between capitalism and democracy (discussed in Chapter 3) – destabilised the liberal world economy, and this in turn disrupted the international political fabric. At the global level, the market system's 'chief institution', its all-powerful law-giver, was the gold standard. Its requirement that domestic price levels fluctuate freely resulted in volatility and unemployment. In such ways, strains shuttled between the national and international spheres. By the close of the nineteenth century, writes Polanyi, the great powers were:

> competing bitterly for free markets to which goods could be exported without causing trouble to themselves. The fierceness of the rivalry for foreign markets and the consequently increased tension between [them] was thus, in the last resort, [due] to the decreasing elasticity of the internal price system.[16]

In the new conditions, commercial peace theory no longer applied. Economic internationalisation served instead to exacerbate inter-state rivalries. Ultimately, the Great War itself was 'the outcome of the attempts at easing the economic strain caused by the pressure of free world markets (Gold Standard) on the increasingly inelastic national systems'.[17]

The aftermath of the war, in Polanyi's narrative, witnessed Herculean efforts to recreate a liberal order but they were futile. The war had failed to remove the strain. It had 'merely reinforced the tendency toward regulated capitalism', which further undermined the vitality of the market economy that had begotten it. The new rigidity was especially damaging at the international level, for the gold standard, free trade and capital export could function properly only if domestic prices continually adapt to global conditions – but 'the capacity for adaptation was diminishing'. Once again, mass unemployment exemplified the problem. To alleviate it, governments reached for social policy levers, but these, viewed by Polanyi through 'Austrian' eyes, served to cushion wages and therefore 'actually prolonged the crisis. Both government and industry were providing employment with the one hand, and creating unemployment with the other'. Following counter-productive attempts to restore the liberal market system (including the gold standard) in the early 1920s, by the end of the decade many countries 'had to realize that major adjustments of the internal price-level had become impracticable'. For, when prices were forced down profits dwindled, given that 'wages and some other items of the costs of production showed a considerable lack of elasticity, on account of the increasing rigidity of the economic system'.[18] In short, efforts 'to restore the gold standard put an intolerable strain on the social system and had to be abandoned.'

By the 1930s, Polanyi was confident that the gold standard would not be restored, 'for governments can and will not allow the economic system of their countries to be the football of uncontrollable international forces'.[19] Its final collapse provoked further bouts of protectionism and confirmed the division of the world economy into relatively autarkic regions. In short, the expansion of liberal capitalism to the global scale brought 'the break-down of the international organisation of economic life', with autarky its 'inevitable result'. Because 'the whole of our national and international system had been shaped by a single intent', the establishment of 'a self-regulating market system', the collapse of liberal civilisation was rapid, complete and ineluctable. And it was final. The prewar liberal economic system 'will not and can not return ... Managed currencies, control of foreign lending and foreign trade have come to stay'. The complete re-integration 'of politics and economics i.e. of society as a whole', Polanyi concluded, was inexorable. The 'haphazard interventionism' of the prewar era would necessarily give way 'to a full blown national unity of the industrial and economic system'.[20]

If the tendency to unity was inevitable and entirely normal (it represented, indeed, 'the re-assertion of the nature of human society'), that did not make it straightforward. In the pre-capitalist world social unity had been secured through custom, or, as in medieval Europe, through the Church and corporate institutions (guilds and monasteries). But in a world of science, technology and a complex division of labour, re-establishing unity would prove difficult – and this explained 'the totalitarian trend' of the 1930s, in the form of fascism, socialism and the New Deal.[21] These three regimes 'owed their common elements to the underlying problem of the integration of the political and economic systems', but they expressed the problem in different ways.[22] Socialism steered toward the abolition of capitalism while fascism undertook its reform, through the introduction of economic planning and the eradication of individual liberty, democracy and international cooperation.[23] In their different ways all three regimes were materialisations of a common conjuncture. 'The outstanding characteristic of our age' was the tendency 'of individual states to develop into more complete and coherent units', with, in particular, the unification of the political and economic spheres.[24] Having been thwarted at the international level, this tendency perforce expressed itself in temporary, national configurations: reactionary (fascist) regimes but also the progressive projects (Roosevelt's New Deal, Stalin's Russia) that for Polanyi were harbingers and pioneers of the great transformation.[25]

THE DISCURSIVE CONTEXT

The Great Transformation is a deeply personal book. No one but Polanyi could have written it. However, it was written not in lonely hermitude but in a cauldron of debate. In the decade following Hitler's seizure of power a series of books appeared that sought to lay bare the roots of western society's spiritual, philosophical and economic crisis. Polanyi was one among many intellectuals whose diagnosis of the civilisational crisis of the interwar period highlighted the pathologies of liberal capitalism. There were Marxists (Walter Benjamin, Theodor Adorno, Erich Fromm) and the occasional Hegelian (Alexandre Kojève), as well as social Christians such as Talcott Parsons, Richard Tawney and Karl Mannheim who identified liberal individualism and the market system as the sources of social atomisation and the subordination of social values to the economic.[26] They all were grappling with the global shift toward corporatism, economic nationalism and planning, and with the rise of fascist and communist regimes. Did these signify an irreparable rupture with liberal civilisation? What were the causes of the Great Depression? What did the rise of economic planning signify? And what of the ascendancy of totalitarian regimes? In this section I survey a number of the outstanding contributions to these debates and Polanyi's responses to them, beginning with corporatism and Keynesianism.

Corporatism's lineage is complex. Its earliest origins expressed aristocratic opposition to the industrial and French revolutions and Catholic reaction to the defeat of the Reformation and 'the agnosticism of industrial society', while a later and quite distinct branch, emerging in the nineteenth century with Saint-Simon as pioneer, gave voice to the utopia of transcending the contradictions of modernity through social-scientific engineering.[27] The 1920s saw corporatism evolve apace. The feudal-reactionary current was developed in Mussolini's Italy ('corporatavismo') and in Austria by fascist sympathisers (Othmar Spann), while Saint Simonianism branched into socialist thought (including guild socialism) and a more mainstream tradition associated with political leaders (Herbert Hoover) and industrialists (Walther Rathenau). Common to all was the belief that the world was passing from an era of extreme individualism to one of associational activities, and that in the economic sphere this required representation of an array of social interests within society's core institutions. Even in liberal Britain, the 1920s witnessed all three major parties execute a corporatist turn. Conservative Party intellectuals came to advocate industrial partnership and the elevating of the worker's 'status', while their Liberal counterparts, notably the 'unabashedly corporatist' economist John Maynard Keynes, advocated that government respond positively toward the rise of cartels, trade associations and forms of monopoly organisation.[28]

Polanyi reported on the corporatist turn, and on the works of Keynes, in columns for the *Österreichische Volkswirt* and other publications. He was no Keynesian. Whereas Keynes wished for economic stabilisation 'in a capitalist sense, we strive for the opposite', he wrote in the 1920s.[29] He also harboured a 'mistrust' of Keynes' theory of crisis. In a letter to Michael, he styled Keynes as a latter-day 'Paracelsus Theophrastus Bombastus: all important, unintelligible, superbly inspiring, and entirely useless in himself'. Like the Swiss practitioner of scientific occultism, the Bloomsbury economist had overcome 'the alchemy of equilibrium theory with the help of a weird realism ... although very few scholars would care to use his medicines today'. However, he did regard the Keynesian School, in which he name-checked Joan Robinson and Roy Harrod, as having 'proved exceedingly fruitful', and he admired some of Keynes' work, not least his essay on 'The End of Laissez-Faire'.[30] It proposed an expansion of 'semi-autonomous bodies within the State', a return 'towards medieval conceptions of separate autonomies', scope for which could be seen in such institutions as 'the universities, the Bank of England, the Port of London Authority, even perhaps the railway companies', and above all in 'the tendency of big enterprise to socialise itself'. These forms of 'semi-socialism', Keynes argued, embodied 'the natural tendencies' of the age.[31] Polanyi found this fascinating. He remarked that although Keynes had deliberately not framed it in this way, his ideals 'approximated to the great achievements in Britain of *communal socialism* and the tremendous *cooperative* movement'. Keynes' ideals, and British economic life in general, Polanyi enthused, 'appear to be moving in this direction'.[32] In 1928 he returned to the theme, with a commentary on the difficulties that the corporatist shift posed for liberal political economy, and Keynes' attitude to this. Although Keynes had not developed a satisfactory theory of the 'controlled' [*gebundene*] economy, he had at least recognised the shift, and his proposal that a liberal course could be navigated by 'regulating monopoly and making it accountable to the collectivity' was interesting too.[33]

Keynes, in short, helped prepare the ground for Polanyi's *The Great Transformation* by way of his prediction that the corporatist shift would continue over subsequent decades, amounting to a sea change in economic policy and ideology 'towards greater national self-sufficiency and a planned domestic economy'.[34] And two other Polanyian ideas, arguably, bear a Keynesian stamp. One is his concept of money as a 'fictitious commodity'. It was Keynes who, of his generation of economists, did the most to debunk the 'commodity theory of money', theorising money instead as an irreducibly social construct. The other is Keynes' analysis of the gold standard: an outworn dogma that negated domestic policy autonomy, and the institution that 'made the market supreme over the industrial system'. According to Rotstein, 'Polanyi got his gold standard position from Keynes'.[35]

Alongside Keynes, Polanyi kept abreast of the mainstream economic literature that was attempting to make sense of the Great Depression. A pamphlet that caught his eye was Erich Welter's *Dreifache Krise: Die Deutsche Wirtschaft im Jahre 1930*. Welter, a business journalist, was in the 1930s a pioneering ordoliberal and was later to join the Mont Pèlerin Society.[36] The section of his treatise that appealed to Polanyi was entitled 'Sand in the Machine'.[37] The metaphor refers to Welter's argument that protectionism slows the wheels of industry: it inhibits the international expansion of the international division of labour, reducing the potential for productivity gains.[38] For Welter this does not mean that state intervention should be abjured, for productivity growth is not the only criterion on which policy should be based. *Dreifache Krise* cites many sound reasons why states involve themselves in economic affairs and holds no truck with the Austrian economists, such as Ludwig von Mises and his English co-thinker Lionel Robbins, who feared that this presages calamity. Polanyi, however, had not only studied the economics of the Austrian school in detail but was 'explicit about the intellectual debt' he owed it, in particular the works of Böhm-Bawerk, Schumpeter and its founding father, Carl Menger.[39] He was intrigued, too, by Robbins' *The Great Depression* – the first major 'Austrian' account of that event. Robbins fiercely opposed economic planning, and defended free trade and the gold standard. Naturally, Polanyi found much of his book objectionable. However, in notes on *The Great Depression* he makes approving references to Robbins' claim that the Great War was the product not of accident but of pre-existing structural tendencies, and he displays a distinct interest in its scene-setting puzzle: given that, in the century prior to 1914, the market system had shown no sign of serious breakdown, why had it teetered on the verge of collapse ever since?[40]

Robbins followed Mises in holding that collective interventions in the market mechanism are inevitably counter-productive.[41] For Robbins, the strength of trade unions, protective tariffs and the cartelisation of industry had conspired to increase the 'rigidities' and 'inflexibility' of particular markets and to decrease the 'elasticity' of the economic system as a whole.[42] Mises argued similarly, in passages from which Polanyi took copious notes, that if a state imposes a price reduction on one good, demand for that good will exceed supply, necessitating rationing, or producers will curtail production, obliging the state to support them by forcing down prices of inputs, including wages – and for this to succeed, price controls must be generalised throughout the economy (or capital and labour would stampede into the remaining free areas). An equally perverse logic applied to trade union demands for higher pay: these raise costs on businesses which, passed on to consumers via higher prices, decrease output and revenues, ensuring, in turn, lower investment and falling wages. If states offer support to the jobless, this simply postpones workers' adjustment to the new economic conditions, resulting in a prolongation of mass unemployment. This final argument particularly impressed Polanyi, even though Mises's conclusion – that the only genuinely viable form of human social relations, given a division of labour, is *laissez-faire* capitalism – was anathema.[43]

The idea that trade union strength and workers' confidence act as a check upon economic growth was, in Polanyi's day as in ours, common currency on the political left and right alike. In William Morris' *News from Nowhere,* for example, it is the centrepiece of 'old Hammond's tale', in which the genesis of the socialist utopia that forms the novel's setting is revealed. As Hammond relates, the transition from industrial capitalism to rural-socialist idyll began when concessions granted to labour served to clog the wheels of industry, causing suffering amongst the masses, who looked to communist ideas, as well as demands by capitalists for the state to intervene, which it did through regulation and nationalisation, unwittingly paving the way to socialist transformation.[44] Morris's fictional chronicle quite precisely anticipates Polanyi's prediction of the breakdown of capitalism. Yet Polanyi, steeped in the literature of Austrian economics and writing in the context of the Great Depression, produced his own distinctive reworking of the idea.

In his journalism and lectures of the 1930s, Polanyi wavered between Austrian and what might be called Welterian positions. At times he adopted the more circumspect approach: 'The liberal economic system *does not work to its best advantage* when it is not free to rearrange the factors of production entirely irrespective of the effects on human life.'[45] More often the perspective was adamant, and 'Austrian': when the autonomy of the market economy is infringed, when its 'automatism' is interfered with, it 'reacts unfavourably', and economic crisis ensues.[46] In the nineteenth century, he argues, the market system could expand relatively smoothly and peacefully: in the heyday of *laissez-faire,* when prices were highly elastic, 'the intrusion of new commodities caused no serious disturbance; neither employment nor profits necessarily suffered'. Accordingly that century did not witness major wars; methods of expansion, as a rule, were 'not violent'.[47] By contrast, at the end of the nineteenth century rising tariffs and wage regulation undermined the price elasticity upon which the smooth functioning of the world market depended. In a lecture on nineteenth-century 'infringements on *laissez-faire*' Polanyi remarks that social insurance, alongside minimum wage and trade union legislation, were 'incompatible with liberal capitalism', for they impaired freedom of the labour market: 'the price of labour was influenced and therefore stabilized by state action'.[48] The 'economic strain' that occurred when increasingly 'inelastic' national economies that were 'unable to adjust themselves to major changes in the international price level' conflicted with the requirements of the gold standard was the underlying cause of the Great War.[49] The 'regulated capitalism' that was constructed in its aftermath attempted to contain these strains but it was inherently inelastic and fragile.

This analysis of the 'disruptive strains' that precipitated the breakdown of liberal capitalism bears a family resemblance to that of the Austrians. In line with Mises and Robbins and anticipating Hayek's *Road to Serfdom,*

Polanyi maintained that a critical factor that generates economic crisis is state intervention, for it renders prices stickier, and this causes markets to malfunction.[50] In *Great Transformation,* he approvingly quotes Mises' argument that if workers did not 'act as trade unionists, but reduced their demands and changed their locations and occupations according to the requirements of the labor market, they could eventually find work', and he proposed that 'any' method of state intervention 'that offers protection to the workers must obstruct the mechanism of the self-regulating market, and diminish the very fund of consumers' goods that provides them with wages'. Each impairment of market freedoms creates anew the need for further regulation, producing tendencies toward price rigidity and government intervention. The result can be economic depressions, and these, Polanyi erroneously claimed during the greatest of them, 'do not pass away unless the price system [becomes] *elastic*'.[51] The Great Depression, he argued, was caused 'by the forces impeding Capitalism in its working, i.e. by the "socialist" measures of governments either subservient to the working classes or unduly influenced by "socialist ideology"'.[52] Where Polanyi departed radically from the Austrian position, of course, is that he interpreted the logic of increasing intervention as inevitable blowback from the deplorable social effects of the 'utopian' market system. Whereas for Mises a transition to socialism in Europe would spell civilisational collapse, swiftly followed by the plundering intrusion of nomadic tribes from Asia (for who would be able to mount resistance 'when the weapons inherited from capitalism, with its superior technology, had been used up?'), for Polanyi the coming of a planned economy was welcome.[53] For him, the 'perverse effects' are the inevitable product of a perverse society: one that is moulded around impersonal market forces, with human labour relegated to the status of commodity. The civilisational crisis of his era instead opened the way towards an advance of human freedom and social unity; the initially perverse logic would ultimately yield a benign outcome. 'The superiority of planned economies over marketing ones,' he prophesied in a draft of *The Great Transformation*, will ensure 'the victory of democratic socialism'.[54]

Just as Polanyi was completing *The Great Transformation,* one other Austrian economist brought out his own gloomy forecast of the 'inevitable decomposition of capitalist society' – a prediction that, he noted, was 'rapidly becoming the general opinion, even among conservatives'. This was Joseph Schumpeter, whose *Capitalism, Socialism and Democracy* appeared in 1942. Capitalism, Schumpeter argued, was being destroyed by its own success. Several mechanisms were at work that combined to lay it low. One was the erosion, in the course of capitalism's evolution, of the *gemeinschaftlichen* associations (including 'the village and the craft guild') through which earlier generations had found collective shelter from economic storms. In breaking them down, capitalism had destroyed not simply the barriers that impeded its progress but also the 'flying buttresses that prevented its collapse'. Secondly, 'bourgeois motivation' had become 'smothered by the unfavourable reactions of society', and was further weakened as private family businesses were superseded by corporate giants. Thirdly, in replacing the entrepreneur by the manager, and atomistic competition by monopolisation, capitalist development decreased the economic centrality and therefore the social legitimacy of the capitalist class. Fourthly, capitalism's tendency to encourage a sense of individual autonomy and critical thought had been turned against itself by the very intellectual layers that it had brought into being – the bureaucrats, intellectuals, professors, lawyers, journalists – and also by the masses, availing themselves of the vote to press for policies of social protection and the regulation of entrepreneurship, policies that tend to erode the principle of 'private property and the whole scheme of bourgeois values'. As late as 1949, Schumpeter still maintained that in the USA and Western Europe *laissez-faire* capitalism was giving way to policies that 'differ but little from genuine socialist planning' in respect of government intervention, redistributive taxation, public control over the labour and money markets, and expansion of the public sector and of social security.[55]

To my knowledge, Polanyi and Schumpeter were not acquainted, but their degree of separation was slight. The Austrian had contributed to the *Volkswirt* when the Hungarian sat on its editorial board. He was a friend of Gustav Stolper and a family friend of Peter Drucker, both of whom were close to Polanyi.[56] But his book elicited only derision from Polanyi: it was of 'little interest'. It was 'an apologia for a lifetime of crypto-Marxism with the silliest reasons imaginable given for his expectation that capitalism is now going to dissolve, and that in the USA!'[57] Was Polanyi protesting too much? Several of Schumpeter's 'silly reasons' bear a resemblance to theses in *The Great Transformation*, notably regarding the fateful consequences of the demolition of *gemeinschaftlich* associations, and the tendency for working-class voters to deploy their democratic vote in ways that dampen the spirits of the market. Polanyi, moreover, had in the 1920s been a follower of Schumpeter's work, regarded him as the least doctrinaire of economic liberals, and as a pioneer of the attempt to re-found the discipline of economics as a study of 'catallactics', that is, as a science of exchange.[58] Polanyi himself had tended, like Schumpeter, to define capitalism in market terms, equating its *laissez-faire* species with the genus itself, assumed to be a domain exclusively of market exchange, contract and profit.[59] With the Austrians and against Keynes, Polanyi believed that the market system relies on self-equilibration and that policy interventions generally aggravate market instability. Indeed, he criticised

Schumpeter over his rejection of the view that protectionism and social legislation 'seriously interfere' with the working of the market system.[60]

Michael Polanyi was equally dismissive of *Capitalism, Socialism and Democracy*, but from a different perspective. For him, the flaws in Schumpeter's book stemmed from the fact that 'the miserable creature ignores Keynesian economics'.[61] Michael was 'a rare bird', observes Philip Mirowski, in that he 'adamantly rejected all talk of planning of science or of the market, and yet stood relatively isolated as a strong supporter of Keynesian macroeconomics'.[62] In Michael's own words, he adopted 'the most "radical" Keynesian attitude which – incidentally – involves the least "planning"'.[63] Karl disagreed with his brother's contention that Keynesian policy was 'compatible with the complete absence of state regulation' but he appreciated Michael's Keynesian analysis of finance, declaring it to be the most interesting contribution of its kind, after Keynes' *General Theory* itself.[64]

In respect of the Keynesian and Austrian traditions, then, Karl and Michael developed positions that mirrored one another. Karl rejected Austrian political and economic theory, above all its exaltation of the market system and its denigration of planning, while accepting central aspects of its definition of capitalism, its theory of value and its explanation of the Great Depression. Michael accepted, and indeed helped to elaborate, Austrian economic theory but was more convinced by the crisis theory of its great rival, Keynes, and by his belief that steady capitalist expansion could be achieved with vigorous assistance from the fiscal and monetary levers at the command of central banks and governments.

The brothers' most profound disagreements, however, were over planning, the Soviet Union and Marxism. Michael was a vocal opponent of all three, and was particularly irritated by those who sought to connect Marxism to Christianity – a quixotic crew that included his own brother, as well as participants in a Christian discussion group, the Moot, of which he was a prominent member. Convened by J. H. Oldham, the Moot was a diverse group. It included liberals and conservatives, and a communist too. Its illustrious adherents included T. S. Eliot and Paul Tillich. Karl Polanyi's friend Sandy Lindsay was a close associate, too.[65] Eliot and Lindsay in particular had come to believe that the interwar crisis could be traced to the erosion of Christian ends by liberalism.[66] What its members had in common was the belief that the rise of fascism and communism 'had revealed a crisis within the whole of western society which could not be ascribed simply to Germanic or Russian peculiarities'. Most of them believed that the threat to virtuous social existence came not only from fascism and communism but also from tendencies within liberal democracies: the centralisation of governmental power, and the rise of mass society, steered by utilitarian interests. They all believed that religious values should play a vital part in formulating a new social morality.[67]

Another prominent Moot member was Karl Mannheim. He was an influential figure in British intellectual life, particularly among Christians in and around the Moot (some of whom adopted his watchword: 'planning for freedom').[68] He was grappling with the rise of fascism and its relationship to democracy and liberal capitalism. In 1933 he put forward the Tocquevillian thesis that democratisation is the inevitable destiny of modern society, 'not only in politics, but also in intellectual and cultural life as a whole', with the twist that the same trend was finding expression in an altogether undemocratic phenomenon: totalitarianism.[69] Published two years later, his *Man and Society in an Age of Reconstruction* presented an argument that in certain respects mirrored the thesis on the incompatibility of liberal capitalism and universal suffrage, discussed in Chapter 3, that was being developed by Karl Polanyi, Bauer, Tawney and (Mannheim's LSE colleague) Laski. Unlike theirs, Mannheim's position was tinged with assumptions of human irrationalism and an elitist dread of the explosive masses.[70] In the distant past, he argued, *Gemeinschaft*-type societies had exhibited a 'horde solidarity' that successfully absorbed latent irrational impulses. Even when *Gemeinschaft* gave way to the liberal order of 'individual competition', popular energies remained partially embedded in organic life because democracy remained partial and popular participation in politics remained passive and insubstantial.[71] But when *Gemeinschaft* bonds dissolved and, simultaneously, the masses swarmed into the political arena, the entire social order became chaotic. At this historical juncture the absence of economic planning became a problem. Whereas in simple societies its absence was unproblematic, rather like the lack of traffic lights at junctions with light traffic density, with the advent of mass society that no longer applied. Just as an increase in traffic at junctions necessitates regulation if anarchy is to be avoided, the massification of society cried out for economic planning.[72] If Mannheim singled out one factor responsible for that 'maladjustment of modern society' which gave rise to fascism it was the clash between the principles of *laissez-faire* and 'planless regulation'. The liberal system of *laissez faire* may promise the automatic adjustment of economic disequilibria, but in the new era of mass society it generated social imbalances and chaos. The future would be marked by the 'tendency towards integrated social and economic units', with, as defining feature, the 'transition from *laissez-faire* to a planned society'.[73] This would occur by way of totalitarian dictatorship or, preferably, by 'planning for freedom'. To this end, sociological *Bildung* and political pedagogy were indispensable. The masses required comprehensive re-education while the intellectually inclined gentleman should be persuaded 'to recognize his role as a member of the "planning elite".[74] Mannheim's attempts to persuade fellow adepts of the benefits of planning centred on his engagement in the Moot.

Mannheim's participation in the Moot embroiled him in a fraternal but fierce debate with Michael Polanyi. Michael thought that his childhood friend was muddying the waters with his concept of 'planning for freedom'. Planning, Michael insisted, designates 'discriminative dispositions concerning an aggregate of particulars' and not 'indiscriminate disposition over an aggregate of particulars' – the latter is simply legislation. A sharp distinction should be drawn between 'discriminative' and 'indiscriminate' dispositions, a distinction that Mannheim's 'planning for freedom' grievously blurs.[75] Michael was in the course of developing his critique of transformative political ideologies and amoral positivism, which he identified as a central cause of the civilisational crisis of the age. The tendency for knowledge to be seen as objective and impersonal, he argued, had sundered science from humanity. Enlightenment rationalism had swallowed steroids, begetting some awful progeny: instrumentalism in the philosophy of science, positivism in the philosophy of social science, and utilitarianism in ethics – approaches, in short, that rejected the truth value and ultimately the authority of traditional social arrangements. The world was not as subject to human order and control as rationalists, utilitarians, tyrants and planners had thought. The glue of society is tradition, and it should not be messed with lightly, as rationalists and planners are wont to do.[76]

In a conversation (loosely defined) that took place in late 1930s and early 1940s London, involving T. S. Eliot, Michael Oakeshott and, at one remove, Karl Popper and Friedrich Hayek, Michael elaborated his conservative philosophical defence of liberal capitalism. It centred on the ineffability of *tradition*, as contrasted with the hubristic, total and rationalist tenets of *ideology*.[77] In this, his trajectory offered an arresting counterpoint to that of his brother. Karl was busy fleshing out a core thesis of *The Great Transformation*: market capitalism radically 'disembeds' economy from society, representing a reckless and violent break with human social traditions. Michael, too, was concerned at modernity's traducing of tradition, but he viewed liberal capitalism as *itself* a reliable social tradition, one that, suitably corrected by laws, regulations and Keynesian intervention, could be comfortably inhabited.[78] In elaborating this case he introduced the idea of 'spontaneous order': a concept that he adapted from gestalt psychology and Smith's 'invisible hand',[79] the providential mechanism that ensures that the self-interested behaviour of multitudinous market actors combine spontaneously to create a mutually beneficial order. But whereas Smith's concept refers to the self-coordination of markets, Polanyi's 'spontaneous order' applied to a variety of social spheres. These include economic behaviour. (He distinguished, for example, between corporate and spontaneous orders: the former, such as a ship's crew, a firm or an army, are hierarchical; the latter are horizontally organised, with development occurring in an unplanned manner through the interaction of numerous self-willed agents, each adjusting their decisions and actions to the outcomes of others.[80]) But the same concept applied equally to the generation of scientific knowledge through the unplanned communication and cooperation of scientists. 'Modern economics,' he wrote Karl,

> is characterised by the interaction of systems of choices operated 'independently' at a large number of centres. This is what I call polycentricity, and I think I have shown that scientific life shows characteristics of polycentricity in close analogy to the market, the differences being due mainly to the fact that the process of public valuation occurs in a different manner.[81]

In developing this position, Michael found himself in dialogue with Hayek. The Austrian economist was, like Michael, an ardent critic of economic planning – and if his *Road to Serfdom* gunned at a single individual it was Mannheim. Hayek also saw Mannheim, alongside Karl's comrade Joseph Needham, as the archetype of scientism – the assumption that the social world can be comprehensively understood, with the knowledge gained capable of being applied to the deliberate engineering of solutions to social problems.[82] Scientism and socialism belonged together as forms of constructed organisation (*taxis*), fundamentally opposed to what Hayek, borrowing from Michael, theorised as spontaneous order (*cosmos*). Where *cosmos* refers to unintended yet coherent web of relations within which agents pursue their various ends regulated only by common procedural rules, *taxis* denotes purposive enterprises seeking to realise substantive collective goals.

Hayekian theory, in Karl Polanyi's judgement, was hobbled above all by its reliance upon the economistic fallacy. Consider, for example, the problem of freedom. Many of the freedoms we cherish – civic liberties, freedom of speech and so on – were, he argued, 'by-products of capitalism'. Would they therefore disappear along with capitalism? Not at all – and in imagining that this was the case, Hayek had fallen prey to the 'illusion of economic determinism'.[83] For Polanyi, contra Hayek, the socialist road pointed directly toward freedom. On this fundamental ethico-political issue they were at loggerheads, but in a number of minor respects their accounts correspond. Both thinkers identified the late nineteenth century as the onset of liberalism's political, economic and intellectual decline, and both viewed the interwar corporatist shift in economic policymaking as propitious to, if not direct evidence of, a transition to socialism. This was a leitmotif in *The Great Transformation* and in *The Road to Serfdom*, which suspected the hydra of socialism in almost every act of planning or direct economic intervention. Both books, Hüseyin Özel points out, use 'similar models to explain the working of capitalism'; despite differences of terminology, they analyse capitalism's institutional structure in essentially the same way.[84] The combination of analytical similarity and normative antithesis is strikingly apparent in respect of the theorisation of spontaneous/constructed orders. In this, Polanyi's position is the very mirror of Hayek's. For the Austrian, macro-economic steering and the welfare state represent the trespass of *taxis* onto the ground of *cosmos*. For the Hungarian, the collectivist countermovement arises *spontaneously,* in resistance to the artificial market machine. In his words, whereas 'laissez-faire economy was the product of *deliberate* state action, subsequent restrictions on it started in a *spontaneous* way', and where the market system was introduced, society '*unconsciously* resisted any attempt at being made into a mere appendage of the market'. [85]

Hayek believed that his dichotomy represented an elaboration of Smithian-Humean theory, but it may more accurately be seen as its vulgarisation, in (at least) two respects. One is that, as William Connolly observes, Hayek exaggerates the self-organising potential of markets 'by implicitly deflating the self-organizing powers and creative capacity of all other systems' – including politics and social movements.[86] The other is that Hayek layered the *cosmos/taxis* couplet atop an assortment of cognate dichotomies: endogenously grown vs exogenously designed, evolutionary rationalism vs constructivist rationalism, market/planning, freedom/despotism, individualism/collectivism, capitalism/socialism, liberalism/totalitarianism and so on. The method is Manichean in that, in the worldview it defines, order exists *either* as *cosmos or* as *taxis.*[87] It is a distinction, moreover, that cannot bear much normative weight because, as Timothy Sandefur has shown, 'the difference between spontaneous and constructed orders collapses on close examination'. What some perceive as the application of a spontaneously evolved rule appears to others as constructivist intervention. In *The Road to Serfdom,* Hayek offers a revealing analogy: 'The attitude of the liberal toward society is like that of the gardener who tends a plant.' What this elides is that the gardener stands outside the garden 'with an exogenous idea of how it ought to look, and he rationally constructs it, prudently allowing plants to grow in some ways and pruning back others'.[88] In Hayek's understanding, the market system relies upon a strong state with a deliberately designed constitution. To that extent it is itself constructivist.

Whether spontaneously evolved or surreptitiously constructivist, the order that Hayek championed was militantly liberal in kind. It is defined in *The Road to Serfdom* through contrasts with its supposed opposite, the 'spectre of totalitarianism', which Hayek characterises through references to a set of regimes (fascist, communist) and theorists (from Comte through

Rathenau to Hitler and Stalin).[89] In this, arguably, he did more than anyone to popularise 'totalitarianism theory'. The term itself, of course, had been in use decades earlier: in Italy in the 1920s, and by Pope Pius XI upon his meeting with Mussolini in 1932.[90] In the early 1930s a current of thought that engaged with the question of totalitarianism emerged among Catholic intellectuals, including Polanyi's friend and mentee Aurel Kolnai. They were reacting to the incendiary writings of Carl Schmitt, specifically his 1931 article on the 'total state', and of Othmar Spann, whose concept of 'totality' was designed to justify the wholesale subordination of civil society to the state. In 1933, Kolnai used 'totalitarianism' to draw attention to structural similarities between fascist and communist regimes.[91] Another Polanyi acquaintance, Borkenau, popularised the term in his 1936 biography of Vilfredo Pareto.

Polanyi, too, used the term – as early as 1933.[92] He was struck by the contemporary tendency toward 'the combination of all forms of power' in a single organisation, the state, and, concurring with Bertrand Russell, predicted that 'the distinction between different kinds of power will soon be of only historic interest'.[93] Unlike Kolnai and Borkenau, however, he was no progenitor of totalitarianism theory. (Indeed, as Kolnai's anti-communism became more pronounced, their relationship grew strained.[94]) Polanyi occasionally referred to similarities between the fascist and communist regimes of the 1930s and 1940s, with reference to such phenomena as economic planning, incomes policy, the centralisa- tion of industrial organisation and the disregard for the value of liberty – and he was presumably aware that Horthyite and fascist governments in his own homeland presided over a 'fully planned economy'.[95] On the whole, however, he emphasised what he saw as the fundamental antithesis between fascism and communism: one represented the victory of the economy over politics, the other signified the reverse.[96] In this, his position was not unlike that of Franz Neumann, a former student of Mannheim. Neumann's *Behemoth* (1942), while admitting some similarities between fascism and Stalinism (and indeed New Deal capitalism), diagnosed fascism as a *sui generis* form of monopoly capitalism, one that ruthlessly advances the strategy of high finance and expresses the primacy of market forces over politics.[97]

Neumann, like Mannheim, belonged to the cohort of gifted Jewish intellectuals who fled to London to escape Central European fascism and then to make sense of it. Another in the same group was Peter Drucker, a former *Volkswirt* colleague of Polanyi. In mid-1930s London the two renewed their bond, and enjoyed long walks discussing the materials that each was shortly to craft into a book. Drucker's was published in 1939 as *The End of Economic Man: A Study of the New Totalitarianism*. It had the distinction of being well-regarded, albeit for entirely different reasons, by Polanyi and Hayek.[98] It diagnosed the collapse of liberal civilisation, with a focus upon the declining popular acceptance of the supremacy of economic values. Tracing the concept of 'economic man' (inaccurately) to Adam Smith, it proposed that its adoption as the 'model of man' and ideological basis of nineteenth-century liberal society had proved unsustainable. Drucker identified two flaws in the classical liberal model: a utilitarian rationalism that assumed everything could be treated as a calculable part of a mechanical sequence, and the prediction, as hubristic as it was erroneous, that freedom and justice could be achieved through market-driven economic development. These shortcomings, translated into policy, had steered the liberal project towards its collapse in 1914. The Great War had revealed to the world that not democracy but imperialist hegemony was the goal of liberal states, and it was followed by the Great Depression, which illuminated the chasm between the liberal ideals of equality and freedom and the unequal and unfree actuality of bourgeois society. As the ideals of freedom and equality lost their purchase on reality, and the popular masses absorbed these lessons, a vacuum arose into which fascism was equipped to march. Totalitarian fascism, Drucker concluded, could be successfully countered and overcome – but not by socialism or by capitalist democracy. Instead, 'a new non-economic concept of a free and equal society' was required.[99] Several or all of these arguments may have influenced Polanyi, and they were indubitably influenced by him. The younger man went on to make his name as an analyst of the modern business corporation, which, he wrote Polanyi, could usefully be understood using the Polanyian concepts of 'reciprocity and redistribution'.[100]

While Drucker was diagnosing the pathologies of liberal indi- vidualism and their role in the rise of fascism, others focused on its geopolitical implications. Acknowledging intellectual debts to Drucker and Mannheim, the British international relations scholar Edward Carr published his *Twenty Years Crisis* in 1939. His book, like theirs, charted the decline of liberal society, but his eyes were on world order and inter- nationalist norms. The nineteenth-century liberal-internationalist idea that the *laissez-faire* economy reflected universally applicable rational principles and enabled interests to harmonise, Carr believed, had been exposed as 'utopian'. Deploying Mannheimian theory on the relationship between knowledge and power, he proposed that the attraction of liberal international ('utopian') thought rested not on the validity of its claims to universality but on British power. Utopianism was not altruistic. Rather, 'the intellectual theories and ethical standards of utopianism, far from being the expression of absolute and a priori principles, are historically conditioned, being both products of circumstances and interests and weapons framed for the furtherance of interests'.[101]

During their heyday, in an era of world-economic growth and 'free spaces' for colonisation and emigration, Carr argued (in echo of Keynes), utopian internationalist ideas appeared common sense, but towards the end of the nineteenth century, economic turbulence and geopolitical closure generated conditions conducive to nationalism and racism. These, when superheated in the furnace of the Great War, brought forth a new age, of chronic conflict and a zero-sum mentality, in which liberal utopianism was starved of oxygen. And then, in the 1930s, the transformation of the world economy saw the end of yet another nineteenth-century liberal illusion: that economics and politics existed – and should exist – as institutionally separate spheres.[102] The imposition of political and social imperatives on the economic sphere, Carr predicted, would continue after the war.[103] Polanyi was impressed by Carr's theses on the geopolitical implications of free-market economics, and in particular by his critique of the *laissez-faire* regime as entailing an unmaintainable divorce between economics and politics.[104] In the 1930s, Carr and Polanyi presented their thoughts on the interwar conjuncture in lectures at Chatham House (at the time the British establishment's foremost venue for geopolitical debate) and from the early 1940s they engaged in occasional correspondence.[105]

In the US, where Polanyi wrote *The Great Transformation* in the early 1940s, debates over the market system and totalitarianism were no less animated than in Britain. Some of the seminal contributions came from Polanyi's colleagues at Bennington College. Drucker was one. His explanation of the demise of liberal capitalism and 'economic man' found fertile soil in the US, given its recent experience of economic disintegration and the New Deal. Erich Fromm was another. In 1942 he published *Fear of Freedom,* which offered a psycho-philosophical account of the origins and evolution of liberal individualism, a diagnosis of its pathologies and a manifesto for its transcendence by means of economic planning and socialism. A third was Horst Mendershausen, a German leftist who had been a comrade of Borkenau in the New Beginning group and who now worked at the National Bureau of Economic Research, with an associate status at Bennington. In 1943 he published *The Economics of War*, parts of which Polanyi read in draft. A treatise on the economics of modern total war, it proposed that the system of 'atomized planning' – Mendershausen's idiosyncratic term for *laissez faire* – had reached the end of its usable life. Throughout the nineteenth century it had functioned effectively but in the course of its expansion it 'tended to destroy the foundations on which its temporary prosperity had rested', and must now be replaced.[106]

On the political right, meanwhile, the discourse of 'totalitarianism' was beginning to find a footing, for example in Isabel Paterson's *The God of the Machine* and James Burnham's thesis on the totalitarian trend towards a 'managerial society'.[107] But of greater salience to Polanyi was the work of Hayek's American allies, who were seeking to re-group around a modified version of classical liberalism. Polanyi took copious notes from Walter Lippmann's books, particularly *The Good Society* (1937).[108] It advertised itself as a manifesto for a virile, reinvigorated liberalism, one that was equipped to beat back the 'collectivism' that had been in the ascendant since around 1870. The collectivist movement, in Lippman's reading, represented 'a rebellion against the market economy'. It had commenced in a gradualist form, as citizens sought 'protection from or mastery of the market,' but invariably it tended to radicalisation, as its adherents came to reject 'the whole conception of an economy in which the division of labour is regulated in markets.'[109] Lippmann divided his diagnosis of liberal decline – not unlike Polanyi's method in *The Great Transformation* but with reversed valence[110] – into two theses: on the maladjustment of economy and society, and on the doctrinal flaws of nineteenth-century economic liberalism. The maladjustment thesis centred on the notion that societies become subject to 'friction and disturbances' when 'the social order is in conflict with the economy'. In circumstances where 'the social heritage and the economy do not form a seamless web', individuals either rebel against the world or renounce it. The 'maladjustment of the social order with the economy' that occurred so dramatically in the nineteenth century had been caused by the industrial revolution. Liberalism emerged to represent 'the logic of the social readjustment required by the industrial revolution' while collectivism swiftly followed, representing the counter-revolutionary response of the retrograde social order.[111]

If a collectivist response was inevitable, however, its menacing extent was not. For this, Lippmann – much to the irritation of the Chicago School economist Frank Knight – apportioned some blame to flaws in classical liberal thought. Its nineteenth-century gurus had committed a perilous error when they convinced themselves of the assumption ('wholly false') that 'a realm of freedom' existed in which 'the exchange economy operated and, apart from it, a realm of law where the state had jurisdiction'. This fallacy spawned a plethora of related errors: the advocacy of an extreme, unalloyed version of *laissez-faire* economics; the pretence that economic behaviour could be modelled strictly along the lines of natural science; and the attempt to found economic theory upon a set of unrealistic assumptions (that economic actors are bloodless and free of attachments, free to move without friction, and in possession of perfect information; and that competition is free and perfect, undistorted by monopolies or legal privileges). The expectation that ensued, of the smooth and automatic advance of free-market society, 'seemed so delightful that the classical economists forgot that they had deduced from their hypothesis the conclusions which they had put into it'. The consequences of these academic errors and false expectations, Lippmann averred, had been 'catastrophic'. Initially, liberals had felt obliged to uncritically defend 'the actually existing law whatever it happened to be', and inevitably became apologists for all the miseries that accompanied these laws. Later, in horrified reaction, many of them bolted from classical liberal positions and converted impulsively to collectivism – with its predictable outcomes of political tyranny, economic ruin and universal misery.[112]

It was to revitalise liberalism and to inure it against the collectivist challenge that Lippmann wrote *The Good Society*, and the results were far from trivial. They included the 1938 Lippman Colloquium in Paris, the baptism of neoliberalism. Organised by the philosopher Louis Rougier to launch the French translation of *The Good Society*, the event was attended by a galaxy of liberal luminaries including Michael Polanyi and of course Hayek, who was inspired by the Paris colloquium to set up the MPS (to which he of course invited Michael Polanyi). Rougier's premise was that the world had become trapped in an infernal cycle whereby 'democrats believed their last defense to be socialism' while 'capitalists believed their only recourse to be fascism'.[113] To break free from the cycle, he and his invited guests believed, required the reinvention of liberalism, liberated from the flaws and fallacies that Lippmann had detected. Karl Polanyi, by contrast, was a convinced believer in the dichotomy that Rougier rejected: that democracy and socialism are natural allies, while capitalists in crisis tend to fascism. He had no truck with the attempts of Lippmann, Hayek, his own brother, et al. to resurrect economic liberalism – and even years later he would remind his wife and daughter of the 'fits' he threw 'about Lippmann's ghastly *The Good Society* and his revival of cheap liberalism'.[114] The desire to repudiate Lippmann surely belonged to the motivations behind *The Great Transformation*.

These, then, were some of the ideas that were in the air when *The Great Transformation* was researched and written. No such survey can aspire to comprehensiveness but I have attempted to sketch the most relevant texts, disputes, inspirations and debates. Polanyi was immersed in critical, and in some cases furious, dialogue with Keynesian, Austrian and early neoliberal theory. Like Kolnai, Drucker and Burnham, he was interested in the concept of totalitarianism but, unlike them, he etched a sharp line between the Nazi and Soviet regimes. He shared a good deal in common with Drucker's critique of economic society, Mannheim's diagnosis of the pathologies resulting from the institutional separation of spheres, and Fromm's prospectus for socialist individualism. Like them, he sought to explain the trend away from 'liberal civilisation', a trend that, he predicted in *The Great Transformation*, was destined to continue.

CONTROVERSIES AND CONTRADICTIONS

The debates and developments reviewed above formed the intellectual backdrop to Polanyi's writing of *The Great Transformation,* but of the authors mentioned, only a few engaged him in direct dialogue. They included his brother Michael, his comrade Tawney, whose comments on *The Great Transformation* I discuss below, and his colleagues Fromm and Drucker.

Drucker was deeply impressed by Polanyi's drafts of *The Great Transformation* but took issue with a series of individual arguments, of which four were important. One concerned Polanyi's assumption that the great transformation away from market economy was unequivocally in train. When writing the book, Polanyi was convinced that the 'profit motive' – which he conceived as a principle that suffuses society, rather than the motivational accompaniment to the capital relation – 'is on the decline', and was destined to give way to economic institutions based upon '*social co-operation* in all its forms'.[115] Relatedly, he maintained, even as late as 1964, that the 'market system is rapidly disappearing in Europe'.[116] Drucker thought these assertions were hyperbolic. The decades that followed the end of the Great War had in fact witnessed 'a fantastic expansion of market-organization' into such territories as Africa, India and even China which, before that time, had remained 'almost entirely outside the scope of the market'. Secondly, he questioned Polanyi's assertion that nineteenth-century British capitalism was 'a market economy *tout court*'. Rather, Drucker suggested to his friend, 'the market axiom was always a liberal Procrustes-bed'. Thirdly, Drucker noted an inconsistency in Polanyi's usage of his 'forms of integration' (reciprocity, redistribution, exchange). At times, Polanyi implies an 'underlying conflict between redistribution-reciprocity on the one hand and market on the other'. At other times there appears to be 'no inherent conflict' between them; rather, a basic problem of any society 'is how to use the various forms in inter-relation and how to link them to each other'.[117] Finally, Drucker dissented strongly from the supposition that, in Polanyi's words, 'a society must collapse if it functions at less than 100% efficiency'.[118] Drucker is referring to what Albert Hirschman has termed a doctrine of 'perverse effect': the idea that, in Polanyi's words, 'interference with markets causes them to function less well'.[119] This was an article of faith among Austrian economists such as Mises and Hayek, who believed that purposive action aimed at improving some feature of the economic order – such as public policy to influence wages and prices – only exacerbates the condition it intends to remedy. One of the elements in Polanyi's theory that distinguishes it from the Marxist and Keynesian traditions is that he accepted this thesis. However, he steered it toward conclusions diametrically opposed to those of Mises and Hayek. Because the liberal-capitalist system is 'utopian', he argued, its 'social effects' inevitably necessitate state interference with its economic cogs. And this, in turn, breeds further con-tradictions: the main effect of regulation is that 'the price system becomes *less elastic*'. Therefore, once a market system is introduced, regulation becomes 'inevitable'. This, with equal inevitability, 'must therefore lead to a crisis of Market-economy which suggests the necessity of Planning'.[120]

In this, Polanyi's theses on protectionism and on perverse effects combine. 'Interference with markets' is essential to protect human beings and their natural habitat, for they require a 'measure of stability and security' that market forces alone cannot provide; hence the need for 'protective measures' in respect of labour and land.[121] But protective measures 'tend to destroy self-regulation'. Therefore, 'government action, while inevitable, is of limited scope'.[122] It tends to be isolated and haphazard in kind, and this, 'in regard to the mechanism of the market', makes the system 'work even less successfully than would have otherwise been the case'.[123] By way of illustration, Polanyi invites us to consider, firstly, 'Speenhamland', the parish relief system that existed during the long stretch of Tory rule that commenced with the premiership of Pitt the Younger and ended with that of the Duke of Wellington. What puzzled him was that there appeared in this period to be no economic pressure compelling England's rural poor to move to the factories.[124] He characterised the era as 'capitalism without a labour-market', postulating that the formation of the latter was thwarted by the Speenhamland system of wage subsidies.[125] Although Speenhamland's ostensible aim was to ameliorate poverty, its unintended consequence was to depress productivity and rural living standards. It was due to the resulting uproar that the case for the market system, advanced by economists such as Ricardo and Malthus, achieved its breakthrough.

Or consider, secondly, unemployment relief in the 1920s and 1930s. In order to alleviate the suffering caused by the ups and downs of the business cycle, governments instituted social measures,

> which by helping to maintain wages actually prolonged the crisis. Both government and industry were providing employment with the one hand, and creating unemployment with the other. But there was no intention, nor even a possibility, of co-ordinating their activities.[126]

Ultimately, then, Polanyi understood the turmoil at the birth of the market system in early nineteenth-century Britain and at its demise one hundred years later as emanating from dysfunctionalities caused by the separation of the spheres. The Speenhamland system was 'incompatible with capitalism' on the grounds that 'if a man earns only part of his living then society owes him the rest'.[127] Something similar applied to interwar Europe, which offered a 'startling parallel' to Speenhamland.[128] In other words, his argument was that the interpenetration of politics and economics prevented market self-regulation, giving rise to irreconcilable contradictions. These led in Speenhamland to the breakthrough of free-market liberalism, and, in interwar Europe, to its demise. Both of these pivotal moments are described in *The Great Transformation* as occurring 'with the force of inevitability'.[129]

Does Polanyi's 'perverse effects' thesis, and his invocations of the inevitable breakdown of market civilisation, attest to a deterministic element in his philosophy? In the view of his friend Felix Schafer, his thesis that interventionism proves 'incompatible with maintaining the self-regulating market and hence brings the market economy to its end', was 'an analogous argumentation to Marx's thesis of the unavoidable replacement of capitalism by the planned economy of socialism'.[130] This is a suggestive interpretation. However, when interpreting predictions by Marx or Polanyi, attention to the meanings of 'unavoidable', 'necessity' and 'inevitability' is essential. Are they being used loosely to refer to generally accepted truths? Or to specify causal relations or strategic formulae of the type 'for Y to occur, X is a precondition'? (As when Polanyi states that in 1918–19 Hungary, 'the workers' parties neglected the *necessity* for a radical redistribution of the land'.[131]) Or are they designating social-scientific laws, such as Marx's on capital accumulation or Polanyi's on democratisation; and, if so, are these portrayed positivistically – as of a piece with natural-scientific laws? Or do they convey a confidence in the necessary *outcome* of a social process or political conflict?[132] This last type was prevalent in Second International social democracy and the communist orthodoxy of the 1930s. Affirmations of the inevitability of victory could serve as a recipe for fatalism and passivity. (Why undergo sacrifice if victory is preordained?) Or to rally the troops: for example, embattled communist activists up against a fascist regime. Such conceptions embodied the comforting notion that *History Is on Our Side*, as Polanyi's Christian-Socialist comrade Needham entitled his book. Polanyi himself was not averse to this language. 'We must teach the *inevitability* of the conflict,' he blazed in 1936, 'the inevitability of the sacrifice' and 'the certainty of ultimate victory'.[133]

Another of Polanyi's Christian Socialist associates was Richard Tawney. The two were on friendly terms, particularly in the 1930s when they met frequently, and the Labour *eminence grise* was one of Polanyi's referees. In 1942 he read a draft of *The Great Transformation*. He found it 'full of suggestive ideas' but was critical on a number of counts.[134] One concerned Polanyi's thesis that the requirements of factory production *necessitated* a transition to the market economy. Tawney regarded this as technological determinism: it overstates the role of 'hardware' innovation.[135] Another controversial point concerned his friend's reading of pre-nineteenth-century English history, in particularly the Tudor enclosures movement.

The nub of the issue was that *The Great Transformation* presents two contradictory historical narratives. One, Tawneyesque, accords a significant role to markets in the late medieval period; these tended to undermine feudal structures and clear a space in which mercantile capitalism could thrive. The other, the book's dominant thread, insists that there was nothing in mercantilism to presage the self-regulating market: the transition to the market economy occurred abruptly in the final years of the eighteenth century and the first of the nineteenth, as the outcome of rapid transformations in the spheres of technology and economic theory, and the stagnation caused by the Speenhamland system.

An early critic of Polanyi's account of Speenhamland arrived in the form of letters from another Labour Party luminary, Douglas Cole, to whom Polanyi had sent a draft of *The Great Transformation*. Cole attempted to persuade his friend that Speenhamland was nothing but a 'war emergency measure, mainly caused by high food prices', that wages were not subsidised to anything like the extent that he believed, and that a labour market did indeed exist across broad sectors of the eighteenth-century British economy.[136] More recent scholarship supports Cole's viewpoint, as well as controverting Polanyi's assumption that the income floor provided by outdoor relief operated in fact as an income ceiling that brought about the immiseration of the rural poor.[137]

In the light of Cole and Tawney's criticisms, Polanyi revised his manuscript, but in the process he injected a new contradictory element. Whereas in the main body of *The Great Transformation* Speenhamland is portrayed as 'protect[ing] *labor* from the dangers of the market system', in the notes appended to the second edition an altogether different meaning of protection is introduced: the system represented a 'protective move of the *rural community*' – by which Polanyi means rural employers – 'in the face of the threat represented by a rising urban wage level'.[138] In this reading, the purpose of Speenhamland was to maintain a rural reserve army by preventing labourers from absconding to the urban industrial centres. Polanyi had rolled two distinct meanings of protection – of workers' living conditions and of rural employers' labour reserve – into one.[139] This was no accidental slip, but was in keeping with his general deployment of 'protection' and 'protectionism'. In a letter to Michael in 1943, he laid out his perspective on the various meanings of protectionism, using the case of India as an example. It could denote, firstly, the protection that India would ideally have instituted in the nineteenth century against the intrusion of exports and techniques from its colonial master which were disrupting traditional social organisation, or, secondly, the quite different type of protection from foreign competition that modern Indian manufacturing industry required. Thirdly, it could signify the protection of India's populace from the general effects of a domestic market economy, and, fourthly, 'the protection of the same people from the dangers of an imperfect market economy (as, for example, that which is causing the present famine in Bengal)'. Of these, the first and fourth examples pertain to societies undergoing a transition to a market economy, while the other two are characteristic of 'mature' market economies. Only the second case exemplifies 'economic protectionism in the classical sense', the others being instances of '*social* protectionism, since social institutions are primarily threatened', or, as in the fourth case, instances where 'the threat is to man's physical existence, the danger arising however not from essentially economic causes but from their interaction with traditional social institutions'. Polanyi was less interested in the second type than in the others, for they 'arise from the introduction of non-economic considerations'.[140] His focus was on the third and also the fourth type, of which Speenhamland was the paradigmatic example.

Inasmuch as Polanyi conceives of social and environmental legislation, subsidies to industry and agriculture, and trade unionism, as protecting workers and nature from the effects of unrestricted market competition, his understanding of protectionism was in line with that of most socialists of the day. However, he also held that while protective interventions serve to restore the social fabric and the natural environment, in economic terms they are detrimental, in that they deduct from the 'social dividend'.[141] This underpins his Speenhamland thesis – a market economy cannot operate efficiently if the welfare net is woven robustly enough to shield workers from hunger and cold – and is bound up with his perverse-effects doctrine. In short, he idiosyncratically melded a socialist understanding of social protection with an 'Austrian' account of its incompatibility with the market system.

SEPARATION AND FUSION OF THE SPHERES

The axial contradiction that the market economy bequeaths to modernity, in Polanyi's view, is that it divides government and business into separate domains. He terms this 'the *institutional* separation of the political and the economic sphere' adding that this is '*my* non-Marxian formulation of the characteristic of 19th-century society' – a position that 'is much more that of Owen or Sismondi than that of Marx, who regarded on the contrary capitalist property as a political institution on which capitalist "dictatorship" rested'.[142] Polanyi was nonetheless aware that the market economy, however disembedded, was and is a politicised and politicising field. To begin with, its rise coincided with, and contributed to, that of the rule of law. When the market became *the* economic institution, its rules became 'identical with the Rule of Law, which reduced all social relations to the one norm of property and contract'. As relations of exchange and credit expanded and intensified, the norms of market behaviour – formal equality and the transacting individual – came to redefine the nature of political authority.[143] Thus, the emergence of the market economy contributed to the consolidation of a specifically *political* polity. However, the two spheres only appear truly separate when considered as abstractions. While the market economy appears to be self-regulating, in reality it 'can neither be established nor kept going without … constant action on the part of the government,' to ensure that it functions 'without fatal harm to the community.'[144]

In his fixation upon the separation of spheres and his assumption that they reconnect principally through government organising the protections necessary for the reproduction of the market and of the social and environmental habitat, Polanyi tends to overstate the 'protective' attributes of states. Consider for example his discussion of the part played by central banking in the double movement. In his analysis, the commodification of money was operationalised through the gold standard. Specie, being a fictitious commodity, generated socially disruptive tendencies, notably deflation. States, in response, attempted to protect society by inventing central banking and creating fiat money. In Polanyi's analysis, central banking was a triumph of the protective countermovement. By the mid-twentieth century it had enabled, across the world, 'the removal of the control of money from the market'.[145] Central banking empowered the state in its regulatory capacity, and formed a buffer between the domestic economy and the world market. In subjecting the monetary system to political direction, the central bank eroded the barrier between politics and economics, and, as lender of last resort, it cushioned the domestic effects of price fluctuations.

But why, Samuel Knafo has asked, should these same processes not be seen as 'integral components of the project of liberal financial governance?' The problem is, Knafo explains, that while Polanyi brilliantly dissects the debilitating consequences of the gold standard he never questions the purposes behind its adoption. He 'takes liberal financial governance at face value' by accepting that the ideal of self-regulation was indeed its telos. Polanyi's understanding of the ideological character of the idea of self-regulation notwithstanding, he never considered 'the possibility that something else was implemented in the name of this idea; that self-regulation constituted a discursive parameter mobilized to justify more concrete and pragmatic projects' of an altogether different kind, namely, the state's acquisition of greater agency over market activities. As Knafo demonstrates in exhaustive detail, the attempts of the Bank of England to impose its authority over the City and the Empire in the late nineteenth century cannot sensibly be understood as a manifestation of a Polanyian double movement, for the gold standard was, from the very beginning, 'a platform upon which state power was built', as much as, or indeed more than, a means of 'unleashing the market'.[146]

This chapter commenced with a survey of the genesis of *The Great Transformation* and of its major theses as they were assembled in the 1930s. Its main section consisted of an overview of the historical and discursive context, paying attention to theories that provoked Polanyi's critical engagement and the arguments that he sought to challenge. It identified numerous aspects of his argument that were being developed more or less simultaneously by others, but when filtered through his Christian-socialist outlook, and his idiosyncratic blend of socialist and Austrian conceptions of protectionism, the result was uniquely his own.

The protagonist of *The Great Transformation* is the market economy; capitalism in its liberal form. Polanyi was aware of the dangers involved in confusing this species of capitalism for the genus itself. In 'The Essence of Fascism', for example, he describes the technique that fascist movements used to focus popular resentment upon

Liberal Capitalism … without any reflection on Capitalism in its non-Liberal, i.e. corporative, forms. Though unconsciously performed, the trick is highly ingenious. First Liberalism is identified with Capitalism; then Liberalism is made to walk the plank; but Capitalism is no worse for the dip, and continues its existence unscathed under a new alias.[147]

What he failed to notice is that social democracy was inventing its own version of the same trick. It identified capitalism with laissez-faire liberalism, and social democracy with the social-protectionist responses to it. Capitalism was no worse for the dip, and continued its existence unscathed under new aliases: corporatism, social democracy, Fordism, embedded liberalism, the mixed economy and so on. Those who enacted the social-democratic version of the trick could learn from *The Great Transformation*, in two ways. First, it showed a method of substituting the dichotomy of capitalism and socialism with that of laissez-faire and regulation. Secondly, it singled out the liberal market economy as the active ingredient in modernity's maleficent turn, and assembled 'regulated' forms of capitalism into heterogeneous categories that received definition only reactively and indirectly, in the mirror of the abstraction that is the free market model. I am not suggesting that *The Great Transformation* purveyed the 'trick' in a simple sense, for it presents regulated capitalism as necessarily fragile and unstable. Its conceptual framework was ill-equipped to deal with it as the durable phenomenon that it turned out to be, failing to anticipate that state intervention could contribute to the stabilisation of market societies. This is one reason why *The Great Transformation* gained only a modest following during the long postwar boom. It is also part of the reason why it is open to interpretation in 'hard' and 'soft' ways, as discussed in the Introduction above. For some, its target is capitalism; for others, it critiques laissez-faire liberalism from a social-democratic standpoint.

Alongside these wrinkles and ambivalences, *The Great Transformation* boasts formidable strengths. Of these, the best known is its sophisticated and passionate critique of the market economy and the political engineering that lay behind its construction. I would also highlight its complex, multi-factoral analysis of the interwar crisis – in particular, its analysis of the ways in which 'strains' shuttled between the political and economic spheres and the national and international scales. With remarkable erudition and narrative skill, Polanyi traced the ways in which the various crises of the age – of democracy, market society, international order and the world economy – interlaced, with each connection multiplying the intensity of the crisis as a whole. It is to one element of that story, the question of world order, that we now turn.

6

Regionalism and the European Union

'We are entering a new era in foreign policy,' declared Polanyi in the mid-1940s. 'Many sense that we are standing at the brink of a great transformation, but the direction the future holds for us is shrouded in thick fog.' To begin to penetrate the fog required understanding 'the new system of international relations'. Inter-state systems, the same text continues, appear in two basic types: 'universalistic, i.e. those that necessarily expand over an entire civilisation, and those that are merely regional orders.' Exemplifying the former was medieval Europe, a realm that, under the overarching governance of the Catholic Church, 'was characterised by an almost unimaginable uniformity', for example in the running of cities, universities and trade. This configuration gave way in the fifteenth century to the modern state system: a non-universalistic order in which 'each individual state stood on its own feet'. In turn, it was supplanted in the nineteenth century by 'a completely new, universalistic order'. The nineteenth-century 'expansion of freedom and the market economy', in Polanyi's reconstruction,

> enfolded all states within a new fabric: the world market of goods, capital and money. ... Trade, industry and capital export were all equally dependent on the functioning of an international financial system, and governments cooperated with each other in order to isolate wars – except for the numerous and endless colonial wars through which the market economy spread itself across the world. The great achievement of capitalism in the sphere of foreign policy was that it spread industrial civilisation through incessant wars while nonetheless managing to avoid general wars which might have destroyed that civilisation. The secret behind the operation was the peace interest, which culminated in the gold standard.

The new liberal-universalist capitalism, given definition and strength by the gold standard, found triumphant expression in the standardised replication, worldwide, of such institutions as constitutions and central banks. But then, in the twentieth century, the utopia of liberal universalism, as represented by Mises, found itself overshadowed by counterparts on the left (the 'international revolutionary socialism' of Trotsky) and the right

(Hitler's 'German dogma' of racial supremacy and Aryan hegemony). What made the 1940s such a momentous decade was that it was witnessing 'the demise of all three forms of universalism: the victory of Stalin over Trotsky, the fall of the gold standard, and the impending downfall of Hitler'. All the societies that arise from the ashes of the old universalisms, Polanyi concluded, will, whether socialist or capitalist, be 'more or less planned economies, and regional in scale'.[1]

In several respects Polanyi's case resembled that which Keynes had outlined ten years earlier. Keynes, a liberal imperialist, held that the nineteenth-century British Empire had laid the foundations of a liberal world economy, and it, in turn, undergirded a relatively pacific international order.[2] London, he insisted, enabled its colonies to develop freely – in contrast to the exclusionary and discriminatory practices of protectionist trading blocs, notably the 'German dream of Mittel-Europa'.[3] Following the onset of the Great Depression, however, Keynes' confidence in the prospects of a universalistic world order crumbled, and he began to advocate protectionist policies. The essay that encapsulates his shift was 'National Self-Sufficiency' (1933). It characterises the preceding age as universalistic. 'The nineteenth century free trader's economic internationalism assumed that the whole world was, or would be, organised on a basis of private competitive capitalism and of the freedom of private contract inviolably protected by the sanctions of law' that tended to conform 'to a uniform type'. The nineteenth century liberal world market had functioned satisfactorily, but the conditions that had sustained it, notably settler colonialism and ease of capital export, no longer held. For at least the next two or three decades Keynes could see no prospect 'of a uniformity of economic systems throughout the world' – and this was no bad thing, for 'we do not wish to be at the mercy of world forces working out some uniform equilibrium according to the ideal principles, if they can be called such, of laissez-faire capitalism … We all need to be as free as possible of interference from economic changes elsewhere, in order to make our own favourite experiments towards the ideal social republic of the future'. To that end, 'greater national self-sufficiency and economic isolation' were welcome.[4] Keynes envisaged that this world-economic shift would be accompanied by a considerable degree of continuity in the units of geopolitical order (empires, nation states, international organisations), albeit perhaps with a stronger showing for regionalism. In an essay of 1938, he proposed the construction, under the aegis of the League of Nations, of 'new regional Leagues – especially a European pact' in which member states would seek mutual agreements on 'collective security, with sanctions, arbitration, defence collaboration, free trade, and help for Jewish refugees'.[5]

In the same period, Polanyi was developing similar ideas, but with a stronger sense that a trend towards regionalism was underway. When young, he had believed in the compatibility between liberal universalism and imperial organisation. The concept of empire was viewed positively by most Europeans of the day, Dominic Lieven reminds us:

> To be an empire was to be powerful, in an era when the gulf between strong and weak states was growing ever wider, and when the weak seemed doomed to marginalization or extinction. Empires were in the van of progress and civilization, bringing all the benefits of western values and technology to the benighted 'lesser races'.[6]

Such beliefs were dearly held by many middle-class Jews of Polanyi's milieu, for whom the empire promised inclusion and progress. The idea of nation, by contrast, appeared rather complex. The invitation of Jews into the Hungarian nation demanded public performances of repudiation of their heritage, and it was little wonder that many of them, including Polanyi and his mentors Pikler and Jaszi, conceptualised national identity as voluntarist (not given) and nations as socially constructed (not primal). Even so, they tended to identify strongly with the Hungarian nation. During his stint as Hungary's Minister for Nationalities, Jaszi adopted a liberal-nationalist approach to the question of the smaller Danubian nations within Greater Hungary. He preached toleration, but with a sense that the hegemony of the Magyars was progressive (in his words, 'the dominance of an economically and politically stronger national group over backward and unorganized peasants') and that the smaller nationalities exhibited 'impetuousness' and a 'narrow exclusiveness'.[7]

Polanyi shared the impatience with 'small nationalities' exhibited by Jaszi and by Fabian thinkers such as Shaw and Wells.[8] With Jaszi, he believed that a long-term movement toward political and economic integration existed, and he condemned as 'ignorant and barbaric' the idea that nations represent the 'ultimate units' of political community.[9] Yet his condemnation did not extend to nations and nationalism *tout court*. That he considered himself an 'internationalist', he was wont to assert, 'should not be confused with disloyalty to one's country or even the colourless existence of the person who feels equally at home everywhere because he has no country of his own'. Humanity, he opined, 'needs nations that have a history', for the content of history is the life of humanity and it 'is lived through nations'.[10] He was a life-long champion of 'true patriotism', which he regarded as 'not only a natural emotion but also a praiseworthy one', in that it lays the 'moral, educational and emotional' basis of government.[11] In 1915, in probably the most foolish decision of his life, he volunteered, cheerfully and dutifully, as an army officer. Later in life, he would recommend that young people be instructed to 'study, choose their profession, subordinate the meanings of their lives' and be prepared to 'suffer poverty' for 'the benefit of their nation', and he bemoaned the 'lack of patriots' that he encountered when, during the war, he emigrated to the USA.[12]

The functionality of the nation-state system, in Polanyi's account, was apparent during the nineteenth century, during which the balance of power system operated effectively. There was no general conflagration, and although the major powers engaged in ceaseless fighting, 'all colonial invasions or suppressions of small states' remained localised. But then, in the early twentieth century, everything changed. The concert of great powers degenerated and the balance of power system gave way to its opposite: bipolar rivalry between the Allies and the Entente. What did the future hold in store? For guidance, Polanyi adopted a thesis that Arnold Toynbee had spelled out in the early 1920s. Noting that in the aftermath of the demise of the Austro-Hungarian Empire and the weakening of Germany and Russia only five great powers remained – France, Italy and Japan (three nation-states) 'and two empires, Britain and the United States' – Toynbee forecast a weakening of the first three 'on the grounds that only empires, and no longer nation states, would be able to compete in future'. To this prediction Polanyi added his own. Following the world war, 'a new order will replace the international market economy system'. In matters of foreign policy, the main question will not be 'socialism versus capitalism, but universal liberal capitalism versus regional organisation'. Which pattern emerged would depend upon the power, strategy and political culture of the great powers. In most major states, flows of currencies, trade and capital were already largely under state control, but the decisive powers were liberal Britain and the United States. The latter, 'currently in a virulently imperialist phase', was the only nation that was committed 'unswervingly to a world order based on the market economy' – a commitment that had been unaffected by 'the unemployment of 1929–36 and the New Deal'. For the overwhelming majority of Americans, 'anything other than the freedom of enterprise, as manifested in a competitive economy, would be intolerable. US foreign policy, consequently, aimed at restoring the pre-1914 world order based on the gold standard, free trade and free movement of capital.' Britain, by contrast, found itself in a contradictory position. On one hand, it was 'the founder of the nineteenth-century world order. Free trade and the gold standard are British institutions, as is the industrial revolution'. It was, moreover, a 'deeply conservative' country in terms of 'its class structure. It is a class society to a much greater extent than any other capitalist state'. On the other hand, Britain had been the first to break 'with the gold standard, and veered off the track of liberal capitalism during the world crisis. Britain has the most comprehensive system of trade unions, its industry is completely cartelised, and its foreign trade and capital markets are completely under state control'.[13] The latter thoughts guided Polanyi in his hope that London would *not* follow its liberal-conservative instincts and assist Washington in re-establishing universal capitalism. Rather, its social-democratic values should persuade it to ally with the comparatively statist powers in constructing a new world of regions. Such hopes came to nothing. London, with Keynes as emissary, helped Washington to reconstruct a form of universal capitalism. But what of Polanyi's prediction of a regionalised world order? Would it fare any better?

EUROPEAN INTEGRATION: A RE-EMBEDDING PROJECT?

It is puzzling that Polanyi expressed scant interest in West European integration, given its status as *the* regionalist experiment of the century. His views on the process are not well documented, but he certainly wrote little, if anything, on the early institutions of European integration, as they were being assembled in the 1940s and 1950s: the ECSC, and the European Economic Community (EEC). Did he see in the EEC's ordoliberal foundations a market fundamentalism that would necessarily prove inimical to his vision of a planned economy? Or did he regard European integration as an inherently social-democratic counter to US-led market liberalism? It is difficult to say.

Among Polanyi's followers, by contrast, the European integration project has attracted eager attention. For some years, the running was made by a Swedish political economist, Björn Hettne. He penned a profusion of essays proposing the case that European integration embodies a socially protective counter-movement to the polarising pressures of economic globalisation, a 'return to the political' that will re-embed the market economy in society. Contemporary globalisation, he advised, should be seen in Polanyian terms,

> as a 'second great transformation,' a 'double movement,' where an expansion and deepening of the market is followed by a political intervention in defence of societal cohesion – the expansion of market constituting the first movement and the societal response the second.[14]

Both the first and second movement assumed regionalist forms, 'with a neoliberal face in the first, and a more interventionist orientation in the second'.[15] Hettne's prediction was that when the Cold War ended, enabling 'a hegemonic position for the market', the stage was set for the second phase of the double movement, 'i.e. when the self-protection of society is activated'. A 'new regionalism' could be seen in emergence, corresponding to the needs of the counter-movement. Whereas the old regionalism 'was created "from above" (i.e. by the superpowers)', the new regionalism emerged from a more 'voluntary [and] spontaneous process "from below"' (with 'below' defined distinctively: 'the constituent states themselves are main actors' and are guided by 'the imperative of cooperation').[16] The new regionalism would transcend the nation-state logic; it heralded 'a segmented world system, consisting of self-sufficient blocs' in which 'political stability and social welfare are major concerns'. In this way, Hettne theorised the 'New Europe' that emerged after 1989 as a paradigm of contemporary neo-mercantilism and 'the model case of the new regionalism'. It embodied 'a trend towards political and economic homogeneity', one that paved the way to ever deeper economic and political integration. Felicitously, the integration process was achieving the construction of a social-democratic 'Fortress Europe', understood as 'a social project to create a true European region, based on a domestic market, a shared culture, and historical identity'.[17]

The EU, in Hettne's vision, did not merely represent the most advanced form of social-democratic regionalism, but, as such, it bore hope as the axis of a new world order. He identified the US as the bastion of a particular approach to world order, a nation-centred Hayekian liberal-market regime. Against it was the EU, the embodiment of a 'Polanyian' demand for the repoliticisation of world order in a regionalist framework. It represented the countermovement on the geopolitical scale. 'The return of "the political"', Hettne proposed, may be realised in several different ways, but the most appropriate of these, 'in today's globalised world, would be a post-Westphalian order, where the locus of power moves up the ladder to the transnational level by the voluntary pooling of state sovereignties'. This tendency would give Europe, through its regionalist propensity, 'a second chance', following its colonial period, 'to influence world order', to pursue *its* values. And these, he felt, radically contrasted with those of the dominant power. Americans are 'from Mars', observed Hettne borrowing from Kagan. They live in a Hobbesian world. The US seeks to 'change the world in accordance with its perceived "national interest"', and 'tends to see political conflict as a struggle between good and evil'. The EU, by contrast, favours 'long-term multidimensional, horizontal, institutional arrangements' based on rational political analysis, pragmatic compromise and dialogue. Europeans are 'from Venus', and are drawn to 'the ideal world of "permanent peace" of Immanuel Kant'. These two 'world order projects', the US Hobbesian-Hayekian hard-power model and the EU's Kantian-Polanyian civic 'inter-regionalism', Hettne concluded, are 'incompatible'. They will inevitably exist in protracted 'struggle'.[18]

Hettne sketched his thesis on a broad canvas, paying comparatively little attention to the specific EU institutions in which the protective countermovement is embodied. Other Polanyian theorists, however, have done so. One is Paul Copeland. He identifies the 'European Social Dimension', as embodied in the Social Protocol of the Maastricht Treaty, as the countermovement to the disembedding tendencies of the Single European Market (SEM) and European Monetary Union (EMU). Although the bulk of EU social policy legislation is soft law (and therefore not legally binding, unlike legislation associated with the SEM and EMU), European integration in the social sphere nonetheless represents Polanyi's countermovement, Copeland suggested, for its aim is 'to protect EU society from the extremes of the pure market'.[19] A second and more influential intervention of this kind was James Caporaso and Sidney Tarrow's essay on 'Polanyi in Brussels'. Following a period of economic liberalism and marketisation in Europe, Caporaso and Tarrow suggested with reference to the ideas of Polanyi and John Ruggie on the 'social embedding of markets', the pendulum has begun to swing back toward social policy and the disciplining of market freedoms by the principle of social justice. Many of the apparent contradictions in the European integration project are best understood as the working through of a 'Polanyian duality', with the 'disembedding of European markets' countered by 'a re-embedding of social regulation at the supranational level'.[20]

Whereas Polanyi's 'countermovement' was powered chiefly by governments but also by social movements, particularly labour, the European countermovement identified by Caporaso and Tarrow is not. Nor could it be. The subjects of grassroots democratic class struggles, notably trade unions and social movements, have been conspicuously absent from the European integration project. Caporaso and Tarrow instead single out the European Court of Justice (ECJ) as the institution that has steered the Polanyian 're-embedding' project, playing a similar role to the neo-Keynesian and social democratic authors of 'the great postwar compromise'. It has engaged in market-making, but crucially, and simultaneously, in market modification too, through the creation of labour rights and social policy 'in something resembling the compromise of embedded liberalism that Ruggie saw in the founding of the Bretton Woods system'. Caporaso and Tarrow gather their evidence 'from the case law of the ECJ regarding the free movement of labor', with particular focus upon the *Acciardi* case, in which the ECJ quashed the decision of the municipality of Amsterdam to pay a lower rate of social security benefits to an Italian citizen, Genaro Acciardi, on the grounds that his wife and child resided in Italy. If the process of market disembedding tends to treat workers as commodities, the ECJ-led re-embedding process has insisted upon their treatment, at the same time, as 'human beings, with families, local commitments, and rights'.[21] The ECJ, they conclude, has constructed an impressive edifice of rights that have invested EU citizenship with social content.

NEGATIVE INTEGRATION

From his mid-century perch it appeared to Polanyi that the world would turn towards either globalisation or regionalisation. As the postwar landscape unfolded, the reality appeared rather untidier. The new era featured globalisation *and* regionalism (in Europe, subsequently in South America, East Asia and beyond) *and* a reinvigoration of the nation-state system, as national liberation movements upended colonial rule. The empires of Western Europe began to relinquish their colonies and, simultaneously, to organise themselves into a regional arrangement. Against Polanyi's expectations, this did not develop as an alternative to 'universal capitalism' but as a process, steered and encouraged by Washington, of consolidating capitalism and forging a common front against the Soviet bloc. The integration project, moreover, exhibited distinctively ordoliberal traits. In 1940s Germany, ordoliberals gained prominent positions, and several contributed to the German policy positions injected into negotiations on the Treaty of Rome.[22] In its political-juridical form, the EEC exhibited unmistakeable affinities with ordo-liberalism: created by a quasi-Schmittian decision to create an economic constitution; driven forward by judge-made law, intergovernmental bargaining, and technocratic institutions; and designed to create a unitary market, with German-style monetary stringency, far-reaching provisions for the removal of national barriers to trade (as the Dutch and Germans demanded), including the elimination of import quotas, low external tariffs, and the restriction of state aids and other national policies that distorted competition.[23] From the Treaty of Rome onwards, guided by an increasingly activist ECJ, and with a competition policy that owed much to German ordoliberal lawyers and economists, integration centred upon repeated pushes toward market 'disembedding', with freedom of goods flows, and increasingly of capital, treated as a fundamental right.[24]

A further twist ensued in the 1980s and 1990s, as the integration project coincided with accelerated neoliberalisation and German hegemony. In the design of EMU, German positions were adopted in two central respects: ordoliberal competition policy provided the main regulatory framework for the internal market, and the prioritisation of price stability was written into the Maastricht Treaty, ensuring a monetarist orientation. EMU, although born on the Maas, was headquartered on the Main, where a sternly ordoliberal *Geist* had long held sway, its emphasis upon price stability precisely synchronised to the needs of German exporters. Like the Single Market, EMU evinced an elective affinity between hegemonic and ordoliberal tendencies. The euro, a project to create a new world money capable of competing with the US dollar, required the creation of deeper and more liquid financial markets – which happened to be centred in the core states. Thanks to Germany's economic weight and higher levels of productivity, but also to the structure of the Eurozone and its adoption of Germany's ordoliberal creed, the corporations of the EU's core states emerged as the chief beneficiaries of Monetary Union. With the euro, German exporters gained stable currency and export markets – including to the countries of the Eurozone periphery which, with Berlin's acquiescence, entered the euro at overvalued exchange rates. In effect, the euro became a mechanism geared to boosting German exports and current account surpluses (financed by current account deficits for peripheral countries) and suppressing German interest rates.[25] This process interacted with Germany's domestic integration project, with ruinous consequences. In 1990, East Germany had converted almost overnight from one of the most to one of the least industrialised regions in Europe. Mass unemployment enabled employers to experiment with practices that trade unions in the West would not countenance. Some firms explicitly used eastern Germany as a greenfield from which to influence work organisation at their western plants. National collective bargaining agreements were ripped up in the east, resulting in a marked regional differentiation of industrial relations. The low wages imposed in the former East were extended westward. Over the next two decades, thanks to a succession of Red-Green and CDU-led governments clamping down on wage growth and squeezing welfare, the proportion of wages and salaries in total GDP plunged to a record low while company profits and income from property hit new highs. The effects ripped through Germany and beyond. Germany's current account surplus soared, but so, inevitably, did its pendant, the entrenched deficits in the countries of the EU periphery – a polarisation that culminated in devastating crisis.[26]

Among Polanyians, unsurprisingly, the ranks of scholars who place faith in the EU as a natural repository of a social-democratic counter-movement have thinned, and alternative Polanyi-inspired perspectives have come to the fore. A noteworthy example is Colin Crouch's *Europe and Problems of Marketization: From Polanyi to Scharpf*. In this monograph, Polanyi figures in his customary role as a social-democratic theorist of the double movement – the tendency of the market economy to destroy institutions, provoking a search for new institutions to shield against the market's negative externalities. But Crouch's emphasis, unlike Hettne's and Caporaso/Tarrow's, is on the propensity of the European marketisation project to undermine the national institutions that had hitherto organised social security. As a result, '"Europe" increasingly appears as a hostile force, setting itself against public policies and practices that protect citizens from the negative consequences of economic uncertainty'. The critical decade, Crouch argues, was the 1990s, which saw not a Polanyian counter-movement but its antithesis: the completion of ESM, the inauguration of EMU and the Stability and Growth Pact (SGP), all of which served to consolidate the EU on neoliberal principles, with stringent constraints on welfare expansion. The ECJ ruled that 'any compulsory social insurance contributions were welfare state contributions, and therefore covered by the [SGP], while any voluntary contributions were necessarily open to the EU's competition laws'. This, Crouch argues, ensured, in general, that European institutions would be 'highly critical of any proposals to extend social protection systems', and, specifically, that trade unions were denied 'the role in European social policy construction that had been promised them'.[27] As a result of the ECJ's determination to reinterpret 'the commitments of member states to create a common market as subjective rights of individuals and firms against these member states' and to extend the sway of what Fritz Scharpf termed 'negative integration' (the removal of obstacles to the EU-wide movement of goods, labour, capital and services) at the expense of 'positive integration' (the creation of social institutions), the defence of social rights is largely left to the nation-state, 'as rights established in the past at national level are pitted against a European drive to reduce them'.[28] EU policymaking, Crouch concludes, has returned to the position that Scharpf once summarised as the dominance of negative over positive integration.

If the ECJ has been the key institution advancing negative integration, what should be made of the Caporaso-Tarrow claim that it has acted to 're-embed' labour markets? The Acciardi case, on which Caporaso and Tarrow base their thesis, is not in fact 'about the promotion of social embeddedness, but rather about market order', in Alexander Ebner's assessment. It promotes the establishment of 'a common European labour market by means of a de-construction of the national limitations of welfare regimes', a process that aims above all to enhance labour mobility, and thereby the EU-wide commodification of labour power.[29] For the SEM and EMU to work as the textbooks say they should, the wheels of labour mobility must be well oiled. According to the Optimum Currency Area theory of Chicago economist Robert Mundell (who has been styled, with only a little hyperbole, the 'father of the Euro'[30]), for a region to qualify as an optimum currency area, high levels of labour and capital mobility are essential. At times of economic crisis, labour mobility acts as an 'adjustment mechanism', with workers in regions of high unemployment moving to boom areas. For the EU, with a diminutive budget available for other means by which to regionally smooth the consequences of crisis, the blockages to labour mobility pose a very real problem. How to fix it? Some obstacles, such as language barriers, are difficult to dismantle. But some can be reduced, and one of these is the non-transferability of social entitlements. It is therefore perfectly plausible that the principal factor motivating the extension of social rights is not a *social* consideration of

EU citizens qua human beings but the *economic* desire to make SEM and EMU function effectively, in neoliberal terms. In a nutshell: if workers are reluctant to move because their (and their relatives') social rights are limited, they need to be awarded wider rights in order to expedite the mobility of labour.

The most searching and meticulous critique of Caporaso and Tarrow's thesis has been advanced by the sociologists Martin Höpner and Armin Schäfer, colleagues of Scharpf and Streeck at Cologne's Max Planck Institute. Höpner and Schäfer broadly share Caporaso and Tarrow's theoretical perspective (albeit with caveats, on which below). But their empirical findings drive them to an antithetical conclusion. They begin by identifying shortcomings in 'Polanyi in Brussels'. First, it conflates 'individual transnational access' to social security and healthcare systems with 'social policy and embeddedness', thereby mis-representing individual social rights as 'the establishment of social policies at the European level'. This can clearly be seen in the case of Signor Acciardi's right to social security on a par with his Dutch neighbours, or, to give another example, in the granting of individual pan-EU rights to the receipt of healthcare, an apparent extension of 'social' rights but one that follows in the wake of the creation of markets in health services by ECJ jurisprudence – an acceleration of the commodification of human livelihoods. When extending social rights to EU citizens, the ECJ simultaneously severs other sets of rights and obligations. The net effect, Höpner and Schäfer suspect, is increased pressure for welfare retrenchment.[31] Secondly and relatedly, 'Polanyi in Brussels' focuses upon only 'one subdimension of EU *social policy*, the free movement of labour', to the neglect of other dimensions of EU social *and economic policy*. For a rounded picture, one needs to take account of all dimensions of European integration, including the social impact of the ECJ's market-making decisions. When these are considered an altogether different picture emerges.

On the whole, negative integration has been pushed further, thanks to the ECJ, than had hitherto been thought possible. Crucially, it

> expanded the so-called horizontal or 'third-party' effect of the European market freedoms to private parties, which implies that European law not only obliges member states, but also private bodies (such as industry associations and trade unions) to refrain from actions that might restrict the fundamental market freedoms.[32]

The paradigm cases were *Viking, Laval, Rüffert*, and *European Commission v Federal Republic of Germany* [case C-271/08], in which the ECJ ruled that trade unions or collective bargaining may not hinder 'the spontaneous order of the markets' (except in specific circumstances, for which the *Gebhard* case [C55/94] has provided the formula).[33] Furthermore, the Court ruled that the logic of economic integration legitimised tax-avoidance practices, and that national efforts to restrict them could not be justified on public-interest grounds. Through such rulings it fuelled tax competition, thereby constraining member states' redistributive capacity. Because European law has tended to favour market liberalisation, proponents of redistributive social policies have had to gear their demands to the national level, but the redistributive capacity of member states has meanwhile diminished, thanks in large part to ECJ case law. If a 'return to the political' is to arise, it will be the result of collective political struggles rather than ECJ rulings. If any 'Polanyian content' is to be found, it will be in public debates over, and protests against, EU market integration.[34]

Caporaso and Tarrow's usage of Polanyian theory has also been subject to critique. One criticism concerns their supposition that in Polanyi's theory all economies are 'embedded'. If 'embedded' is understood as a synonym of 'instituted', this is non-contentious,[35] and finds agreement among those who, like Polanyi, define the capitalist market economy, in the Austrian manner, 'almost exclusively as a domain of exchange, contract and profit', and those who do not.[36] Markets self-evidently require an array of institutional supports (property rights, forms of law, means of enforcement of contracts etc.). Economic behaviour is always woven into legal, political, customary and ideological fabrics, and the stability and predictability of markets depends upon their connections to wider webs of social relations. However, this reading obscures the distinctiveness of Polanyi's case. It sees all economies as 'instituted' but only some as 'embedded'. (The idea of the 'always socially embedded market', Christian Joerges points out, 'fails to distinguish between the policies which stabilise the market mechanism and the counter-movements which strive for its replacement'.[37]) A second criticism pertains to Caporaso and Tarrow's interpretation of the double movement thesis. They read it in an 'oversimplified' way, argue Höpner and Schäfer, as a process that tends to 'balance efficiency and equity'. In Höpner and Schäfer's interpretation, by contrast, the double movement proceeds 'neither automatically nor smoothly' but instead embodies 'contradictory impulses' and is freighted with 'political conflict',[38] including countermovements that seek to re-embed the market. In respect of the EU, these contradictory and conflictual impulses can be seen in three main areas: 'the separation of politics from the economy; the interplay of the international economic regime and domestic politics; and the tension between free markets and democracy'.

In Polanyi's era, the movements for and against free markets 'could not be resolved in any productive way. Instead, fascism resolved the deadlock between the two contending sides of the double movement – capitalism and democracy – by eradicating the latter'. Today, Höpner and Schäfer argue, the suppression of democracy is advanced in the EU not by fascist but by 'Hayekian' means. The ECJ rulings that appeared to Caporaso and Tarrow as the nucleus of supranational social policy, a Polanyian form of 'embedded liberalism', appear on inspection to closely resemble Hayek's vision of market-enforcing 'integration through law': a recipe for reduced social protection and redistribution at the national level.[39]

In making this argument, Höpner and Schäfer cite a widely noted essay by Perry Anderson which identifies a remarkable resemblance between the EU, and EMU in particular, and a vision outlined by Hayek in his 1939 paper, 'The Economic Conditions of Interstate Federalism'. In this text, Hayek maintained that although the main purpose of inter-state federation may be the securing of peace, a tremendously welcome side effect would be a Europe-wide shift toward liberal political economy, with a division of competencies that naturally guard against excessive taxation and undue interventionism, given that constituent states would compete for mobile resources, precluding inflationary demands (which, for Hayek, were essentially the consequence of polarised class relations within independent national states). For Hayek, then, a federal Europe with an independent central bank would not mean 'a super-state, but *less* state'.[40] The greater the heterogeneity of member states, the less the prospect of concurrence over macro-economic regulation (for it requires some common agreement over purposes and values) and the greater the pressure to effect the regulation of society's affairs 'nomocratically' (via a set of universal, abstract and predictable rules that set the framework for action within which individuals are able to pursue their own goals) rather than 'teleologically', by establishing a set (or hierarchy) of goals or purposes, for example with the aim of attaining a particular pattern of distribution of economic and social resources.[41] In short, Hayek was the prophet of 'the depoliticisation of economic governance by means of supranational structures of law',[42] and a prophet, moreover, who was heeded by policymakers, including not least the architects of the European Central Bank (ECB).[43] Hayek endorsed supranationalism as a way of protecting capital from the interventions of people seeking a 'just distribution' of wealth, limiting the effect of mass democracy on political decision-making, and as a device to disempower the working class by forcing governments to steer against popular aspirations to security of welfare and employment.

In the analysis of Anderson, Scharpf, and Höpner and Schäfer, the EU has largely succeeded in turning Hayek's blueprint into reality, thanks to the synergy between the principle of negative integration through law and the heterogeneity of EU member states which, 'just as Hayek predicted, makes positive, market-restricting regulation at the European level unlikely' and decreases the likelihood of 'coordinated resistance to integration-enforcing ECJ case law'.[44] Secluded from popular accountability and oriented around a project of market unification, the EU evolved as a market and legal order that was ideally suited to the neoliberal regime when it entered its ascendancy in the 1980s. From its inception, integration had been driven by judge-made law and technocratic politics, both of which were inspired by the highly restrictive understanding of democracy that defined (in Peter Lindseth's phrase) the 'post-war constitutional settlement' – the distancing of European polities from the ideals of parliamentary sovereignty and the delegating of power to unelected bodies such as constitutional courts.[45] Until the 1980s, 'politics' and 'law' worked hand in glove, with legal supranationalism complemented by political bargaining. Over subsequent decades, the relationship between law and the political was repeatedly 'reinstitutionalised', as integration through law gained ever greater dominance within the European project.[46] Of course, as Anderson qualifies the case, 'with its dense web of directives, and often dubious prebends' the EU is 'far from a perfect Hayekian order. But in its political distance from the populations over which it presides, it approaches the ideal he projected'. The European Parliament still survives ('a memento of federal hopes forgone'), and agricultural and regional subsidies continue to absorb much of the EU budget. 'But of a 'social Europe' … there is as little left as a democratic Europe'.[47]

CONCLUSION

In a partial sense, Polanyi's prediction of the rise of regionalism has been borne out, but the results have not, as anticipated, tilted global politics toward social democracy, let alone socialism. Any lingering illusions in the social-democratic configuration of the European project were pitilessly dispelled in the first decades of the present century. The utility of Polanyian theory in comprehending European (dis)integration lies not in his theory of regionalism but in the political-economic dynamics analysed in *The Great Transformation*, in particular, his analysis of the gold standard, the resemblance of which to EMU has oft been noted. Just as, in the nineteenth century, the gold standard required that national economies experiencing an outflow of gold be obliged to adopt deflationary policies, and displaced responsibility for those policies by linking the domestic currency to an international fixed rate regime, so today the Eurozone's neoliberal straight-jacket constrains the powers of sovereign governments and imposes the burden of adjustment disproportionately upon weaker economies.[48] Euroland's exclusion of the possibility of devaluation, Streeck observes,

> is akin to the nineteenth-century gold standard, whose devastating impact on the capacity of the then-emerging nation-states to defend their peoples from the unpredictability of free markets, together with its

ramifications for the stability of international relations, was analysed so impressively in Polanyi's *The Great Transformation*.

The challenge to the gold standard, in Polanyi's analysis, arose from democracy and industrial struggles, for its functioning depended upon the insulation of central bankers and government officials from popular pressure. In Europe today, a similar situation applies. With the democratic gloss peeling away and the old rhetoric of the 'social dimension' unceremoniously dropped now that its purpose – to assuage critics of the SEM – had been fulfilled, the European integration process reveals itself to be managed by capital. The EU, in Streeck's words, is designed to ensure 'that democracy is tamed by markets instead of markets by democracy': that the economy is depoliticised while politics is de-democratised. This is exemplified in the operation of EMU, representing as it does, the EU's mission: to liberate 'the capitalist economy from democratic distortion'.[49] This was nowhere clearer than in 2012, when, at the bidding of the 'troika', elected governments in Italy and Greece were removed and replaced with technocrats, in what amounted to what one *Financial Times* columnist termed a 'humiliating and overt loss of national sovereignty'.[50] In the case of Greece, supervision mechanisms were put in place in all government ministries, turning it into Euroland's first colony.[51] Regionalism may have attenuated the powers of nation states, but the new arrangement bears a disconcerting resemblance to empire.

7

Intellectuals and the Red Scare

In 1947, Polanyi was appointed to a visiting professorship at Columbia University. He hoped that Ilona would be able to join him in New York, but her application for a visa was refused, obliging her to remain in London. In the following March, his Faculty canvassed its members on the future challenges that faced the institution. Polanyi duly submitted his recommendations. He advised that 'universities in the free democracies of the world should shoulder the task of counteracting the tendency towards cultural conformity which seems almost inherent in modern complex society'. Universities should resist 'the silent pressure of the intolerance' that emanated from 'modern mass democracy', and seek to prevent public opinion 'from becoming a vehicle of standardization of attitudes'. Admittedly, he continued, 'any discussion of the tasks of the University in regard to the maintenance of a sound public opinion on cultural and intellectual matters is beset at the moment by the dilemma of national security versus civic liberties'. To the extent that this dilemma was real, its solution would require something that universities were ideally placed to foster, namely, 'a judicious spirit which is open both to the obvious realities of the situation and the transcendent principle of political freedom'.[1]

The university authorities evidently did not take Polanyi's advice on board, for in early 1949, Columbia's President, Dwight Eisenhower, sent a letter to 'Mr and Mrs Polanyi' that contained little of the judicious spirit. 'At Columbia we are engaged in a crusade,' the letter growls, a crusade for which 'your help' is required. One can imagine the thoughts of Mr Polanyi – and of Mrs Polanyi, given her communist past – as they learned of the crusade's target. 'The communists,' Ike's communiqué continued, 'will always try to move in on the country's school system, realizing that success would assure control of the country. The communists have felt that they could have no better target than the underpaid school teacher.' With the dedicated support of faculty members and their spouses, students must be educated to 'understand America', in order to ensure that the nefarious designs of the communists come to naught.[2]

Ilona's visa refusal of 1947 and Eisenhower's letter of 1949 were straws in the wind. A wave of repression was about to crest: the Second Red Scare. It had been building for some time – arguably, since Roosevelt encouraged J. Edgar Hoover to place communists under surveillance.[3] Communists were targeted as Public Enemy No. 1 but the broader purpose was to expunge socialist ideas from the New Deal coalition, to curb its 'social democratic potential', as one historian has put it.[4] Not all historians see matters this way. A recent treatise by Jennifer Delton contends that, far from subverting the New Deal, the red scare 'preserved and expanded it'. The best-known anti-communist measures 'were carried out not by conservatives but by liberals seeking to uphold the New Deal': the Truman administration's expulsion of communists from government agencies; blacklisting by liberal Hollywood executives; labour leaders such as Walter Reuther purging communists from their unions, in order to consolidate their power within the CIO. Even Eisenhower, in this optic, was at core a liberal New Dealer in conservative clothing. Although committed to conservative financial principles and a mafia-style foreign policy – organising coups d'etat, arranging the murder of democratically elected leaders (Mossadeq, Árbenz, Lumumba), napalming Vietnam, planning the Bay of Pigs invasion – his administration also expanded social welfare and public works programmes, notably road building.[5] Eisenhower sought to slow and constrain New Deal programmes but not to abolish them. The flaw in Delton's thesis is that it rests upon two simplistic assumptions: that New Dealers formed a unitary camp, and that it could be equated with support for 'big government'. In fact, the red scare clove that camp in two. Some New Dealers of the anti-communist liberal stripe joined the witchfinders. But, aside from communists, the greatest terror was inflicted upon the people around them: 'the other labour unionists, academics, or entertainers who watched them thrown out of the workplace and said nothing'.[6] They were preponderantly left New Dealers of one stripe or other: socialists and social democrats who favoured redistribution, strong trade unions and a tolerant attitude to communism. This was Polanyi's milieu.

Polanyi's spell at Columbia coincided almost exactly with the Second Red Scare, which lasted from 1947 to 1957 and was closely associated with Senators McCarran and McCarthy. A measure of the fanaticism of McCarran's Internal Security Act (1950) is that it even caught in its net Michael Polanyi, an anti-communist of impeccable credentials. In 1951, he was denied a visa – and had to surrender a Chicago University chair – on the grounds that he had once delivered a lecture to a communist-linked organisation. The witchfinders had clawed at Ilona, a predictable target, and now even at Michael. Next, they began to intrude into Karl's professional environment. The anti-communist mania did not bypass academia. In the late 1940s over thirty states 'required academics at public universities to take loyalty oaths, and those who would not take them for whatever reason, including on grounds of conscience and constitutionality, lost their jobs'. A Communist Party member, it was presumed, was unfit to teach, and this justified dismissal, or denial of tenure or promotion. Later, this was extended to cover academics who invoked the Fifth Amendment, or who were fellow travellers, or merely radical in their politics – supportive, for instance, of New Deal-type economic policies such as regulation and national economic planning, or civil rights, or Henry Wallace's 1948 presidential campaign.[7] As Ellen Schrecker has documented, the enforcement of McCarthyism by the university system silenced an entire generation of progressive and radical intellectuals and 'snuffed out all meaningful opposition to the official version of the Cold War.'[8]

In 1952, one of Polanyi's closest collaborators, Moses Finley, was brought before the House Un-American Activities Committee (HUAC). Already in 1939 the FBI had filed him as 'a notorious Stalinist',[9] and twelve years later their suspicions were heightened when a denunciation arrived from the Columbia sinologist, Karl Wittfogel. At the HUAC, Finley invoked the Fifth, but this did not prevent him from being fired from his post at Rutgers later that year. Polanyi also knew personally at least three Columbia anthropologists on whom the FBI had its eye. One was John Murra, an expert on the Inca Empire.[10] Another was Conrad Arensberg, one of Polanyi's closest collaborators, who joined the anthropology department in 1952. A third was a research student, Rosemary Arnold, who Polanyi appointed to the position of Executive Secretary of his 'Interdisciplinary Project' in the early 1950s. When the heat was turned on Arnold, she approached Polanyi for counsel:

> I am in need of your advice – to say nothing of the consolation of talking it over with you and Ilona. I have some reason to believe that I may not escape the congressional inquiries this session as, for a while, I thought I might. (Imagine! – *me* of all people! They certainly must be scraping the bottom of the barrel.) There is nothing definite, straws in the wind merely, but I have decided it is foolish to be unprepared. It is not a question of my basic attitude, of course – it will be a decided pleasure to spit in their face, however discreetly. But it is a question of tactics, and while I should like to take a completely independent line, not even availing myself of a lawyer, still I must find out what legal questions are involved in invoking the 5th Amendment or not doing so.[11]

In his reply, Polanyi was, understandably, parsimonious. Arnold's attitude 'sounds reasonable and judicious,' he wrote. He enclosed a copy of a Faculty resolution on issues of general relevance but said no more.[12] He later destroyed some of his correspondence with Arnold, and urged Arensberg to follow suit, but the reasons for that decision are unknown.

Anthropology, evidently, was a discipline in which the FBI took a beady-eyed interest. It tended to attract students and scholars of an anti-racist persuasion, and this was particularly so at Columbia where the department's guiding eminence across the first four decades of the century had been the cultural pluralist anthropologist Franz Boas. Boas encouraged in his students, such as Ruth Benedict and Gene Weltfish, anti-racism and an appreciation of Native American cultures, both of which were symptoms of a subversive mentality in the FBI's view of the world.[13] Boas was a co-leader, with Finley, of the (Communist-linked) American Committee for Democracy and Intellectual Freedom. As Hoover saw it, he was 'one of the leading "stooges" for Communist groups in the US'.[14]

The FBI had its own stooges and snitches in the anthropology department: professors and students who fed it their suspicions about the subversive attitudes of their colleagues. The anthropologists George Murdock and Esther Goldfrank passed on their concerns that Arensberg was exhibiting an unhealthy interest in Marxism and consorting with suspected communists.[15] In the end, he escaped a summons to HUAC but his colleague Weltfish was not so fortunate.[16] She denied any personal sympathies with the communist cause, but her profile was typical of FBI targets in the period: she belonged to several known communist-led organisations, and was an outspoken critic of gender and racial oppression. Moreover, she had publicly voiced her fear that the US was deploying biological weapons in the Korean war – an accusation that had been made by Chinese Communist Party leaders and was echoed by her (and Polanyi's) friend, the sinologist Joseph Needham.[17] Weltfish had been on the FBI's radar throughout the 1940s, and in autumn 1952 she was summoned to the HUAC. A few months later she was summarily dismissed from her Columbia lectureship. Her graduate students felt obliged to mask their Marxist views. (One, Eleanor Leacock, phrased her theoretical approach so diplomatically during her oral examination – because she felt obliged to keep 'my Marxist "neo-evolutionary" views to myself' – that one faculty member faulted her for expressing 'no point of view'.[18])

The man at Columbia's helm during the Weltfish affair was a former security wonk at the State Department, Grayson Kirk. In 1951 he had been elevated to the University's presidency when Eisenhower was seconded to NATO, and in 1953 he was confirmed in post. One of his first acts as president, in 1951, was to ban a communist, Howard Fast – whose just-published novel, *Spartacus*, was to inspire the 1960 film – from speaking on campus.[19] However, in deference to the liberal opinions of a large number of faculty, he felt obliged to resist the calls of anti-communists to fire left-wing figures.[20] (One such, who happened to be close to Polanyi's milieu, was the sociologist C. Wright Mills.[21]) Publicly, Kirk undertook not to authorise any screening of faculty for communists, on the grounds that such measures would 'reduce our aim of freedom of inquiry', albeit with the rider that the freedom of inquiry did not apply to communists.[22] He categorically rejected any suggestions that in firing Weltfish the University had taken its cue from government, insisting that her dismissal had been 'under tenure rules' and not on political grounds. Yet this was a flat falsehood. Even as he paid lip service to academic freedom, Kirk had been secretly discussing, with university trustees, administrative methods by which to dispose of leftists, and by his own admission he revised a rule on tenure specifically in order to facilitate the dismissal of Weltfish.[23] Not only did Kirk lie, but he displayed a dazzling proficiency in Orwellian newspeak in his insistence that the decision to fire Weltfish had been motivated by the need to *protect* academic freedom.[24] Columbia University under Kirk was busily engaging, in secret, in the very blacklisting and purging that, in public, it scorned. In this, it was no exception. Like every other major US institution, the academy failed to put up serious resistance to McCarthyism. It largely played its patriotic part.[25]

At Columbia the red scare loomed over the department of anthropology in particular but it made its presence felt across the institution. In 1952, after two dozen Columbia professors voiced concerns over the propriety of vice-presidential candidate Richard Nixon's campaign expense fund, a dirty tricks media smear campaign was launched, which revealed that nine of the 'pinko' professors were known to the HUAC.[26] They included three of Polanyi's closest colleagues: Robert MacIver, Robert Merton and Paul Lazarsfeld. Typical of red-baiting campaigns, it was not only persecutory in purpose but the empirical basis for the claims that particular individuals sympathised with communism was fabricated from flimsy factoids. Lazarsfeld is a case in point. He was open about his youthful immersion in Vienna's socialist movement, but it was well known that his activism had not survived his move to the United States, and many students assumed that his political affiliations were conservative.[27] Similar applied to MacIver and Merton, neither of whom was a communist or fellow traveller. Merton's thought crime was to have been on suspiciously amicable terms with his colleague Bernhard Stern, a communist chum of Finley and Boas, and to have published in *Science and Society,* a Marxist journal of which Stern was a moving spirit. (In the following year, Stern himself was hauled before the Internal Security Senate subcommittee, where he invoked the Fifth.[28] Columbia considered dismissing him, concurrently with Weltfish. But he was spared her fate due to his slightly more secure contract and more vocal support from colleagues, notably Merton.[29])

In 1953, Polanyi moved to Canada, from where he would travel to Columbia during the summer and winter semesters to carry out research and teaching, in an adjunct capacity. Students and former students kept him abreast of developments – and non-developments: 'Nothing untoward here, except the steady hot wind from McCarthy'.[30] The hot wind, unfortunately, did not respect the Canadian border. Among visitors to Polanyi's house on the outskirts of Toronto, his daughter recalls, 'was Marshall

McLuhan. It was he who told us, with some embarrassment', that the head of his department of political economy advised 'that contact with Polanyi could prejudice his application for Ford funding'.[31]

Toward the end of 1953 the red scare reached its peak. At times it resembled a theatre of the absurd – as when an Indiana textbook commissioner drew attention to the distressing possibility that Robin Hood may have been a communist, and recommended a purge of textbook references to Quakers on grounds of their pacifism. One forceful counterblast to this nonsense came from Ed Murrow. Two decades earlier, when working at the Institute of International Education (IIE), Murrow had been responsible for Polanyi's initial invitation to America. Now a prominent CBS journalist, he was under suspicion over engagement in subversive activities, including – a favourite McCarthyite smear – having been 'on the Soviet payroll'. Murrow, himself of Quaker background, commented publicly on the absurdity of adding Quakers such as William Penn, alongside Robin Hood, to a 'gallery of Red rogues of the past'.[32] In several ways, he utilised his position as a broadcaster to roll back McCarthyism. One involved deploying the hallowed values of his profession to debunk the aura of 'investigative reason' that McCarthyism claimed for itself. Famously, he produced what has been described as television's first-ever piece of investigative reporting, in a report that dramatised the case of an employee forced out of the air force because of his father's allegedly subversive activities, highlighting the McCarthyite tendency to impute guilt by association.[33] Another exploited the potential of editing. A programme featuring film clips of McCarthy was edited to give prominence to moments in which he burped, or picked his nose. But perhaps Murrow's most effective move, in April 1954, was simply to invite McCarthy to defend himself on camera. The senator agreed, and, with his customary grace, proceeded to harangue and flail at his host. Murrow, ranted McCarthy, 'is a symbol, a leader and the cleverest of the jackal pack which is always found at the throat of anyone who dares to expose individual Communists and traitors'; he had when young belonged to 'the Industrial Workers of the World, a terrorist organization'; he was a lifelong friend of Harold Laski, 'the greatest Communist propagandist of our time in England'; and he had in the 1930s 'engaged in propaganda for Communist causes. For example, the IIE, of which he was the Acting Director, was chosen to act as a representative by a Soviet agency to do a job which would normally be done by the Russian secret police'.[34] But McCarthy had misjudged his audience. His gibbering paranoia did not go down well. It was a debacle that, combined with Murrow's other investigative and probing McCarthy-related broadcasts, gave him a strong claim to have contributed to the Wisconsin senator's downfall. By the end of the year, McCarthy's career, if not the crusade for which he stood, was as good as over.

MARX BEHIND A MASK

Polanyi's life was shaped and scarred by the red scare. It prevented his wife and his brother joining him in America. It singled out his first US employer, the IIE, for censure, and it encircled him at Columbia, lashing at his students and colleagues. It attacked not only communists and ex-communists, such as Ilona, but also those who espoused (or had in their misspent youth espoused) a left social-democratic credo – and this included many of his friends and acquaintances, including Lazarsfeld, Murrow and Laski.[35] What, though, is known of Polanyi's attitude to the scare? How did he respond to it? Did he attempt to analyse and explain it?

Clearly, Polanyi was badly seared when McCarthyite repression homed in on his loved ones. He would also, presumably, have appreciated the irony that at the very moment at which he gained a secure and well-paid position, for the first time in his life, the McCarthyite menace began to loom. There is evidence to suggest that he initially underestimated the witch hunt, and Columbia's willingness to join it. In 1949 he spoke almost nonchalantly of the 'dilemma' that had arisen, 'of national security versus civic liberties',[36] and, even after having received Eisenhower's 'crusade' letter, he continued to view Columbia as a fundamentally liberal institution.[37] Self-evidently, he was appalled by the anti-communist panic that accompanied the onset of the Cold War, and he was contemptuous of those such as Arthur Koestler and George Orwell who were helping to give it intellectual respectability.[38]

The McCarthyite inquisitions set the temper of the times and altered the political discourse. Radicals and left-liberals felt apprehensive, or frightened, under attack, and in some cases were personally harassed. To different degrees all were discouraged, cowed, even broken. This contributed to a paradoxical phenomenon, whereby social scientists were incentivised to depoliticise their research, emphasising the technical tools at their command, insisting on their autonomy and social detachment and pretending that scholars can stand apart from the value-soaked practices of knowledge production and utilisation – even though this tendency was itself the product of politics, in the form of the red scare.[39] Self-censorship was standard practice among left-wing Americans in the 1950s, and it was all but impossible to openly discuss Marxism in the academy.[40] It was impossible, in any US university, 'to refer to socialism in any form',[41] recalls Kari Polanyi-Levitt. Progressive academics 'restricted and censored the content of their lectures ... and/or redirected their research and publications to safe, more conventional areas'.[42] Some would 'lard their publications with random virulent condemnations of communism' that in retrospect seem abject but were viewed as necessary to get, or hold down, a job.[43] All were obliged to adjust their behaviour in some fashion.

Was Polanyi subject to this imperative? In 1945 he remarked, in a comment piece published by a provincial British newspaper, that 'wholesale attacks on Marxism still make me react in favour of a creed which has earned the fanatical detestation of fascists the world over'.[44] In McCarthyite America that commitment was put to the test. Of course he knew, his friend and student Anne Chapman recalls, 'that in a sense he was vulnerable, not least because of his wife'. (That some academics were investigated by the FBI solely on the grounds of the political affiliations of their spouses was common knowledge.) 'He was aware of the dangers, and felt isolated in a sense. If he wasn't on the list it was because he had never been a Communist Party member'.[45] In terms of his recorded statements and behaviour he showed little sign of belonging to the category of academics – roughly five per cent, according to one study – who felt 'paralyzed' by McCarthyite red-baiting.[46] Indeed, he chose to collaborate with tainted individuals such as Arensberg and Finley: the former as director of his major research project of the 1950s, the latter as his research assistant and, according to Polanyi's express wish, the co-author of an article on ancient Greece.[47] Admittedly, he supped with these red devils only from 1953, when fears of dismissal from his post at Columbia were nugatory, but my hunch is that he would have behaved similarly in previous years.

Chapman claims that Polanyi refused to allow the frenzy of reaction to meaningfully influence his published views. As a 'fervent socialist and pacifist' it would not have been surprising if he had refrained from referring to these convictions in his *Trade and Market in the Early Empires*, 'given the persecution of the resident communists and their "fellow travellers", pacifists and socialists included, that hit a high point of political hysteria with McCarthy a few years before and was still being fomented at the time'.[48] Nevertheless, she argues, in that volume he consciously elected to include a reference to socialism. It is found in this passage:

> Outside of a system of price-making markets, economic analysis loses most of its relevance as a method of inquiry into the working of the economy. A centrally planned economy, relying on nonmarket prices is a well-known instance … The choice between capitalism and socialism, for instance, refers to two different ways of instituting modern technology in the process of production.[49]

An alternative perspective is associated with Rhoda Halperin. Her emphasis (discussed in Chapter 2) is on the ground that Polanyi shared with Marx. The younger man's project amounted to a development of, more than a departure from, Marx's.[50] This premise permits her to propose that the conceptual shift conveyed for example in the dwindling of references to Marx and to capitalism in Polanyi's work of the 1940s and 1950s was not genuine and meaningful but an Aesopian adaptation to the McCarthyite climate. Polanyi's American years, she points out, coincided with a period during which 'the maintenance of an academic appointment almost demanded that he shroud his Marxism in non-Marxist terminology, in short, that he mask his Marxism'. So, for example, Polanyi does not discuss private property – a 'puzzling omission, unless one understands it as an example of Polanyi's attempt to mask his Marxism'. Similarly, he was 'extremely careful to avoid the terms capitalist, precapitalist, and noncapitalist in his post-1950 writing [and] systematically substituted the word market for capitalist'. For Halperin, Polanyi's substantivist economics represented a veiled 'critique of capitalism', one that was framed technically, as 'a critique of economic concepts'.[51]

Halperin errs in thinking that questions of property ownership ever occupied a central position in Polanyi's conceptual field. He had less reason to 'mask' his concepts than she supposes, as they were less Marx-influenced than she thinks. And although she correctly notes that Polanyi's conceptual language shifted, with 'capitalism' giving way to 'market system' and 'market economy', she fails to note that he was frequently using the latter term already in the 1920s. Outside the Marxist camp, in those days,[52] 'capitalism' was largely shunned, and for the same reasons as during the McCarthy era. 'Market economy' was common, including in Polanyi's own usage. Admittedly, in the 1930s he had also used 'capitalism' frequently but from around 1940 its frequency declined. This coincided with his relocation to America but *before* the red scare. The masking process, moreover, had real discursive effects, for example, the delegitimation of the term capitalism and the elevation in its place of 'market economy' and 'market system', terms that, J. K. Galbraith has argued, are 'bland, benign' and ultimately 'erroneous', their popularity derived from a desire to distance contemporary society from the unsavoury associations of capitalist power. In the 'market system,' he continues, history is absent. 'No individual or firm is dominant. No economic power is evoked. There is nothing here from Marx or Engels. There is only the impersonal market, a not wholly innocent fraud.' It would have been hard, he concludes, 'to find a more meaningless designation'.[53]

Whether Polanyi, in his writings and lectures of the 1950s, intentionally or sub-consciously prismed out ideas from the infra-red band of the spectrum is hard to ascertain. He may well have benefited materially from playing down his more radical views in his funding application to the Ford Foundation, an organisation that operated as a conscious instrument of covert US foreign policy and a willing tool of its Cold War apparatus.[54] Certainly, some of his bitterest invective against Marxism is found in his writings of the 1950s, and, long after the McCarthyite episode had passed, he was still encouraging Marxists to disguise their views.[55] But in Polanyi's case the thickness of the veil is doubly difficult to determine because his trajectory was in any case away from the Marxist terrain that had fascinated him during his years in Vienna and Britain. He continued to identify as a socialist but increasingly emphasised the insufficiency of what he saw as traditional socialist agendas (particularly in his reflections on 'freedom and technology'). That his socialist enthusiasm abated somewhat even as his research idealised the socially embedded exchange systems of pre-capitalist societies is perhaps explicable in terms of his awareness of his 1950s audience, for whom socialism seemed a more exotic and outlandish proposal than, say, market-free commerce in Early Dynastic Ur. Ultimately, though, whether the tempering of his radicalism in the 1950s should be put down primarily to audience awareness in the context of the red scare (the 'mask' argument), or personal circumstances (career success), or the stabilisation of capitalism and international relations following the interwar crisis (from mass unemployment to full employment), or the accumulation of evidence of Stalin's crimes (on which see Chapter 4), is impossible to say.

HERMENEUTICS OF A MORAL PANIC: *THE NEW AMERICAN RIGHT*

On the face of it, McCarthyism appears to have left little imprint upon Polanyi's analysis of contemporary socio-political developments. If so, this would be remarkable, given that so many in his milieu were mesmerised by America's totalitarian turn, and were analysing it in their work. Following his move to Canada, he would return each month to his New York apartment where he would find his lodger, Nicholas Halazs, busy at work on a thinly disguised allegory on McCarthyism, *Captain Dreyfus: The Story of a Mass Hysteria*. Some of Columbia's brightest graduate students were researching the topic – for example Immanuel Wallerstein, whose essay on McCarthyism as a phenomenon of American political culture was beginning to circulate.[56] Meanwhile, Polanyi's closest colleague, MacIver, was directing a major research project investigating the trammelling of academic freedom in the McCarthyite era, the findings of which were published in 1955 as *Academic Freedom in Our Time*. Or consider another Columbia academic, Marie Jahoda. An old friend of Otto Bauer and of Polanyi's nephew Hans Zeisel, Jahoda was quick off the mark.[57] Already in 1951, with assistance from Merton, she secured funding to study the impact of the 'Loyalty and Security Program', Truman's loyalty order on federal employees. She packaged the study as an aid to the state in policy design, but it concluded with a warning that the McCarthyite panic threatened to corrode the fabric of civil society and 'undermine the great traditions of American democracy'.[58] Then there was Jahoda's former husband, Lazarsfeld. He applied his training in quantitative analysis of survey data on topical social problems to the question of the influence of McCarthyism within academia, and published his findings as *The Academic Mind: Social Scientists in a Time of Crisis*. (It was prepared with Wagner Thielens and David Riesman, and with drafting assistance and comments from Jahoda, Zeisel and Edward Shils, as well as Lazarsfeld's Columbia colleagues, Merton and Richard Hofstadter, who was concurrently collaborating with MacIver on *Academic Freedom in Our Time*).

The Academic Mind, the product of a large foundation grant that funded a very substantial survey, furnished positive confirmation of an anecdotally well-established truth: numerous colleges and universities did indeed experience 'unusual stress' in the early to mid-1950s, resulting in a rise in distrust among faculty members and the dismissal of a significant number of them. It reported the pressures that lecturers were under to play safe, and to crop curricula, weeding out controversial topics. In some classrooms this produced a palpable chill. ('You no longer get the Marxist view brought up in class,' one professor lamented. 'In 1946 to 1949 they made this place hum.') And it rendered in statistical and diagrammatic form some manifest realities: McCarthyism did constrain the freedom of expression, and teachers with a more 'permissive' political stance did tend to feel cowed, experiencing a sense of 'apprehension' that resulted in very widespread self-censorship. However, even more than Jahoda's study, *The Academic Mind* affected a detached neutrality toward its subject. It stuck strictly to description and detailed analysis of reported behavioural tendencies by academics in the face of McCarthyism, eschewing any attempt to explain that phenomenon itself and – apart from a fleeting reference to the Salem witch trials – guarded assiduously against the appearance that it might be passing judgment.[59]

While the 'methods man', Lazarsfeld, focused upon compiling and analysing individual reactions to McCarthyism, his theory-minded colleagues attempted to explain the phenomenon. Their project grew out of a Columbia faculty seminar on political behaviour, a seminar that was to exert a profound influence upon social-scientific thought in the US and beyond. Its first fruit was a volume, *The New American Right*. Its editor, Daniel Bell, and most contributors, including Hofstadter and Nathan Glazer, were based at Columbia, while contributors from other institutions included Riesman and Talcott Parsons. Hofstadter was the link figure. He was pivotal to the political behaviour group and, together with Bell, developed an influential thesis, later dubbed 'the end of ideology', that sought to define a stance for contemporary intellectuals that would prevent them from succumbing to the sort of 'perfectionist ideology' that had incited the enmity of the McCarthyites.[60] In the same period, Hofstadter knew Polanyi and almost certainly attended his seminar on economic institutions.[61]

In his contribution to *The New American Right,* Hofstadter set the agenda by characterising McCarthyism as a wave of dissent that was characterised by 'a relentless demand for conformity'.[62] He, Bell and their colleagues, writes Ellen Schrecker, 'were vociferous in their denunciations of the conformity of American life. McCarthyism, suburbia, television, tailfins, "kitsch", Communism, and Nazism – they were all, in one way or another products of mass society'.[63] In the same year, Polanyi was riffing on the same theme. He gave the first of a series of lectures that identified 'the omnipresent tendency towards uniformity and conformity, or briefly, averagism' as the defining pathology of the age. The trend to conformity was the product of the conjunction of 'the machine' (which reconstructed society around itself), market society and mass democracy; the outcome was the trapping of individuals within complex structures 'from which no release is possible'. Conformism was smothering the 'freedom to differ', and it dovetailed with an authoritarian turn in American political life which, although not as egregious as in Nazi Germany and Communist countries, nonetheless 'overshadows American life', posing a serious threat to freedom. This was the sociological soil in which McCarthyism could grow, and explanations of McCarthyism should begin with it, rather than with the phenomenon itself. 'A thousand pocket McCarthys,' he argued,

> pursuing their several fads, each on his own, do not add up to the damage done by a single one brandishing the cat o' nine tails of conformism. Not McCarthy was responsible for McCarthism [*sic*] – he merely picked up the deadly poison of conformism that the educators of the nation had concocted for medical purposes and left lying around. … An inconspicuous culture trait, the polite social habit of conforming, had dissolved the Constitution of the United States.[64]

In his Tocquevillian explanation of McCarthyism as a symptom of mass society, Polanyi resembled Hofstadter. But he, unlike Polanyi, emphasised McCarthyism's character as a social movement. Its force, Hofstadter believed, derived from a pervasive sense of anxiety that had arisen when the relatively agrarian society of the mid-nineteenth century, characterised by 'relative ethnic homogeneity', opened out to the 'heterogeneity' and 'rootlessness' of the urban industrial present, with its 'scramble for status and its peculiar search for secure identity'. With America's elite deficient in 'political and moral autonomy', and with a mass culture that was 'populistic' in temper, the ingredients were present for a flare up of unsettled citizens in what Hofstadter, borrowing from Adorno, termed 'pseudo-conservative' agitation.[65] These arguments reappear throughout *The New American Right.* Collectively, its contributors presented McCarthyism as a social movement, an offshoot of the Populist tradition that had emerged out of the great agrarian revolt of the 1890s. They explained its genesis in terms of what Lipset and Bell (marrying Weber to Freud) refer to as 'status anxieties' that had become inflamed by industrialisation and mass immigration. A salient example of such frustrations was the spectre of 'racial equality' which, according to Riesman and Glazer, had emerged as a 'formidable reality' in America's ever-swelling suburbs, disrupting recent immigrants' aspirations, unleashing fears of displacement and unsettling the uneducated and impoverished layers of earlier (predominantly white) immmigrants.[66]

The key chapter in the *The New American Right* was Parsons' diagnosis of 'social strains in America'. The Harvard sociologist proposed that McCarthyism be understood as 'a relatively acute symptom of the strains' that accompanied 'a major change in the *situation and structure* of American society'. By 'situation', he refers to America's precipitous geopolitical ascendancy. The US suddenly found itself embroiled in a major war, after which it was obliged 'to prevent Soviet domination of the whole continent of Europe', but this unexpected and 'grand-scale resumption of responsibility', following years of isolation, 'imposed serious internal strains'. This situation, moreover, intruded upon a society that was undergoing wholesale 'structural' change, as industrialisation discombobulated political and cultural norms. The effect of 'industrialism' was above all that the structures (he mentions family and kinship, religion, social stratification and government) 'which would interfere with the free functioning of the economy, and of their adaptation to it, are minimized'. All such structures were obliged to adapt to the requirements of 'American industrialism', and it had, uniquely, 'developed overwhelmingly under the aegis of free enterprise'.[67]

From these premises, Parsons constructed an argument that resembled, albeit in conservative form, Polanyi's 'double movement'. On one hand, as the industrialisation process advanced, the US experienced 'a steady increase in the amount of public control imposed on the economy, with the initiative mainly in the hands of the Federal government'. On the other, the hegemony of the free-enterprise system had naturally led Americans to assume that, except in unavoidable and clearly established cases, 'responsibilities should not be undertaken by government'. It was therefore no surprise 'that the opening up of vast new fields of governmental responsibility should meet with considerable resistance and conflict'. This socio-economic contradiction underlay an impasse at the level of politics, and it is here that the strains occurred which manifested in McCarthyism.[68] A contradiction had arisen between the 'natural tendency' of the state, in industrial society, to become dominated 'relatively unequivocally' by the business community, and the American 'situation' in which – *pace* Marxist propaganda – business leaders hesitated to grasp the responsibility, leaving a vacuum that was filled by individuals of 'miscellaneous' social origin: professional politicians, labour officials and sundry East Coasters (who 'exhibit a more or less "aristocratic" tinge'). Given that it was itself shuddering from the same general social strains, the political elite was hardly in a position to master them. Far from being dominated by capitalists, it was 'fluid and relatively unstructured', and this gave it a fragile quality at this critical time. For the conjuncture, overdetermined by the Soviet threat, demanded that American society be 'mobilized', a process that required stout leadership at the governmental level as well as patriotic commitment from the many diverse elements of the population. The enormous, inevitable increase in pressure 'to subordinate private interests to the public interest' (that is, 'loyalty'), in its turn clashed with the traditional American presumption in favour of the former, and generated further social strains, anomie and political maladies. This, then, was Parsons' explanation of 'the current flare-up of stress in the form of McCarthyism'. The 'strains of the international situation' impinged upon the domestic strains mentioned above, and were compounded by the status sensitivities of second-generation immigrants, producing 'high levels of anxiety and aggression, focused on what rightly or wrongly are felt to be the sources of strain and difficulty'. Communism, understandably, emerged as the focus of popular anxieties, for it connected 'the objective external problem and its dangers with the internal strain'. Soviet Russia was correctly identified as a terrible international threat, and its US supporters were rightly identified as conspiratorial and seditious. Communism, moreover, having simultaneously identified itself with universalistic and emancipatory well-springs, had proven able to seduce 'large elements of liberal opinion', including the considerable numbers of intellectuals who became 'fellow-travelers'. Hence the 'special order of ambivalence' that came to be attached to it. Its members were clearly a disloyal 'enemy within' yet they also symbolised the highbrow East Coast elite that was out of touch with the ordinary Joe. McCarthy, as he denounced conspiring communists and their intellectual stooges in the name of 'the people', was able to tap into traditions of populist agrarian and other radicalism that located the source of people's grievances in the conspiracy of corrupt East Coast politicians and their Wall Street puppetmasters. Of course, McCarthyism drew support from 'certain vested-interest elements' too, but its continuities with progressive populism did give it the appearance of 'a popular revolt against the upper classes'. There was, Parsons conceded, an irrational element in this explosive revolt, with its scapegoating and aggression, but this should be understood as the growing pains of a normal teenage society. After all, he reassured readers, social scientists have securely established the axiom that 'neither individuals nor societies can undergo major structural changes without the likelihood of producing a considerable element of "irrational" behavior'.[69]

In these ways, Parsons' chapter partook of the general anxiety while offering grounds for confidence. Its conclusion offers a series of straightforward solutions: to 'improve our understanding', to 'realize our strength' and to 'trust in it', to 'encourage the ordinary man to accept greater responsibility' and develop 'the necessary implementing machinery' to this end, and to judiciously incorporate 'business and nonbusiness elements' in the political elite, with input from academics and clergy in particular. This programme, Parsons recommended, was feasible and 'within the great American tradition'. It would enable right-thinking Americans to regain their 'national self-confidence' following the McCarthyite wobble, 'and to take active steps to cope with the situation with which we are faced'.[70]

FROM MASS SOCIETY TO PLURALISM

The New American Right represented an untenable and in places maladroit explanation of McCarthyism. But it was one that successfully served as a launch pad for pluralism, the paradigm that came to dominate political science for the next two decades. The pluralist school included David Truman, Hofstadter, Lipset, Riesman, Shils and Bell, and it interleaved – with Parsons the hinge – with the ascendant paradigm in sociology, structural-functionalism. Polanyi engaged with all these scholars (with the possible exceptions of Shils and Bell), through conversations, correspondence and invitations to his seminar.

The analytical ineptitude of *The New American Right* and the triumph of the pluralist school are linked, for the analytical flaws were crucial to the success of the rhetorical construction of the paradigm, in particular its conjuring of a spectre, a hydra comprised of a multitude of mobs: populism (its anti-semitic strands foregrounded) and its putative McCarthyite offshoot, as well as Nazism and its totalitarian twin to the East, and, by association, contemporary communism in the USA. A pioneering critique of the pluralists' reading of McCarthyism was offered in the 1960s by Michael Rogin. He contended that they misunderstood agrarian populism (it was democratic and was not anti-industrial), that none of its core social constituencies were later to lend significant support to McCarthyism, and that although McCarthyism contained anti-industrial and anti-cosmopolitan elements, these were present more among the Senator's elite support than his mass base, and they revealed McCarthyism's roots 'not in agrarian radicalism but in traditional conservatism'. Unlike the agrarian populists, Senator Joe made relatively little impact on Joe Public. McCarthyism 'influenced few voters and enjoyed its greatest success among elites' – and to the extent that it did enjoy popular support, this was the result of the Cold and Korean wars 'far more than anti-industrial sentiments and authoritarian preoccupations'. It is ironic, Rogin remarks at the end of his demolition of its argument, that pluralism, 'partially stimulated and rendered plausible by McCarthyism, fails to comprehend the Senator and his following'.[71]

What lay behind the pluralists' misdiagnosis of McCarthyism in *The New American Right*? Part of the explanation can be traced to their reaction to fascism and communism. In the US, the intellectual response to these perils was dominated by a series of contributions, notably by Jewish refugees from Central and Eastern Europe with an eye on the spectres of Hitler and the gulag, which laid the basis of what came to be dubbed 'mass society theory'. The seminal texts include Mannheim's *Man and Society in an Age of Reconstruction* (1935/1940), Lederer's *State of the Masses* (1940), Fromm's *The Fear of Freedom* (1942) and *Man for Himself* (1947) and Riesman's *The Lonely Crowd* (1950), as well as Adorno and Horkheimer's *Dialectic of Enlightenment* (1944) and Hannah Arendt's *Origins of Totalitarianism* (1951). This was a milieu with which Polanyi was very familiar, in many cases personally. (Mannheim was his compatriot and referee, Lederer was an in-law, Fromm a friend, Riesman a correspondent and Arendt his 'erstwhile combatant'.[72]) Mannheim's theory of mass society was discussed in Chapter 5 and need not detain us here. Arendt's book has been described as 'Tocquevillian', in that it explores the relationship between processes of restlessness and atomisation characteristic of modernity, the deracination of social and family ties and the anomic anxiety of the masses, the resulting susceptibility to totalitarian movements, and the attainment of absolute power by a master-figure or movement, culminating in the total administration of society by the Leviathan state.[73] For their part, Fromm, Adorno and the other scholars at the Institute for Social Research (ISR) transposed the fears that reactionaries had traditionally associated with 'crowds' and 'mobs' – aggregates of human beings whose atomisation and de-individualisation manifests in destructive, irrational behaviour and the imperative to conform – on to capitalist *Gesellschaft* itself. Their concept of mass society was amenable to the left, with the bureaucratisation of public life, mass consumption and the culture industry figuring as the techniques by which individuals are manipulated to conform to the requirements of the capitalist machine. The Freudo-Marxist critique of American 'mass society' developed by Fromm influenced his student (and patient) Riesman's Freudo-Tocquevillian critique of leisure-society conformity. *The Lonely Crowd* elevated middle-class angst to the pivotal subject of scientific concern and – doubtless as a result – became the best-selling sociology book of all time.[74]

Many of the pluralists had themselves subscribed to one or other concept of 'mass society'. Shils, for example, had held 'a view of modern life that stressed the dangerous attenuation of belief systems, the threat posed by unanchored masses, and a general fear of social disorder', a society mutilated by disintegrative and socially disembedding tendencies that he depicted with reference to Tönnies's Gemeinschaft-Gesellschaft couplet.[75] But they were now, in the 1950s, subjecting the theory of mass society to critique.[76] Moreover, where the emphasis of Fromm and Adorno, and to a degree of Arendt too, was on the way in which the weakening of social ties by industrialisation, the culture industry and totalitarian states produced sameness, standardisation, a pervasive conformism and mass *passivity*, the spectre for the pluralists was social movements and mass *activity*. For them, fascism and communism were the spawn of mass movements, and in their minds the image of the concentration camp was wedded to what Bell, with hindsight, described as their 'fear of mass action, a fear of too much activism'.[77] In short, the pluralists set out to bring the 'fear of the crowd' back into social and political theory. With this in mind, their misreading of McCarthyism as a mass movement, in which agrarian populism articulated naturally with racist and anti-communist hysteria, should be seen as symptomatic. They were reading contemporary history through the prism of their own plebeiophobia.

The correlate of the pluralists' misidentification of McCarthyism as a mass movement thrown up by 'social strains' was an exculpatory argument concerning the incumbent political class. The pseudo-conservative 'flare up', in their reading, was essentially devoid of political content. It was a psycho-social spasm. The effect was to absolve the political establishment, and the Democratic Party in particular, of responsibility for the red scare. Their analysis ignored the fact that the fuel which Senator Joe ignited had been fermenting, over decades, in Washington and New York. It ignored the central dynamic of the red scare: established institutions (the FBI, big business, Republican Party and right-wing Democrats) cracking down on the left and the labour movement. What came to be known as McCarthyism, as David Price has argued, 'was part of a long, ignoble American tradition of repressing the rights of free association, inquiry and advocacy of those who would threaten the status quo of America's stratified political economic system'. The 1920s had seen fears of a global Judaeo-Bolshevik conspiracy whipped up – with lavish astroturfing – by business leaders such as Henry Ford, and in the same decade the FBI's self-aggrandisement commenced, soon to be expedited by Roosevelt. The loyalty-security paranoia with which McCarthy made his name were not his invention, nor were they a product of the Cold War. They had been unleashed, years earlier, by Democrats, by the Hatch and Smith Acts and Truman's Loyalty Order. It was Democratic presidents – Roosevelt and Truman – together with such 'honourable' GOP worthies as Hiram Bingham who developed the repressive procedures that were later refined 'into a true art form of the absurdist inquisition' by McCarran, McCarthy and their gang.[78] These senators, moreover, were not fringe lunatics, but were well connected. McCarthy was appointed to his Senate committee by Robert Taft. He trod the campaign trail with Eisenhower, and was close to such prominent Democrats as Joe Kennedy. It was right-wing Democrats around Truman who accused Wallace of being a tool of the Kremlin (due to the fact that the Communist Party supported his ticket). And when Truman was replaced by Eisenhower the witch-hunts continued. The new president opted not to confront McCarthy but to outbid him with his own anti-communist crusade, featuring a drive to deport resident aliens, in particular editors and journalists who were suspected of being 'critical of the American Celebration',[79] and the purging of hundreds of 'subversive' books from governmental libraries – with bipartisan support, it need hardly be added.[80] In this sense, McCarthyism was the continuation of routine politics, with its scapegoating of subversives and its recourse to fearmongering to swing popular support behind authoritarian policies. It was the creation of conservative and liberal powerholders – the very same elites to whom the pluralists were turning in their quest for an orderly society.[81]

The prospectus advanced by the pluralists can be summarised epigrammatically: 'Our leaders are innocent, but they must lead!', and 'Be anxious, but relax!' The first refers to the pluralists' fabrication of a sociological alibi for the political elite, by way of an explanation of McCarthyism in terms of the 'social strains' attendant upon modernisation and the recrudescence of populism to which those strains purportedly gave rise. At the same time, the red scare revealed the fickleness of public opinion, which for the pluralists – who had all, when young, admired Roosevelt for his strong leadership – provided further evidence that Machiavelli's advice on political leadership remained valid. If the political elites were not culpable for the McCarthyite excesses, their wisdom and statecraft were indispensable to securing political order and prosperity. The second apophthegm, prescribing simultaneous vigilance and confidence, derives from the pluralists' conception of industrialisation: a rocky ride to sunny uplands. Industrialisation, for the pluralists, is modern history's motor force. It uproots traditional social relations yet its success 'enables group politics to dominate a society'. Group politics directs political motivation to its proper concern: 'social cohesion in a constitutional, industrial society'. It serves to institutionalise conflict at the level of group leaders, who are 'socialized into the dominant values and associations of industrial society'. In this way, pluralism took the traditional liberal concern for rationality, together with conservativism's fixation upon social order and fear of the unattached individual, and an insistence upon the social centrality of associations (which had been the emphasis of prewar pluralists: Figgis, Laski, Cole), and bound these several elements together to create a distinctive political theory 'aimed at the stability of the social system'.[82]

Because industrialisation tends naturally to bring into being a particular type of individual, with a rational, instrumental orientation, together with a vibrant civil society composed of autonomous functional associations (religious groups, professional organisations, and so on) that integrate individuals into the social order, the pluralists radiated confidence in the future stability of capitalist society, and to that extent their body of theory is uncritical, even 'complacent'. Wright Mills branded it 'the American Celebration'.[83] However, they exuded anxiety too, derived from their concern that a subsidiary tendency of the industrialisation process, with its abstract rules, economic dynamism and suburbanisation, could attenuate traditional social ties and undermine community, producing a volatile mass with a propensity to seek relief from social strains by engaging in extreme behaviour.[84] This set the limits of pluralist tolerance. Associations were to be encouraged, but not anti-industrial or anti-capitalist mass movements that might channel the totalitarian impulses, the irrational desires and despair, of the *hoi polloi*.

The pluralist worldview, then, exhibited a peculiar coupling of liberal confidence and conservative vigilance. By way of illustration, consider the case of Shils. In the 1930s he had developed a leftish version of mass society theory, but in the following decades he turned against it, accusing it of 'German sociological romanticism' – of idealising pre-modern harmonious *gemeinschaft*.[85] Now, he subscribed to the pluralist hypothesis that industrialisation tends to generate stability, with individuals successfully embedded in society through 'primary groups'. American capitalism, he argued, had been demonstrably stabilised by Roosevelt and his successors: there was no need to rock the boat. Shils attacked McCarthyite over-reach (such as the 'insane' McCarran Act) and was incensed when paranoid State Department intervention squelched his attempt to secure a post at Chicago for Michael Polanyi (to whom he dedicated his book on McCarthyism, *Torments of Secrecy*).[86] The best defence against such excesses was to rally the pluralist centre ground: to defend America's civil society, law and established political procedures. However, that defence also required the policing of deviant behaviour, for the successful integration of individuals into associational groups, and for the cohesion of society as a whole, Shils argued in a series of chapters co-authored with Parsons in 1951, requires the unification of the political community around a 'shared pattern' of norms and values.[87] The social world is first and foremost a moral world; it is glued together by shared beliefs, and it is this value consensus that forms the basis upon which American social order was constructed. That bedrock was being eroded by embittered leftists – not least the leftist proponents of mass society theory whose 'grim critique of American society and culture' Shils castigated as 'a potentially cancerous element in America's plural politics'. For him, the critics' exaggerated picture risked becoming 'a kind of tragic self-fulfilling prophecy – by poisoning the well of public sentiment that the precious Anglo-American liberal order drinks from, either directly or by producing nativist, anti-intellectual backlashes whipped up by spurned and opportunistic politicians'. This analysis authorised anti-leftist vigilance of a bullish kind, and it is little wonder that Shils hired his services to the national security state. He was prepared to work on projects that 'abused the principles' of democracy, and associated himself, alongside Lipset, Bell and Michael Polanyi, with the CIA-funded Congress for Cultural Freedom.[88] He made his name as the scourge of the ISR, and was not above indulging in mundane harassment of its social-democratic employees – Jahoda, for example.[89] (Shils, she recalls, accused her 'of being a Communist fellow-traveller'. He was 'the quintessential *Kommunistenfresser*, seeing a Communist hidden under every bed in America'.[90])

To summarise, the contributors to *The New American Right* were, in the main, former radicals – including former card-carrying communists – *en route* to Cold War liberalism. The Cold War, one of their number recalls, served to hasten a 'closing of the ranks, a disposition to stress common objectives, a revulsion from Marxism and its tendency to think of social conflict as carried *á outrance*'.[91] They sought to eradicate the germs of totalitarianism by affirming the strength of America's immune system, in the form of its pluralist political norms and the vibrant intermediary institutions of civil society, and by firming up a definition of democracy on elitist (Madisonian-Schumpeterian) lines, the better to keep at bay both the desires for direct democracy that periodically well up from the bowels of populism and the false promises of democratic perfection that lure the poets and philosophers – having drunk from the well of moral absolutism – toward treacherously meliorist projects of one sort or another. The pluralists' sociological account of McCarthyism absolved the US Establishment in general and the Democratic Party in particular of responsibility for the McCarthyite mania, and defined the social anxieties that underlay it as the accoutrements of prosperity and international prowess. At the level of theory, the project affirmed the newly hegemonic paradigm in sociology, structural functionalism, and constructed a new orthodoxy in political science, pluralism. These paradigms provided cover for the rightward shift of the liberal intelligentsia. They celebrated the status quo and 'the end of ideology' while enjoining a vigilant suspicion toward communists in particular and radicals in general.

CONCLUSION

Polanyi's spell at Columbia coincided not only with the red scare but also with a momentous resculpting of the social-scientific landscape. He knew personally several of those who were at work on that project, including most of the contributors to *The New American Right*. That volume emerged from a seminar at Columbia contemporaneous with his, and it tapped into currents in political and social theory that were dear to him: functionalism and pre-war pluralism. Its contributors tended to 'sociologise' McCarthyism, emphasising the conformist tendencies that arise within 'mass society' and the social strains attendant upon modernisation. These were central tropes within Polanyi's analysis of the era, too. Yet Parsons and the pluralists were harnessing them to a conservative-liberal agenda that he found abhorrent. This is, I believe, one reason why Polanyi, in his final years, was fixated upon Parsonian economic sociology – to the extent that his very last public address, in Budapest in 1963, was devoted almost entirely to exposition and critique of Parsons. He viewed Parsons with intense ambivalence. On one hand, there were biographical affinities between the two. Parsons had grown up in a social-Christian family, moved to London to study with Laski and Malinowski, and strongly supported Roosevelt's New Deal.[92] His concern for social integration resembled Polanyi's for social unity. Polanyi found himself attracted to Parsons' theory of 'pattern maintenance': that society maintains its organisation through the alignment of individual mores with social requirements – in Polanyi's paraphrase, 'through the maintenance of its "patterns" and the management of "strains"'.[93] On the other hand, Parsons' understanding of 'the place of the economy in society' was 'relatively unfruitful', because it succumbs to the 'economistic fallacy'.[94] A similar ambivalence applied to his opinion of Parsons' political outlook. On one hand, he was zealously anti-communist. When, in 1963, Polanyi grumbled that 'the enemies of socialism in the United States are purposefully and effectively at work in the field of the social sciences', it is likely that the Harvard sociologist was among those he had in mind.[95] On the other hand, Parsons supported a *modus vivendi* with the Soviet Union, and when Polanyi began work on a journal of Western-Soviet rapprochement (*Co-Existence*), he invited Parsons to contribute.[96]

Co-Existence was Polanyi's final project, and in a sense it was a direct, political and practical response to the red scare. It directly contradicted the official Cold War narrative. But his most influential and lasting response was indirect in nature: his research programme in economic history. It arose in a specific context, when the discipline of economics was being rewrought in the McCarthyite furnace. Keynesian and institutionalist traditions, alongside Marxism, were targeted. The first American textbook to give an accurate rendering of Keynes' ideas, Lorie Tarshis' *The Elements of Economics*, was attacked as communistic and withdrawn from library shelves. The doyen of neo-Keynesianism, Paul Samuelson, recalls that the climate created by the red scare 'drove me a little to the right, as people vulgarly measure these things'.[97] In this context, Polanyi's research in economic history was invaluable. He too may have 'masked' some of his views, and was possibly nudged 'a little to the right'. Certainly his disagreements with Marxism became sharper. Nonetheless, in developing his distinctive critique of mainstream economics – that it fails to appreciate the historical uniqueness of the modern market system and its ideological appurtenances – he helped to revitalise the 'old institutionalism', and in a way that, *sotto voce,* incorporated his socialist leanings. These can be seen in the form taken by his excavations in ancient history, as he searched for examples of societies that had successfully embedded 'economy' within 'society'.

8

Redistribution and Market Exchange in Mesopotamia

'The problems of the present,' Polanyi mused in the late 1950s, 'are reflected in the fields of anthropology and ancient history. It is from these critical sources that we need to augment our terminological and methodological armoury.'[1] During his North American years, he devoted himself to sketching the main lines of a 'general economic history', a framework through which to make sense of modes of economic organisation even where systems of interconnected price-making markets are marginal or absent, in the hope that lessons could be applied to the reform or transcendence of contemporary capitalism. The principal findings were published in three volumes: *Dahomey and the Slave Trade*, *The Livelihood of Man* and an edited collection, *Trade and Markets in the Early Empires*.

Polanyi's research programme focused upon trade, markets and money. These, he held, are the basic economic institutions but have been widely misunderstood. Because in recent times they had fused into a single interconnected market system, modern minds – and modernist historians – tend to assume that the same triadic nexus existed in earlier epochs, and that markets functioned as the generative and coordinating instance, with trade existing as movements of goods through markets, facilitated by money. In fact, he proposed, trade, markets and money are best understood as discrete and separately institutionalised phenomena.[2] Archaic societies were predominantly integrated by redistributive means, with strong elements of reciprocity and in some cases of market exchange. Markets existed in many archaic economies but did they not play the supreme coordinating role that they do in modern capitalism. When interpreting this argument, a sharp eye on usage of the term 'market' is required. It can refer to a market *place,* or to exchange motivated by individual gain, or to a mechanism that determines the distribution of resources through supply–demand feedback (Polanyi's 'price-making market system'). These should not, Polanyi cautioned, be conflated.

Concerning Mesopotamian economic life, Polanyi proposed three main theses. The first, on trade, was specific to the Assyrian city of Assur and its trading colonies. Whereas market trade involves two or more parties and is mediated by a negotiated contract, Assyrian traders operated 'dispositionally', issuing unilateral declarations of will. The Old Assyrian trader, Polanyi argued, was a variant of the Akkadian *tamkārum*: a salaried individual acting quasi-publicly within the framework of the palace hierarchy and engaging in risk-free commercial exchange. The second concerned money and banking. Money in Mesopotamia was of a 'special-purpose' kind. In early Babylonia, for example, under the First Babylonian Dynasty, 'silver functioned as a standard of value, while in the decisive sector of the economy, the temples, accounts were carried on in the units of the means of payment, which was barley. Barley was, in effect, the only means of payment in regard to taxes, rent, wages, and so on'.[3] Banking centred on the 'staple finance' practices of large estate managements. These operations (inventories, accounting and so on) deployed money in the 'special-purpose' sense, with one staple selected as the standard of value. The point for Polanyi was that Mesopotamian banking developed not as an expedient for exchange but to serve redistribution.

The third thesis, on markets, is presented in two variants. In one, which I call the 'qualified' version, Polanyi maintained that trade and entrepreneurial activity in Babylonia did not 'originally' take a market form. The other, the 'absolute' version, goes further. It claims that Babylonia 'possessed neither market places nor a functioning market system of any description'.[4] Polanyi based the latter claim on the research of Ronald Sweet and Leo Oppenheim. In a letter to his brother, Michael, he reports that Sweet had sifted through 7,000 documents from the Old Babylonian period but not a single case 'of profit made on price differentials has turned up yet'.[5] As to Oppenheim, his essay published in *Trade and Markets* focuses upon Southern Mesopotamian cities, which he portrays not as a 'redistributive' system centred on temple and palace, as Polanyi was wont to do, but, rather tentatively, as a binary system built upon the symbiosis between redistributive temple (and palace) institutions and the communally organised city. Although Oppenheim was well aware that large-scale private merchant ventures were ubiquitous and that towns would typically possess a *kar* (or *karu*: 'harbour' or 'port', a special extramural district in which merchants would gather to engage in long-distance trade), he also remarked upon the lack of a central market place, in contrast to the cities of medieval Europe.[6] It is this observation that struck Polanyi, and there is some evidence that he saw the 'absolute' thesis ('marketless Babylon') as a pioneering discovery. In a letter to a friend he commented that Oppenheim was of the opinion that 'archaeological evidence speaks against the existence of "market-places" within the cities of the ancient Near East'.[7] To Robert Merton he enthused that 'our work on the "Cappadocian" tablets (on so-called early Assyrian trade) has caused the breakthrough' on the question of marketless Mesopotamia.[8] In correspondence with another friend, Walter Neale, he advanced the rather stronger claim that Oppenheim 'recognized that no markets were present in Babylonia and that no word for "market" existed'.[9] And, in a letter that he received from his editor at Routledge & Kegan Paul, the latter communicated his 'delight' upon hearing Polanyi's 'good news about absence of markets in Babylonia'.[10]

In this chapter, I explore Polanyi's account of trade, markets and money in Mesopotamia. I assess the merits and demerits of his contribution, with reference to Assyriological and anthropological literatures. I examine, in particular, his functionalist method and his taxonomy of 'mechanisms of integration', and suggest that Polanyi played a role – variously as foil, mentor and indirect stimulus – in an important phase in the progression of critical anthropological thought toward its reunion with global historiography.

TRADE, MONEY AND CREDIT

How well do Polanyi's analyses of ancient Mesopotamian economies stand up in the light of subsequent scholarship? The short answer is: less successfully than his other forays into comparative economic history. Two of his theses were, at best, overstated. One of these, 'marketless Babylon', finds little support, although his more 'qualified' formulations on Mesopotamian markets remain influential, as discussed below. His thesis that Old Assyrian trade was conducted by *tamkāru* along non-market lines has proved susceptible to critique, with tablets from the Assyrian trading colony at Kanesh providing significant evidence of merchants acting for personal gain. That markets existed in Assyria where goods could be sold at a profit, the Assyriologist Klaas Veenhof argues, 'does not fit well into Polanyi's system'.[11] In respect of the Old Babylonian period as a whole, in the judgment of John Gledhill and Mogens Larsen, Polanyi's conceptualisation of the *tamkārum* does not apply, for it is doubtful whether the trader in Mesopotomia was ever an official, in the sense of a person who, as a member of a bureaucratic organisation, acts on behalf of the state, drawing a salary and/or land.[12] The Assurian *tamkārum*, they add, acted principally in response to changes in supply and demand. Polanyi's suggestion that, given negotiated prices, trade was essentially risk-free is refuted by the numerous documented references to losses sustained – not to mention the letters from the wives of the Assyrian merchants at Kanesh who complain that their spouses were only interested in money.[13]

What can be safely stated is that in Old Assyria the boundaries between public and private were rarely clear-cut, and the *tamkārum* was not a rigidly defined position. He could be a trader who travels with his merchandise, or a functionary whose task it was to facilitate trade – as banker, merchant or moneylender who gives out commercial loans. That the role is best summarised as that of an independent merchant within a market system cannot be taken as given, for alternative interpretations are available. Mario Liverani has argued that Assurian trade is best understood as embedded within a redistributive economy, with trading operations subdivided into three processes: the initial relationship between a palace or temple and merchants, their activities after leaving home base, and the settling of accounts between merchants and central agencies at the end of the process. In the intermediary stage merchants could trade freely, playing on price differentials to augment their gains but in the other stages an administered relationship obtained.[14] If one casts the net wider, in space or time, other, more 'Polanyian', trading relationships have been recorded. Take, for example, the merchants at Nuzi described by Carlo Zaccagnini. They demonstrated a significant degree of independence but in the context of a professional and subordinate relationship to the palace.[15] Or the *dam.gàr* of Ur III. Discussing Marvin Powell's contention that these traders were independent and profit-oriented, Robert Englund has suggested that while this may conceivably apply in the case of Nippur, if so, it represented an outlier. In towns such as Girsu and Umma, by contrast, *dam.gàr* were unambiguously employees of the state, and their capital was state property.[16] If we skip forward fourteen centuries or so we come to the Neo-Babylonian *tamkārum*: a 'slightly enigmatic' figure but one who, in Michael Jursa's assessment, tended to be state-sponsored.[17] Finally, consider the Neo-Assyrian *tamkārum* studied by Karen Radner. She portrays these as royal agents, legitimated by the king and equipped with quasi-diplomatic status, who travelled near and far to furnish the monarch with items required for the running of state affairs. Typically, they would belong to the household of a member of the king's family or of a high official, and would likely be linked to the armed forces; some even commanded military personnel. Radner compares them to Francis Drake or Hernando Cortez, who enjoyed military and diplomatic competences granted by an imperial ruler and were tasked to seek out and acquire the gold and other luxury items that their monarch required – although the typical *tamkārum*, unlike Drake or Cortez, could hardly be described as a freebooter.[18]

As regards Polanyi's third thesis, I shall consider it in two parts: money, then banking. On money, it is clear that from around 2500 BC in Babylonia (and several centuries later in Assyria) silver began to resemble Polanyi's 'all-purpose' money in certain respects. Yet in which respects, and how rapidly, is open to debate. Some Assyriologists claim that silver, as far back as the third millennium, assumed the mantle of the principal definition of economic value, and that it was regularly exchanged for other commodities – and not only in long-distance or high-value trade.[19] Others maintain that its 'all-purpose' nature only manifested itself within certain economic spheres. For much of the third millennium, they argue, economic exchange in southern Mesopotamia was mediated by a variety of forms of money in the 'redistributive' ration systems of temple and palace, and by various monies but also, importantly, by small-scale barter at the local level.[20] A substantial part of rural rents, taxes and agricultural exchanges were paid with 'special-purpose' currencies (such as barley or dates) or in labour services, while hired labour was remunerated in fixed rations (of grain, oil or wool). Silver was employed for pensatory payments (payments by weight) and in the incurrence and discharge of debts, but was never coined, and in important spheres – from village exchange to the prebendal system – it was marginal.[21] In Oppenheim's judgment, payments for real estate, slaves, goods and services during the Old Babylonian period were only rarely made in silver, even though prices were generally quoted according to that standard.[22] On similar lines, Mitchell Rothman maintains that tablets that record actual transactions almost never mention silver changing hands, unless silver itself was the object of exchange. Nor was there 'a standard of account in ancient Mesopotamia. ... In short, silver did not function as real money'.[23]

If monetisation was minimal until the beginning of the first millennium, between the eighth and sixth century BC that changed dramatically. Babylonia was now at the heart of an empire that drew large amounts of silver, by trade or by compulsion ('the spoils from Assyria, the tribute from Syria') from across the region. The enhanced surplus available to the Neo-Babylonian monarchy accelerated monetisation and the spread of markets. Although the economy could, arguably, still be described as binary, the demarcation was no longer clear, at least not by the sixth century. While some activities associated with the use of silver were exclusively conducted in that metal, it now played a role in all sectors, even the core areas of the redistributive institutional households. These were increasingly dependent on hired labour, their external economic exchanges were conducted chiefly in silver (most of it acquired via cash crop production), as were around a sixth or seventh of internal temple transactions. In comparison with Old Babylonians, their sixth-century descendants were considerably more likely to use silver in market exchange (and no longer essentially of high-value items) and in dowries, and significant numbers received it as at least a component of their wage.[24] Nonetheless, it would be far-fetched to describe even Neo-Babylonian silver as all-purpose money. Unlike present-day money, it was 'never a universally acceptable currency'.[25]

Turning to banking and credit, here too, Polanyi's theses find some qualified support among contemporary Assyriologists. There is no doubt that he underestimated the role of private money-lending. However, his contention that temple and palace institutions in the second and third millennia were the principal providers of harvest credit is plausible. There is, moreover, little evidence of productive loans to industrial entrepreneurs for achieving gain through the accrual of interest. Interest rates, Jursa points out, were 'potentially subject to negotiation between the parties concerned, but custom and in part also interference by cities or the crown strongly promoted a standard rate'. Financial instruments were essentially limited to claims and liabilities, while deposit banking and capital markets, where they existed at all, were rudimentary, and while credit for productive purposes was available, 'the mechanisms which brought investors and businessmen together were as likely to have been social as strictly economic'. Even in first-millennium Babylonia, according to Jursa, only a modest proportion of private and institutional wealth was reinvested in the business economy – ten or fifteen per cent is his estimate. Much institutional wealth passed through commodity markets but only rarely was it 'fed directly into business ventures of any kind'.[26]

THE MARKET AND THE WHEEL

Polanyi's claim of 'marketless Babylon' is easy to dismiss, but what of his 'qualified' claim, that markets, at least for long spells, were marginal to Mesopotamian economic life? The generality of the thesis means that it can accommodate the identification of specific markets, so long as they are minor relative to economic life overall. Even it, however, is contradicted by some economic historians. Morris Silver, for example, holds that ancient Mesopotamia was unequivocally a marketised society: it played host to 'ubiquitous multinational firms' and experienced lengthy periods of 'unfettered market activity'.[27] A similar case has been made by David Warburton. His self-styled Keynesian economic history of the ancient Near East, *Macroeconomics from the Beginning*, takes some pot shots at Polanyi and at all who have drunk from his poisoned well. The allocation and distribution of resources in Mesopotamia, in Warburton's depiction, occurred primarily through 'markets' and 'market forces'.[28] It was a market economy, and all its institutions were 'subject to the rule of the market'.[29]

Polanyian Assyriologists concede that research in recent decades has revealed Mesopotamian economic processes and relations that would have surprised the master. These include evidence of land sales in Ur III and, above all in the first millennium BC, a significant degree of market exchange, private land ownership and the contractual alienation of land, as well as the hiring of free labour on a significant scale. That said, too many criticisms of Polanyi's Mesopotamian theses miss their target due to insufficient care in reading his texts. Warburton's *Macroeconomics* abounds with misinterpretations of this sort. It jumps from the valid assertion that Polanyi erred in his interpretation of the data from Kanesh to the unwarranted conclusion that he based his 'entire theory' upon this mistake.[30] It proposes that the evidence for profit-seeking trade in Assyria's Cappadocian colonies proves that Polanyi's idea of 'redistribution' is ill-chosen, as if profit-seeking exchange cannot coexist with prices administered by the large institutions.[31] A few pages later it claims that Polanyi held that the presence of non-market 'forms of economic activity in antiquity demonstrated that markets did not exist', and that this was based on Polanyi's assumption 'that the existence of the market would effectively eliminate' all other such forms.[32] Here, Warburton seems not to have grasped that Polanyi's 'mechanisms of integration' are ideal types; that in actually existing societies they coexist. Nor does he appear to understand the conceptual distinctions that Polanyi makes between 'market places', 'price-making markets' and the 'market system'. Likewise, Silver's talk of 'unfettered markets' should be treated with caution. It bears the imprint of the 'economistic fallacy' – Polanyi's term for the tendency of economic historians to project the contemporary experience of 'market society' upon pre-modern societies. On substantive issues, Silver, crucially, fails to demonstrate that a market existed for the fundamental means of production: agricultural land. At least in the third and early second millennia, much of Mesopotamia's southern alluvium was dominated by *oikos* economies: colossal bureaucratic palace and temple complexes that controlled not only distribution but much production too – with their own land, herds and workshops. Although land could be sold, this was rare, and would typically have taken the form of a sale to a single buyer by multiple sellers who owned it in common. Some sorts of private land ownership seem to have existed but these were of marginal importance relative to the institutional (temple and palace) and village-based domestic and communal sectors. The latter sector, Warburton claims, consisted of private property in the modern sense. But the reasoning he deploys to make the case is speculative. Records of purchase and ownership of agricultural land from the towns of Emar and Mari 'would imply that the palaces of the second millennium B.C. were purchasing private property which had been recognised as such'. Data from these same towns 'would imply that the ownership of grain lands may only have become a royal affair during the second millennium'. And 'any large scale purchases of grain land during the third millennium demand' (that is, imply) the existence of 'private ownership at that time, and any purchases of grain imply private sales, and therefore private possession of grain, which would again imply private possession (even if as legally "shared ownership") of land during the third millennium'.[33]

Even if one allows for an inevitable documentary bias towards the palace and temple institutions that kept records, at least under the Ur III dynasty they controlled most productive land and it was not generally subject to free sale. This was moreover, Johannes Renger has argued, a situation that continued into the Old Babylonian period.[34] Although a different regime of land tenure existed in northern Babylonia, with greater scope for land rental contracts between private individuals, there is no definite evidence supporting the existence of a land market with price-clearing markets at standardised prices set by supply and demand. Land sales did not occur 'on the market' at a price set by supply and demand within an institution of regular exchange. Instead they were occasional, and were often made under duress (for example, military attack or drought) or to relatives. Of course, by the first millennium the picture had changed. Babylonian fields and gardens in private hands could be more freely bought and sold, and by the time of Nabonidus most of the temple's arable land was farmed by sharecroppers and no longer by its own labour force. Yet even now, Jursa has argued, the land market was not fully synchronised with commodity markets. It was subject to factors that did not affect them (and which remain poorly understood), and, crucially, it was set within a heavily subsistence-geared economy in which only a fraction of the product was brought to market.[35]

In the light of the contributions over the last twenty years by Renger, Englund, Liverani, Zaccagnini, Michael Hudson and others, it appears that, confutation of Polanyi's 'marketless Babylon' thesis notwithstanding, several of his more qualified theses on Mesopotamian economic life stand up to scrutiny. Unlike modern market society, in which owners and labourers have no means of reproducing themselves other than by selling and buying, in which money provides the necessities of life and usurps nature as the essential immediate condition of human existence, and in which customs and values are powerfully shaped by the imperatives that pulse from a distinct market sphere, the economies of ancient Mesopotamia were heavily geared to subsistence production. For the mass of producers, subsistence was underwritten by direct access to their own plot or communal land. Relatively little surplus was available for exchange, the commodification of labour and land was peripheral, and markets were restricted mainly to goods, rather than land or labour-power. An economic structure of this type underpinned cultural and ethical dispositions that were quite unlike those that prevail in market societies. A societal ethic of individual gain-seeking did not come into being, personal wealth accumulation was widely distrusted, and self-aggrandisement risked punishment by a goddess of social justice.

None of this should be taken to imply that the Mesopotamian economy lacked dynamism, or technological and economic innovation. The Mesopotamians, after all, invented glass and the seeder plough, not to mention the wheel. They developed advanced irrigation and sanitation systems and innovated in numerous other fields of endeavour. Polanyi's 'primitivist' account was not blind to this. It did not depict Mesopotamia as suffering from a dearth of economic innovation, as some have supposed,[36] and he was aware that the region (notably Babylonia in the sixth century) enjoyed periods of 'efflorescence' – phases in which growth in commerce and population and urbanisation are accompanied by stable or rising incomes and economic and cultural specialisation and complexity. His argument, rather, was that such periods featured increased commerce, money use and business transactions alongside 'the eclipse of the market'.[37] The error lay not in a denial of 'efflorescence' but in the perception of 'eclipse'.

One element in Polanyi's historical misreading, Hudson suggests, is that he imagined markets 'to be inherently private', and missed 'their initially public aspect'.[38] The critique is somewhat overstated. Polanyi identifies armies as 'the chief promoters of markets' in Hellenic society, and he was interested – intensely so – in the nurturing of markets by the Greek *poleis* (as we discuss in Chapter 9). That said, he did indeed define markets as sharply distinct from non-economic institutions, with 'market exchange' strongly connoting private economic activity and 'redistribution' identified with public institutions.[39] This, Hudson shows, hinders understanding of privatisation processes. Whereas Polanyi thought that markets first emerged among military camp followers, foreign merchants and money lenders, Hudson maintains that they arose on the fringes of the temple and palace complexes in Sumer and Babylon.[40] The temples were administered as corporately autonomous bodies. By distributing goods at standard prices they created conditions propitious to the emergence of independent merchants and market exchange. In this way, 'private' enterprise emerged from the 'public' sector. It developed at the top of society, as self-seeking proliferated among *tamkāru* who, in their official roles, belonged to the public bureaucracy. (On similar lines, Oppenheim had earlier drawn attention to New Babylonian privatisation processes centred on the palace bureaucracy.[41])

As an interim conclusion, I would suggest that, exaggerations and errors in Polanyi's account notwithstanding, there is much to be said for his contribution. His observations on banking, finance and administered prices continue to be quarried for insights by scholars working in the field today. His discussion of the role of markets in Mesopotamia remains relevant, as does Oppenheim's argument on the economically marginal character of market places in southern cities in some periods. Clearly, markets played an important role in certain sectors during certain epochs and yet, given the subsistence orientation of most producers, a market system could not come into being. Mesopotamia knew neither a market economy in the Polanyian sense nor capitalism in the Marxian sense. On the other hand, new evidence and interpretations have substantially altered the Assyriological field that Polanyi was ploughing. There is a near consensus that he understated the degree of market development, the presence of the profit motive, and the extent of private enterprise in Mesopotamia. In delineating too stark a divide between administered and market trade, and relatedly, between public and private power, his framework is not suited to explaining dynamics of privatisation or the emergence of markets within the 'public' sector. Arguably, however, the weakest aspect of Polanyi's approach to archaic societies is not this or that specific thesis, but his functionalist tendency to downplay their internal contradictions. This leaves his framework ill-equipped to explaining socio-economic change.

MUTINY OF THE GODS

The disciplinary focus of Polanyi's Mesopotamian studies lies in economic history and the critical discussion has largely revolved around his theses on markets. But his typology of economic integration drew heavily upon research from another discipline: anthropology. Polanyi immersed himself in writings by the functionalist anthropologists Malinowski and Firth, as well as by anthropologist colleagues at Columbia. In the postwar years, Columbia's anthropology department was dominated by the Boasian tradition and reactions against it. Boas' method had developed in reaction against the cultural evolutionism of Victorian nineteenth-century anthropology which, at its ethnocentric worst, posited a progressive evolution of social forms from primitive tribal ignorance to their telos in the advanced civilisations of Western Europe and North America. Boas eschewed attempts to map laws of historical evolution and cultural integration, arguing instead for an empiricist, idiographic and relativist method. Apprehending individual societies as *sui generis* complexes of material and symbolic elements, anthropologists should focus upon fieldwork-based description, analysis of how the elements articulate, and interpretation of their symbolic field.

Boas' method can in a broad sense be described as functionalist,[42] by which I refer to approaches that explain social phenomena and human behaviour in terms of their beneficial effects upon the social organism. It was a perspective that, in the narrower sense, was adopted by several of his students. Ruth Benedict, in particular, kept the functionalist flame alight at Columbia. The cultural traits present in any given society, she argued, 'tend to be integrated', that is, they constitute 'a more or less consistent pattern of thought and action'. Citing Malinowski, she proposed that anthropological research should study a society's 'living culture', considered holistically: 'to know its habits of thought and the functions of its institutions.'[43] By the time of Polanyi's arrival at Columbia, functionalism was formidably well represented in the Department of Anthropology. His closest collaborator, Arensberg, was a functionalist anthropologist and a pioneer of 'community study' research. (It studies communities, assumed for the purposes of analysis to be bounded and culturally homogenous

– in Arensberg's words, a community 'is "a whole", a "full round of local life"'.)[44] Through Arensberg, Polanyi got to know graduate students in anthropology, including Chapman, while, outside the anthropology department, his closest friends and collaborators at Columbia included Robert MacIver, a communitarian-functionalist sociologist, and Robert Merton, a prominent functionalist sociologist and student of Parsons.[45]

Polanyi's brand of functionalism has been described – accurately, I think – by Hann as 'radical'. In contrast to Malinowski, whose methodology was 'synchronicist' and whose political views were conservative (including a 'patronizing attitude to non-European peoples, loyalty to colonial institutions' and a tendency 'to treat Western values as of universal applicability'), Polanyi's political leanings were to the left and his scholarship exhibited a search for 'patterns in history'. His method was, unlike Malinowski's, a 'functionalism of *institutions*'. Hann also explores the similarities between the two imperial compatriots. Both, when young, had been enthusiasts for Machian positivism and for Bücher's economic history, and both held a romantic conception of culture. Polanyi's overriding goal in later life, like Malinowski's, 'was to show how the economy meshed in with other cultural institutions in different societies'.[46] Both believed that neoclassical economics applies to capitalist societies 'in which individuals are out to get the most they can' but not to non-capitalist societies 'in which kinship, religion, and politics constrain individual choice'. This position, the anthropologist Donald Donham has argued, in helping to establish 'the "otherness" of other cultures', served to affirm anthropology's position within the academic division of labour inherited from the colonial era. It spoke to 'deeply ingrained rhetorical needs in anthropology', and helps to explain the appeal of Polanyi's research programme to anthropologists.[47]

Functionalism permeates Polanyi's economic historiography. Consider his major preoccupation: 'redistribution', a mechanism of integration in which the appropriative and locational movements are toward and from a centre. In pre-class societies, redistribution appeared in, for example, the coordinated hunt: in formal terms, goods (such as game) are acquired, transferred to a central place and then redistributed for consumption. The process 'integrates' the economy and, in social terms, consolidates 'communal solidarity'. Redistribution later came into its own with storage-based civilisations such as ancient Mesopotamia in which a central group takes command of the appropriation and redistribution of goods. In Polanyi's studies of Mesopotamia and other archaic economies the functionalist accent can be seen in his conception of redistribution as simply a 'form of integration', with emphasis on the role of economic practices in strengthening social bonds, and playing down questions of power or exploitation. For example, he portrays the redistributive process as essential to social existence and social cohesion, as those at the centre distribute resources to supply the 'army, bureaucracy, and labour force', without considering the fact that the resources had been extracted *by* army and bureaucracy *from* the labour force. On Babylonia in the age of Hammurabi, he describes trading relations between farmer and palace/temple authorities as if they were conducted on a free and equal basis. Concerning Mesopotamian history more broadly, he salutes the irrigational-imperial states for their creation of the rules and institutions that embodied 'justice, law, and individual freedom'.[48]

Understated if not entirely ignored in Polanyi's accounts are the mechanisms by which humans appropriate natural resources, as well as relations of power and social class. These are hardly recondite aspects of Mesopotamian society. By way of illustration, consider the legend of Enki and Ninmah and the Atrahasis Epic. These, the earliest recorded creation myths, were written on Sumerian clay tablets early in the second millennium. The narrative begins prior to the creation of humankind, in a world populated by deities. They are hierarchically organised. A lesser race of gods maintains the irrigation networks and tills the fields to supply the divine community. It was from the contradictions of this hierarchical set-up that humanity was born. When the lesser gods discovered class struggle and refused to work, their overlords – Enki, Enlil, Anu and the mother goddess (Mama) – decided to create a new race to take on the task of labour. They slaughtered one of the cleverer worker gods (perhaps the rebel ringleader) and, combining his divine flesh with earthly clay, brought humans into being. In the story that follows, the human population is driven higher and lower in number – an instability of human existence that is fundamentally driven by clashes of interests among the gods: Enlil, god of the earth and weather, sends plagues, floods, drought and famine to cull the human population while Enki, god of wisdom and fresh water, preserves and nourishes it.[49]

That Sumer's creation mythology foregrounds an episode of industrial action, with humans called into existence to serve as strike breakers, is eye-catching. This was a society, the first of its kind for which extensive documentation is available, in which a minority gained control of a significant surplus that could be stockpiled, hoarded in granaries, measured and redistributed. The irrigation systems on which Sumerian agriculture relied required continuous supervision, and those who supervised them, and the granaries that stored surplus produce, became a group over and above society, demanding praise and obedience. The grain storehouses were the first temples, their superintendents the first priests. The temples were institutional centres of class power. Their functions included supervising irrigation projects, redistributing economic produce, and encoding public duties and private-property rights.[50] Over the fourth and third millennia, economic resources were increasingly centralised in the temple and palace households, which consumed roughly half the annual crop.[51] What once had been the 'community's' product became in practice the property of the new urban class of clerics and administrators, an elite that utilised its control of resources and state power to extract surplus product from the peasantry and to compel peasants to conduct public works in return for wages in cash or kind. In certain periods, corvée labour was in widespread use, for agricultural labour, brick-making and constructing canals and defensive installations, and in Old Babylonian times, slave owning was still common.[52] One form of dependent labour consisted in so-called house-born slaves – 'people with lesser rights who worked for the master of a specific house, the patron of an extended family' – but a larger segment worked for the temples and palaces. These should be considered 'a kind of temple-slaves', according to Gebhard Selz, for they were 'the property of these institutions, temples or palaces. They were sometimes bought in exchange for goods, or came into the cities as prisoners of war'. Above them in the social pyramid were 'a group that partly depended on fiefs: during part of the year they sustained themselves by their own harvest, but in return for the use of land they had to fulfil certain obligations towards the institutions and the state' – such as military service and public construction work.[53] At the apex were the temple and palace officials. Here we see the material basis of the Atrahasis myth. The temple was a major landowner and patron of a largely dependent workforce. It organised the collection, storage and distribution of food, vast amounts of which, although dedicated to the gods, was in fact consumed by mortal members of the divine household: the temple personnel.[54] The task for the rest was to play the role of the humans in the myth: accept their place in the divinely organised social order, perform their duties and follow the rules in order not to provoke divine retribution. The message would hardly have been clearer if it had been displayed – as in John Carpenter's *They Live* – as hortatory slogans on public walls.

GLOBAL UPHEAVAL AND REDISTRIBUTIVE CANNIBALISM

Given its fixation upon the role of culture in *resolving* social contradictions, functionalism was ill-equipped to explain its role in *justifying* them. It came under fire, relatedly, for conveying an 'inherently conservative political message' (in view of its tendency to take social and economic integration, or the functional unity of society, as a given rather than as a variable); for the static nature of its analysis (with its assumptions that institutions exist in order to satisfy the needs of the community as a whole and that social practices serve to maintain the stability of society, considered as a culturally unified whole); for envisaging the state as society's heart due to its central locus in circulation and the services it performs on behalf of society at large (which at worst could validate state-enacted practices of oppression, exploitation and the abuse of power); and for downplaying or overlooking colonialism, imperialism and other forms of geopolitical power projection.[55] During Polanyi's Columbia years, these critiques began to be aired, and alternatives emerged in the form of neo-evolutionism, cultural materialism and Marxism, in all of which his anthropologist colleagues, and in some cases his protégés, played seminal roles. Arguably the key figure was Julian Steward. He developed a materialistic approach, for which he coined the term 'cultural ecology'. It featured a much sharper and more consistent focus than that of his contemporaries (including Polanyi) on human societies' technological capacities, organisation of the labour process and metabolism with the natural environment.[56] His 'neo-evolutionist' method was post-Boasian, in the sense that it assumed multilineality and did not entertain the ethnocentric fantasy of unilineal evolutionism – that all roads point west.

In 1950, an organisational crucible of new ideas at Columbia, the Mundial Upheaval Society, was set up. Its members included Morton Fried, Sidney Mintz and Eric Wolf, as well as Murra. They all took an interest in Polanyi's work, as did several other Steward-linked anthropology graduate students, notably Marvin Harris and Marshall Sahlins.[57] Mintz penned an admiring review of Polanyi's *Trade and Markets* for the journal of the American Anthropological Association.[58] Wolf brought together Polanyi's discussion of 'the intrusion of capitalist norms and practices into noncapitalist and precapitalist social orders' and Trotsky's idea of uneven and combined development, in his research on 'skewed' societies that had succumbed to Bonapartist forms of government.[59] Fried, who must have known Polanyi,[60] and Sahlins, a Polanyi mentee, integrated Polanyi's reciprocity-redistribution-exchange triad into their work, but with a twist: they re-read redistribution through the lens of social stratification.[61] They did not consider storage functionally, as the means of supplying and consolidating the community, but as a mode of power centralisation, one that signified indeed the *separation* of the central elite from the community at large. In *The Evolution of Political Society,* Fried mapped Polanyi's mechanisms of integration to particular modes of stratification. Whereas goods in egalitarian societies circulate through *reciprocal* exchange, in rank societies 'the major process of economic integration is *redistribution*, in which there is a characteristic flow of goods into and out from a finite center. Invariably that center is the pinnacle of the rank hierarchy or, as complexity mounts, the pinnacle of a smaller component network within a larger structure'.[62] Harris, similarly, distinguished two types of redistribution. One, in egalitarian societies, is an intensified example of reciprocity, where a generous provider gives and expects nothing in return. The other evolves in a context of the emergence of classes and states, of increasing coercion and warfare. Here, the redistributor retains the largest share, and accumulates possessions.[63] In the embryonic states of Mesopotamia, he argued, redistributive chiefs 'gradually set themselves above their followers and became the original nucleus of the ruling class'. Ultimately, they created a stratified society 'in which the many debased themselves on behalf of the exaltation of the few'. In *Cannibals and Kings*, Harris adapted the concept of redistribution to explain the formation of class cohesion (as opposed to societal or community cohesion). In a memorable passage on the Aztec Empire he proposed that priests 'can legitimately be described as ritual slaughterers in a state-sponsored system geared to the production and redistribution of substantial amounts of animal protein in the form of human flesh'. The critical question therefore is

> not how much these cannibal redistributions contributed to the health and vigor of the average citizen but how much the cost/benefits of political control underwent a favourable shift as a result of using human flesh to reward selected groups at crucial periods. If an occasional finger or toe was all anyone could expect, the system would probably not have worked. But if the meat was supplied in concentrated packages to the nobility, soldiers, and their retainers, and if the supply was synchronized to compensate for deficits in the agricultural cycle, the payoff for Moctezuma and the ruling class might have been sufficient to stave off political collapse.[64]

In late 1940s Puerto Rico, the Mundial Upheavalists took part in a ground-breaking collaborative research project. It was led by Steward and Murra, with participation of Mintz and Wolf.[65] To some, it appeared as an application of the 'community study' approach, but Steward was adamant that it was not: Puerto Rican society was 'complex' and 'heterogenous', and the project compared four of the island's regions, 'each with a distinctive combination of environment, crops, and institutional arrangements'.[66] It was a study of a rapidly changing society, affected powerfully by relations of extra-insular power, and in the throes of what mainstream social science was beginning to refer to as 'modernisation'. As such, it contributed to what Howard Brick describes as anthropology's momentous postwar shift away from its inherited 'focus on "primitive" peoples' and toward the study of '"peasant" communities recognizably tied to the modern world'. The Puerto Rico project represented, moreover, 'a turn toward more "materialist" conceptions of political economy and a distinctive kind of historical awareness that militated against conventional notions of culture as a static form'.[67]

The Columbia graduate students and junior professors around Wolf, Mintz, Fried, Sahlins and Leacock revolutionised anthropology.[68] They broke with established traditions that fixated on the 'ethnographic present', as if 'primitive' peoples live outside history. They demonstrated that historical change can be driven by ordinary people.[69] They elevated the study of relations of domination – by class, gender, race and empire – to a central position within the discipline. Despite McCarthyism, they welcomed the advice of Marxists (such as Leacock's advisor, Weltfish) that anthropologists should never ignore the colonised history of the peoples they study but neither should they document the impact of colonisation as if it is a one-way process, ignoring their subjects' 'active participation in their own history'.[70] Learning from anti-colonial scholars and from dependency theory, they began to develop an understanding of the way in which *global* relations shape human cultures, and to advance a 'deep-historical critique of Western domination of the wider colonial and postcolonial world'.[71]

This came at a critical intellectual conjuncture. Mainstream social science in the 1950s and 1960s was busy reinventing the Victorian, west-centric paradigm of progress, in the form of modernisation theory (which was later to morph into globalisation theory). The post-Boasian anthropologists at Columbia were arguing for a different understanding of progress. Eschewing both apparent poles of debate – an ethnocentric modernisation theory that cloaks hierarchy and domination in the language of growth and progress, and a moral relativism that, unable to provide categories of judgment, 'tolerates everything' – they were motivated by a commitment, as Steward put it, to 'fight intolerance and conquest – political and economic as well as military –in all their forms', and to envision progress not in non-Eurocentric terms but instead, as the young Sahlins put it, in opposition to the 'older, entrenched social orders' of the world's dominant powers.[72] In short, they supplied the ingredients not only of a counter-narrative to modernisation theory but, more broadly, of what Brick describes as a set of pioneering '"world", "global" and "transnational" approaches' that continue to shape social-scientific scholarship today.[73]

CONCLUSION

In comparison with his research on the origins and nature of the modern market system, Polanyi's studies of ancient and 'archaic' economic history are not well known. Of his empirical theses on Mesopotamia, some have been refuted while others remain influential and continue to inspire archaeologists and Assyriologists today. His methodology was functionalist, but in an unusual and 'radical' sense: he tends to assume that pre-modern societies are successfully integrated while modern market society is not (or, in an alternate formulation, the latter succumbs to disruptive strains to the extent that integration is institutionalised through the utopia of the self-regulating market). Although Polanyi's approach pays comparatively little attention to the human metabolism with the natural environment, or to the 'hidden abodes' of social reproduction,[74] or to questions of class, gender, imperialism, colonialism or racism, it nonetheless carried a powerfully critical edge. Polanyi reminds economic historians that phenomena need to be grasped in a way that recognises that 'agent and participant understanding of social and economic activity is integral to and partially constitutive of the characteristics of such activities', as Alasdair MacIntyre once put it.[75] Above all, Polanyi provided a salutary warning of the hazards of the 'economistic fallacy' – the assumption that concepts developed within modern market societies can be unproblematically applied to earlier social formations. That his empirical research and methodological innovations were motivated in part by a search for alternatives to capitalism is frowned upon by some yet this provided the spark, the social vision, that underlay his research on ancient economic history, with its searching questions and imaginative transhistorical comparisons. It also explains why many engaged intellectuals, despite their differences with his methodological framework, found inspiration in his writings. They include the Polanyi protégé Immanuel Wallerstein and others of the world-systems school, such as Giovanni Arrighi and Christopher Chase-Dunn, who utilise Polanyi's forms of integration in their theories of global historical dynamics.[76] Less famously but equally importantly, they include the neo-evolutionist young Turks at Columbia, to whose work the discipline of anthropology, and 'transnational' critiques of globalisation theory, owe so much.

9

Markets in Ancient Greece: The Challenge of the New Institutionalism

Polanyi was a lifelong Hellenophile.[1] His classical education included hearty servings of ancient Greek and Roman literature and philosophy. From childhood on, in the words of his daughter, 'he adored the Greeks', avidly read Greek literature and enjoyed reciting Greek poetry.[2] He was well versed, too, in nineteenth-century German Romantic philosophy, a current that envisioned ancient Greece as a model of a fully realised, integrated society, one that formed a contrast to contemporary Germany while also demonstrating, tantalisingly, the potential for cultural and philosophical radiance within a matrix of political fragmentation.[3] Along with Lukacs and other radical intellectuals of Hungary's 'Great Generation', he reacted with revulsion against the materialistic, utilitarian civilisation of his day, and idealised ancient Greece as a non-alienated culture, one that could serve as an instrument of criticism of the present and a model of integrity and synthesis for the future.[4]

Alongside Hellenic culture and philosophy it was the ancient economy – or, more accurately, the relationship between economy and politics – that engaged Polanyi in an in-depth and sustained manner. His interest was fuelled by two political and intellectual considerations. The first was his conception of the pressing needs of the postwar global political economy. Two forms of economic organisation, plan and market, appeared to be vying for dominance within industrialised countries and on the world scale, and an 'age of transformation' was underway that would witness the demise of the market. 'A re-viewing of economic history,' he wrote, is required in order 'to equip ourselves and the next generations' for the approaching transition.[5] Studying ancient Greece would help shed light on this defining issue of the age, for both systems had their origins in Hellenic civilisation.[6] These thoughts guided his questions concerning the ancient Greek economy: was it 'administered or competitive?' 'Bureaucratic or free?' If these were not alternatives, how then were these apparent opposites institutionally reconciled?[7] Did markets *integrate* the economy? How did democracy fit into the overall picture, and in particular, how did it relate to the market? Secondly and relatedly, he believed that the impending demise of the mid-twentieth century market economy was precipitating a grave crisis in the disciplines of economics and economic history.

A new 'general economic history' was required, by which he meant a framework that would enable accurate classification and analysis of the range of forms of economic organisation, including those in which interconnected price-making markets played little or no part. At Columbia, he and his collaborators launched a research programme to this purpose, using anthropological ideas and methods to examine the nature of markets, trade and money in a range of 'primitive' and archaic societies (including ancient Greece). In the process they developed new concepts, including the 'substantive economy' and 'forms of integration', designed to facilitate analysis of the institutional arrangements governing the production, exchange and valuation of goods in a diverse assortment of market and non-market societies.

Polanyi's purpose in examining the stages of Greek economic history in detail, arguably, to face a stern test implied by his own position: could he demonstrate that advanced forms of money, markets and trade, which he had sought to conceptually separate and divorce from models based on 'modernist' economic theory, could exist in a premodern society without having to give up his embeddedness thesis? Although part of the argument was about the political implications of the Greek *polis* and its redistributive systems for twentieth-century politics and political economy, the more analytical question – the challenge that Polanyi's model posed – has remained a bone of contention for economic historians of antiquity. As in Polanyi's day, much of the more recent debate on this revolves around his specific claims on the nature of markets in antiquity. Making sense of his approach to ancient Greece, and therewith the relevance of his writings on that period for economic historians and anthropologists alike, requires a critical look at his main contentions about ancient markets and their implications. We will approach this in the following way. First we survey Polanyi's understanding of the ancient Greek economy and his account of its development. Next, we offer an interpretation of how he sought to differentiate ancient markets from the 'modernist interpretation' of them. Central to his argument against the modernists were three different claims about such markets: one based on the absence of 'supply and demand', one based on the motives of historical agents, and one based on their empirical significance. Since the last of these has been extensively discussed in the existing literature, we shall concentrate on the first two. We then look at how economic historians have sought to incorporate both Polanyi's argument and his opponents' counterarguments into a single framework in order to leapfrog the primitivism-modernism controversy, namely by reframing the interpretative question as a matter of institutional variation. Finally, we conclude with the suggestion that despite its flaws, Polanyi's project, as illustrated by the ancient Greek case study, still has theoretical insights to offer that the 'new institutional' approach does not fully capture.

PRIMITIVE SUPERPLANNERS AND OTHER CHIMERAS

The key institutional innovation of the ancient Greeks was the *polis*. Even in its earliest form (850–750 BC) the *polis*, as a community of free citizens, exhibited an egalitarian potential, albeit restricted to a small elite. At this stage, in Polanyi's reading, the Athenian *polis* possessed considerable 'redistributive' power, but, not yet disciplined by democracy, it was prone to misuse (exemplified by the export of grain during periods of famine, a policy which 'no healthy society would tolerate').[8] His account of the democratisation process in Athens is conventional. It begins with the Solonic crisis. Solon presented himself as the reconciling political leader, championing justice – in the form not of property redistribution but 'Respect for Law' – as the antidote to the disruptive drives of hubris, lust, and envy.[9] (His poetry describes how he demolished the *horoi* boundary stones, liberating those who had been forced to 'crouch 'neath a master's frown, in vilest slavery'.[10]) But the effects of his reforms were complex. He resisted 'what must have been tremendous popular pressure to seize the large estates and redistribute the land', which earned him the animosity of the poor, yet the abolition of debt bondage was in the economic interests of the poor citizenry, and was a crucial factor in raising the status of the citizen, and enabling the rudiments of a self-governing civic community to be fashioned.[11] These measures served in addition to enhance the role of the rising commercial elite in management of the *polis* (by loosening the grip on government of the aristocrats of the great *oikoi*), while the abolition of debt bondage curbed the concentration of landed property, expanded contractual tenancy and accelerated the monetisation of economic relations – including, a generation after Solon, the use of coin.

In Polanyi's narrative, the post-Solonic tyrants are given their due for having created conditions propitious to centralised economic administration by the *polis*.[12] Under the tyrant Peisistratos and then Cleisthenes, policy tools for economic administration were strengthened, embedding the economy within society in a new way. Although the presence of 'market elements' was growing (to the vexation of the aristocrats, who viewed the market as 'a rather dubious institution'[13]), the system remained essentially 'redistributive': the economy that resulted was one factor 'that gave the classical polis its enduring strength, its elasticity and its highly specific character'.[14] Crucially, the tyrants and Cleisthenes reduced aristocratic power, and introduced reforms in the interests of 'the common people', such as ostracism, and the deme-based system of local justices.

All this prepared the ground for the democratic breakthrough. The reforms of sixth-century Athens, from Solon to the Peisistratids, ensured that 'the equalitarian legacy of primitive society' and an elevated status of the individual citizen were incorporated into the constitution of the new and proto-democratic civic community, which then achieved its climax in the classical era.[15] With the advent of democracy, 'the economy became located in Greek society in a novel way', with reciprocal and market exchanges coordinated by *polis*-led redistribution.[16] This was a conclusion that chimed with Polanyi's values. Individual autonomy, political citizenship, democracy and community had evolved in unison, at the expense of hierarchy and aristocratic command, and, moreover, in a way that was pregnant with solutions for contemporary socialist strategy. Whereas 'to the modern mind, with its marketing orientation, freedom and a centralization of power commonly appear as opposites', the Athenians had introduced the most far-reaching form of ancient democracy within a state entity that possessed 'complete and unchallengeable power' and which was regarded as the institutional embodiment of justice and morality.[17]

Polanyi's interpretation confronts two sets of difficulties. One is the pervasive unfreedoms that characterised the Athenian regime.[18] Women suffered oppression in the political and economic spheres, and the economy at *polis* level, at least in the fifth century, was organised as a 'military-coinage-slavery complex', to borrow David Graeber's term.[19] The acquisition of a substantial segment of social wealth occurred by means of slave labour and other forms of direct coercion (imperial tribute, piracy, plunder). Slaves were heavily used in Athens' two major industries, agriculture and silver mining. The latter, indeed, was wholly reliant on slaves, and was the industry in which conditions were at their most harsh and dangerous, with slaves regularly worked to death.[20] The Laureion mines represented an exceptional boost to the *polis*' coffers. (When a bemused queen, in Aeschylus' *The Persians,* demanded to know the source of Athenian wealth, the answer came: they have a 'spring of silver, a treasurehouse of the earth'.[21]) Their bounty propelled the Attic drachma to its hegemonic position as the currency of the Eastern Mediterranean, and facilitated imperial expansion.[22]

Athenian imperialism was not known for its gentleness – witness Thucydides' Melian Dialogue – and it brought an influx of slaves and tribute, as well as access to new silver mines. Slave agriculture, imperial tribute and slave-mined silver combined to yield monetary and commercial supremacy, with Athens' port of Piraeus becoming a magnet that attracted trade from across the Aegean, the Black Sea, Cyrenaica, Sicily and beyond. Monetary and commercial supremacy, through their stimulation of shipping, 'produced naval superiority, which in its turn sustained the empire'.[23] The empire brought in the slaves, the tribute and the triremes, enabling the expansion of markets and coinage, and the consolidation of democracy.

This set of difficulties did not detain Polanyi. He refers to the position of women and slaves only in passing. Where he discusses the silver mines his focus is not on production relations but revenues and ownership (their proceeds were 'regarded as belonging to the people'), and while he understands that modern minds tend to see empire as a 'total defection from democratic principles', such a view misconceives the nature of classical democracy: for Athens to survive, 'it had to create an empire'.[24] It was another tangle of knots that truly absorbed him. If classical Athens were read as a market society it would lend credence to the thesis that citizenship, democracy and market society arise together. This is what one might call the 'optimistic modernist reading': classical Athens as an embryonic capitalist economy, providing history with the original model of an institutional arrangement conducive to wealth accumulation and economic growth, and featuring private property, democratic politics, a market economy and an individualistic ethic.[25]

In reviving the so-called primitivism-modernism debate over the interpretation of the economic institutions of antiquity, a debate that dates back to the Bücher-Meyer controversy,[26] Polanyi raised 'the question of the applicability of modern economic theory to non-market economies' that had been central to that debate.[27] He saw the embeddedness of markets in antiquity as implying that market exchange was not the primary 'mode of integration' of the provision and distribution of goods, of 'livelihood' as he put it, in premodern societies. Rather, the dominant forms of integration were combinations of reciprocity, redistribution and householding. For this argument, his discussion of the Greek case was of particular importance because of the high development in an early stage of history of both market and state in the classical *polis*. The particular form in which the two were integrated into a social system demonstrated, for Polanyi, how even (relatively) advanced forms of political and economic organisation could coincide with a fundamentally non-capitalist, that is to say not market-based, mode of economic integration. As he put it, the Greeks – by which he refers to the classical and Hellenistic eras, including Ptolemaic Egypt – were 'the initiators of all advanced human economy'.[28] They 'almost singlehandedly developed both types of economy', the market and exchange type as well as the planning and redistributive type, 'to their highest forms reached up til then'.[29]

We should perhaps pause on this point, for it reveals a nuance of Polanyi's primitivism that is often overlooked. If the basic primitivist methodological injunction is, put simply, 'don't assume that the ancients thought and behaved as we do!', this need not imply, as political correlate, that 'their institutions are so alien that we cannot learn from them'. As indicated above, Polanyi's interest in ancient institutions was driven in part by contemporary political considerations. He was drawn to ancient Athens by its configuration of democracy, redistribution and market exchange, but Egypt caught his eye too. 'Ptolemaic Egypt stands out in the Hellenistic world,' he enthused. It was 'the wealthiest country of the world', producing a substantial agricultural surplus and supporting a large and largely free population (in contrast to, say, Roman Italy, with its gargantuan private estates and expropriated peasantry).[30] Under the Ptolemies, in Polanyi's analysis, 'the methods of storage and redistribution inherited from the ancient Pharaohs were raised to the level of sophisticated economic planning'. He calls this 'Hellenic central planning' and, elsewhere, 'an elaborate planned economy'. Thanks to their control of state and temple granaries, the Ptolemaic planners also succeeded in constructing a trans-regional grain market; for Polanyi this is one of several pieces of evidence that indicates that the apogee of ancient markets (*circa* 332 BC to 200 AD) was simultaneously the high point of ancient planning.[31]

On the Ptolemaic period, recent historiography suggests that Polanyi (and Michael Rostovtzeff on whose studies he drew) can be criticised for assuming, in a sense, too much 'modernity' in their view of ancient 'central planning'. The work of J. G. Manning, for example, has shown that despite its efficient administrative and information gathering capacities, Ptolemaic Egypt was in most salient respects a typical pre-modern form of state, and less institutionally centralised and homogenous than is often assumed. Although it was economically interventionist, and political rulers utilised their powers to control production, their interventions were by no means comprehensive or intensive. Farmers farmed and merchants traded without much detailed involvement of the state, apart from its inevitable appetite for 'its share' of output. The government issued decrees, but these were generally more reactive to evolving realities than comprehensive directives from the centre.[32] The Ptolemies drew up plans, but a plan is not the same as a planned economy.

POLANYI'S DUAL FUNCTIONALISM:
INSTITUTIONS, MARKETS AND THE ECONOMY

Polanyi's argument about markets in antiquity rests on conceptual differentiations which must be understood if his work is to be properly assessed. In particular, he differentiates markets, money and trade as separate phenomena that economic historians, reasoning backwards from modern conditions, have wrongly tended to see as institutionally unified. With respect to ancient markets he focuses on 'ports of trade' that were nodal to long-distance elite trading, and the role of the *marketplace* as a social and physical place for the exchange of local surpluses.[33] To observe the existence and functions of such marketplaces did not, for Polanyi, entail the existence of market exchange as a mode of integration: they do not operate according to the 'supply and demand mechanism', and he also questioned, for specific cases and periods, their empirical significance. The conceptual division he drew among trade, money and markets distinguishes his approach from mainstream conceptualisations of the Market. As the anthropologist James Carrier explains, 'people in many times and places have engaged in trade, have given and received objects and services among themselves and with those in neighbouring societies, without necessarily having the notion of the Market. Equally, many people have developed markets, more or less elaborate institutions devoted to facilitating or channelling this trade, without necessarily having the notion of the Market. And again, many people engage in commerce, by which I mean market trade as a significant rather than an incidental part of their economic lives, without thereby developing the notion of the Market'.[34]

Although Polanyi did not deny the existence of market exchange in antiquity altogether, he did often make claims that downplayed its empirical significance compared to the state-led redistribution mechanisms he saw as more characteristic of antiquity. We shall not discuss this empirical point at length, for three reasons. First, it has been treated in detail elsewhere.[35] Secondly, Polanyi was by no means consistent on the 'quantitative' degree of market exchange in antiquity. Thirdly, his framework for comparative history – differentiating classical markets rather than denying them – was of greater importance to him than the specifics of the volume of goods traded in particular times or places. Such questions, moreover, can only be settled by empirical archaeology, and estimates are likely to remain quite varied within a wide bandwidth of possibilities for the foreseeable future. It is therefore, in our view, more important to concentrate on what Polanyi himself saw as decisive: the criteria of supply and demand and motivation for interpreting the *function* of markets; how they operated as organs of 'society' as a whole. Indeed, some of the apparent contradictions in Polanyi's claims about markets in antiquity seem to rest on differentiating the motivations of agents rather than volume of exchange *per se*. The central question is often claimed to be whether individual agents sought to obtain *profit* in a more or less modern sense, that is, 'gain made in relationship to prices', in such markets as antiquity did possess. But for Polanyi, profit motivation was not sufficient to establish the 'modernist' case. One could on this view have capitalist activity, motivated by profit, without having capitalism as a system, and indeed without much market exchange at all. On this interpretation we can say that capitalist motivation was, for Polanyi, not in contradiction with his general embeddedness thesis as long as it did not become the general motivation of *society*. As Hann notes, much of Polanyi's historical work 'brings out the positive role played by markets in pre-industrial societies all the way back to ancient Athens, with the implication that well integrated societies will feature *combinations* of market institutions with other economic processes'.[36]

The classical Greek *polis* was important for Polanyi because, as he interpreted its political-economic structure, individual profit motivation and reciprocal relations could coexist with the overarching dominance of redistributive relations. In Greece, redistribution, reciprocity and exchange were integrated into an organic or embedded whole in the *polis'* orientation to provide for its self-preservation through ensuring the livelihood of its members. The state's motivation to ensure the survival of the *polis* as an organic collective was the determining factor, so that much of the economy was undertaken or regulated by the *polis* itself for this purpose: 'The transcending responsibility of the city for the livelihood of its citizens was a fundamental feature of Greek city economy. [...] not only the supply of necessary articles imported from abroad was organized under state direction, but the revenues of the citizens themselves were drawn in large part from the state.'[37] The democratic form of the *polis* strengthened this tendency by incorporating more market exchange, without fundamentally altering the general orientation of the *polis* as a collective agent.

At the heart of Polanyi's concept of embedded ancient markets is therefore, rather, the thesis that they were not subject to supply and demand 'laws', and that although individual profit orientation may have been common within their limited sphere, this orientation had no power to affect social 'regulation', beyond the 'sovereignty of individual wants'.[38] The latter was a matter of 'modes of integration': in other words of an *institutional order* presupposing a *societal integration* on the basis of a shared moral code. This understanding also shows why the emphasis on the empirical extent of market activity, private ownership, market-places and so forth in various societies of antiquity that has characterised much of the primitivism-modernism debate since Polanyi is to some extent misplaced. Although Polanyi certainly did not refrain from occasionally overly strong empirical claims about trade volume and property rights, his primary arguments in favour of his modified form of primitivism do not require such claims *per se*.

At bottom, Polanyi's understanding of ancient economies rests on a dual claim about a particular set of 'institutional foundations': the absence of supply and demand laws as an integrative principle, as an institution in the Northian sense (being a rule), and the presence of a particular kind of 'instituted process' that embeds economic life such that people do not aim at safeguarding their 'individual interest in the acquisition of material possessions but rather at ensuring social good will, social status, social assets'.[39] Such a society demands of the economic historian to take fundamentally *non-economic* elements to be necessary for explaining the functioning of the production and distribution of goods at the societal level, even where market exchange is common. In other words, it is a functionalist claim about the particular role of societal motivational and value-oriented institutions: 'the inclusion of the noneconomic is vital. For religion or government may be as important for the structure and functioning of the economy as monetary institutions or the availability of tools and machines ... The instituting of the economic process vests that process with unity and stability; it produces a structure with a definite function in society ... it centers interest on values, motives, and policy'.[40] Let us now examine each of these in order in the context of the debates on the ancient Greek economy, beginning with the 'law of supply and demand'.

ANCIENT GREEK MARKETS: A LAW OF SUPPLY AND DEMAND?

To evaluate Polanyi's claim about the absence of supply and demand laws as institutions that regulate market exchange in ancient Greece, we must first get a clearer sense of what he meant by the concept. Arguably, his most precise definition is: 'The supply-demand-price mechanism (which we popularly call the market), is a modern institution of specific structure, which is easy neither to establish nor to keep going'.[41] Rather strikingly, 'the market' and 'the supply-demand-price mechanism' are here equated, suggesting Polanyi was describing with reference to the supposed laws of microeconomics the more general social institution that James Carrier mentioned above, the Market. This may be seen as a case of synecdoche, where the model of the market foundational for neoclassical economics has come to stand for the Market as a whole, in its modern guise as a 'mode of integration' based on the universality of 'fictitious commodities' as such.

On this reading, the Market is an instituted process of its own, rather than being part of such a process. It is defined by the way 'the movement of goods is controlled by prices. ... The fact that market prices are "fluctuating or changing" and of a "competitive nature" is obviously decisive'. As Maucourant and Plociniczak note, two earlier statements of Polanyi give a clearer view of his approach to prices, which now appear to be one with the 'supply-demand mechanism': 'Acts of exchange on the personal level produce prices only if they occur under a system of price-making markets, an institutional set-up which is nowhere created by mere random acts of exchange,' but 'even price-making markets are integrative only if they are linked up in a system which tends to spread the effect of prices to markets other than those directly affected'.[42] The latter qualification seems important, for it moves Polanyi further from the denial of market exchange *per se* that he is often associated with. But insofar as it makes a weaker claim, it is also more difficult to test empirically. If we take the above statements together, it seems fair to say that the market as an independent instituted process requires for Polanyi two things: (i) the presence of price fluctuation as the primary driver of the distribution of goods in an ongoing market exchange relation ('fluctuating or changing'), and, (ii) that such a relation be wide in scope, not limited to one or two specific kinds of trade ('linked up in a system').

For the classical period, Polanyi posits a sharp distinction between two types of trade. One was the market trade at the *agora*, a municipal market economy. It was 'purely internal to the polis',[43] was heavily regulated, with 'rigid boundaries; specifications of who may and who may not trade, and with whom; official market inspectors as well as municipal spies; commodities sold directly by the peasant either for money or in barter'.[44] The democratic *polis* determined currency rates, market access, supply and, to a considerable extent, prices.[45] Because it 'depended entirely on the postulate of the iron discipline' of the *polis*, the market was 'organically incapable' of transcending its territorial limitations.[46] 'Local trade – and no other trade – was market trade.' The other type was inter-*polis* trade. Whereas the *agora* evolved internally, it 'was a foreigner's show', and whereas market exchange throve in the *agora,* there was no significant market organisation outside the *polis*. Inter-*polis* trade exhibited only marginal 'market elements' – it was largely administered, and in part organised, on traditional gift-exchange lines. From at the latest Aristotle's time onwards, however, a supply-demand regulated market *did* come to exist. Two such markets, in fact: the grain trade at the 'international' – or rather, inter-*polis* – level, and the slave trade at Delos. But even so, Polanyi seems to argue, it was limited to those two markets initially. Only after the death of Alexander the Great did this phenomenon come to disembed itself from the *polis* and its self-regulation. And even then, Polanyi remained ambiguous about its implications, emphasising the tendency to 'price uniformity in the entire area' resulting from a 'free' market in grain in this period which was, however, orchestrated by a bureaucratic centralist state: Ptolemaic Egypt.[47]

Given these considerations, how might we evaluate Polanyi's claim that classical Greek markets (and possibly Hellenistic ones) were not integrated by a supply-demand-price mechanism? While there remains considerable disagreement about the interpretation of the evidence, some relevant observations from recent economic historical work can be made. Within local market settings, when we look at profit and exchange between city and countryside in the Athenian *polis*, for example, the weight of evidence indicates a good deal of direct market exchange and high levels of profit on agricultural production and sale to the city, sustained by strongly monetised local land markets. Within these markets price responsiveness appears to have been considerable, not least because of ongoing high demands for cash money on the part of the landowners for taxes and liturgic purposes.⁴⁸ In short, there existed a rather livelier trade in land and labour than Polanyi's model suggests. The distinction he drew, however, between local and inter-*polis* trade has stood the test of time quite well. 'The physical distinction between *emporia* and *agorai*,' Sitta von Reden and Dominic Rathbone observe, 'is a direct manifestation of commercial exchange taking place at two levels between Greek cities: firstly at the local level, largely regulated by free supply-and-demand mechanisms, and secondly a connection with the external world, which was far more controlled by political interference, incentive structures created by public institutions, and direct legislation. These two markets ... were not fully related to each other, and their interdependent price formation was frequently controlled by administrative regulation'.⁴⁹

In the production and distribution of the key commodity, grain, much recent evidence points to a substantial role of non-market allocation systems. It was common for benefactors to provide grain to the general population, sometimes by intervening in existing markets at prices below the going rate. This was often done under considerable political and civic pressure, especially in times of need, and in exchange for public approbation in the form of inscriptions, statues and the like. But most economic historians would not see this as evidence one way or the other for the 'embeddedness' of markets in the stronger sense suggested by Polanyi: even in our own market society, charity and public provision are by no means not unheard of. More salient is to find measures of market integration and of the responsiveness of prices to shocks in supply or demand. Usually, evidence of price uniformity across market-places, and of price fluctuations within markets in response to external shocks, can be seen as evidence of market integration and (therefore) performance in the 'modernist' sense, as has been studied in the case of grain markets throughout history.⁵⁰

At least for grain, according to some studies, prices were set within an integrated market across a broad region, but others contend that 'local markets set prices with relatively little integration between *poleis* even at relatively short distances'.⁵¹ In this regard, the Greek case looks superficially good for Polanyi's argument, but much hinges on data that are either absent or difficult to interpret in a quantitative way. Extant prices, von Reden and Rathbone note, 'cannot tell us much about the nature of markets and price formation in the Classical and Hellenistic world'. Even so, they do make several general observations. One concerns the grain trade in classical and Hellenistic Greece. There existed 'strong notions of a "normal price" for grain which were different in different economic zones and under different economic circumstances'. Such region-wide stability of price expectations over generations and even centuries, they add, 'suggests a large degree of institutional pressure and little impact of changing economic trends and market forces'. During periods of shortage, sharp deviations from normal price levels were common, both within and between regions, but the distribution of grain during such periods was handled as 'a social rather than an economic problem'.[52]

This position finds considerable support among ancient historians. The Hellenistic market, in the view of Gary Reger, 'was probably only partially, imperfectly, and transitorily integrated – it linked local markets which exercised mutual affects on each other, but acted only slowly, and sometimes not at all, to correct price fluctuations', and public entities 'sought to control prices by non-market intervention'.[53] From some parts, for example Hellenistic Babylonia, documented price series are detailed enough for the conclusion to be drawn that the integration of its food market with the rest of the Seleucid realm was 'poor'.[54] In an influential article on price development on Delos, Reger argues strongly against the idea of price responsiveness to general economic trends, identifying no meaningful correlation between price behaviour in one good as compared to another within the same market-place and over the same time period. For him, this argues – in fact against Polanyi's comparatively modernist take on Delian markets – that 'this strongly suggests that any explanation for a particular individual price history must be sought in the particularities of that good, and not in a general appeal to a common price-setting market for imported goods'.[55] For Léopold Migeotte, similarly, the modernist image of a 'single vast market serving the whole Mediterranean or even the entire ancient world, a market … in which prices for the same products would be more or less the same everywhere and would all fluctuate together' has been conclusively refuted. The bulk of production was consumed locally, either directly or via local markets; there existed 'a multitude of regional markets, all with their own networks and their own prices, [and] even though a labor market was created from time to time, chiefly by public enterprises, the Greek world as a whole never knew of such a thing'.[56] Nor was this pattern altered by Rome's conquest of the eastern Mediterranean. The grain market in the Roman Empire, according to Paul Erdkamp's authoritative study, 'seems largely to have operated within restricted, sometimes isolated, regions'.[57]

On balance, these studies on market integration and price fluctuation lend some credence to a Polanyian primitivist position. However, market integration can be assessed in different ways, and the picture is rather different if one sees it as measurable by evidence of market volume, a wide range of commodified goods and markets for land and labour. Much depends therefore on the definition of market integration. Different types of evidence can be adduced to support or oppose the existence of a supply-demand mechanism according to Polanyi's criteria. Since his criteria are rather imprecise and contextual, they cannot easily be resolved for the ancient Greek case given the lack of quantitative evidence on the sources of price formation and fluctuation. In effect, we are dealing with different types of evidence because we are dealing with different kinds of models, and the validity of Polanyi's approach to the Greek case, and indeed to pre-modern economic history in general, depends a good deal on which model is being contested.

We would distinguish three different approaches to markets in economic history that are relevant to Polanyi's position. Two are forms of 'modernism': the argument based on quantitative measures of market integration, which have been applied particularly notably to the Roman case,[58] and the argument based on the extent of commodification of land and labour and the volume of exchange. The third form, however, has to do with Polanyi's substantivist claims in which the embeddedness of the economy is contrasted not with modernism but with *formalism* (Polanyi's term for social-scientific methodologies that assume the basic unit of analysis to be rational autonomous individual utility maximisers operating in a condition of scarcity, to be apprehended using techniques of marginalist economics). This is not a matter of the interpretation of empirical evidence *per se*, but of a methodological question: the application of contending economic theories. The formalist perspective sees Polanyi's arguments as fundamentally mistaken, not because of this or that degree of price responsiveness, but because the method of economics applies to any situation in which opportunity costs exist, and therefore to any kind of society subject to scarcity of means or competition between ends. Supply and demand is in this sense inescapable, as is 'the Market' in the abstract, whatever the specifics of market-places, trade or money may be. From the formalist viewpoint, Polanyi can't see the wood for the trees. As one recent critic of his approach puts it, the market in economic theory is 'nothing more than the abstract intersection of supply and demand for scarce goods and services. Economics is relevant wherever you cannot have your cake and also eat it'.[59]

Of course, Polanyi was well aware of this line of reasoning, which he dubbed the 'economistic fallacy', and wrote extensively against it. His core arguments against it are twofold: he denied that scarcity in this sense existed in the embedded economies in question, and he challenged the model of rationality that this approach presupposes, questioning whether it really is universally applicable. Against scarcity, he argued that the term could only meaningfully describe situations in which there was a fundamental insufficiency of goods from the point of view of psychological needs, which he rejected as irrelevant to the 'good life' of much of pre-modern life. Insofar, moreover, as goods were not generally commensurable via money prices, and insofar as individuals did not exercise meaningful individual choice over conventionally given standards of living or non-market distribution systems, the concept was all the more inapplicable.[60] He also dismissed the rationality assumption of the individual utility maximiser as inapplicable to societies where embeddedness of economic behaviour was sufficiently strong that self-preserving and redistributive motivations predominated at the societal level. We have seen a practical example of such a view in Polanyi's interpretation of the Greek *polis*.

In this contest of economic models, the evidence of market exchange and price movements possesses little traction. What matters is, rather, a kind of anthropological difference in perspective, a different world-view regarding the nature of human behaviour. Polanyi's substantivist perspective, as opposed to the formalist, has perhaps for this reason from the very beginning been influential in economic anthropology, and controversial, too – indeed, the height of the controversy has been called a golden age for economic anthropology. Neither side is likely to find empirical evidence to contradict its perspective. Even so, Polanyi recognised this inescapable anthropological dimension perhaps more clearly than the formalists did, at least inasmuch as he saw his perspective as one in need of anthropological substantiation where the latter usually do not. As discussed below, that Polanyi's substantivist research programme drew on anthropological theory rather than conventional methodology in economics gave him a distinct advantage in putting flesh on the otherwise rather bare bones of his institutionalist analysis. But precisely because anthropology is concerned with developing different approaches to human nature than those trained in economics are used to, this aspect of Polanyi's vision has not found much support even among sympathetic economic historians.

In view of this impasse, more and more scholars have sought to find a way 'beyond' the primitivism-modernism and especially the substantivism-formalism debate. Many now hold that if we are to understand historical differentiation between economies over time we must find a way of reconciling the best insights of both sides. Here, an important development has been the rise of the New Institutional Economics and its influence on the writing of economic history, exemplified by the New Institutionalist Economic History (NIEH) of Douglass North and colleagues. Its emergence was provoked in part by Polanyi's own emphasis on the *institutional structure* that defines the nature and degree of 'embeddedness' of markets, money and trade in a particular historical economy. Equally, the NIEH has gained considerable influence within economic history, and has served to moderate and reformulate many of the old 'formalist' certainties. It seems that the New Institutionalist approach offers a means of overcoming the impasse. But does it?

THE MODERNITY OF ANCIENT ATHENS:
A NEW INSTITUTIONALIST APPROACH

Much of the reception of Polanyi's claims about ancient economic history has been hostile or indifferent, although a significant number, if a minority, of scholars have seen merit in its fundamentals.[61] However, the most common view seems to be that the debates between formalists and sub-stantivists, and primitivists and modernists, were altogether mistaken, and that a contemporary analysis is better served by avoiding such dichotomies altogether. Instead of the Polanyian schema of modes of integration, or the straightforward interpretation of Greek or Roman economies as early forms of capitalist market economy, we now have a toolset that allows for an intermediate synthesis: the economic and political analysis of institutional variation.

A major impetus behind this New Institutionalist turn is, it seems, its promise of transcendence of the primitivism-modernism debate by offering a way to apply mainstream economic theory without abandoning the relevance for historical explanation of the specificities of norms, laws and 'culture' in a broad sense. Several major studies of the ancient Greek economy are founded on the premise that 'the inspiration of the neo-institutional economists allows us to go beyond the old debates between primitivists and modernists or substantivists and formalists'.[62] Within economic anthropology itself, New Institutionalism has also been presented as a way of avoiding the perceived dead ends of substantivism.[63]

The promise of the New Institutionalism to achieve this aim is at first sight considerable, as a discussion of North's NIEH may clarify. With well-defined concepts of institutions as 'rules of the game' combined with a boundedly rational choice framework borrowed from the pioneering work of Herbert Simon, it allows for a framework of interpretation that unites the strengths of economists' model-building with the flexibility that comes with permitting institutional variation as the independent variable within those models.[64] In this way, otherwise potentially intractable problems of interpretation, caused by the apparent contrast between the 'regulation' of society by religion, culture, law and state on the one hand, and the self-regarding motives of gain in the market-place on the other hand, can be avoided. Rather than resorting to potentially vague claims about 'integration' or 'embeddedness', the NIEH applies the same method-ological principles of rationality and incentives regardless of institutional specifics. Those specifics can then be defined as the independent variables according to two measures: the level of transaction costs and the stability and incentive-enhancing structure of property rights (or their absence). Finally, states and civil societies 'getting the institutions right' (or not) becomes the main mode of economic historical explanation.

In a peculiar way, it accepts the primitivists' emphasis on the qualitative difference between ancient economies and modern ones, but explains this in different terms: as the result of bad institutions and/or high transaction costs constraining what might otherwise have been flourishing economies. For the primitivists these – drastic institutional variation and limited markets – are the proofs of difference, something that calls for different theoretical models of such economies. But in this approach they are reinterpreted through a 'modernist' lens. Such institutional constraints act at best merely as substitutes, imposed by dire necessity, for the trappings of our modern market societies, and at worst are a sign of the folly of restricting the freedom of the entrepreneurial individual.

This combination of modelling flexibility at the level of historical specifics combined with the precision (not to say prestige) of conventional economic microfoundations is understandably appealing. In its Northian form, the New Institutionalism seems to offer a middle way between the potential vagueness of Polanyian models of embeddedness and the stark reductionism of rational efficiency models of markets and institutions, with their neglect of historical specifics and their 'Panglossian' propensities. In view of this potential, it has become something of a commonplace to reflect back on the primitivism-modernism debate as a chapter that is now closed. In recent works one finds repeatedly the observation that the debate was 'sterile', debased by strawmanning, and that it failed to recognise common ground in the analysis of historically specific institutions within a larger (mainstream) economic framework focusing on property rights and economic growth.[65]

Is this attitude justified? To a degree. With his emphasis on institutional integration as one of the two criteria of embeddedness, Polanyi himself certainly opened the door to the application of institutional economic theory to studying what precisely that embeddedness might consist of, what its rules were, and how these affected familiar economic variables like prices, growth, living standards and trade volume. Moreover, in so doing such an approach can be seen as giving flesh to the otherwise rather spectral concept of embeddedness. At the very least, the NIEH provides tools that allow economic historical arguments about antiquity to take place with more precision and 'operationalisability' than Polanyi's general claims about embeddedness. While we are sceptical of the claim that general theories about the effect of institutions or transaction costs are really more refutable than rival approaches, the possibility of estimating transaction costs gives another empirical result to stimulate more accurate models.

That said, there are reasons – empirical and theoretical – to doubt whether New Institutionalist approaches such as the NIEH will actually succeed in putting the primitivism-modernism debate to bed. On the empirical side, consider by way of example the work on the ancient

Athenian economy of the new institutionalist economist Anastassios Karayiannis and his colleagues George Bitros and Aristides Hatzis. Classical Athens, in their optic, provided history with the original model of an institutional arrangement conducive to creating a progressive market society. Particularly in the fifth century, a robust legal system with clearly instituted property rights produced confidence in the enforcement of contracts and security of transactions, as well as a strong sense of economic justice. Crucial, too, was 'the importance of morality and social norms', including individualism, 'reciprocity, the value of reputation and the wide acceptance of business ethics … as transaction cost-saving devices'. The upshot was 'a full-fledged free market society', in which 'market-driven production and distribution of goods and services secured enough surpluses of mining and manufacturing goods to exchange for the required imports of grain', and which suffered 'economic problems similar to market societies of today'.[66] Karayiannis and Bitros illuminate the case by comparing Athens with its main rival, Sparta, in 490–338 BC. Sparta's economy was based on brutal exploitation of the helots, and its institutional order suppressed 'the natural urging of human beings to amass wealth in the form of fixed and personal property assets'. Its road to expansion lay therefore through conquest. In contrast, Athens was an embryonic capitalist economy in which 'labor was the source of private property and accumulation of wealth'. Its citizens 'were asked to be industrious'; to achieve growth they looked above all to their own labour. While Sparta stagnated, Athens 'progressed economically', thanks to its 'homogeneity' and above all to its 'great institutions of private property, democracy, and free markets'. Enjoyment of those magnificent institutions was denied to slaves; and slavery, they tentatively concede, 'may reflect badly on Athens, if looked through the lenses of present day views'. But the Athenian policy regime, they add in mitigation, was nonetheless meritocratic: it permitted 'ample leeway for the economic and social advancement of slaves'.[67]

Karayiannis' studies exhibit new institutionalist methodology being put to work not in transcending but in recapitulating a modernist reading of ancient Greece – and a cliché-ridden one at that. If their vulgarity cannot be laid at the door of the New Institutionalism as a whole,[68] the modernist bias can. For example, while the NIEH affected to address 'Polanyi's challenge', and has taken aspects of it in creative directions, it has also pursued a reinvention of the economistic fallacies against which Polanyi had inveighed. Specifically, it ignores Polanyi's critique of the transhistorical application of rationality assumptions based on modern market society. Despite its ambitions to extend the scope of explanation to the domain of the social and institutional framework in which economic phenomena are embedded, the NIEH leans strongly on a theoretical approach derived from what Polanyi would have called 'formalist' economic theory. This does not mean that the NIEH relies on a rational-choice or efficiency approach to institutional analysis. Rather, there is a conceptual tension in its concept of rationality. On one hand we have the entrepreneurial, self-regarding individual, however boundedly rational, who pursues her own interests and seeks to obtain rents and even change institutions accordingly. On the other, there is the level of structural constraints, such as collective institutions and the transaction costs that result from them. These are not assumed to emerge from self-regarding reason, but may serve collective cooperation or even simply derive from 'irrational' beliefs. How a more traditional microeconomic rationality is to be reconciled with the importance of norms and beliefs at the societal level is never quite explained, despite attempts to square the circle by social contract theory or evolutionary reasoning. As discussed below, the NIEH's apparent strength – its flexibility of application to in principle any institutional economic order – is therefore also its weakness. If anything can be explained as a constraint on individual action, what remains of the parsimony and mathematical applicability of traditional models of economic rationality? If anything goes, indeterminacy looms. That this should be so can be explained by looking at the dual origins of the NIEH approach.

HAS THE NEW INSTITUTIONALISM RENDERED POLANYI'S INTERVENTION OBSOLETE?

The modernist interpretation of the economies of antiquity was first developed in the late nineteenth century. It was no coincidence that the same historical moment witnessed the rise of marginalist economics and the sociology of Herbert Spencer.[69] Whereas for classical political economists such as Smith, historically specific institutional factors were germane to the analysis of any particular economy, for marginalism these can be bracketed out of consideration: all effective social organisations are merely disguised versions of the 'ur-market', expressing the imputed behaviour of the rational individual.[70] As to Spencer, in his polemical simplification of the Smithian concept of spontaneous order, the policy regime that Smith opposed, mercantilism, is bundled together with all pre-commercial stages of society, in opposition to commercial (in his lexicon 'industrial') society. Primitive 'militant' societies are characterised by command and control, with governments or chieftains calling the shots; the result is economic backwardness, social tension and international conflict. In industrial society, by contrast, individuals work for one another, motivated by a blend of egotism and sympathy.[71] The central mechanism that enables this felicitous outcome is the market. (A 'substantially-independent co-ordinating agency', in Spencer's words.)[72] It embodies the principle of evolutionary spontaneous order, and the civilisational consequence is peace, prosperity and progress. Spencer's dichotomy was vulgarised further by Hayek (whose Manichean worldview of *cosmos* or as *taxis*; spontaneous and planned orders, is discussed in Chapter 5) before finding its way to the NIEH, albeit in refined forms, for example as North's dichotomy of 'natural states' and 'open access orders'. The difference between these, says North, is that the former are institutionally inflexible and limit competition in the 'personal' interests of dominant individuals or elites, whereas the latter boast 'adaptive efficiency' and harness competition for good.[73]

The NIEH can be said to rest on two foundations. Firstly there is the institutionalist approach of Smith, which takes the natural entrepreneurial orientation of the individual as its point of departure, but seeks to understand the institutional structure of each historical stage of the economy and how it might have led to 'commercial society'. Smith was no modernist. He was aware that what he called 'the stage of commerce' was of recent provenance, and that earlier social formations had been quite different in character. But he did supply modernism with vital ingredients: the axiom that the marketing mentality comes naturally to human beings, the concept of spontaneous order (the invisible hand), and a Whiggish philosophy of progress toward commercial society. The other is the Spencer-Hayek lineage of the evolution of spontaneous order, that is, how market exchange makes order – and with it the desirable economic outcomes of the free market – possible where otherwise there would be chaos.

Joined together, these traditions entail several interconnected assumptions: the economic is ultimately always about (monetary) exchange; there are no fundamental domains of incommensurability between different realms of economic activity; the self-regarding actions of individuals in exchange are the (unintended) basis of human cooperation and thereby of social life itself; only by letting exchange operate freely can such cooperation lead to economic success; and all societies can be measured according to the extent to which their institutional framework enables 'capturing the gains from trade'. Institutions themselves are understood as the rules and norms of 'the game'. Institutions, in turn, 'structure incentives in *human exchange, whether political, social, or economic*'.[74] This short sentence reveals the profound degree to which formalist analysis is inherent to the NIEH project: institutions structure incentives not just in the economic sphere proper, but in all other spheres as well, insofar as these are concerned with 'human exchange'.[75] In short, for the NIEH the unfolding of efficient markets and their potential is both premise and *explanandum* of economic history. The market itself is rarely 'institutionalised': what is studied is the effect of institutions as an independent variable on the performance of 'the market' as a dependent variable.

With regard to the argument in this chapter, the new institutionalism exhibits two basic shortcomings. One is that it tends to posit the market as a natural institutional arrangement. This tendency is manifested rhetorically and conceptually. New Institutionalist theorists are prone to using market vocabulary. For example, in their strategic interaction with existing institutional orders, individuals are for North 'entrepreneurs', who change institutions 'at the margins' – even when those institutions are informal and involve norms, conventions and culture. Politics is spoken of throughout as the operation of a 'political market'.[76] This use of language is expressive of a deeper conceptual problem. Oliver Williamson's work, Daniel Ankarloo and Giulio Palermo observe, 'depicts micro-economically rational agents selecting, voluntarily through conscious choice, markets over hierarchy, capitalism over feudalism, wage labour over serfdom, by calculating their respective efficiency. ... But there is a tension in this account of both rational choice and selection arguments of efficiency. If markets are assumed to exist prior to selection, nobody historically could have chosen them for their efficiency (i.e., the market cannot be explained from an efficiency point of view). Alternatively, if markets are seen as consciously chosen, markets cannot be seen as the unintended, "spontaneous" result of evolution, of a societal "natural selection"'.[77] Or consider North's attempt to meet what he called 'The Challenge of Karl Polanyi' by showing that New Institutional Economics plus traditional choice theory can explain non-market institutions. In the process he defines 'families, firms, guilds, manors, trade unions, cooperatives' as 'substitutes for price-making markets'. The term 'substitutes', Francesco Boldizzoni points out, is revealing. It

> is not neutral and indeed here does not mean 'alternatives'. Substitutes expresses the idea that the natural allocation system is the market, and the others are surrogates for it, intervening when conditions are imperfect and unfavorable. In other words, according to North, it is not the emergence of the market system that requires explanation, but why other institutions 'allocate resources in place of markets.' This is an extraordinary starting point. First the market is said to be the exception, and then it is taken as a yardstick.[78]

To put the point polemically, the story begins with abstract markets and ends with abstract markets, with institutions in between. In the NIEH model, 'the social' is reduced to a set of institutions conceived as rules, which are changed according to marginalist notions of individual optimisation and which are inherited at societal level in a quasi-evolutionary pattern of path dependence. At the micro-level, the NIEH interprets institutions (including beliefs, motives and norms) simply as additional constraints on individual optimisation, while simultaneously rejecting the relevance of optimising and equilibrium models at the macro-level. At the macro-level, in turn, the reduction of 'the social' to rule-like institutions leads to what Ankarloo has called an 'as-if market' view of history: institutions are essentially substitutes for, or complements to, the market-like entrepreneurial rationality of individuals; through their impact on the costs of transaction and production, they account for differential 'economic (or societal) performance'. (Note that 'economic performance' and 'societal performance' are understood as essentially synonymous.)

In other words, as Ankarloo and Palermo put it, New Institutionalist theory tends to transform the market, without an evident analytical justification, 'from a historically defined institution into a universal category'.[79] This is not because its institutionalism, its concern for embeddedness, is indistinguishable from the neoclassical approach in the strict sense. It is rather because New Institutionalist authors are above all else keen to preserve within their framework the centrality of the market to understanding human sociality. They too frequently assume from the get-go, as Ankarloo points out, that the strategic structure of any artifactual framework will take the form of an abstract market and that beliefs and preferences interact with institutions (rules) only within this market-like structure.[80] Yet the emergence of such abstract markets, with the self-regarding behaviour that characterises their structure and with the beliefs that determine whether this kind of allocation system or another is the form taken by 'the economic', is what needs to be explained in the first place. Rather than seeing market exchange as an instituted process embedded in a larger social whole, and therefore in need of explanation, New Institutionalism often elides this distinction, construing institutions and their political-cultural formation as the outcome of a kind of spontaneous social contract of incipient market exchange.[81]

The NIEH's second shortcoming is that, in its efficiency approach to institutional formation, it holds that institutional orders are 'chosen' according to their properties of minimising transaction costs given incentive structures. While this may be relevant for the study of firms versus private contracting in capitalist society, it does not shed much light on the historical formation of institutions. In North's attempt to answer 'Polanyi's challenge' this efficiency approach is dropped. But he substitutes for this an account of how institutions structure incentives and how this permits institutional change (or not) as essentially analogous to the prisoner's dilemma in game theory, complemented with some basic cognitive science to emphasise the importance of 'beliefs' and 'mental models' as constraints on rationality and sources of imperfect information.[82]

This produces two major weaknesses for economic-historical purposes. For one thing, the concern for beliefs and mental models comes as an *ad hoc* complement to the basic microeconomic framework, and therefore only appears as arbitrary constraints on the operation of rational choice, rather than as a serious consideration of motives, preferences, and beliefs in a particular historical society. It misses the point of Polanyi's critique of the 'economistic fallacy', or at least fails to engage with this broader question about the economic language of values, choices and preferences and how they might be recontextualised.[83] For another, both conventional game theory and the incorporation of all these bounds on rational choice as additional constraints share one major problem: indeterminacy. This is perhaps the greatest weakness of the 'institutional turn' in economic history, and it stems from the flaws of the economic theory on which it draws. The advantage of rational choice economics, and the main reason for using it despite its well-understood shortcomings, is that it gives a non-psychological, parsimonious and determinate result. The more one introduces *ad hoc* modifications, the less likely it is to lead any determinate outcome. If no particular model of rationality is assumed, social institutions could affect individual choice and economic behaviour in highly varied ways, and since institutions are themselves social phenomena in need of explanation, the approach risks extreme indeterminacy. If virtually anything can give rise to a particular institutional order, and from a particular institutional order no particular economic behaviour can be assumed, nothing is actually explained by reference to institutions. It becomes a word no clearer than 'embeddedness', and the institutionalist turn threatens to reduce to not much more than the cliché that institutions and history matter. If, however, it is assumed that individuals behave essentially according to rational choice models of self-serving behaviour, then reference to transaction costs, property rights and other constraints becomes more meaningful. This is the path taken by the NIEH authors. But they do so at the cost of returning us to the modernist-formalist position from which the debate began. 'Bringing in' institutions does not enable the primitivism-modernism controversy to be overcome; at least not without a good deal of careful thought about the methodology employed. This indeterminacy is already present in Douglass North's own work.[84] Yet it is generally given little attention in the work of most ancient economic historians, who are happy to simply take NIEH theory on board to avoid the 'sterility' of the primitivism-modernism debate.

CONCLUSION

Polanyi's own solution to this problem was to deny the applicability of conventional models of rationality to economic behaviour in antiquity, and to rely largely on *sui generis* references to anthropological concepts of motivation. Most importantly, he was attached to the notion that meaningful institutional 'choice' operated not at the level of individuals or even the state *per se*, but at the level of a community as a whole. For him, the Greek *polis* was a perfect example of this principle, with its combination of state redistribution and market exchange, both embedded in a larger regulation or integration on the basis of the norms of citizenship, reciprocity and community survival. Polanyi's observations on classical Greece are for that reason a cornerstone for his larger comparative project of forms of pre-modern economic integration, in the course of which he revolutionised the primitivism-modernism controversy.

While both primitivist and modernist readings have their avowed partisans, there appears to be an emerging consensus that the debate has run its course. Better quantification, improved statistical techniques, and advances in archaeology play a role in this, but a more important cause is the conviction that the economic theory of institutional variation can unite the best insights of substantivism with the more 'scientific' and widely respected methods of economics. This line of thinking suggests that Polanyi's synthesis between economic anthropology and the primitivist approaches of 'old' institutionalism is out of date, and that the future of economic studies of ancient Greece rests primarily with applying the methods of (for example) the NIEH. Seeking to explain historical specificities by institutional variation and its effects on property rights, market performance and transaction costs, often summarised under the slogan that 'institutions matter', has supplanted the two Polanyian trinities: the modes of integration and the distinctions between markets, money and trade.

Yet it seems to us that the debates Polanyi was engaged in are not so easily avoided. Institutional variation is too often merely a redescription of the problem that does not provide a determinate analytical framework for explaining precisely how institutions affect economic behaviour. Moreover, the market often ends up being taken for granted, so that institutions are no more than *ad hoc*, exogenously given *constraints* within a model not fundamentally different from our understanding of market exchange in the modern world. In James Carrier's terms, we could say an overreliance on New Institutionalism threatens to miss Polanyi's point: that one must distinguish *a* market from *the* Market. If so, the institutionalist approach is really a means of bringing the modernist viewpoint in the debate in through the back door, and this would suggest that the debate between modernists and primitivists is not so dead as has been claimed. Of course, the NIEH provides a far richer theoretico-historical argument than the 'formalism' of neoclassical economics against which Polanyi polemicised, but at the cost of leaving wide open the question of how individual choice relates to allocation systems at the macro-level.

Polanyi's embeddedness approach does not necessarily provide more precise answers to these questions. His empirical claims about the economy of ancient Greece are still heavily contested. As the debate currently stands, he appears to have been more right than he thought about the larger picture, and yet frequently wrong about the specifics of market trade in classical and Hellenistic Greece. His debates with formalists were severely weakened by his unwillingness (or inability) to critique their claims to have provided a valid method for understanding market societies. As has been widely noted, this left his analysis of the workings of the modern economy curiously disembodied, and lacking in attention to relations of power and exploitation. However, his substantivist 'challenge' remains. Polanyi recognised the need to bring anthropology back into the study of economic history if the analysis of institutional variation was ever to be adequately theoretically grounded. He consciously used the insights of anthropologists into the relations between agency and structure, not content to leave it to the 'formalism' of the economists' choice theory. If the New Institutionalist turn has entailed an acknowledgement that pre-modern economic systems were in some qualitatively important sense different from our own, this could be read as a meaningful nod to Polanyi's substantivist critique. But the methodological shortcomings and indeterminacy of the NIEH approach shows that Polanyi's challenge requires more than this toolset to be fully answered. From that viewpoint, one might say that the reports of Polanyi's death have been exaggerated.

Notes

INTRODUCTION

1. Martin Wolf (2016) 'Britain's Friends Are Right to Fear Brexit', *Financial Times*, 20 April.
2. Anne Applebaum (2016) 'Is This the End of the West as We Know It?', *Washington Post*, 4 March.
3. 'The Strangest Tory Ever Sold', *Economist,* April 1998, www.economist.com/node/124878
4. Paul Mason (2015) 'Enter Europe's New Populist Left Movement', http://blogs.channel4.com/paul-mason-blog/enter-europes-populist-left-movement/2835
5. Robert Brenner (1985) 'The Paradox of Social Democracy', in Mike Davis, Fred Pfeil and Michael Sprinker, eds., *The Year Left: An American Socialist Yearbook,* Verso.
6. Eric Hobsbawm (1984) *Worlds of Labour: Further Studies in the History of Labour,* Weidenfeld and Nicolson, p. 260.
7. Tariq Ali (2015) 'The New World Disorder', *London Review of Books*, 9 April.
8. Kari Polanyi-Levitt (1994) 'Karl Polanyi as Socialist', in Kenneth McRobbie, ed., *Humanity Society and Commitment: On Karl Polanyi,* Black Rose, p. 115.
9. Tim Stroshane (1997) 'The Second Contradiction of Capitalism and Karl Polanyi's The Great Transformation', *Capitalism, Nature, Socialism*, 8(3), p. 107.
10. This section is derived in part from an article published in *New Political Economy* in 2010, available at www.tandfonline.com/10.1080/13563460903290920
11. Iván Szelényi (1991) 'Karl Polanyi and the Theory of a Socialist Mixed Economy', in Marguerite Mendell and Daniel Salée, eds, *The Legacy of Karl Polanyi; Market, State and Society at the End of the Twentieth Century,* Macmillan.
12. Sylvia Walby (2015) *Crisis,* Polity, pp. 24-32.
13. Andrew Schrank and Josh Whitford (2009) 'Industrial Policy in the United States: A Neo-Polanyian Interpretation', *Politics & Society*, 37(4) p.522.
14. Jürgen Habermas (2001) *The Post-national Constellation,* Polity, p. 85.
15. Maurice Glasman (2014) contribution at 'The Power of Market Fundamentalism' seminar, House of Lords, July.
16. Karl Polanyi Archive (hereafter KPA) KPA-55-2, Ilona Duczynska (1965) to George Dalton, 4 April.
17. Kari Polanyi-Levitt, interview, Montreal, 23 June 2006.
18. Timothy David Clark (2014) 'Reclaiming Karl Polanyi, Socialist Intellectual', *Studies in Political Economy,* 94(1), pp. 61–84.
19. Cf. Claus Offe (1984) *Contradictions of the Welfare State,* Hutchinson.
20. Hannes Lacher (1999) 'Embedded Liberalism, Disembedded Markets: Reconceptualising the *Pax Americana*', *New Political Economy*, 4(3), pp. 343–60.
21. Jan Drahokoupil (2004) 'Re-Inventing Karl Polanyi: On the Contradictory Interpretations of Social Protectionism', *Czech Sociological Review*, 40(6), p. 845.
22. For elaboration, see Gareth Dale and Nadine El-Enany (2013) 'The Limits of Social Europe: EU Law and the Ordo-liberal Agenda', *German Law Journal,* 14(5), pp. 613–50.

23. See also Gareth Dale (2010) *Karl Polanyi: The Limits of the Market*, Polity, pp. 12–13, 101–02; Johanna Bockman (2011) *Markets in the Name of Socialism: The Left-Wing Origins of Neoliberalism*, Stanford University Press.

24. Karl Polanyi (2001) *The Great Transformation: The Political and Economic Origins of Our Time*, Beacon Press, pp. 87, 257.

25. KPA-9-3, Karl Polanyi (1934–46) Notes on Lippmann.

26. Polanyi, *The Great Transformation*, pp. 192, 223.

27. Rod Alence (2001) 'Colonial Government, Social Conflict and State Involvement in Africa's Open Economies: The Origins of the Ghana Cocoa Marketing Board, 1939–46', *Journal of African History*, 42(3), p. 408.

28. Tracy Williams (2009) 'An African Success Story: Ghana's Cocoa Marketing System', IDS Working Paper 318.

29. KPA-15-4, Karl Polanyi, 'The Shock Absorbing Function of Autonomous Central Banking under the Postulate of Stable Exchanges'.

30. Just as 'commodityness' is not solely a matter of alienability and price responsiveness, so commodification is not a simple reflex of market expansion. It also depends on, and is driven forward by, an array of other social institutions, such as factories, commercial enterprises and state bureaucracies – as Martha Lampland has shown with respect to Soviet-era Hungary, and Jason Moore with respect to humanity's interaction with the natural environment. Martha Lampland (1995) *The Object of Labor: Commodification in Socialist Hungary*, University of Chicago Press; Jason Moore (2014) *Capitalism in the Web of Life: Ecology and the Accumulation of Capital*, Verso.

31. Rhoda Halperin (1988) *Economies across Cultures: Towards a Comparative Science of the Economy*, Macmillan, p. 30.

32. KPA-16-2, Karl Polanyi (1945–46) 'Europe Today and Tomorrow'; KPA-8-7, Karl Polanyi (1934–46) 'The Rise and Decline of Market Economy'. For discussion, Dale, *Karl Polanyi*, Chapter 2; KPA-15-4, Karl Polanyi (1936–40), Morley lectures; KPA-31-10 (n.d.) 'The Trend Towards an Integrated Society'.

33. It is, according to some scholars, 'the dominant question' in political thought today. Jennifer Schuessler (2013) 'In History Departments, It's Up with Capitalism', *New York Times,* 6 April.

34. Karl Polanyi (2016) 'Civil War', in Gareth Dale, ed., *Karl Polanyi: The Hungarian Writings,* Manchester University Press.

35. KPA-18-8, Karl Polanyi (early 1940s) 'The Fascist Virus'.

36. Polanyi, *The Great Transformation*, p. 259.

37. Douglass North (1977) 'Markets and Other Allocation Systems in History: The Challenge of Karl Polanyi', *Journal of European Economic History*, 6(3), pp. 703–16.

CHAPTER 1

1. This chapter is based upon Gareth Dale (2011) 'Positivism and "Functional Theory" in the Thought of Karl Polanyi, 1907–1922', *Sociology Compass*, 5(2), pp. 149–64.

2. Tibor Frank (2007) 'The Social Construction of Hungarian Genius (1867–1930)', www.franktibor.hu/index.html?hu_uj_kozl.html, p. 23.

3. Ernest Gellner (1998) *Language and Solitude: Wittgenstein, Malinowski and the Habsburg Dilemma*, Cambridge University Press, p. 12.

4. Gellner, *Language and Solitude*.

5. Endre Ady, quoted in John Lukacs (1993) *Budapest 1900: A Historical Portrait of a City and its Culture*, Weidenfeld, p. 198.

6. I have reproduced the names of Hungarians, such as Jaszi, who gained recognition in the Anglosphere in anglicised form. For all others, Hungarian orthography is used.

7. Rudolf Tökés (1967) *Béla Kun and the Hungarian Soviet Republic: The Origins and Role of the Communist Party of Hungary in the Revolutions of 1918–1919*, Praeger, pp. 17–18.

8. Jaszi, quoted in Mary Gluck (1985) *Georg Lukács and his Generation, 1900–1918*, Harvard University Press, p. 104.

9. Krishan Kumar (1978) *Prophecy and Progress: The Sociology of Industrial and Post-industrial Society*, Penguin, pp. 9, 15, 42.

10. KPA-30-18, Karl Polanyi (1950) 'The Contribution of Institutional Analysis to the Social Sciences'.

11. KPA-15-8, Karl Polanyi (1943–44) Lectures, 'Government and Industry', University of London; KPA-51-1, Karl Polanyi (1959) to Paul Medow and to 'George', 30 September.

12. KPA-51-1, Polanyi (1959) to 'George'.

13. Karl Polanyi (2016 [1910]) 'Preface to Ernö Mach's *Die Analyse der Empfindungen*', in Dale, *Polanyi: The Hungarian Writings*.

14. In Friedrich Adler (1918) *Ernst Machs Ueberwindung des mechanischen Materialismus*, Wiener Buchhandlung, pp. 51–52.

15. Peter Manicas (1987) *A History and Philosophy of the Social Sciences*, Blackwell, p. 189.

16. Michael Polanyi (1958) *Personal Knowledge: Towards a Post-critical Philosophy*, Routledge & Kegan Paul, p. 9.

17. SPSL-536-1, Karl Polanyi (1934) to Walter Adams, 31 March.

18. SPSL-536-1, Polanyi to Adams.

19. Péter Hanák (1998) *The Garden and the Workshop: Essays on the Cultural History of Vienna and Budapest*, Princeton University Press, p. 152.

20. Roy Bhaskar (1989) *Reclaiming Reality: A Critical Introduction to Contemporary Philosophy*, London: Verso, p. 49; Alasdair MacIntyre (2007) *After Virtue: A Study in Moral Theory*, Duckworth.

21. Chris Hann (1992) 'Radical Functionalism: The Life and Work of Karl Polanyi', *Dialectical Anthropology*, 17, p. 147.

22. SPSL-536-1, Polanyi to Adams.

23. Lukacs, quoted in Michael Löwy (1979) *Georg Lukács – From Romanticism to Bolshevism*, New Left Books, p. 113.

24. SPSL-536-1, Polanyi to Adams; SPSL-536-1, Karl Polanyi (1934) to Zoe Fairfield, 24 March.

25. Karl Polanyi (1921–23) 'The Resurrection of Jesus', in Dale, *Polanyi: The Hungarian Writings*; KPA-4-9, Karl Polanyi, 'Early Christianity and Communism'.

26. Karl Polanyi (2016 [1919]) 'Oration to the Youth of the Galilei Circle', in Dale, *Polanyi: The Hungarian Writings*.

27. KPA-45-8, Abraham Rotstein (1957) 'Notes of Weekend XII with Karl Polanyi', p. 28.

28. Polanyi, 'Wissenschaft und Sittlichkeit', pp. 184, 195.

29. KPA-2-2, Karl Polanyi (1920–22) Draft manuscript (n.t.).

30. KPA-2-3, Karl Polanyi (1920–22) 'Wissenschaftliche Politik ohne Skepsis und die Privilegien der Soziologie'.

31. SPSL-536-1, Polanyi to Adams.

32. SPSL-536-1, Polanyi to Fairfield.

33. KPA-2-1, Karl Polanyi (n.d.) 'Sein und Denken'.

34. Karl Polanyi (1921) 'Believing and Unbelieving Politics', in Dale, *Polanyi: The Hungarian Writings*.

35. Polanyi, 'Worauf es heute ankommt'.

36. For detailed analysis, see Gareth Dale (2014) 'The Iron Law of Democratic Socialism: British and Austrian Influences on the Young Karl Polanyi', *Economy and Society*, 43(4), pp. 650–67.

37. This critique can point to the abolition of the wage labour system or merely to socio-political measures that ensure workers' incorporation as citizens into the body politic. This was a defining ambiguity of guild socialism.

38. In Raymond Williams (1958) *Culture and Society, 1780–1850*, Chatto & Windus.

39. For example, Oswald Mosley (1968) *My Life*, Thomas Nelson & Sons, p. 173.

40. Helge Peukert (2001) 'The Schmoller Renaissance', *History of Political Economy*, 33(1), p. 115.

41. In Göran Therborn (1976) *Science, Class & Society: On the Formation of Sociology & Historical Materialism*, New Left Books, p. 202.

42. KPA-32-6, Karl Polanyi (1953–55) 'On Forms of Trade in the Ancient Near East'.

43. In Peukert, 'Schmoller Renaissance', p. 99.

44. Schmoller [1874], in Heino Heinrich Nau, ed. (1998) *Gustav Schmoller. Historisch-ethische Nationalökonomie als Kulturwissenschaft. Ausgewaehlte methodologische Schriften*, Metropolis, pp. 82, 89, 96.

45. Schmoller [1902] in Peukert, 'Schmoller Renaissance'. p. 109.

46. Douglas Brown (1988) *Towards a Radical Democracy: The Political Economy of the Budapest School*, Unwin Hyman, p. 48.

47. Steven Lukes (1973) Émile Durkheim: His Life and Work, Allen Lane, p. 89.

48. Durkheim, quoted in Heino Heinrich Nau and Philippe Steiner (2002) 'Schmoller, Durkheim, and Old European Institutionalist Economics', *Journal of Economic Issues*, 36(4), p. 1018.

49. Nau and Steiner, 'Schmoller, Durkheim', p. 1018.

50. George McCarthy (2009) *Dreams in Exile: Rediscovering Science and Ethics in Nineteenth-Century Social Theory*, State University of New York Press, p. 122.

51. Nau and Steiner, 'Schmoller, Durkheim', p. 1016.

52. H. E. Barnes (1920) quoted in Mike Gane (1992) 'Institutional Socialism and the Sociological Critique of Communism', in Mike Gane, ed., *Radical Sociology of Durkheim and Mauss,* Routledge.

53. KPA-1-2, Karl Polanyi (1909) 'Scientific Method', *Huszadik Század*, 10(2); KPA-4-10, Karl Polanyi (early 1920s) Notes on readings.

54. Kari Polanyi-Levitt, interview, 6 October 2007, and email to the author, 29 October 2007.

55. Fritz Pappenheim (1959) *The Alienation of Modern Man: An Interpretation Based on Marx and Tönnies*, Monthly Review Press, p. 80; David Inglis (2014) 'Tönnies Today: A Living Legacy in the Sociology of Globalization and Globality', in Massimo Pendenza, ed., *Classical Sociology Beyond Methodological Nationalism*, Brill, p. 59.

56. Jose Harris (2001) 'General Introduction', in Ferdinand Tönnies, *Community and Civil Society*, Cambridge University Press, p. xxiv.

57. Ferdinand Tönnies (2001 [1922]) *Community and Civil Society*, ed. Jose Harris, Cambridge University Press, p. 210.

58. Jose Harris (2001) footnote 33, in Tönnies, *Community and Society*, p. 210.

59. Tönnies, *Community and Society,* p. 76; Ferdinand Tönnies (1974) *On Social Ideas and Ideologies*, Harper & Row, pp. 173–74.

60. Tönnies, *Community and Society* pp. 65, 82, 93, 98, 101, 258.

61. Karl Polanyi (1977) *The Livelihood of Man*, Academic Press, p. 49.

62. Owen, *A New View,* p. 181.

63. G. D. H. Cole (1925) *Robert Owen*, Ernest Benn, p. 154.

64. KPA-21-22, Karl Polanyi (1937) 'Community and Society. The Christian Criticism of Our Social Order'.

65. KPA-20-6, Karl Polanyi (n.d.) 'Democracy vs. Total Crisis'.

66. KPA-18-8, Karl Polanyi (n.d.) 'The Fascist Virus'.

67. Karl Polanyi (2001) *The Great Transformation*, Beacon Press, pp. 75, 79; cf. KPA-15-10, Karl Polanyi (1944) 'The Study of Human Institutions (Economic and Social)'.

68. Inglis, 'Tönnies Today', p. 46.

69. Kurtuluş Gemici (2008) 'Karl Polanyi and the Antinomies of Embeddedness', *Socio-Economic Review*, 6(1), pp. 5–33.

70. As paraphrased in Alasdair Macintyre (2006) *Edith Stein: A Philosophical Prologue, 1913–1922*, Rowman & Littlefield, p. 127.

71. Gemici, 'Karl Polanyi'.

72. Karl Polanyi (2002 [1934]) 'Tory Planwirtschafter', in Michele Cangiani and Claus Thomasberger, eds, *Chronik der großen Transformation*, Band 1, Metropolis, pp. 96, 103.

73. Terry Eagleton (1990) *The Ideology of the Aesthetic*, Blackwell, p. 319.

74. Adam Tolnay (2003) Review of Lee Congdon's 'Seeing Red: Hungarian Intellectuals in Exile and the Challenge of Communism', *Journal of Cold War Studies*, Fall.

75. David Lockwood, quoted in Alex Callinicos (2007) *Social Theory: A Historical Introduction,* Polity, p. 135.

76. KPA-2-1, Polanyi, Draft manuscript.

77. KPA-18-10, Karl Polanyi (1934) 'What Three-fold State?', *New Britain*, 2(43), pp. 503–04.

78. Talcott Parsons (1935) 'Sociological Elements in Economic Thought', *Quarterly Journal of Economics*, 49(4), p. 664–67.

CHAPTER 2

1. KPA-20-2, Karl Polanyi (1938-39) 'Tame Empires'. This chapter includes reworked material from Gareth Dale (2014) 'Karl Polanyi in Vienna: Guild Socialism, Austro-Marxism, and Duczynska's alternative,' *Historical Materialism*, 22(1), pp. 34–66.

2. SPSL-536-1, Karl Polanyi (1934) to Zoe Fairfield, 24 March; SPSL-536-1, Karl Polanyi (1934) to Walter Adams, 31 March.

3. KPA-37-8, Karl Polanyi (1958) 'The Galilei Circle fifty years on'.

4. SPSL-536-1, Polanyi to Adams.

5. A mirror image of Dalton's argument is found in Duran Bell (2002) 'Polanyi and the Definition of Capitalism', in Jean Ensminger, ed., *Theory in Economic Anthropology*, AltaMira.

6. Fred Block (2001) 'Karl Polanyi and the Writing of *The Great Transformation*'. Paper presented at the Eighth International Karl Polanyi Conference, 'Economy and Democracy'. UNAM, Mexico City, 14–16 November.

7. Engels, quoted in John Lie (1991) 'Embedding Polanyi's Market Society', *Sociological Perspectives*, 34(2), p. 231; John Elster, ed. (1986) *Karl Marx: A Reader*, Cambridge University Press, p. 35.

8. Karl Polanyi (2005) 'Über die Freiheit', in Michele Cangiani and Claus Thomasberger, eds, *Chronik der großen Transformation*, Band 3, Metropolis, p. 165.

9. Rhoda Halperin (1984) 'Polanyi, Marx, and the Institutional Paradigm in Economic Anthropology', *Research in Economic Anthropology*, 6, pp. 247, 268.

10. Rhoda Halperin (1988) *Economies across Cultures: Towards a Comparative Science of the Economy*, Macmillan, p. 5.

11. Justin Elardo (2012) 'Economic Anthropology After the Great Debate', in Ty Matejowsky and Donald Wood, eds, *Political Economy, Neoliberalism, and the Prehistoric Economies of Latin America*, Emerald.

12. Halperin assumes that by 'society' Marx 'meant institution', that is, 'simply an organizing principle operating in a sociocultural unit'. Equally idiosyncratically, she sees Marx as the inspiration for 'old institutionalist' economics *tout court*, including Thorstein Veblen, Wesley Mitchell and John Kenneth Galbraith. Halperin, 'Polanyi, Marx'.

13. Michael Burawoy (2003) 'For a Sociological Marxism: The Complementary Convergence of Antonio Gramsci and Karl Polanyi', *Politics & Society*, 31(2), pp. 193–261. See also Noel Castree (2010) 'Crisis, Continuity and Change: Neoliberalism, the Left and the Future of Capitalism', *Antipode* 41(1), pp. 185–213.

14. Tamás, Gáspár Miklós (2006) 'Telling The Truth About Class', www.gerlo.hu/kommunizmus-vita/tgm/telling_the_truth_about_class.pdf

15. Tamás, 'Telling The Truth'.

16. Karl Kautsky (1892) *The Class Struggle*, www.marxists.org/archive/kautsky/1892/erfurt/ch04.htm

17. Karl Kautsky (1909) *The Road to Power*, Samuel Bloch, pp. 36–40.

18. Ervin Szabó (1982 [1904]) *Socialism and Social Science*, edited by György Litván and János Bak, Routledge, p. 65.

19. Alan Shandro (1997) 'Karl Kautsky: On the Relation of Theory and Practice', *Science & Society*, 61(4), p. 478.

20. Jules Townshend (1989) 'Reassessing Kautsky's Marxism', *Political Studies*, 37(4), p. 663.

21. Karl Polanyi (1922) 'Karl Kautsky and Democracy', in Dale, *Polanyi: The Hungarian Writings*.

22. Peter Gay (1952) *The Dilemma of Democratic Socialism: Eduard Bernstein's Challenge to Marx*, Columbia University Press, p. 54; Manfred Steger (1997) *The Quest for Evolutionary Socialism; Eduard Bernstein and Social Democracy*, Cambridge University Press, p. 68.

23. Ernest Belfort Bax (1896) 'Our German Fabian Convert; or, Socialism According to Bernstein', www.marxists.org/archive/bax/1896/bernstein/bernstein1.htm

24. Steger, *Evolutionary Socialism*.

25. This was not a technical quibble. Without premises of value, Marx's work would be 'a merely implicit critique of capitalism, lacking an integral investigation into the nature of capitalism: he would be an anti-capitalist romantic'. The relevance to Polanyi's work is obvious. Inspired by Bernsteinian revisionism, he tended to theorise market behaviour on marginalist lines. This left his case against market society resting heavily upon a postulated moral distinction between ordinary and fictitious commodities. Agnes Heller (1974) *The Theory of Need in Marx*, Allison & Busby, p. 39.

26. Steger, *Evolutionary Socialism*.

27. Barry Hindess (1983) *Parliamentary Democracy and Socialist Politics*, Routledge, p. 38.

28. Margaret Cole (1974) 'H. G. Wells and the Fabian Society', in A. J. A. Morris, ed., *Edwardian Radicalism 1900–1914*, Routledge & Kegan Paul, p. 112.

29. Eduard Bernstein (1893) 'Ferdinand Lassalle', www.marxists.org/reference/archive/ bernstein/works/1893/lassalle/chap10.htm

30. Shandro, 'Karl Kautsky', p. 481.

31. Steger, *Evolutionary Socialism*, p. 248.

32. Steger, *Evolutionary Socialism*, p. 142.

33. Bernstein, paraphrased in Carl Schorske (1983 [1955]) *German Social Democracy, 1905–1917: The Development of the Great Schism*, Harvard University Press, p. 18.

34. Bernstein, *Evolutionary Socialism*.

35. Andrew Janos (1982) *The Politics of Backwardness in Hungary, 1825–1945*, Princeton University Press, p. 187; Paul Ignotus (1961) 'The Hungary of Michael Polanyi', in P. Ignotus, E. Shils and A. Koestler, eds, *The Logic of Personal Knowledge*, Routledge, p. 6.

36. Ferenc Múcsi (1990) 'The Start of Karl Polanyi's Career', in Kari Polanyi-Levitt, ed., *The Life and Work of Karl Polanyi*, Black Rose, p. 29.

37. Cited in Peter Thomas (2009) *The Gramscian Moment*, Brill, p. 2.

38. In Lenin's case: his later writings, not *Materialism and Empirio-criticism*.

39. On Kautsky's equivocation on the mass strike, see Dick Geary (1987) *Karl Kautsky*, Manchester University Press, pp. 62–63; Shandro, 'Karl Kautsky', p. 496; Daniel Gaido (2008) 'Marxism and the Union Bureaucracy: Karl Kautsky on Samuel Gompers and the German Free Trade Unions', *Historical Materialism*, 16(3), p. 132.

40. The circumstantial evidence for this is that the copy in Polanyi's library is more thumbed and more heavily marked up than any other book. According to Maucourant and Cangiani, 'Introduction', in Cangiani and Maucourant, eds, *Essais de Karl Polanyi*, Seuil, 2008, citing Alfredo Salsano, Polanyi 'avait avant tout sous les yeux "la richesse et l'originalité du marxisme hongrois, caractérisé par un intérêt précoce pour le thème de l'aliénation, dont témoignaient le jeune Lukács, aussi bien que Béla Fogarasi et Pál Szende; ce sont ces derniers qui, restés en contact avec Polanyi après la guerre, le poussèrent à lire Marx à travers la problématique de la réification"'.

41. George Lukács (1987) *History and Class Consciousness*, Merlin, p. 27

42. Ervin Szabó (1982 [1904–09]) *Socialism and Social Science*, edited by György Litván and János Bak, Routledge, pp. 41, 109, 142.

43. Szabó, *Socialism*, pp. 32–33, 37, 113.

44. Michael Löwy (1979) *Georg Lukács – From Romanticism to Bolshevism*, New Left Books, p. 81.

45. György Litván and János Bak (1982) 'Editors' Introduction', in György Litván and János Bak, eds, *Socialism and Social Science: Selected Writings of Ervin Szabó*, Routledge, pp. 14–15.

46. Lukács, Georg (1983) *Record of a Life: An Autobiographical Sketch*, Verso, pp. 39–40.

47. SPSL-536-1, Polanyi to Adams; Karl Polanyi (1919) 'Weltanschauungskrise', *Neue Erde*, Heft 31/32.

48. Later in life, Polanyi qualified his critique. Technology and ecology, he acknowledged, 'decisively limit the basic structure of human society', even to the point of 'deeply influencing' its ideology, and yet, contra Marx, only in a market economy 'do economic factors not only limit, but *determine* culture. Only here does the economy *determine* the shape and form of society'. But even in this modified critique Polanyi was only reiterating a point made by Douglas Cole, and which Marx had pre-emptively rebutted in *Capital*. It had first been raised by an American journalist,

who Marx cites in *Capital*. In his judgment, Marx's view that 'the economic structure of society is the real basis on which the juridical and political superstructure is raised and to which definite social forms of thought correspond; that the mode of production determines the character of the social, political, and intellectual life generally', was 'very true for our own times, in which material interests preponderate, but not for the Middle Ages, in which Catholicism, nor for Athens and Rome, where politics reigned supreme'. To this, Marx responded that 'the Middle Ages could not live on Catholicism, nor the ancient world on politics. On the contrary, it is the mode in which they gained a livelihood that explains why here politics, and there Catholicism, played the chief part'. KPA-35-10, Karl Polanyi (1949) 'Economic History and the Problem of Freedom'; Marx, *Capital*, www.marxists.org/archive/marx/works/1867-c1/ch01.htm

49. KPA-1-25, Karl Polanyi (1918) 'The Programme and Goals of Radicalism', in Dale, *Polanyi: The Hungarian Writings*; KPA-45-14, Abraham Rotstein (1957) Notes of Weekend XIX with Karl Polanyi, p. 14.

50. KPA-37-2, Karl Polanyi (n.d.) 'The Methodological Problems Connected with the Question of Capitalism in Antiquity'; KPA-18-36, Karl Polanyi (n.d.) 'Western Socialism: A Tract on Values and Power'.

51. KPA-35-10, Polanyi, 'Economic History'; KPA-15-6, Karl Polanyi (1939) 'Deutsches Leben und Schrifttum'; KPA-37-6, Karl Polanyi (1957) 'The Machine and the Discovery of Society'.

52. Polanyi, 'Sein und Denken'.

53. Polanyi, 'Wissenschaft und Sittlichkeit', p. 195.

54. KPA-2-1, Karl Polanyi (n.d.) 'Sein und Denken'; KPA-15-4, Karl Polanyi (1936–40) Morley College lectures.

55. KPA-8-14, Karl Polanyi (1934–46) Notes on readings.

56. Polanyi, 'Early Christianity and Communism'; KPA-15-4, Polanyi, Morley lectures. For Dühring's position, see Eugen Dühring (1900) *Kritische Geschichte der Nationalökonomie und des Socialismus von ihren Anfängen bis zur Gegenwart*, 4th edn, Leipzig, esp. p. 502.

57. KPA-37-10, Karl Polanyi (1958) 'From the Diary of an Antimarxist'.

58. KPA-8-14, Polanyi, Notes; Karl Polanyi (1968) *Primitive, Archaic, and Modern Economies*, Beacon Press.

59. Polanyi, explicated by Abe Rotstein (KPA-24-6, Drafts, 1951–60) and by Felix Schafer (KPA-29-10, Karl Polanyi's Life in Vienna, 1973–74).

60. KPA-31-3, Karl Polanyi (1947) 'General Economic History', No. 5.

61. See, for example, Dühring's critique of Marx's alleged reduction of human life to base material motives. Eugen Dühring (1900) *Kritische Geschichte der Nationalökonomie und des Socialismus von ihren Anfängen bis zur Gegenwart*, 4th edn, Leipzig, p. 499.

62. Antonio Gramsci (1971) *Selections from the Prison Notebooks,* ed. Quintin Hoare and Geoffrey Nowell Smith, Lawrence & Wishart, p. 163 and *passim*; Lucio Colleti (1972) *From Rousseau to Lenin: Studies in Ideology and Society,* Monthly Review Press; Daniel Bensaid (2009) *Marx for Our Times: Adventures and Misadventures of a Critique*, Verso, p. 264; David Harvey (2001) *Spaces of Capital: Towards a Critical Geography*, Edinburgh University Press, p. 268; Peter Manicas (1987) *A History and Philosophy of the Social Sciences*, Blackwell, pp. 113–15.

63. Karl Marx and Friedrich Engels (1845) *The Holy Family*, www.marxists.org/archive/marx/works/1845/holy-family

64. Engels (1895) Introduction to *Class Struggles in France*, www.marxists.org/archive/marx/works/1850/class-struggles-france/intro.htm On Engels' criticism of the SPD

leaders who mutilated his text see, for example, Friedrich Engels (1895) 'Letter to Laura Lafargue', 28 March, www.marxists.org/francais/marx/works/00/sda/sda_6_4. htm. For discussion, see Till Schelz-Brandenburg (2010) 'Einführung', MEGA, Band 32, Akademie Verlag, http://mega.bbaw.de/struktur/abteilung_i/dateien/mega_i-32_inhalt-einf.pdf

65. Don Lavoie (1985) *Rivalry and Central Planning*, Cambridge University Press.

66. Colin Barker (2008) 'Class Struggle', www.academia.edu/8596730/_CLASS_STRUGGLE_ (Emphases in original).

67. Marx, quoted in Agnes Heller (1974) *The Theory of Need in Marx*, Allison & Busby, pp. 74–75. When capitalism is analysed historically, he adds, the illusion of regarding economic tendencies as 'natural laws of production' vanishes.

68. Quoted in D. G. Leahy (1996) *Foundation: Matter the Body Itself*, SUNY Press, p. 82.

69. Barker, 'Class Struggle'.

70. Harvey, *Spaces of Capital*, p. 268.

71. Neil Davidson (2012) *How Revolutionary Were the Bourgeois Revolutions?*, Haymarket, p. 5.

72. More recently, Colin Leys has offered a related critique. Polanyi, he argues, is silent on the subject of the class character of capitalist countries. Yet the state, which in his model regularly reasserts the interests of society against those of capital ('the self-regulating market'), itself rests on class forces, and his disinclination to specify these forces leaves this salutary historical function of the state ultimately unexplained. Eugene Genovese (1968) Review of Karl Polanyi, 'Dahomey and the Slave Trade', *The Journal of Economic History*, 28(1), p. 149; Colin Leys (2001) *Market-Driven Politics: Neoliberal Democracy and the Public Interest*, Verso.

73. Dühring, *Kritische Geschichte*, esp. p. 502. For Keynes, see Doug Henwood (1998) *Wall Street: How It Works and for Whom*, Verso.

74. Ellen Wood (1999) *The Origin of Capitalism: A Longer View*, Verso, p. 111.

75. Adam Smith (1993) *The Wealth of Nations*, Oxford University Press, p. 36; Geoffrey Pilling (1972) 'The Law of Value in Ricardo and Marx', *Economy and Society* 1(3), pp. 281–307.

76. Simon Clarke (1982) *Marx, Marginalism and Modern Sociology: From Adam Smith to Max Weber*, Macmillan.

77. Ben Fine (1982) *Theories of the Capitalist Economy*, Edward Arnold, p. 22.

78. Karl Marx (1863) *Theories of Surplus Value*, Part II, Chapter X, www.marxists.org/archive/marx/works/1863/theories-surplus-value

79. Pilling, 'Law of Value', p. 297; Jacques Melitz (1970) 'The Polanyi School of Anthropology on Money: An Economist's View', *American Anthropologist*, 72(5), pp. 1020–40; Clarke, *Marx, Marginalism*.

80. Marx, speaking of the newly published first volume of *Capital*, said that one of its two 'best points' is 'the two-fold character of labour according to whether it is expressed in use-value or exchange-value, which is brought out in the very First Chapter'. Karl Marx, letter to Engels of 24 August 1867, https://marxists.anu.edu.au/archive/marx/works/1867/letters/67_08_24.htm

81. Scott Meikle (1991) 'Aristotle and Exchange Value', in David Keyt and Fred Miller, eds, *A Companion to Aristotle's Politics*, Wiley-Blackwell, p. 175.

82. Clarke, *Marx, Marginalism*, p. 45.

83. KPA-21-3, Karl Polanyi (1936) 'Social Values in the Post-war World'.

84. SPSL-536-1, Polanyi to Adams.

85. Polanyi, 'Über die Freiheit', pp. 139ff.

86. KPA-20-12, Karl Polanyi (1938) 'Notes of a Week's Study on *The Early Writings of Karl Marx* and Summary of Discussions on *British Working Class Consciousness*'.

87. KPA-15-1, Karl Polanyi (1934-35) 'Marxian Philosophy', p. 2.

88. Polanyi, 'Über die Freiheit', p. 139.

89. KPA-21-2, Karl Polanyi (1936) 'The New Social Order from the Point of View of Christian Principles'.

90. KPA-21-22, Karl Polanyi (1937) 'Community and Society. The Christian Criticism of Our Social Order'.

91. KPA-20-12, 'Notes of a Week's Study'.

92. Kari Polanyi-Levitt, interview, Montreal 14 July 2006.

93. There was one moment, the mid-1930s, during which the above critique of Polanyi does not apply, or at least not with force. In several publications he developed a more nuanced understanding of the integral relation between Marx's theories of value and commodity fetishism. For example, KPA-19-22, Karl Polanyi (1930s) 'Christianity and Economic Life'.

94. Hüseyin Özel (1997) 'Reclaiming Humanity: The Social Theory of Karl Polanyi', PhD dissertation, University of Utah, p. 108.

95. KPA-2-22, Karl Polanyi (1924-27) 'Pure Economic Theory'; KPA-2-10, Karl Polanyi and Felix Schafer (1920s) 'Hans Mayer's Lösung des Zurechnungsproblems'; KPA-2-20 Karl Polanyi (1930-31) 'Einführung in die Volkswirtschaftslehre'; KPA-29-10 Schafer, 'Vienna'; Franz Oppenheimer (1910) *Theorie der reinen und politischen Ökonomie; Ein Lehr- und Lesebuch für Studierende und Gebildete*, Georg Reimer, p. 79.

96. Emil Lederer (1922) *Grundzüge der Oekonomischen Theorie*, Mohr, pp. 4, 10, 13 and *passim*.

97. KPA-29-10 Schafer, 'Vienna', p. 60.

98. KPA-2-22, Karl Polanyi, 'Pure Economic Theory'.

99. Fred Block (2001) 'Karl Polanyi and the Writing of *The Great Transformation*', Paper presented at the Eighth International Karl Polanyi Conference, Mexico City, p. 17.

100. Fred Block and Margaret Somers (2014) *The Power of Market Fundamentalism: Karl Polanyi's Critique*, Harvard University Press, p. 99.

101. Block, 'Karl Polanyi', p. 17.

102. Don Robotham (2009) 'Afterword: Learning from Polanyi', in Chris Hann and Keith Hart, eds, *Market and Society: The Great Transformation Today*, Cambridge University Press, p. 280

103. Marx (1973) *Grundrisse*, Penguin, p. 101.

104. Antonio Gramsci (1971) *Selections from the Prison Notebooks*, Lawrence & Wishart, p. 160.

105. For example, Philip Mirowski (2013) *Never Let a Serious Crisis Go to Waste*, Verso; Jamie Peck (2013) *Constructions of Neoliberal Reason*, Oxford University Press.

106. Maria Szecsi (1979) 'Looking Back on *The Great Transformation*', *Monthly Review*, 30(8), p. 35.

107. Kari Polanyi-Levitt and Marguerite Mendell (1987) 'Karl Polanyi: His Life and Times', *Studies in Political Economy*, Spring, pp. 11, 27-28.

108. For example, Marx, *Grundrisse* pp. 507-15; Marx, *Capital* Vol.1, chapters 26-33.

109. Douglas Brown (1988) *Towards a Radical Democracy: The Political Economy of the Budapest School*, Unwin Hyman, p. 48; Somers (1990), pp. 153, 156.

110. Polanyi upbraided Marx for assuming parliamentary government 'to be intrinsically of the devil'. This may have appeared to be the case in Europe, he argued, but was not universal – as demonstrated in North America. 'In the United States a people chose

to govern itself by a parliament from the beginning', and Canada's citizenry 'chose a parliament and threw out executive rule'. KPA-21-19, Karl Polanyi (n.d.) 'A Christian View of Marxism' and 'Marxism and Christianity'.

111. Michael Burawoy (2010) 'From Polanyi to Pollyanna: The False Optimism of Global Labor Studies', *Global Labor Journal*, 1(2), p. 307. Burawoy's emphasis here differs significantly from that put forward in his 2003 essay discussed above.

112. Mike Haynes and Rumy Husan (1998) 'The State and Market in the Transition Economies: Critical Remarks in the Light of Past History and the Current Experience', *Journal of European Economic History*, 27(3), pp. 609–44.

113. Jill Lewis (1991) *Fascism and the Working Class in Austria, 1918–1934: The Failure of Labour in the First Republic*, Berg, p. 79.

114. Karl Polanyi (1935) 'The Essence of Fascism', in Karl Polanyi et al., eds, *Christianity and the Social Revolution*, Gollancz.

CHAPTER 3

1. This chapter includes reworked material from Gareth Dale (2014) 'Karl Polanyi in Vienna: Guild Socialism, Austro-Marxism, and Duczynska's Alternative', *Historical Materialism*, 22(1), pp. 34–66.

2. Fareed Zakaria (2007) *The Future of Freedom: Illiberal Democracy at Home and Abroad,* W.W. Norton.

3. Editorial (2011) 'The Economics of the Arab Spring', *Financial Times*, 24 April.

4. Hamish McRae (2009) 'The Chinese Are Our Teachers Now', *Independent,* 29 July, www.independent.co.uk/voices/commentators/hamish-mcrae/hamish-mcrae-the-chinese-are-our-teachers-now-1763951.html

5. Stephen Gill (1998) 'European Governance and New Constitutionalism: Economic and Monetary Union and Alternatives to Disciplinary Neoliberalism in Europe', *New Political Economy*, 3(1), pp. 5–26; Teivo Teivainen (2002) *Enter Economism, Exit Politics: Experts, Economic Policy and the Damage to Democracy*, Zed.

6. Claude Ake (1997) 'Dangerous Liaisons: The Interface of Globalization and Democracy', in Axel Hadenius, ed., *Democracy's Victory and Crisis*, Cambridge University Press.

7. Wendy Brown (2015) *Undoing the Demos: Neoliberalism's Stealth Revolution*, Zone Books.

8. Wendy Brown (2010) 'We Are All Democrats Now ...' *Theory & Event*, 2(1).

9. Alain Badiou (2012) *Polemics*, Verso; Nick Hewlett (2010) *Badiou, Balibar, Ranciere: Re-thinking Emancipation*, A&C Black.

10. David Blunkett (2012) 'In Defence of Politics Revisited', http://davidblunkett. typepad.com/files/in-defence-of-politics-revisited.pdf p. 13.

11. Patrick Wintour (2012) 'David Blunkett Attacks Germany in Blueprint to Engage Voters', www.guardian.co.uk/politics/2012/sep/16/david-blunkett-germany-voters

12. Blunkett, 'In Defence', p. 24.

13. Quoted in Michael Foot (2011 [1973]) *Aneurin Bevan: A Biography: Volume 2: 1945–1960*, Paladin, p. 19.

14. KPA-18-8, Karl Polanyi (n.d.) 'The Fascist Virus'.

15. Ellen Wood (1995) *Democracy against Capitalism: Redefining Historical Materialism*, Cambridge University Press, p. 203.

16. Charles Tilly (2007) *Democracy*, Cambridge University Press.

17. Antony Arblaster (2002) *Democracy*, 3rd edn, Open University Press, p. 48.

18. Sidney Webb (1889) 'The Basis of Socialism', in George Bernard Shaw, ed., *Fabian Essays in Socialism*, Humboldt.

19. Sidney and Beatrice Webb (1920) *A Constitution for the Socialist Commonwealth of Great Britain*, Longman, Green and Co.

20. George Bernard Shaw (2006 [1889]) *Fabian Essays in Socialism*, Cosimo, p. 50.

21. Wells, quoted in Elliott Abramson (2012) 'The Fabian Socialists and Law as an Instrument of Social Progress: The Promise of Gradual Justice', *St. John's Law Review*, 62(2), p. 229.

22. Hal Draper (1966) 'The Two Souls of Socialism', www.marxists.org/archive/draper/1966/twosouls/index.htm

23. Rhiannon Vickers (2004) *The Labour Party and the World, Volume 1: The Evolution of Labour's Foreign Policy, 1900–51*, Oxford University Press, p. 38.

24. Webb, quoted in Abramson, 'Fabian Socialists', p. 214.

25. Abramson, 'Fabian Socialists', p. 227.

26. John Street (1989) 'Fabian Socialism, Democracy and the State', in Graeme Duncan, ed., *Democracy and the Capitalist State*, Cambridge University Press, p. 162.

27. Abramson, 'Fabian Socialists', pp. 214–17.

28. Sidney Webb (1893) 'English Progress Towards Social Democracy', http://nzetc.victoria.ac.nz/tm/scholarly/tei-Stout86-t3.html; Street, 'Fabian Socialism'.

29. Abramson, 'Fabian Socialists', p. 216.

30. In Ashu Pasricha and K. S. Bharath (2009) *The Political Thought of Annie Besant*, Concept Publishing, p. 106.

31. Margaret Cole (1974) 'H. G. Wells and the Fabian Society', in A. J. A. Morris, ed., *Edwardian Radicalism 1900–1914*, Routledge & Kegan Paul, p. 108.

32. Sidney and Beatrice Webb (1897) *Industrial Democracy*, Longmans, p. 36.

33. Webb, *Industrial Democracy*, p. 36; Ralph Miliband (1982) *Capitalist Democracy in Britain*, Oxford University Press, p. 23.

34. Patrick Parrinder (2013) 'Introduction', in Patrick Parrinder and John S. Partington, eds, *The Reception of H. G. Wells in Europe*, Bloomsbury, p. 9. Incidentally, it was the reading of Wells by a Hungarian physicist, Leo Szilard, that inspired the invention of the nuclear bomb.

35. Andrew Arato (1985) 'Austromarxism and the Theory of Democracy', in Anson Rabinbach ed., *The Austrian Socialist Experiment: Social Democracy and Austro-marxism, 1918–1934*, Westview, p. 138.

36. Karl Polanyi (2016) 'The Constitution of Socialist Britain', in Dale, *Polanyi: The Hungarian Writings*.

37. KPA-19-23, Karl Polanyi (n.d.) 'Ignoring the Obvious'.

38. KPA-20-4, Karl Polanyi (1939-40) 'Common Man's Masterplan'. Polanyi's admiration for the Plymouth Puritans and frontier pioneers' tolerance and patience with minorities conveys a rose-tinted view of Europe's colonisation of the Americas – a perspective, incidentally, that he shared with his sister, Laura. She, with his assistance, published a defence of John Smith, the freebooting English colonialist and mercenary. Laura Polanyi Striker and Bradford Smith (1962) 'The Rehabilitation of Captain John Smith', *The Journal of Southern History*, 28(4), pp. 474–81.

39. Gay, *Dilemma*, p. 240.

40. Steger, *Evolutionary Socialism*, p. 129.

41. Gay, *Dilemma*, p. 239.

42. Stephen Eric Bronner (2013) *Socialism Unbound: Principles, Practices, and Prospects*, Columbia University Press, p. 65.

43. Bronner, *Socialism Unbound*, p. 64.

44. Bernstein, *Evolutionary Socialism.*
45. Quoted in Klaus Leesch (2012) 'Eduard Bernstein und die Fabian Society: Der Einfluss englischer sozialreformerischer Vorstellungen auf das Bernsteinsche Marxismusverständnis und sein Konzept von Sozialdemokratie', http://library.fes. de/pdf-files/bibliothek/bestand/70943/veroeffentlichungsfassung-29062012.pdf; p. 20.
46. Bronner, *Socialism Unbound*, p. 64.
47. Karl Polanyi (2016) 'Karl Kautsky and Democracy', in Dale, *Polanyi: Hungarian Writings.*
48. Sidney and Beatrice Webb (1920) *A Constitution for the Socialist Commonwealth of Great Britain*, London: Longman, Green and Co., p. xi.
49. Karl Polanyi (2016) 'The Rebirth of Democracy', in Dale, *Polanyi: Hungarian Writings.*
50. Polanyi, 'Rebirth of Democracy'.
51. Karl Polanyi (1924) 'The Week of the Lawless', *Bécsi Magyar Újság*, 24 January.
52. Karl Polanyi (1924) 'Ramsay Macdonald Comes out Victorious', *Bécsi Magyar Újság*, 6 March; KPA-1-51, Karl Polanyi (early 1920s) 'The Labour Government and Protectionism', *Bécsi Magyar Újság*; KPA-1-51, Karl Polanyi (1924) 'The Cabinet of Somnambulists and Lords', *Bécsi Magyar Újság*, 31 January.
53. KPA-1-51, Karl Polanyi (1923) 'What Will Happen in Britain?', *Bécsi Magyar Újság*, 12 December.
54. Frank Kirkpatrick (2005) *John Macmurray: Community Beyond Political Philosophy*, Rowman & Littlefield, pp. 21, 39.
55. Laski, 1933, in Paul Foot (2005) *The Vote: How It Was Won, and How It Was Undermined*, Penguin, p. 315.
56. Laski, 1932, in Foot, *The Vote*, p. 315.
57. Ross Terrill (1973) *R. H. Tawney and His Times; Socialism as Fellowship*, Harvard University Press, p. 146.
58. In Lawrence Goldman (2013) *The Life of R. H. Tawney: Socialism and History*, A&C Black, p. 173.
59. R. H. Tawney (1964 [1931]) *Equality*, Unwin.
60. Graeme Duncan (1989) *Democracy and the Capitalist State*, Cambridge University Press, p. 171.
61. In Terrill, *Tawney*, p. 147.
62. In Ralph Miliband (1979 [1961]) *Parliamentary Socialism: A Study in the Politics of Labour*, Merlin Press, p. 155.
63. Ilona Duczynska (1978) *Workers in Arms: The Austrian Schutzbund and the Civil War of 1934*, Monthly Review Press, p. 41.
64. In Raimund Loew (1979) 'The Politics of Austro-Marxism', *New Left Review*, I/118 November-December.
65. Ilona Duczynska (1975) *Der demokratische Bolschewik: Zur Theorie und Praxis der Gewalt*, List Verlag, p. 92.
66. Duczynska, *Workers in Arms*, p. 132.
67. Gerhard Botz (2001) 'Der "15 Juli 1927": Ablauf, Ursachen und Folgen', in Norbert Leser and Paul Sailer-Wlasits, eds, *1927, als die Republik brannte: von Schattendorf bis Wien*, Edition va bene.
68. Duczynska, *Workers in Arms*, p. 134. With extraordinary chutzpah, Bauer later claimed credit for 'the heroic act of the February uprising of the *Schutzbündler*' – even though he had cast aspersions on their loyalty, restricted internal SDAP debate over *Schutzbund*-related affairs, and acted consistently to undermine their prospects

of success. Although he admitted some responsibility for its defeat, he negated the import of that regret by claiming that the arrival of the Dollfuss dictatorship was inevitable. Otto Bauer (1976) *Werkausgabe,* Band IV, Europa Verlag, p. 326; Ewa Czerwínska-Schupp (2005) *Otto Bauer. Studien zur sozial-politischen Philosophie,* Peter Lang, p. 550.

69. The idea that parliament constitutes an essential instrument of proletarian power was an axiom of social democracy, from the Erfurt programme onward. Jukka Gronow (1986) *On the Formation of Marxism: Karl Kautsky's Theory of Capitalism, the Marxism of the Second International and Karl Marx's Critique of Political Economy,* Finnish Society of Sciences and Letters.

70. Arato, 'Austromarxism', p. 137.

71. Loew, 'Austro-Marxism'.

72. Julius Braunthal (1961) 'Otto Bauer, Ein Lebensbild', in *Otto Bauer, Eine Auswahl aus seinem Lebenswerk,* Verlag der Wiener Volksbuchhandlung, pp. 40, 51, 68.

73. The only other plausible contender for the laurels would be Ludwig von Mises. Hans-Hermann Hoppe claims that Mises single-handedly prevented Bolshevik revolution in Austria. Hoppe concedes that the fate of the revolution lay in Bauer's hands but suggests that Mises persuaded Bauer that it would be a disastrous course. However, Mises was pushing at an open door. Hoppe, Hans-Hermann (1995) 'Einführung', in Ludwig von Mises, *Liberalismus,* Akademie Verlag, p. 13.

74. Loew, 'Austro-Marxism'.

75. Bauer, *Werkausgabe,* Band II, pp. 72, 802–05, 960.

76. Bauer, in Tom Bottomore and Patrick Goode, eds (1978) *Austro-Marxism,* Clarendon Press, pp. 166–67.

77. KPA-8-7, Karl Polanyi (1934–46) 'The Christian and the World Economic Crisis'.

78. KPA-19-17, Karl Polanyi (n.d.) 'The Eclipse of Panic and the Outlook for Socialism'.

79. KPA-18-6, Karl Polanyi (1934) 'Fascism and Marxian Terminology'; KPA-31-10, Karl Polanyi (n.d.) 'Five Lectures on the Present Age of Transformation: The Trend Towards An Integrated Society'.

80. KPA-31-10, Polanyi, 'Present Age'.

81. KPA-15-2 Karl Polanyi (1937–38) 'Conflicting Philosophies in Modern Society'.

82. As a more recent account of the period puts it, 'democracy failed to deliver sustained growth in the 1920s because of conflicts between fiscal and monetary policy, the former in the hands of universal suffrage parliaments, the latter still largely controlled by financial élites'. Niall Ferguson (2002) *The Cash Nexus: Money and Power in the Modern World, 1700–2000,* Penguin, pp. 364–65.

83. Karl Polanyi (1937) *Europe To-Day,* Workers' Educational Trade Union Committee, p. 55.

84. KPA-19-16, Karl Polanyi (late 1930s) 'What Is the Real Character of the Economic Crisis?'.

85. KPA-20-8, Karl Polanyi (n.d.) 'Synopsis of "The Fascist Transformation"'; Polanyi, *The Great Transformation,* p. 25; KPA-19-17, Polanyi, 'Eclipse of Panic'; KPA-20-2, Polanyi, 'Tame Empires'.

86. Given that Brüning and von Papen directly preceded Hitler, it is curious that today's German elite harbours a collective fear of *inflation,* derived from the experience of the early 1920s, but not at all of *technocracy,* with reference to the Brüning and von Papen administrations. Polanyi, *The Great Transformation,* pp. 25, 247.

87. KPA-9-2, Karl Polanyi (1934–46) Notes on readings; KPA-18-6, Polanyi, 'Fascism'; KPA-20-8, Polanyi (1934–35) 'Synopsis'; KPA-21-2, Karl Polanyi (1936) 'The New

Social Order from the Point of View of Christian Principles'; KPA-20-2, Polanyi, 'Tame Empires'.

88. KPA-21-5, Karl Polanyi (1936) 'The Nature of the Present World Crisis'; KPA-31-10, Polanyi, 'Present Age'. Reflecting this polarisation in reality, social theory was polarising too, with 'democratic philosophy tending to be socialistic' and 'laissez-faire philosophy tending to be antidemocratic'. KPA-15-2, Polanyi, 'Conflicting Philosophies'.

89. Karl Polanyi (1927) 'The Goals of Hungarian Democracy', in Dale, *Polanyi: Hungarian Writings*.

90. KPA-17-1, Karl Polanyi (1938-39) 'Canterbury XII'.

91. Charles Maier (1987) *In Search of Stability: Explorations in Historical Political Economy*, Cambridge University Press, p. 168.

92. Wolfgang Streeck (2014) *Buying Time: The Delayed Crisis of Democratic Capitalism*, Verso, p. 57.

93. Ed Miliband (2012) 'The BBC's Sources, the Octonauts and a Call from David Cameron', *New Statesman,* 11 July, www.newstatesman.com/politics/politics/2012/07/ed-milibands-week-its-not-scale-our-problems-concerns-me-so-much-smallnes; cf. Ed Miliband (2012) 'Ed Miliband Interview: I Want to Save the Capitalism my Father Hated,' www.telegraph.co.uk/news/politics/ed-miliband/9544522/Ed-Miliband-interview-I-want-to-save-the-capitalism-my-father-hated.html

94. Ralph Miliband (1992) 'Fukuyama and the Socialist Alternative', *New Left Review* I/193, May-June, p. 109.

95. Karl Polanyi (2005) 'Faschismus und Marxistische Terminologie', in Cangiani, Polanyi-Levitt and Thomasberger, eds, *Chronik der großen Transformation*, Band 3, Metropolis, p. 243.

96. In Bob Jessop (2007) 'Dialogue of the Deaf: Some Reflections on the Poulantzas-Miliband Debate', in P. Wetherly, C. W. Barrow and P. Burnham, eds, *Class, Power and the State in Capitalist Society: Essays on Ralph Miliband*, Palgrave Macmillan.

97. Miliband, 'Fukuyama', p. 109; Ralph Miliband (1989) 'Reflections on the Crisis of Communist Regimes', *New Left Review,* I/177, September-October.

98. Ralph Miliband (1982) *Capitalist Democracy in Britain*, Oxford University Press, p. 16.

99. Jürgen Habermas (1988 [1973]) *Legitimation Crisis*, Polity, pp. 58, 61.

100. Nancy Fraser (2015) 'Legitimation Crisis? On the Political Contradictions of Financialized Capitalism', *Critical Historical Studies,* 2(2), p. 170.

101. Evelyne Huber et al. (1999) 'The Paradoxes of Contemporary Democracy', in Lisa Anderson, ed., *Transitions to Democracy*, Columbia University Press, p. 168.

102. Jamie Martin (2015) 'Just Be Grateful', *London Review of Books*, 23 April.

103. Philip Green (1985) *Retrieving Democracy: In Search of Civic Equality*, Methuen, p. 19. See also Göran Therborn (2001) 'Capitalism', entry in P. B. Clarke and J. Foweraker, eds, *Encyclopaedia of Democratic Thought*, Routledge.

104. Christopher Lasch (1995) *The Revolt of the Elites and the Betrayal of Democracy*, W.W. Norton.

105. Barry Gills, Joel Rocamora and Richard Wilson, eds (1993) *Low Intensity Democracy: Political Power in the New World Order*, Pluto.

106. Streeck, *Buying Time*, p. 75.

107. Wolfgang Streeck (2009) *Re-Forming Capitalism: Institutional Change in the German Political Economy*, Oxford University Press, p. 10.

108. Wolfgang Streeck (2014) Interview with Ben Jackson, Renewal, 22(3/4), www.renewal.org.uk/articles/interview-capitalism-neo-liberalism-and-democracy

109. Wolfgang Streeck (2011) 'The Crises of Democratic Capitalism', *New Left Review* 71, September-October; Streeck, *Buying Time*, pp. 21, 57.

110. Wolfgang Streeck (2013) *Gekaufte Zeit. Die vertagte Krise des demokratischen Kapitalismus,* Suhrkamp, p. 28; Wolfgang Streeck (2014) 'How Will Capitalism End?', *New Left Review* 87, May-June.

111. Wolfgang Streeck (2012) 'Citizens as Customers', *New Left Review* 76, July-August; Streeck, 'How Will Capitalism?'.

112. Wolfgang Streeck (2012) 'Markets and Peoples', *New Left Review,* 73, January-February; Streeck, *Buying Time.*

113. Streeck, 'How Will Capitalism End?'.

114. Streeck, 'The Crises'.

115. KPA-15-4, Karl Polanyi (n.d.) 'Socialism'.

116. KPA-20-16, Karl Polanyi (1939) 'Coercion and Defence'.

117. Karl Polanyi (1925) 'Neue Erwägungen zu unserer Theorie und Praxis'. *Der Kampf,* Jänner.

118. KPA-9-2, Polanyi, Notes; KPA-18-6, Polanyi, 'Fascism'.

119. Lucio Colleti (1972) *From Rousseau to Lenin: Studies in Ideology and Society,* Monthly Review Press, pp. 107–08.

120. For example, Carol Pateman (1970) *Participation and Democratic Theory,* Cambridge University Press.

121. Karl Marx (1850) *Class Struggles in France,* www.marxists.org/archive/marx/works/1850/class-struggles-france/. Some (for example, Adam Przeworski (1985) *Capitalism and Social Democracy,* Cambridge University Press, p. 39) read the same passage as proposing that universal suffrage in the political sphere naturally progresses to democracy in the economic sphere, but that is in my view a misreading.

122. Marx, *Class Struggles in France.*

123. Karl Marx (1844) *On the Jewish Question,* www.marxists.org/archive/marx/works/1844/jewish-question. Some, such as Claude Lefort, read this text as a wholesale rejection of bourgeois rights. In fact it argues against those who see political emancipation as a false goal, that political emancipation is a condition for human emancipation. Claude Lefort (1986) 'Politics and Human Rights', in Lefort, ed., *The Political Forms of Modern Society,* Polity.

124. Jason Moore (2014) *Capitalism in the Web of Life: Ecology and the Accumulation of Capital,* Verso.

125. Nancy Fraser (2015) 'Legitimation Crisis? On the Political Contradictions of Financialized Capitalism', *Critical Historical Studies,* 2(2), p. 161; Nancy Fraser (2014) 'Behind Marx's "Hidden Abode": For an Expanded Conception of Capitalism', *New Left Review,* 86, March-April, p. 70.

126. Marx, *Class Struggles in France.*

127. Fraser, 'Behind', p. 68.

128. Fred Block and Margaret Somers (2014) 'The Return of Karl Polanyi', *Dissent,* www.dissentmagazine.org/article/the-return-of-karl-polanyi

129. KPA-15-2, Polanyi, 'Conflicting Philosophies'.

CHAPTER 4

1. In Gyorgy Litvan (1991) 'Democratic and Socialist Values in Karl Polanyi's Thought', in Margucrite Mendell and Daniel Salée, eds, *The Legacy of Karl Polanyi; Market, State and Society at the End of the Twentieth Century,* Macmillan, p. 255.

2. Karl Polanyi (1922) 'Lloyd George', *Bécsi Magyar Újság,* 24 October.

3. Karl Polanyi (2016) 'The Test of Socialism', in Gareth Dale, ed., *Karl Polanyi: The Hungarian Writings*, Manchester University Press; KPA-2-2, Karl Polanyi (1920–22) Draft manuscript.

4. Aurel Kolnai (1999) *Political Memoirs*, Lexington, p. 133.

5. KPA-21-1, Karl Polanyi (1936) 'The Paradox of Freedom'.

6. KPA-21-33, Karl Polanyi (n.d.) 'Christian Left Study Circle'.

7. KPA-18-1, Karl Polanyi (1931) 'Austria and Free Trade', p. 363; Karl Polanyi (2002 [1933]) 'Fünfjahrplan abgebremst', in Michele Cangiani and Claus Thomasberger, eds, *Chronik der großen Transformation*, Band 1, Metropolis, pp. 304–06; Tibor Frank (1999) 'Situation Berlin. Ungarische Wissenschaftler und Künstler in Deutschland, 1919–1933', *IMIS Beiträge*, Heft 10.

8. Kari Polanyi-Levitt, interviews, 1 June, 6 September and 13 December 2008, Montreal; KPA-15-2 Karl Polanyi (1937–38) 'Conflicting Philosophies in Modern Society'; KPA-20-14, Christian Left Group/Karl Polanyi (1939) 'Russia in the World', *Bulletins for Socialists*, no. 4.

9. KPA-17-18, Karl Polanyi (1937) 'Modern Governments – Progress or Regress?'; KPA-18-6, Karl Polanyi (1934) 'Fascism and Marxian Terminology', p. 129; Kolnai, *Political Memoirs*, p. 133.

10. Mohammad Nafissi (2005) *Ancient Athens and Modern Ideology: Value, Theory and Evidence in Historical Sciences*, University of London Institute of Classical Studies, p. 169.

11. PFP-212-326, Karl Polanyi (1958) to Misi, 5 January.

12. KPA-8-2, Karl Polanyi (1934–46) 'Russia and the British Working Class'; KPA-15-10; Polanyi, 'Study of Human Institutions'. Emphasis added.

13. MPP-17-7, Karl Polanyi (mid-1930s) to Misi.

14. KPA-7-3, Karl Polanyi (1934–46) Notes on readings; KPA-20-19, Karl Polanyi (1934) Lectures; KPA-21-2, Karl Polanyi (1936) 'Xty and the Social Order'.

15. KPA-18-10, Karl Polanyi (1934) 'What Three-fold State?'; KPA-35-10, Karl Polanyi (1949) 'Economic History and the Problem of Freedom'.

16. KPA-15-4, Karl Polanyi (1936–40) Morley College lectures.

17. KPA-8-2, Karl Polanyi (early/mid-1940s) 'Social Factors in Recent European History'.

18. KPA-17-18, Polanyi, 'Modern Governments'.

19. KPA-18-9, Karl Polanyi (1934) 'Marxism Re-stated'. See also Karl Polanyi (2005) 'Sozialistische Rechnungslegung', in *Chronik der großen Transformation*, Band 3, ed. by Michele Cangiani et al., Metropolis.

20. MPP-17-7, Polanyi to Misi.

21. KPA-30-6, Karl Polanyi (1963) 'Hazánk Kötelessége', *Kortárs*, pp. 1843–44; KPA-8-14, Karl Polanyi (1934–46) Notes on readings.

22. KPA-16-16, Karl Polanyi (1938–39) 'International Affairs'; KPA-18-38, Karl Polanyi (n.d.) 'The Roots of Pacifism'; KPA-20-14, Polanyi/Christian Left, 'Russia'.

23. KPA-16-14, Polanyi, 'International Affairs'.

24. KPA-7-3, Polanyi, Notes. In combining a political stance close to Stalinism with an admiration for Trotsky's person and contribution to the socialist cause, Polanyi resembled his friend Laski. Isaac Deutscher (2003) *The Prophet Outcast: Trotsky 1929–1940*, Verso, p. 217.

25. KPA-8-4, Karl Polanyi (1934–46) 'Stages of the Russian Revolution'; KPA-20-2, Karl Polanyi (1938–39) 'Tame Empires'; Karl Polanyi, (1937) *Europe To-Day*, Workers' Educational Trade Union Committee. Elsewhere he identifies 'an element of truth'

in Trotsky's theory of permanent revolution, viz. 'the crises of democracy and capitalism'. KPA-15-4, Polanyi, Morley lectures.

26. KPA-20-14, Polanyi/Christian Left, 'Russia'.
27. Karl Polanyi (2003 [1927]) 'Die neue Weltlage', in Michele Cangiani and Claus Thomasberger, eds, *Chronik der großen Transformation*, Band 2, Metropolis, p. 64.
28. Karl Polanyi (2003 [1934]) 'Wo hält Sowjetrußland?', in *Chronik der großen Transformation*, Band 2, Metropolis, pp. 308–09; KPA-20-2, Karl Polanyi (1938–39) 'Tame Empires;' KPA-42-17, Karl Polanyi (n.d.) 'Plan for Work', pp. 7–8.
29. KPA-20-14, Polanyi/Christian Left, 'Russia'; Georgi Derluguian (2013) 'The Lessons of Communism', in Immanuel Wallerstein et al., eds, *Does Capitalism Have a Future?*, Oxford University Press.
30. Ralph Miliband (1973) *Parliamentary Socialism: A Study in the Politics of Labour*, Second edition, Merlin Press, p. 198.
31. Michele Cangiani (2009) 'The Unknown Karl Polanyi', *International Review of Sociology: Revue Internationale de Sociologie*, 19(2), p. 369.
32. Michael Newman (1993) *Harold Laski: A Political Biography*, Macmillan, p. 186; Paul Corthorn (2006) *In the Shadow of the Dictators: The British Left in the 1930s*, Tauris, p. 67.
33. Paul Flewers (2008) *The New Civilisation? Understanding Stalin's Soviet Union 1929–1941*, Francis Boutle, pp. 48, 50, 114.
34. Noreen Branson (1997) *History of the Communist Party of Great Britain, 1941–1951*, Lawrence & Wishart, p. 5.
35. KPA-18-23, Karl Polanyi (1943) 'Why Make Russia Run Amok?', p. 406.
36. KPA-17-14, Karl Polanyi (1936) 'World Politics Today'.
37. MPP-17-5, Karl Polanyi (1935) to Misi, 31 November.
38. KPA-7-3, Polanyi, Notes.
39. KPA-19-8, Karl Polanyi (n.d.) 'The Meaning of Parliamentary Democracy'.
40. KPA-18-39, Karl Polanyi (1938) 'The Meaning of Peace'.
41. KPA-19-8, Polanyi, 'Meaning of Parliamentary'.
42. As Polanyi put it in his notes, 'A democracy may have to set up [a dictatorship] to defend itself. Dictatorship in USSR turned an illiterate into a literate country, i.e. democracy'. KPA-7-3, Polanyi, Notes.
43. Here, as often, Polanyi's view resembled Bauer's. Otto Bauer (1976) *Werkausgabe*, Band IV, Europa Verlag, pp. 178–79, 214.
44. Karl Polanyi (1935) 'The Essence of Fascism', in Karl Polanyi et al., eds, *Christianity and the Social Revolution*, Gollancz. Cf. Aurel Kolnai (1999) *Political Memoirs*, Lexington, p. 133.
45. KPA-15-2, Polanyi, 'Conflicting Philosophies'. Karl Polanyi (2002 [1936]) 'Russischer Verfassungswandel', in Michele Cangiani and Claus Thomasberger, eds, *Chronik der großen Transformation*, Band 1, Metropolis, pp. 316–17.
46. KPA-16-16, Karl Polanyi, 'The Russian Trials in World Politics'; KPA-20-10, Auxiliary Christian Left (1938) Newsletters; KPA-20-14, Polanyi/Christian Left, 'Russia'.
47. KPA-15-3, Karl Polanyi (1938) 'Perilous Europe'.
48. KPA-17-1, Karl Polanyi (1938–39) 'Canterbury XII'.
49. KPA-20-14, Polanyi/Christian Left, 'Russia'.
50. Judith Szapor (2005) *The Hungarian Pocahontas: The Life and Times of Laura Polanyi Stricker, 1882–1959*, East European Monographs, p. 97.
51. An example is Friedrich Adler. See Deutscher, *Prophet Outcast*, p. 298. Even Laski, who had published a book as late as 1935 that extolled the Soviet justice system, condemned the Moscow trials as 'a travesty of justice' and an imitation of 'German

methods'. (Paul Corthorn (2006) *In the Shadow of the Dictators: The British Left in the 1930s*, Tauris, p. 99.) Many social democrats, however, remained aloof – including H. G. Wells and the Webbs. Deutscher, *Prophet Outcast*, p. 300.

52. Jean Richards, telephone interview, 17 August 2011.
53. MPP-17-6, Karl Polanyi (1936) to Misi 17 January.
54. Walter Gulick (2003–04) 'Letters about Polanyi, Koestler, and Eva Zeisel', *Tradition and Discovery* 2, pp. 6–10.
55. MPP-17-11, Michael Polanyi (1944) to Karl, 16 June.
56. MPP-17-11, Karl Polanyi (1944) to Misi, 11 July. An additional factor in play may have been Karl's 'doubts' over Eva's character: 'her lifestyle, her exhibitionism.' Interview with Kari Polanyi-Levitt, Montreal, 13 December 2008. The sentiment was reciprocated. Eva and Karl 'didn't have quite such a great rapport as Karl did with others', and in this, I would speculate, Karl's position with respect to her prison experience played a part. Interview with Kari Polanyi-Levitt, Montreal, 13 December 2008. Jean Richards, telephone interview, 17 August 2011.
57. Nigel Harris (1968) *Beliefs in Society: The Problem of Ideology*, Penguin, p. 125.
58. Polanyi had likely read a recent work by Wells in which he reiterated his apocalyptic outlook: 'We human beings are facing gigantic forces that will either destroy our species altogether or lift it to an altogether unprecedented level of power and well-being. These forces have to be controlled or we shall be annihilated.' H.G. Wells (1942) *The Outlook for Homo Sapiens: An Unemotional Statement of the Things that are Happening to Him Now, and of the Immediate Possibilities Confronting Him*, Secker and Warburg, p. 198.
59. KPA-17-10, Karl Polanyi (1942) to Misi, 26 October.
60. KPA-18-25, Karl Polanyi, (1943) 'Friends of Democratic Hungary: America'.
61. MPP-17-11, Karl Polanyi (1945) to Michael, 10 June.
62. KPA-20-1 Karl Polanyi (mid-1940s) 'A moszkvai konferencia utan'; KPA-45-12 Abraham Rotstein (1957) 'Notes of Weekend XVII with Karl Polanyi', p. 62.
63. KPA-30-6, Karl Polanyi (1963) 'Hazánk Kötelessége', *Kortárs*; KPA-30-2, Polanyi on Polanyi (1958–1960); KPA-37-10, Karl Polanyi (1958) 'From the Diary of an Antimarxist'.
64. PFP-212-326, Karl Polanyi (1959) to Misi, 21 October; KPA-40-3 Karl Polanyi (1957) to Carter, 11 January.
65. MPP-17-12, Karl Polanyi (1958) to Misi, 5 March; KPA-53-2, Karl Polanyi (1963) to Terry Hopkins, 15 December.
66. KPP-1-4, Karl Polanyi (1961) to Erich Fromm, 14 January.
67. Pasternak's novel concludes in the 1920s but an epilogue alludes to the catastrophe of forced collectivisation and its relationship to the terror. Vadim Rogovin associates this with Trotsky's argument that the terror was implemented in response to the mass discontent that collectivisation generated. KPA-50-3, Karl Polanyi (1958) to Paul Medow, 11 November; Boris Pasternak (1958) *Doctor Zhivago*, Collins, p. 453; Vadim Rogovin (1998) *1937: Stalin's Year of Terror*, Mehring Books, p. xvii.
68. KPA-37-10, Polanyi, 'Diary of an Antimarxist'; KPA-45-11, Abraham Rotstein (1957) 'Notes of Weekend XV with Karl Polanyi', p. 42.
69. KPP-1-4, Polanyi to Fromm; KPA-37-10, Polanyi, 'Diary of an Antimarxist'; Karl Polanyi to György Heltai, in Dale, ed., *Karl Polanyi: The Hungarian Writings*, Manchester University Press.
70. In Hüseyin Özel (1997) 'Reclaiming Humanity: The Social Theory of Karl Polanyi', doctoral dissertation, University of Utah, p. 121.
71. KPA-40-1, Karl Polanyi (1954) 'Peisistratus: The Tyrannis Episode'.

72. KPA-39-6 Karl Polanyi (1954) 'Tyrannis and Democracy'. On Dionysus worship, cf. Barbara Ehrenreich (2008) *Dancing in the Streets: A History of Collective Joy*, Granta, and Robert Connor (1996) 'Civil Society, Dionysiac Festival, and the Athenian Democracy', in Josiah Ober and Charles Hedrick, eds, *Dēmokratia; A Conversation on Democracies Ancient and Modern,* Princeton University Press.

73. Karl Polanyi (1977) *The Livelihood of Man,* Academic Press, pp. 40–41, 60.

74. György Konrád and Ivan Szelényi (1979) *The Intellectuals on the Road to Class Power*, Harvester Press, pp. 47–63.

75. Although drawing heavily upon works by Konrád and Szelényi, Burawoy's theory of the Soviet system, in *The Politics of Production* (Verso, 1985), finds theoretical inspiration in other sources too, from Marc Rakovsky to Janos Kornai. See also Linda Fuller (1999) *Where Was the Working Class? Revolution in Eastern Germany*, University of Illinois Press.

CHAPTER 5

1. This chapter includes reworked material from Gareth Dale (2008) 'Karl Polanyi's *The Great Transformation*: Perverse Effects, Protectionism, and *Gemeinschaft*', *Economy and Society*, 37(4), pp. 495–524.

2. In 1943, Karl wrote his brother that *The Great Transformation* 'runs strictly along the lines of the original outline' that he had mapped out, 'point for point', in 1939. MPP-17-10, Karl Polanyi (1943) to Misi, 8 July.

3. KPA-47-11, Karl Polanyi (1941) to Marschak, 29 January.

4. Adam Smith (1993) *An Inquiry into the Nature and Causes of the Wealth of Nations*, Oxford University Press, p. 299.

5. KPA-11-8, KP 'Notes on Readings'. 1934–46.

6. KPA-8-7, Karl Polanyi (1934–46) 'The Rise and Decline of Market Economy'.

7. KPA-18-8, Karl Polanyi (n.d.) 'The Fascist Virus'.

8. KPA-8-7, Polanyi, 'Rise and Decline'; KPA-21-22, Karl Polanyi (1937) 'Community and Society. The Christian Criticism of Our Social Order'.

9. KPA-16-2, Karl Polanyi (1945–46) Lecture course: Syllabus.

10. KPA-21-1, Karl Polanyi (1936) 'The Paradox of Freedom'; KPA-35-10, Karl Polanyi (1949) 'Economic History and the Problem of Freedom'.

11. KPA-15-2 Karl Polanyi (1937-38) 'Conflicting Philosophies in Modern Society'; KPA-8-7, Polanyi, 'Rise and Decline'; KPA-16-15, Karl Polanyi (1937–40) 'Lectures on Modern European History'.

12. KPA-15-2, Polanyi, 'Conflicting Philosophies'.

13. KPA-15-4, Karl Polanyi (1936–40) Morley College lectures.

14. KPA-31-10, Karl Polanyi (n.d.) 'The Trend Towards an Integrated Society'.

15. KPA-19-5, Karl Polanyi (1941) 'Plan of a Book on the "Origins of the Cataclysm"', p. 4.

16. KPA-16-15, Polanyi, 'Lectures'; KPA-19-5, Polanyi, 'Plan', p. 5.

17. KPA-15-4, Polanyi, Morley lectures.

18. KPA-16-15, Polanyi, 'Lectures'; KPA-15-2, Polanyi, 'Conflicting Philosophies'; KPA-20-16, Karl Polanyi (1939) 'Coercion and Defence'.

19. KPA-18-38, Karl Polanyi (n.d.) 'The Roots of Pacifism'.

20. KPA-15-2, Polanyi, 'Conflicting Philosophies'; KPA-19-5, Polanyi, 'Plan'; KPA-8-7, Karl Polanyi (1934–46) 'The Christian and the World Economic Crisis'.

21. KPA-20-16, Polanyi, 'Coercion'.

22. KPA-19-5, Polanyi, 'Plan', p. 6.

23. KPA-8-7, Polanyi, 'Christian'; Karl Polanyi (2005) 'Faschismus und Marxistische Terminologie', in Cangiani, Polanyi-Levitt and Thomasberger, eds, *Chronik der großen Transformation*, Band 3, Metropolis, p. 237.

24. KPA-20-16, Polanyi, 'Coercion'.

25. KPA-16-15, Polanyi, 'Lectures'.

26. Howard Brick (2006) *Transcending Capitalism: Visions of a New Society in Modern American Thought*, Cornell University Press, p. 129; Nils Gilman (2006) 'The Prophet of Post-Fordism: Peter Drucker and the Legitimation of the Corporation', in Nelson Lichtenstein, ed., *American Capitalism: Social Thought and Political Economy in the Twentieth Century*, University of Pennsylvania Press.

27. Nigel Harris (1972) *Competition and the Corporate Society: British Conservatives, the State and Industry, 1945–1964*, Methuen, p. 51.

28. Harris, *Competition*; Edmund Phelps (2007) 'Corporatism and Keynes: His Views on Growth', http://capitalism.columbia.edu/files/ccs/CCSWP20_Phelps.pdf

29. Karl Polanyi (2002) 'Zur Sozialisierungsfrage', in Cangiani, Polanyi-Levitt and Thomasberger, eds, *Chronik der großen Transformation*, Band 3, Metropolis.

30. MPP-17-9, Karl Polanyi (1941) to Misi, 22 August.

31. John Maynard Keynes (1926) 'The End of Laissez-Faire', www.panarchy.org/keynes/laissezfaire.1926.html

32. KPA-1-34, Karl Polanyi (1926) Untitled review.

33. Polanyi (2002) [1928]) 'Schmalenbach und Liberalismus', in *Chronik der großen Transformation, Band 1*, ed. by Michele Cangiani and Claus Thomasberger, Metropolis.

34. John Maynard Keynes (1933) 'National Self-Sufficiency', *The Yale Review*, 22(4), pp. 755–69.

35. KPA-45-3, Abraham Rotstein (1956) 'Notes of Weekend II with Karl Polanyi', p. 25; Keynes, quoted in Harris, *Competition*, p. 51.

36. I am not suggesting that Polanyi sympathised with ordoliberalism, but others have done, notably Rainer Hank. (Fittingly, in the *Frankfurter Allgemeine Zeitung*, which Welter edited for several decades.) Hank avers that Polanyi shared Alfred Müller-Armack's belief that 'das Prinzip der Freiheit auf dem Markt' should be joined with the principle of 'sozialen Ausgleichs'. But this is a superficial comparison. It occludes the extent to which the ordoliberal economist adopted positions abhorrent to Polanyi. Müller-Armack admired *Mein Kampf*, regarded the Nazi regime as an 'accentuated democracy', and called for the 'complete integration of society into the state', with the ultimate purpose of liberating the 'entrepreneur', The thesis that Polanyi shares with ordoliberals is that states play a crucial part in the creation of the market order, but numerous others – including Marx – argued similarly. See Rainer Hank (2014) 'Karl Polanyi: Der entfesselte Kapitalismus', *Frankfurter Allgemeine Zeitung*, 19 December; Werner Bonefeld (2012) 'Freedom and the Strong State: On German Ordoliberalism', *New Political Economy*, 17(5) p. 635; Ralf Ptak (2009) 'Neoliberalism in Germany: Revisiting the Ordoliberal Foundations of the Social Market Economy', in Philip Mirowski and Dieter Plehwe, eds, *The Road from Mont Pèlerin: The Making of the Neoliberal Thought Collective*, Harvard University Press, p. 122.

37. KPA-10-4, 'Notes on Readings'.

38. Eric Welter (1931) *Dreifache Krise: Die Deutsche Wirtschaft im Jahre 1930*, Societäts-Verlag, p. 47

39. Dale, *Karl Polanyi*; Kurtuluş Gemici (2015) 'The Neoclassical Origins of Polanyi's Self-Regulating Market', *Sociological Theory*, 33(2), pp. 125–47.

40. KPA-10-4, Karl Polanyi (1934-46) Notes on readings.

41. Ludwig von Mises (1995 [1927]) *Liberalismus*, Akademie Verlag, pp. 68–69.

42. Lionel Robbins (1934) *The Great Depression*, Books for Libraries Press, pp. 59–60, 189.

43. KP 10-2, 'Notes on readings'; Mises, *Liberalismus*, pp. 73–75.

44. William Morris (1992 [1890]) *News from Nowhere*, Routledge, pp. 90–93.

45. KPA-11-8, Polanyi, 'Notes'. Emphasis added.

46. KPA-15-2, Polanyi, 'Conflicting Philosophies'.

47. KPA-16-15, Polanyi, 'Lectures'.

48. KPA-16-13, Karl Polanyi (1938–39) Lecture XXIII. This argument was repeated in *The Great Transformation*, with a nod to Mises.

49. KPA-16-16 Karl Polanyi (1938–39) WEA Lecture IX; KPA-15-4, Polanyi, Morley lectures.

50. KPA-16-14, Karl Polanyi (1939–40) lectures on 'Modern European History'. Cf. Polanyi's belief that where 'non-market relationships are involved in buying and selling they must be regarded as flaws in the market system'. KPA-31-11, Karl Polanyi (1953–55) 'The Institutionalization of the Economic Process'.

51. Polanyi, *The Great Transformation*, pp. 176, 231; KPA-15-4, Polanyi, Morley lectures.

52. KPA-19-18, Karl Polanyi (n.d.) 'Interventionism and the Alternative'.

53. Ludwig von Mises (1932) *Die Gemeinwirtschaft: Untersuchungen über den Sozialismus*, Gustav Fischer, p. 475.

54. KPA-20-3, Karl Polanyi (1938–39) Book plan. Polanyi, like the Austrians, tended to regard 'Planning and Socialism' as fundamentally the same, in the long run. (Cf. Robbins, *The Great Depression*, p. 146). Yet he does display a recognition, albeit usually held in the background, that 'the capitalists' too 'are out for planning'. And he warned his students that 'unless the working class is politically up to the mark, the *new planning* will keep them in permanent subservience'. KPA-15-8, Karl Polanyi (1943–44) Lecture 18.

55. Joseph Schumpeter (1954 [1943]) *Capitalism, Socialism and Democracy*, Fourth edn., Unwin, pp. xiii–xiv, 139, 143, 156, 418.

56. Robert Allen (1991) Opening Doors: The Life and Work of Joseph Schumpeter, Transaction, p. 42.

57. KPA-57-8, Karl Polanyi (1943) to Misi, 25 October.

58. MPP-17-13, Karl Polanyi (n.d.) to Misi.

59. Incidentally, Schumpeter's seminal essay on the 'sociology of imperialisms' is constructed on the same equation.

60. KPA-19-8 Karl Polanyi (n.d.) 'Crisis of 1920s'.

61. KPA-57-5, Michael Polanyi (1943) to Karl, 17 December.

62. Philip Mirowski (2004) *The Effortless Economy of Science?*, Duke University Press, p. 77.

63. Michael Polanyi, quoted in Phil Mullins and Struan Jacobs (n.d.) 'Michael Polanyi and Karl Mannheim', www.missouriwestern.edu/orgs/polanyi/tad%20web%20archive/tad32-1/tad32-1-fnl-pg20-43-pdf.pdf

64. MPP-17-11, Karl Polanyi (1945) to Misi 1 November; KPA-9-3, Karl Polanyi (1934–46) Notes on Lippmann.

65. Eliot went on to join Isaiah Berlin and Richard Crossman in founding the British Society for Cultural Freedom, affiliated to the CIA-backed Congress for Cultural Freedom.

66. Julia Stapleton (2001) *Political Intellectuals and Public Identities in Britain since 1850*, Manchester University Press.

67. Keith Clements, ed. (2010) *The Moot Papers: Faith, Freedom and Society 1938–1944*, Continuum, p. 8.

68. Matthew Grimley (2004) *Citizenship, Community, and the Church of England: Liberal Anglican Theories of the State between the Wars*, Clarendon Press, p. 207.

69. Christian Borch (2012) *The Politics of Crowds: An Alternative History of Sociology*, Cambridge University Press, p. 174.

70. Jefferson Pooley (2006) 'An Accident of Memory. Edward Shils, Paul Lazarsfeld and the History of American Mass Communication Research', DPhil, Columbia University, p. 96.

71. Colin Loader (1985) *The Intellectual Development of Karl Mannheim*, Cambridge University Press, pp. 128ff.; Pooley, 'Accident of Memory'.

72. Karl Mannheim (1940) *Man and Society in an Age of Reconstruction*, Routledge, p. 157. Conceivably, Polanyi borrowed the image. In his Morley lecture notes (KPA-15-4) we find: 'The regulation of society does not mean the restriction of free exchange or enterprise. Regulation of traffic is not meant to prevent man from criss-crossing the road.'

73. Mannheim, *Man and Society*, pp. 162, 250.

74. Stefan Collini (2006) *Absent Minds: Intellectuals in Britain*, Oxford University Press, p. 318; David Kettler and Meja Volker (n.d.) 'Karl Mannheim's Jewish Question', www.bard.edu/contestedlegacies/lib/kettler_articles.php?

75. Mullins and Jacobs, 'Polanyi and Mannheim'.

76. Walter Gulick (n.d.) 'Michael and Karl Polanyi: Conflict and Convergence', *First Principles*, www.firstprinciplesjournal.com/articles.aspx?article=1518&loc=qs

77. Pooley, 'Accident of Memory', p. 130.

78. Thus, for Michael, contra Hayek (and Popper), the 'free society is not an Open Society, but one fully dedicated to a distinctive set of beliefs'. Michael Polanyi, quoted in R. T. Allen (1998) *Beyond Liberalism: The Political Thought of F. A. Hayek & Michael Polanyi*, Transaction, p. 169.

79. It perhaps also contains a trace of the concept of 'sobornost' found in the novels of Dostoyevsky and Tolstoy.

80. Struan Jacobs (2000) 'Spontaneous Order: Michael Polanyi and Friedrich Hayek', *Critical Review of International Social and Political Philosophy*, 3(4), p. 58.

81. MPP-17-12, Michael Polanyi (1953) to Karl, 3 December.

82. Pooley, 'Accident of Memory', pp. 143–47.

83. Karl Polanyi (1947) 'On Belief in Economic Determinism', *Sociological Review*, 39(1), p. 102.

84. Hüseyin Özel (n.d.) 'The Road to Serfdom in the Light of *The Great Transformation*: A Comparison on the Basis of Unintended Consequences', http://yunus.hacettepe.edu.tr/~ozel/HayekvsPolanyi.pdf

85. Polanyi, *The Great Transformation*, p. 141, emphasis mine.

86. William Connolly (2013) *The Fragility of Things: Self-Organizing Processes, Neoliberal Fantasies, and Democratic Activism*, Duke University Press, p. 66.

87. Christina Petoulas (2001) *Hayek's Liberalism and its Origins: His Idea of Spontaneous Order and the Scottish Enlightenment*, Routledge, p. 12.

88. Timothy Sandefur (2009) 'Some Problems with Spontaneous Order', *The Independent Review*, 14(1), pp. 5–25.

89. Friedrich Hayek (1986 [1944]) *The Road to Serfdom*, ARK paperbacks.

90. Ira Katznelson (2003) *Desolation and Enlightenment: Political Knowledge after Total War, Totalitarianism and the Holocaust*, Columbia University Press, pp. 22–23.

91. KPA-4-1, Aurel Kolnai (1933) 'Totaler Staat und Zivilization'; James Chappel (2011) 'The Catholic Origins of Totalitarianism Theory in Interwar Europe', *Modern Intellectual History*, 8(3), pp. 561–90.

92. KPA-2-21 Karl Polanyi (1933) 'Die Wirtschaft ist für den Faschismus'.

93. Bertrand Russell (1938) *Power: A New Social Analysis*. In Polanyi's copy of Russell's book these lines are annotated 'very good'. Cf. KPA-9-3, Karl Polanyi (n.d.) Notes on Bertrand Russell.

94. At one point in the 1930s, Kolnai, when talking to a British immigration official, made a point of dissociating himself from the leftism of the Gollancz publishing house. Polanyi 'severely reprimanded' him for this. Francis Dunlop (2002) *The Life and Thought of Aurel Kolnai*, Ashgate, p. 153 (and cf. p. 195).

95. KPA-18-10, Karl Polanyi (1934) 'What Three-fold State?', *New Britain*, 2(43); Martha Lampland (2016) *The Value of Labor: The Science of Commodification in Hungary, 1920–1956*, University of Chicago Press, p. 160.

96. KPA-2-21, Polanyi, 'Wirtschaft ist für'.

97. Mannheim, too, criticised those who identified fascism with Bolshevism. Duncan Kelly (2002) 'Rethinking Franz Neumann's Route to *Behemoth*', *History of Political Thought,* XXIII(3), pp. 458–96; William Jones (1999) *The Lost Debate: German Socialist Intellectuals and Totalitarianism*, University of Illinois Press, p. 7.

98. KPA-8-13, Karl Polanyi (1934–46) Notes on readings.

99. Peter Drucker (1939) *The End of Economic Man: A Study of the New Totalitarianism*, Heinemann, p. 227.

100. KPA-49-4, Peter Drucker (1955) to Karl 14 June.

101. Ian Hall (2012) *Dilemmas of Decline: British Intellectuals and World Politics, 1945–75*, University of California Press.

102. E. H. Carr (2001 [1939]) *The Twenty Years' Crisis*, Palgrave, pp. 108–20.

103. John Ruggie (2002) 'At Home Abroad, Abroad at Home: International Liberalization and Domestic Stability in the New World Economy', in Eivind Hovden and Edward Keene, eds, *The Globalization of Liberalism,* Palgrave Macmillan, p. 99.

104. KPA-9-4, Karl Polanyi (n.d.) Notes on E. H. Carr.

105. Jo-Anne Pemberton (2001) 'Towards a New World Order: A Twentieth Century Story', *Review of International Studies*, 27(2), pp. 265–72.

106. Horst Mendershausen (1943) *The Economics of War*, Prentice-Hall, pp. 56–57.

107. Daniel Immerwahr (2009) 'Polanyi in the United States: Peter Drucker, Karl Polanyi, and the Midcentury Critique of Economic Society', *Journal of the History of Ideas*, 70(3), pp. 445–66.

108. Karl Polanyi (1934–46) Notes on readings.

109. Walter Lippmann, (1943 [1937]) *The Good Society*, Billing and Sons, pp. 172–73.

110. As Polanyi puts it (*The Great Transformation,* 2001 edn, p. 148), Lippmann offered 'an account of the double movement substantially similar to our own, but [he] put an entirely different interpretation on it'.

111. Lippmann, *The Good Society*, pp. 211, 225, 235–37.

112. Lippmann, *The Good Society*, pp. 191, 198–99, 206.

113. Rougier's own biography appeared rather to confirm the democrat-socialist/liberal-fascist dichotomy: he collaborated closely with Marshal Pétain and, later, with the Nouvelle Droite. Angus Burgin (2012) *The Great Persuasion: Reinventing Free Markets since the Depression*, Harvard University Press.

114. Karl Polanyi (n.d.) to Kari and Ilona, provisionally filed in KPA File 131.

115. 'In this sense,' he thought, 'the Co-operative Movement may regard itself as the pioneer of a new society.' KPA-17-24, Karl Polanyi (1945) 'Rise and Decline of the Profit Motive', London Co-operative Society Weekend School.

116. János Gyurgyák, ed. (1986) *Karl Polanyi, 1886–1964*, Fővárosi Szabó Ervin Könyvtár, p. 181.

117. KPA-49-4, Peter Drucker (1955) to Polanyi, 2 October.

118. KPA-47-15, Peter Drucker (1945) to Polanyi, 21 May.

119. Albert Hirschman (1991) *The Rhetoric of Reaction: Perversity, Futility, Jeopardy*, Harvard University Press, pp. 27ff.; KPA-16-14, Polanyi, 'Modern European History'.

120. KPA-16-14, Polanyi, 'Modern European History'.

121. KPA-20-6, Karl Polanyi, (n.d.) 'Democracy vs Total Crisis'.

122. KPA-15-8, Polanyi, 'Government and Industry'.

123. KPA-19-17, Karl Polanyi (n.d.) 'The Eclipse of Panic and the Outlook for Socialism'.

124. KPA-9-1, Karl Polanyi (1934–46) Notes on readings.

125. KPA-8-12, Karl Polanyi (1934–46) Notes on readings.

126. KPA-20-16, Polanyi, 'Coercion'.

127. KPA-16-13, Karl Polanyi (1938–39) Lecture XXIV; KPA-16-11, Karl Polanyi (1937–38) Lecture 21.

128. KPA-19-5, Polanyi, 'Plan', p. 8.

129. Fred Block (2001) 'Karl Polanyi and the Writing of *The Great Transformation*', Paper presented at the Eighth International Karl Polanyi Conference, Mexico City.

130. KPA-29-10, Felix Schafer (1973–74) 'Karl Polanyi's Life in Vienna'.

131. KPA-18-26, Karl Polanyi (1944) 'Towards a New October Revolution in Hungary'.

132. Terry Eagleton (2011) *Why Marx Was Right*, Yale University Press.

133. KPA-21-5, Karl Polanyi (1936) 'The Nature of the Present World Crisis'.

134. KPA-47-12, Richard Tawney (1942) to Polanyi, 16 September.

135. KPA-47-12, Karl Polanyi (1942) to John, 12 September.

136. KPA-48-1, G.D.H. Cole (1946) to Polanyi, 11 February, and as reported by Polanyi (MPP-17-10, Polanyi (1943) to Misi, 9 November.

137. For example, Samantha Williams (*Poverty, Gender and the Life-Cycle under the English Poor Laws*, Oxford, 2012) shows that the majority of relief was provided to elderly and lone-parent families, and that Speenhamland-type relief was offered at times of crisis, mainly after 1815, and did not fundamentally alter social behaviour.

138. Polanyi, *The Great Transformation*, pp. 80, 299–301. Emphasis added.

139. For detailed discussion, see Gareth Dale, *Polanyi: Limits of the Market*, Chapter 2.

140. MPP-17-10, Michael Polanyi (1943) to Karl, 9 December. In contrast, recent accounts of the 1943 Bengal Famine highlight the role of British imperialism and racism – for example, Madhusree Mukerjee (2010) *Churchill's Secret War: The British Empire and the Ravaging of India during the Second World War,* Basic Books.

141. KPA-19-17, Polanyi, 'Eclipse of Panic'.

142. MPP-17-10, Karl Polanyi (1943) to Michael, 1 November.

143. KPA-42-1, Karl Polanyi (1960–63) 'Economy and Society in the Negro Kingdom of Dahomey'. On this, see Alexander Ebner (2011) 'Transnational Markets and the Polanyi Problem', in Christian Joerges and Josef Falke, eds, *Karl Polanyi, Globalisation and the Potential of Law in Transnational Markets*, Hart Publishing, p. 22, and Craig Muldrew (1998) *The Economy of Obligation: The Culture of Credit and Social Relations in Early Modern England*, Macmillan, p. 327. Unlike Polanyi, Muldrew centres this development in the sixteenth and seventeenth centuries.

144. KPA-15-10, Karl Polanyi (1944) 'The Study of Human Institutions (Economic and Social)'; KPA-15-8, Polanyi, 'Government and Industry'.

145. Polanyi, *The Great Transformation*, p. 260.
146. Samuel Knafo (2013) *The Making of Modern Finance: Liberal Governance and the Gold Standard*, Routledge, pp. 32, 175.
147. Karl Polanyi (1935) 'The Essence of Fascism', in Karl Polanyi et al., eds, *Christianity and the Social Revolution*, Gollancz.

CHAPTER 6

1. KPA-8-7, Karl Polanyi (mid-1940s) 'The New ABC of Foreign Policy'. This chapter includes reworked material from Gareth Dale and Nadine El-Enany (2013) 'The Limits of Social Europe: EU Law and the Ordo-liberal Agenda', *German Law Journal*, 14(5), pp. 613–50. I discuss Polanyi's international relations theory in Gareth Dale (2015) 'In Search of Karl Polanyi's International Relations Theory', *Review of International Studies*, http://journals.cambridge.org/abstract_S0260210515000273
2. Carlo Cristiano (2014) *The Political and Economic Thought of the Young Keynes: Liberalism, Markets and Empire*, Routledge.
3. John Maynard Keynes (1929) *The Economic Consequences of the Peace*, Harriman House. See also Donald Markwell (2006) *John Maynard Keynes and International Relations: Economic Paths to War and Peace*, Oxford University Press, p. 20.
4. John Maynard Keynes (1933) 'National Self-Sufficiency', *The Yale Review*, 22(4), pp. 755–69.
5. Markwell, *John Maynard Keynes*, pp. 196–97.
6. Dominic Lieven (2000) *Empire: The Russian Empire and Its Rivals*, Yale University Press.
7. Oscar Jaszi (1944) 'Nationalism and Nationalities', in M. B. Schnapper, ed., *Regionalism and World Organization: Post-war Aspects of Europe's Global Relationships*, American Council on Public Affairs, pp. 84–85, 90.
8. Margaret Cole (1974) 'H. G. Wells and the Fabian Society', in A. J. A. Morris, ed., *Edwardian Radicalism 1900–1914*, Routledge & Kegan Paul, p. 109.
9. KPA-21-2, Karl Polanyi (1936) 'Xtianity and the New Social Order'; Jaszi, 'Nationalism', pp. 95–96.
10. KPA-56-13, Karl Polanyi (1960) to Irene, 22 September.
11. Karl Polanyi (1947) *The Citizen and Foreign Policy*, Workers' Educational Association, p. 10.
12. KPA-52-2, Karl Polanyi (1962) to John, 1 May.
13. KPA-8-7, Polanyi, 'New ABC'.
14. Björn Hettne (2005) 'Beyond the "New" Regionalism', *New Political Economy*, 10(4), p. 548.
15. Hettne, 'Beyond', p. 548.
16. Björn Hettne (1993) 'Neo-Mercantilism: The Pursuit of Regionness', *Cooperation and Conflict*, 28(3), pp. 221–22; Björn Hettne (2002) 'The Europeanisation of Europe: Endogenous and Exogenous Dimensions', *Journal of European Integration*, 24(4), p. 326.
17. Hettne, 'Neo-Mercantilism', p. 221; Björn Hettne (1997) 'Europe in a World of Regions', in Richard Falk and Tamas Szentes, eds, *A New Europe in the Changing Global System*, United Nations University Press, p. 17.
18. Björn Hettne (2005) 'Regionalism and World Order', in Mary Farrell, Björn Hettne and Luk van Langenhove, eds, *Global Politics of Regionalism: Theory and Practice*, Pluto, pp. 273, 285–86; Björn Hettne (2005) 'Beyond the "New" Regionalism', *New Political Economy*, 10(4), p. 566.

19. Paul Copeland (2009) 'International Political Economy and European Integration: Applying Karl Polanyi's *The Great Transformation*', IPEG Papers in Global Political Economy, p. 40.

20. James Caporaso and Sidney Tarrow (2009) 'Polanyi in Brussels: Supranational Institutions and the Transnational Embedding of Markets', *International Organization*, 63(4), p. 599.

21. Caporaso and Tarrow, 'Polanyi in Brussels', p. 599.

22. Alexander Ebner (2006) 'The Intellectual Foundations of the Social Market Economy: Theory, Policy, and Implications for European Integration', *Journal of Economic Studies,* 33(3), p. 216.

23. Bernard Moss (2000) 'The European Community as Monetarist Construction: A Critique of Moravcsik', *Journal of European Area Studies*, 8(2), p. 259.

24. Wolfram Kaiser (2007) *Christian Democracy and the Origins of European Union*, Cambridge University Press, p. 305.

25. Costas Lapavitsas et al. (2010) 'Eurozone Crisis: Beggar Thyself and Thy Neighbour', Research on Money and Finance Occasional Report.

26. Gareth Dale (2004) *Between State Capitalism and Globalisation,* Peter Lang; Gareth Dale (2015) 'What Reunification Wrought', www.jacobinmag.com/2015/10/germany-cold-war-reunification-berlin-wall-stasi

27. Colin Crouch (2013) *Europe and Problems of Marketization: From Polanyi to Scharpf*, Firenze University Press, pp. 14, 20.

28. Fritz Scharpf (2010) 'The Asymmetry of European Integration, or Why the EU Cannot Be a "Social Market Economy"', *Socio-Economic Review* 8(2), p. 221; Crouch, *Europe*, p. 31.

29. Ebner, 'Transnational Markets', p. 37.

30. Greg Palast (2012) 'Robert Mundell, Evil Genius of the Euro', *Guardian,* 26 June, www.guardian.co.uk/commentisfree/2012/jun/26/robert-mundell-evil-genius-euro; Paul Krugman (2012) 'Mundell and the Euro', http://krugman.blogs.nytimes.com/2012/05/28/mundell-and-the-euro

31. Martin Höpner and Armin Schäfer (2010) 'Polanyi in Brussels? Embeddedness and the Three Dimensions of European Economic Integration', MPIfG Discussion Paper 10/8, Max-Planck-Institut für Gesellschaftsforschung, Köln. In this sense, Alain Supiot has archly observed, EU law resembles that of Communist China: in ECJ case law, 'as under Communist rule, loud proclamation of the fundamental rights of workers is accompanied by prohibition of their attempts to defend their interests freely and collectively'. Alain Supiot (2012) 'Under Eastern Eyes', *New Left Review* 73, January-February, pp. 35–36.

32. Höpner and Schäfer, 'Polanyi in Brussels?'.

33. Supiot, 'Eastern Eyes', pp. 31–32.

34. Martin Höpner and Armin Schäfer (2012) 'Embeddedness and Regional Integration: Waiting for Polanyi in a Hayekian Setting', *International Organization*, 66(3), p. 438; Höpner and Schäfer, 'Polanyi in Brussels?'.

35. For discussion, see Gareth Dale (2010) *Karl Polanyi: The Limits of the Market*, Polity, p. 202 and *passim*.

36. Ebner, 'Transnational Markets', p. 31.

37. Christian Joerges (2011) 'A New Type of Conflicts Law as the Legal Paradigm of the Postnational Constellation', in Joerges and Josef Falke, eds, *Karl Polanyi, Globalisation and the Potential of Law in Transnational Markets*, Hart Publishing, p. 473.

38. Höpner and Schäfer, 'Embeddedness', p. 434.

39. Höpner and Schäfer, 'Polanyi in Brussels?'.

40. Perry Anderson (1997) 'The Europe to Come', in Anderson and Peter Gowan, eds, *The Question of Europe*, Verso.

41. Perry Anderson (2009) *The New Old World*, Verso, p. 30; Raymond Plant (2010) *The Neo-liberal State*, Oxford University Press, p. 84.

42. Werner Bonefeld (2012) 'Neoliberal Europe and the Transformation of Democracy: On the State of Money and Law', in Petros Nousios, Andreas Tsolakis and Henk Overbeek, eds, *Globalisation and European Integration: Critical Approaches to Regional Order and International Relations*, Routledge, p. 51.

43. Hayek's proposal for a money-issuing authority insulated from political pressures was a central element in the Maastricht Treaty. According to Niels Thygesen, a member of the Delors Committee that drew up the first detailed blueprint for monetary union, the Hayekian concept was valued as a method by which to reduce the scope for 'lax' monetary policy. In the recollection of Otmar Issing, the first chief economist of the ECB, 'many strands in Hayek's thinking … may have influenced the course of the events leading to Monetary Union in subtle ways. What has happened with the introduction of the euro has indeed achieved the denationalisation of money, as advocated by Hayek'. Quoted in Harold James (2012) *Making the European Monetary Union*, Harvard University Press.

44. Höpner and Schäfer, 'Polanyi in Brussels?'.

45. In Jan-Werner Müller (2012) 'Beyond Militant Democracy?', *New Left Review* 73, January-February, p. 40.

46. Michelle Everson and Christian Joerges (2012) 'Reconfiguring the Politics–Law Relationship in the Integration Project through Conflicts–Law Constitutionalism', *European Law Journal*, 18(5), p. 645.

47. Anderson, *New Old*, pp. 66, 541.

48. Peter Burnham (2011) 'Towards a Political Theory of Crisis: Policy and Resistance across Europe', *New Political Science*, 33(4), pp. 493–507.

49. Wolfgang Streeck (2012) 'Das Ende der Nachkriegsdemokratie', *Süddeutsche Zeitung*, www.sueddeutsche.de/wirtschaft/ein-neuer-kapitalismus-das-ende-der-nachkriegsdemokratie-1.1427141; Wolfgang Streeck (2014) *Buying Time: The Delayed Crisis of Democratic Capitalism*, Verso, pp. 106, 116, 175.

50. Gideon Rachman (2012) 'Democracy Loses in Struggle to Save Euro', *Financial Times*, 10 September.

51. Wolfgang Münchau (2012) 'Greece Must Default if It Wants Democracy', *Financial Times*, 19 February.

CHAPTER 7

1. KPA-35-9, Karl Polanyi (1948) 'Notes on the Future Tasks of the Columbia University Submitted to the Department of Economics', 12 March.

2. KPA-48-4, Dwight Eisenhower (1949) to Mr and Mrs Polanyi, 3 February.

3. Ellen Schrecker (1998) *Many Are the Crimes: McCarthyism in America*, Little, Brown.

4. Landon Storrs (2013) *The Second Red Scare and the Unmaking of the New Deal Left*, Princeton University Press, p. 1.

5. Jennifer Delton (2013) *Rethinking the 1950s: How Anticommunism and the Cold War Made America Liberal,* Cambridge University Press, pp. 13–29.

6. Jonathan Neale (2015) 'Thinking about Feminism and Islamophobia 4: McCarthyism Old and New', https://sexismclassviolence.wordpress.com/2015/04/07/thinking-about-feminism-and-islamophobia-4-mccarthyism-old-and-new

7. Frederic Lee (2004) 'History and Identity: The Case of Radical Economics and Radical Economists, 1945–70', *Review of Radical Political Economics*, 36, p. 180.

8. Ellen Schrecker (1986) *No Ivory Tower: McCarthyism and the Universities*, Oxford University Press, p. 341.

9. David Price (2004) *Threatening Anthropology: McCarthyism and the FBI's Surveillance of Activist Anthropologists*, Duke University Press.

10. Anne Chapman, telephone interview, 19 July 2009.

11. KPA-49-1, Rosemary Arnold (1953) to Polanyi.

12. KPA-49-1, Karl Polanyi (1953) to Arnold, 23 June.

13. Storrs, *Second Red Scare*, p. 42.

14. Daniel Tompkins (2013) 'Moses Finkelstein and the American Scene: The Political Formation of Moses Finley, 1932–1955', in W. V. Harris, ed., *Moses Finley and Politics*, Brill.

15. David Price (2008) 'Materialism's Free Pass: Karl Wittfogel, McCarthyism, and the "Bureaucratization of Guilt"', in Dustin Wax, ed., *Anthropology at the Dawn of the Cold War*, Pluto, pp. 42–43; Price, *Threatening Anthropology*, p. 230. On Arensberg's involvement in the politically sensitive area of supervising interned Japanese-Americans during World War II, which may well have crossed the Boasian line from 'confronting power with truth' to 'supplying information to power'; see David Price (2008) *Anthropological Intelligence: The Deployment and Neglect of American Anthropology in the Second World War*, Duke University Press, Chapter 7.

16. Price, *Threatening Anthropology*.

17. Simon Winchester (2008) The Man Who Loved China: The Fantastic Story of the Eccentric Scientist Who *Unlocked the Mysteries of the Middle Kingdom*, Harper Perennial, pp. 210–11; Robert McCaughey (2003) *Stand, Columbia: A History of Columbia University in the City of New York*, Columbia University Press, pp. 345ff.

18. Leacock, quoted in Catherine McCoid (2008) 'Eleanor Burke Leacock and Intersectionality: Materialism, Dialectics, and Transformation', *Race, Gender & Class*, 15(1-2), p. 237.

19. McCaughey, *Stand, Columbia*. The FBI had leaned on publishers to ensure they rejected Fast's novel, forcing him to publish it himself. Frances Stonor Saunders (1999) *Who Paid the Piper? The CIA and the Cultural Cold War*, Granta, p. 53.

20. McCaughey, *Stand, Columbia*, p. 345.

21. Mills and Polanyi were not close. However, Mills did express a desire to attend Polanyi's faculty seminar, and Polanyi certainly encouraged him to do so. KPA-49-1, Karl Polanyi (1953) to Arthur R. Burns, 30 March; see also correspondence in KPA-49-2.

22. George Striker (1953) 'Kirk Sees No Faculty Probe for Reds Here', *Columbia Daily Spectator*, XCVII, 12 May.

23. McCaughey, *Stand, Columbia*, p. 345.

24. Gilana Keller (2012) 'Behind the Lion Curtain: McCarthyism at Columbia in the 1950s', www.columbiacurrent.org/2012/12/behind-the-lion-curtain-mccarthyism-at-columbia-in-the-1950s-essay

25. Schrecker, *No Ivory*, p. 340.

26. *Columbia Daily Spectator*, XCVII(11), 13 October 1952 and XCVII(11), 9 October 1952, p. 1; Seymour Martin Lipset (2001) 'The State of American Sociology', in Stephen Cole, ed., *What's Wrong with Sociology*, Transaction, p. 251.

27. David Sills (1987) *Paul Lazarsfeld, 1901–1976: A Memoir*, National Academy of Sciences.

28. Striker, 'Kirk Sees'.

29. His gender may have been a factor too. Price, *Threatening Anthropology*, p. 151.

30. KPA-49-3, Char (1954) to Karl Polanyi, 12 November.

31. Kari Polanyi-Levitt, email to the author, 20 May 2015. Polanyi himself had won a major Ford Foundation grant, which was renewed until 1958. Nonetheless, the anxiety that McLuhan reported was certainly not baseless.

32. A. M. Sperber (1986) *Murrow: His Life and Times*, Michael Joseph, p. 426.

33. Schrecker, *Many Crimes*, p. 292. Murrow's nose for deception was not always so sensitive. On his gullibility vis-à-vis the tobacco industry, see Erik Conway and Naomi Oreskes (2010) *Merchants of Doubt: How a Handful of Scientists Obscured the Truth on Issues from Tobacco Smoke to Global Warming*, Bloomsbury, p. 19.

34. Joseph McCarthy (1954) Reply to Edward R. Murrow, *See it Now* (CBS-TV, April 6), www.lib.berkeley.edu/MRC/murrowmccarthy2.html

35. During his spell in America, well before McCarthy, Laski was subjected to anti-socialist harassment. 'I am glad I had a return ticket,' he said upon returning to Britain from his last visit in 1948. In Ralph Miliband (1993) 'Harold Laski: An Exemplary Public Intellectual', *New Left Review* I/200, July-August.

36. KPA-35-10, Karl Polanyi (1949) 'Economic History and the Problem of Freedom'.

37. KPA-48-4, Karl Polanyi (1949) to Sandy Lindsay, 10 June.

38. Polanyi regarded Orwell's *1984* as a 'lurid intellectual obscenity', and regretted the 'taint' that it had left upon the Zeitgeist. KPA-57-8, Karl Polanyi (1956) to Michael, 23 February; see also correspondence in KPA-49-5 and KPA-45-16. When summing up McCarthyism in 1956, however, he borrowed a metaphor from Orwell's best-known novel: 'the awful military danger threatening from the East caused a panic, producing the "1984" leadership of a whole generation'. PFP-212-326, Karl Polanyi (1956) to Misi, 23 February.

39. Theodore Porter (2012) 'Foreword', in Mark Solovey and Hamilton Cravens, eds, *Cold War Social Science: Knowledge Production, Liberal Democracy, and Human Nature*, Palgrave Macmillan.

40. Price, *Threatening Anthropology*.

41. KPA-55-6, Kari Polanyi-Levitt (1983) to Louis Dumont, 14 December.

42. Lee, 'History and Identity', p. 180.

43. Neale, 'McCarthyism Old and New'.

44. KPA-18-31, Karl Polanyi (1945) 'What Kind of Adult Education', *The Leeds Weekly Citizen*, 21 September.

45. Anne Chapman, telephone interview, 19 July 2009.

46. Paul Lazarsfeld and Wagner Thielens, with David Riesman (1958) *The Academic Mind: Social Scientists in a Time of Crisis*, The Free Press of Glencoe, p. 95.

47. KP-49-3, Karl Polanyi (1954) to Finley, 28 May. Finley turned down the invitation.

48. Anne Chapman (n.d.) 'Karl Polanyi (1886–1964) for the Student', www.thereed foundation.org/rism/chapman/polanyi2.htm

49. Polanyi, in Chapman, 'Karl Polanyi'.

50. Rhoda Halperin (1984) 'Polanyi, Marx, and the Institutional Paradigm in Economic Anthropology', *Research in Economic Anthropology*, 6, pp. 247, 268.

51. Halperin, 'Polanyi, Marx', pp. 256–58; Halperin, Rhoda (1988) *Economies across Cultures: Towards a Comparative Science of the Economy*, Macmillan, p. 41.

52. There was no consensus term. In the early twentieth century, for example, Schmoller proffered this rather inelegant substitute for 'capitalism': 'die modernen geldwirtschaftlichen, unter dem liberalen System der Gewerbefreiheit, der freien Konkurrenz und des unbeschränkten Erwerbtriebes ausgebildeten Betriebsformen.' Gustav Schmoller (1998 [1902]) 'Historisch-Ethische NationalÖkonomie als

Kulturwissenschaft. Ausgewaehlte methodologische Schriften', in Heino Nau, ed., Metropolis, p. 211.

53. John Kenneth Galbraith (2004) *The Economics of Innocent Fraud*, Houghton Mifflin, pp. 6–8.

54. Saunders, *Who Paid?*, pp. 139, 144.

55. 'Karl tried to persuade me not to "come out" as a Marxist – I would be more influential if I chose that path. He didn't say I should *abandon* Marxist ideas, just disguise them.' Interview with István Mészáros, 12 December 2010.

56. Wallerstein was at the time an officer of the World Assembly of Youth, an organisation set up by Labour Party leaders in Britain's Foreign Office and largely funded by the CIA, but his political direction was veering leftward. Immanuel Wallerstein (2000) *The Essential Wallerstein*, The New Press, p. xvi; Howard Brick (2015) 'Peasant Studies Meets the World System: Eric Wolf, Immanuel Wallerstein, and Visions of Global Capitalism', in Howard Brick, Robbie Lieberman and Paula Rabinowitz, eds, *Lineages of the Literary Left: Essays in Honor of Alan M. Wald*, Maize Books.

57. Marie Jahoda (1997) *'Ich habe die Welt nicht verändert': Lebenserinnerungen einer Pionierin der Sozialforschung*, Campus; R. M. Cooper, ed. (1992) *Refugee Scholars: Conversations with Tess Simpson*, Moorland Books, p. 78.

58. Marie Jahoda and Stuart Cook (1952) 'Security Measures and Freedom of Thought: An Exploratory Study of the Impact of the Loyalty and Security Program', *Yale Law Journal* 61(3), pp. 295–333. Jahoda followed this up with a study of the effects of blacklisting upon employees in radio and television: Marie Jahoda (1956) 'Anti-Communism and Employment Policies in Radio and Television', in J. Cogley, *Report on Blacklisting II, Radio-Television*, The Fund for the Republic.

59. Lazarsfeld and Thielens, *Academic Mind*, pp. 35–230, and an anonymous academic quoted in Price, *Threatening Anthropology*, p. 33.

60. Marian Morton (1972) *The Terrors of Ideological Politics: Liberal Historians in a Conservative Mood*, The Press of Case Western University, p. 109. See also Carl Landauer (2000) 'Deliberating Speed: Totalitarian Anxieties and Postwar Legal Thought', *Yale Journal of Law & the Humanities*, 12(2), pp. 171–248.

61. Certainly, Hofstadter expressed a wish to attend, and was invited. KPA-49-1, Polanyi to Burns, Karl Polanyi (1955) to Arthur R. Burns, 9 September; KPA-49-2, Karl Polanyi, Notes on those to be invited to the University Seminar.

62. Richard Hofstadter (1964 [1955]) 'The Pseudo-Conservative Revolt', in Daniel Bell, ed., *The Radical Right: The New American Right*, Doubleday.

63. Schrecker, *Many Crimes*, p. 410. Bell, however, would not sign up to a general condemnation of McCarthy. Saunders, *Who Paid?*, p. 199.

64. KPA-37-3, Karl Polanyi (1957) 'Freedom in a Complex Society'; KPA-36-9, Karl Polanyi (1955) 'Freedom and Technology'.

65. Hofstadter, 'Pseudo-Conservative', p. 69.

66. David Riesman and Nathan Glazer (1964 [1955]) 'The Intellectuals and the Discontented Classes', in Daniel Bell, ed., *The Radical Right: The New American Right*, Doubleday.

67. Talcott Parsons (1964 [1955]) 'Social Strains in America', in Daniel Bell, ed., *The Radical Right: The New American Right*, Doubleday. Emphasis added.

68. '... and not, as Marxists would hold' – adds Parsons, obtusely – 'in the structure of the economy.' Parsons viewed Marxism as its German academic critics had: as a wooden, evolutionary, materialistic determinism. Cf. Alvin Gouldner (1973) *For Sociology: Renewal and Critique in Sociology Today*, Pelican, p. 164.

69. Parsons, 'Social Strains'.

70. Parsons, 'Social Strains'.
71. Michael Rogin (1967) *The Intellectuals and McCarthy: The Radical Spectre*, MIT Press, pp. 29–31.
72. KPA-50-2, Terry Hopkins (1958) to Karl Polanyi, n.d.
73. Corey Robin (2004) *Fear: The History of a Political Idea*, Oxford University Press; Jacques Rancière (2006) *Hatred of Democracy*, Verso, p. 20.
74. Paul Buhle (1987) *Marxism in the USA: From 1870 to the Present Day*, Verso, p. 213; Neil McLaughlin (2001) 'Critical Theory Meets America: Riesman, Fromm, and *The Lonely Crowd*', *The American Sociologist*, Spring.
75. Jefferson Pooley (2006) 'An Accident of Memory. Edward Shils, Paul Lazarsfeld and the History of American Mass Communication Research', DPhil, Columbia University, p. 25.
76. Daniel Bell (1956) 'The Theory of Mass Society: A Critique', *Commentary* 22, July, p. 79.
77. David Brown (2006) Richard Hofstadter: An Intellectual Biography, University of Chicago Press, p. 73. On Truman's dread of collective action, see Ira Katznelson (2003) *Desolation and Enlightenment: Political Knowledge after Total War, Totalitarianism and the Holocaust*, Columbia University Press, p. 174.
78. Price, *Threatening Anthropology*, pp. 2, 21–22. On Bingham's dishonourable antics in the earlier phase of his career, see Neil Smith (2003) *American Empire: Roosevelt's Geographer and the Prelude to Globalization*, University of California Press.
79. David Caute (1978) *The Great Fear: The Anti-Communist Purge Under Truman and Eisenhower*, Simon & Schuster, p. 239.
80. Price, *Threatening Anthropology*.
81. Athan Theoharis (n.d.) 'The Politics of Scholarship: Liberals, Anti-Communism, and McCarthyism', www.writing.upenn.edu/~afilreis/50s/theoharis.html
82. Rogin, *Intellectuals and McCarthy*, p. 10.
83. Mills, quoted in Javier Trevino (2012) *The Social Thought of C. Wright Mills*, Sage, p. 22.
84. William Kornhauser (1960) *The Politics of Mass Society*, Routledge.
85. Christian Borch (2012) *The Politics of Crowds: An Alternative History of Sociology*, Cambridge University Press, p. 224.
86. Pooley, 'Accident of Memory', p.160. In a letter to Shils, Michael Polanyi praises the book, commenting that he sees himself and Shils as belonging to 'a very small band' of 'fighters for freedom'. Quoted in Phil Mullins (n.d.) 'Moodey on Shils, Polanyi and Tradition', www.missouriwestern.edu/orgs/polanyi/.../TAD39-3-fnl-pg29-37-pdf
87. Talcott Parsons and Edward Shils, eds (1951) *Toward a General Theory of Action*, Harper & Row.
88. Pooley, 'Accident of Memory', p. 29.
89. Martin Jay (1985) *Permanent Exiles: Essays on the Intellectual Migration from Germany to America*, Columbia University Press, p. 51.
90. Jahoda, *Lebenserinnerungen*, p. 125.
91. Hofstadter, quoted in Frederick Lynch (1977) 'Social Theory and the Progressive Era', *Theory and Society*, 4, p. 166.
92. Jens Nielsen (1991) 'The Political Orientation of Talcott Parsons: The Second World War and Its Aftermath', in Roland Robertson and Bryan Turner, eds, *Talcott Parsons: Theorist of Modernity*, Sage.
93. Karl Polanyi (1963) 'Lecture at Kulturális Kapcsolatok Intézete'.
94. KPA-49-4, Karl Polanyi (1955) to Hopkins, 15 March.
95. KPA-30-6, Karl Polanyi (1963) 'Hazánk Kötelessége', *Kortárs*.

96. Nielsen, 'Political Orientation'.

97. Jamie Peck (2010) *Constructions of Neoliberal Reason*, Oxford University Press, p. 95.

CHAPTER 8

1. KPA-51-1, Karl Polanyi (1959) Letter to György Heltai, 19 December. This chapter is based upon Gareth Dale (2013) 'Marketless Trading in Hammurabi's Time: A Reappraisal', *Journal of the Economic and Social History of the Orient*, 56(2), pp. 159–88.

2. KPA-42-14, Karl Polanyi (n.d.) 'Market Elements and Economic Planning in Antiquity'.

3. KPA-42-14, Polanyi, 'Market Elements'.

4. Karl Polanyi (1957) 'Marketless Trading in Hammurabi's Time', in Karl Polanyi et al., eds, *Trade and Market in the Early Empires*, The Free Press, pp. 16, 25. Emphasis added.

5. MPP-17-11, Karl Polanyi (1958) to Misi, May.

6. Leo Oppenheim (1957) 'A Bird's-Eye View of Mesopotamian Economic History', in Polanyi et al., eds, *Trade and Market in the Early Empires*. See also Leo Oppenheim (1967) 'A New Look at the Structure of Mesopotamian Society', *Journal of the Economic and Social History of the Orient*, 10(1), pp. 1–16.

7. KPA-49-1, Karl Polanyi (1953) to 'Bill', 4 March.

8. Karl Polanyi (1955) to Merton, 14 June. I am grateful to Dan Tomkins for passing me a copy of this letter.

9. KPA-52-3, Karl Polanyi (n.d.) to Walter.

10. KPA-50-1, Norman Franklin (1957) to Polanyi, 8 March.

11. Klaas Veenhof (1972) *Aspects of Old Assyrian Trade and its Terminology*, Brill, p. 356.

12. John Gledhill and Mogens Larsen (1982) 'The Polanyi Paradigm and a Dynamic Analysis of Archaic States', in Colin Renfrew et al., eds, *Theory and Explanation in Archaeology*, Academic Press, p. 205.

13. Mogens Larsen (1982) 'Caravans and Trade in Ancient Mesopotamia and Asia Minor', *Society for Mesopotamian Studies Bulletin* 4, pp. 42, 893ff.

14. Mario Liverani (2005) 'The Near East. The Bronze Age', in J. G. Manning and Ian Morris, eds, *The Ancient Economy: Evidence and Models*, Stanford University Press, p. 53.

15. Carlo Zaccagnini (1977) 'The Merchant at Nuzi', in J. D. Hawkins, ed., *Trade in the Ancient Near East: Papers Presented to the XXIII Rencontre Assyriologique Internationale*, British School of Archaeology in Iraq.

16. Robert Englund (1990) *Organisation und Verwaltung der Ur III-Fischerei*, Dietrich Reimer, pp. 16–17.

17. Michael Jursa (2010) *Aspects of the Economic History of Babylonia in the First Millennium BC: Economic Geography, Economic Mentalities, Agriculture, the Use of Money and the Problem of Economic Growth*, Ugarit-Verlag, p. 580.

18. Karen Radner (1999) 'Traders in the Neo-Assyrian Period', in Jan Gerritt Dercksen, ed., *Trade and Finance in Ancient Mesopotamia*, Leiden, pp. 101–03.

19. Marvin Powell (1999) 'Wir müssen unsere Nische nutzen: Monies, Motives, and Methods in Babylonian Economics', in Jan Gerritt Dercksen, ed., *Trade and Finance in Ancient Mesopotamia*, Leiden, p. 5. See also Charpin et al., (2004) *Mesopotamien: Die altbabylonische Zeit*, pp. 900–09; A. C. V. M. Bongenaar (1999) 'Money in the Neo-Babylonian Institutions', in Jan Gerritt Dercksen, ed., *Trade and Finance in Ancient Mesopotamia*, Leiden, p. 162; Veenhof, *Aspects*, p. 350.

20. Ianir Milevski (2011) *Early Bronze Age Goods Exchange in the Southern Levant: A Marxist Perspective*, Equinox.

21. G. van Driel (2002) *Elusive Silver: In Search of a Role for a Market in an Agrarian Environment*, Nederlands Instituut voor het Nabije Osten, p. 328; Raymond Goldsmith (1987) *Premodern Financial Systems: A Historical Comparative Study*, Cambridge University Press, pp. 10, 13, 145.

22. Leo Oppenheim (1977) *Ancient Mesopotamia: Portrait of a Dead Civilization*, revised edn, University of Chicago Press.

23. Mitchell S. Rothman (2000) 'The Commoditization of Goods and the Rise of the State in Ancient Mesopotamia', in Angelique Haugerud, et al., eds, *Commodities and Globalization: Anthropological Perspectives*, Rowman and Littlefield, p. 174.

24. Oppenheim, *Ancient*, p. 87; Jursa, *Aspects*, pp. 500, 564, 570, 668, 777–79, 787, 810.

25. Bongenaar, 'Neo-Babylonian Institutions', p. 174; See also Mark Peacock (2013) *Introducing Money*, Routledge.

26. Jursa, *Aspects*, pp. 791–98.

27. Morris Silver (1983) 'Karl Polanyi and Markets in the Ancient Near East: The Challenge of the Evidence', *Journal of Economic History*, XLIII(4), p. 795.

28. Warburton distinguishes between markets, which 'appear to be the only known means of distribution documented in human history', and market forces, which do not make their historical entrance until circa 1900 BC. David Warburton (2003) *Macroeconomics from the Beginning: The General Theory, Ancient Markets and the Rate of Interest*, Recherches et Publications, pp. 294, 355.

29. Warburton, *Macroeconomics*, p. 184

30. Warburton, *Macroeconomics*, p. 177.

31. Michael Hudson (2005) Review of Warburton, *Macroeconomics from the Beginning*, *Journal of the Economic and Social History of the Orient*, 48, p. 120.

32. Warburton, *Macroeconomics*, p. 181.

33. Warburton, *Macroeconomics*, p. 133.

34. Johannes Renger (1994) 'On Economic Structures in Ancient Mesopotamia', *Orientalia*, 63, pp. 157–208.

35. Jursa, *Aspects*, pp. 27, 32, 791, 798.

36. Michael Hudson (2012) 'Entrepreneurs: From the Near Eastern Take-off to the Roman Collapse', in David Landes, Joel Mokyr and William Baumol, eds, *The Invention of Enterprise: Entrepreneurship from Ancient Mesopotamia to Modern Times*, Princeton University Press, p. 9.

37. KPA-42-14, Polanyi, 'Market Elements'.

38. Michael Hudson (2000) 'Karl Bücher's Role in the Evolution of Economic Anthropology', in Jürgen Backhaus, ed., *Karl Bücher: Theory–History–Anthropology–Non-Market Economies*, Metropolis, p. 320. Of course, the modern distinction of public and private cannot be straightforwardly transferred to ancient Mesopotamia, where the public sector was in an important sense antithetical to a third category, the 'communal'. See Jan Gerritt Dercksen (2004) *Old Assyrian Institutions*, Nederlands Instituut voor het Nabije Osten, and Peacock, *Introducing*.

39. Karl Polanyi (1977) *The Livelihood of Man*, Academic Press, pp. 47, 127.

40. Hudson, 'Karl Bücher's'.

41. Leo Oppenheim (1964) *Ancient Mesopotamia: Portrait of a Dead Civilization*, pp. 85–86.

42. Robert Lowie (1937) *The History of Ethnological Theory*, Farrar & Rinehart, p. 142.

43. Ruth Benedict (1973 [1934]) *Patterns of Culture*, Houghton Mifflin Harcourt, pp. 46–49.

44. Conrad Arensberg (1954) 'The Community-Study Method', *American Journal of Sociology*, 60(2), p. 111; Alexander Moore (1998) *Cultural Anthropology: The Field Study of Human Beings,* Rowman & Littlefield.

45. Anne Chapman, telephone interview, 19 July 2009; Leah Gordon (2015) *From Power to Prejudice: The Rise of Racial Individualism in Midcentury America*, University of Chicago Press, p. 47.

46. Chris Hann (1992) 'Radical Functionalism: The Life and Work of Karl Polanyi', *Dialectical Anthropology*, 17(2), pp. 148–50. See also Marvin Harris (2001 [1968]) *The Rise of Anthropological Theory: A History of Theories of Culture*, Rowman Altamira, p. 558, and Chris Hann (2008) 'Towards a Rooted Anthropology: Malinowski, Gellner, and Herderian Cosmopolitanism', in Pnina Werbner, ed., *Anthropology and the New Cosmopolitanism: Rooted, Feminist and Vernacular Perspectives*, Berg.

47. Donald Donham (1999) *History, Power, Ideology: Central Issues in Marxism and Anthropology*, University of California Press, p. 13.

48. Polanyi, *Livelihood*, pp. 61, 65, 73, 115.

49. Frans van Koppen (2007) 'Aspects of Society and Economy in the Later Old Babylonian Period', in Gwendolyn Leick, ed., *The Babylonian World*, Routledge, p. 219.

50. Michael Mann (1986) *The Sources of Social Power*, Vol. 1, Cambridge University Press, p. 126.

51. Anne Goddeeris (2007) 'The Old Babylonian Economy', in Gwendolyn Leick, ed., *The Babylonian World*, Routledge, p. 198.

52. Driel, *Elusive Silver*, p. 260; Jursa, *Aspects*, p. 660.

53. Gebhard Selz (2007) 'Power, Economy and Social Organisation in Babylonia', in Gwendolyn Leick, ed., *The Babylonian World*, Routledge, p. 282.

54. Richard Seaford (2004) *Money and the Early Greek Mind: Homer, Philosophy, Tragedy*, Cambridge University Press, p. 74.

55. Henrika Kuklick (2009) 'Functionalism', in Alan Barnard and Jonathan Spencer, eds, *The Routledge Encyclopedia of Social and Cultural Anthropology*, Second edn, Routledge; Robert McCormick Adams (1991) 'Contexts of Civilizational Collapse: A Mesopotamian View', in Norman Yoffee and George Cowgill, eds, *The Collapse of Ancient Civilizations,* University of Arizona Press, p. 23.

56. Blair Gibson and M. N. Geselowitz identify compatibilities among the ideas of Steward and Polanyi. If so, they are surely not pronounced. To my knowledge they did not display any significant interest in one another's work. Blair Gibson and M. N. Geselowitz (2013) *Tribe and Polity in Late Prehistoric Europe: Demography, Production, and Exchange in the Evolution of Complex Social Systems*, Springer. For a critique of Steward, see Marc Pinkoski (2008) 'American Colonialism at the Dawn of the Cold War', in Dustin Wax, ed., *Anthropology at the Dawn of the Cold War*, Pluto.

57. Anne Chapman, telephone interview, 19 July 2009.

58. Sidney Mintz (1958) Review of *Trade and Market in the Early Empires*, *American Anthropologist*, 60(3), pp. 583–86.

59. Brick, 'Peasant Studies'.

60. Certainly the degree of separation was small: Fried's first PhD student was Sahlins, a Polanyi mentee.

61. According to Harris, the link between redistribution and social stratification was first suggested by Sahlins. Marvin Harris (2011 [1977]) *Cannibals and Kings: The Origins of Cultures*, Knopf Doubleday, p. 299.

62. Morton Fried (1967) *The Evolution of Political Society: An Essay in Political Anthropology*, McGraw-Hill, pp. 116–17.

63. Marvin Harris (1975) *Culture, People, Nature: An Introduction to General Anthropology*, Second edition, Thomas Crowell, p. 289.

64. Harris, *Cannibals and Kings*, pp.71, 81, 164.

65. Steward selected a group of graduate students 'who shared a background of "progressive politics and socialist beliefs" and who found his "matter-of-fact materialism" and tolerant liberalism a congenial framework in which to pursue their own more radical agenda for "stretching anthropological paradigms"'. George Stocking (2006) 'Unfinished Business: Robert Gelston Armstrong, the Federal Bureau of Investigation, and the History of Anthropology at Chicago and in Nigeria', in Richard Handler, ed., *Central Sites, Peripheral Visions: Cultural and Institutional Crossings in the History of Anthropology*, University of Wisconsin Press, p. 119.

66. Howard Brick (2012) 'Neo-Evolutionist Anthropology, the Cold War, and the Beginnings of the World Turn in US Scholarship', in Mark Solovey and Hamilton Cravens, eds, *Cold War Social Science: Knowledge Production, Liberal Democracy, and Human Nature*, Palgrave Macmillan, p. 162; Herbert Lewis (2013) 'Columbia University', in Jon McGee and Richard Warms, eds, *Theory in Social and Cultural Anthropology: An Encyclopedia*, Sage, p. 126.

67. Brick, 'Peasant Studies'.

68. Of these, Leacock appears to have been the least aware of Polanyi's work. But her father, the literary critic Kenneth Burke, may have known him personally: they both taught at Bennington College. Burke arrived in 1943, just as Polanyi was leaving.

69. Sarah Hill (2015) 'The Sweet Life of Sidney Mintz', *The Boston Review,* 31 December.

70. Kristin Alten (1998) 'Eleanor Burke Leacock', www.indiana.edu/~wanthro/theory_pages/Leacock.htm

71. Brick, 'Neo-Evolutionist', p. 166.

72. Steward, quoted in Jerry Gershenhorn (2004) *Melville J. Herskovits and the Racial Politics of Knowledge*, University of Nebraska Press, p. 211; Sahlins, quoted in Brick, 'Neo-Evolutionist', p. 160.

73. Brick, 'Neo-Evolutionist', pp. 157–58.

74. Nancy Fraser (2014) 'Behind Marx's "Hidden Abode": For an Expanded Conception of Capitalism', *New Left Review,* 86, March-April.

75. In Rob Knowles and John Owen (2008) 'Karl Polanyi for Historians: An Alternative Economic Narrative', *The European Legacy*, 13(2), p. 181.

76. Christopher Chase-Dunn (1991) *Global Formation: Structures of the World-economy*, Rowman & Littlefield.

CHAPTER 9

1. The lead author of this co-authored chapter is Matthijs Krul.

2. Kari Polanyi Levitt, interview, Montreal, 13 December 2008.

3. Jeremy McInerney (2001) 'Ethnic Identity and *Altertumswissenschaft*', in David Tandy, ed., *Prehistory and History: Ethnicity, Class and Political Economy*, Black Rose.

4. Gareth Dale (2009) 'Karl Polanyi in Budapest: On His Political and Intellectual Formation', *Archives Européennes de Sociologie*, 50(1), pp. 97–130.

5. KPA-22-3, Karl Polanyi (1947–1957) 'Plan and Market in Early Society'.

6. KPA-39-1, Karl Polanyi (1954) 'Greece'; Karl Polanyi (1977) *The Livelihood of Man*, Academic Press, p. 274.

7. KPA-35-11, Karl Polanyi (1950-55) 'Draft Manuscript, *Livelihood of Man*'.

8. KPA-39-4, Karl Polanyi, 'Draft Manuscript: The Solonic Crisis and the City Economy'.

9. [Arist.] *Athenian Constitution* (c. 325 BC), IV.

10. [Arist.] *Athenian constitution*, XII, 4; Solon Fr. 36.

11. KPA-39-4, Polanyi, 'Solonic Crisis'.

12. KPA-39-6, Karl Polanyi (1954) 'Tyrannis and Democracy'.

13. KPA-40-2, Karl Polanyi (1954) 'The Economy of the Classical Polis', p. 3.

14. KPA-39-6, Polanyi, 'Tyrannis and Democracy'.

15. KPA-11-7, Karl Polanyi (1934–46) Notes on readings. On egalitarian tendencies of sixth century Greece, see Ian Morris (1996) 'The Strong Principle of Equality and the Archaic Origins of Greek Democracy', in Josiah Ober and Charles Hedrick, eds, *Dēmokratia; A Conversation on Democracies Ancient and Modern*, Princeton University Press.

16. KPA-39-4, Polanyi, 'Solonic Crisis'.

17. KPA-40-2, Polanyi, 'Classical Polis'.

18. Similar points can be made with regard to the archaic period, which we do not discuss here. Polanyi's discussion of archaic gift exchange emphasises its creation of social solidarity through the symbol-invested circulation of goods. Other historians demur, pointing out that 'gifts' are essentially what lords extort from their subordinates, for exchange with other lords. Compare, for example, Peter Rose (2012) *Class in Archaic Greece*, Cambridge University Press, pp. 71–72, and Polanyi, *Livelihood*, pp. 60, 110–12.

19. David Graeber (2011) *Debt: The First 5,000 years*, Melville House, p. 229.

20. Rose, *Archaic Greece*, p. 40.

21. Leslie Kurke (1999) *Coin, Bodies, Games, and Gold: The Politics of Meaning in Archaic Greece*, Princeton University Press, p. 306.

22. Sitta von Reden (2010) *Money in Classical Antiquity. Key Themes in Ancient History*, Cambridge University Press, Chapter 3.

23. Michael Doyle (1986) *Empires*, Cornell University Press.

24. KPA-40-2, Polanyi, 'Classical Polis', p. 22.

25. For a recent example, see George Bitros and Anastassios Karayiannis (2010) 'Morality, Institutions and the Wealth of Nations: Some Lessons from Ancient Greece', *European Journal of Political Economy*, 26(1), pp. 68–81.

26. On this controversy, see André Reibig (2001) 'The Bücher-Meyer Controversy: The Nature of the Ancient Economy in Modern Ideology', University of Glasgow doctoral thesis: theses.gla.ac.uk/4321/

27. Sally Humphreys (1969) 'History, Economics, and Anthropology: The Work of Karl Polanyi', *History and Theory* 8(2), p. 181.

28. Polanyi, *Livelihood*, p. 146.

29. KPA-22-10, Karl Polanyi (n.d.) 'The Role of Market Methods in the Western World up to the High Middle Ages'.

30. On Douglass North's theory, discussed below, Roman imperial institutions should have been conducive to growth, given 'the large potential market of the empire, the long periods of peace across much of the empire, the relatively low average taxes, and the legal system protecting property rights. And yet, the area of the empire in which these characteristics were most strongly felt, tribute-exempt Italy, did not lead the empire in sustained growth'. Dominic Rathbone (2000) 'Ptolemaic to Roman Egypt: The Death of the *Dirigiste* State?', in Elio Lo Cascio and Dominic Rathbone, eds, *Production and Public Powers in Classical Antiquity*, Cambridge Philological Society, p. 50; Richard Saller (2005) 'Framing the Debate over Growth in the Ancient Economy', in J. G. Manning and Ian Morris, eds, *The Ancient Economy: Evidence and Models*, Stanford University Press, p. 236.

31. KPA-23-3, Karl Polanyi, 'Capitalism in Antiquity'; Polanyi, *Livelihood*, pp. 145, 273.

32. J. G. Manning (2010) *Egypt Under the Ptolemies, 305–30 BC*, Princeton University Press.

33. Karl Polanyi (1963) 'Ports of Trade in Early Societies', *The Journal of Economic History* 23(1), pp. 30–45.

34. James Carrier, ed. (1997) *Meanings of the Market: The Free Market in Western Culture*, Berg, p. 26.

35. Gareth Dale (2010) *Karl Polanyi: The Limits of the Market*, Polity.

36. Chris Hann (1992) 'Radical Functionalism: The Life and Work of Karl Polanyi', *Dialectical Anthropology* 17(2), pp. 141–66.

37. KPA-40-2, Polanyi, 'Classical Polis'.

38. Jerôme Maucourant (2002) 'Polanyi on Institutions and Money: An Interpretation Suggested by a Reading of Commons, Mitchell and Veblen', in Fikret Adaman and Pat Devine, eds, *Economy and Society: Money, Capitalism and Transition*, Black Rose.

39. Karl Polanyi (1968) *Primitive, Archaic, and Modern Economies*, Beacon Press, p. 65.

40. Karl Polanyi (1957) 'The Economy as Instituted Process', in Karl Polanyi et al., eds, *Trade and Market in the Early Empires: Economies in History and Theory*, The Free Press, pp. 249–50.

41. Polanyi, *Livelihood*, p. 6.

42. Polanyi, 'Economy as Instituted', pp. 251, 255; Jerôme Maucourant and Sébastien Plociniczak (2013) 'The Institution, the Economy and the Market: Karl Polanyi's Institutional Thoughts for Economists', *Review of Political Economy* 25(3), pp. 525–26.

43. KPA-40-2, Polanyi, 'Classical Polis', p. 5.

44. Polanyi, *Livelihood*, p. 187.

45. Polanyi, *Primitive, Archaic*, p. 311.

46. KPA-22-10, Polanyi, 'Market Methods'.

47. Polanyi, *Livelihood*, pp.187, 198, 229–30; KPA-41-1, Karl Polanyi (1954) 'Local Markets and Overseas Trade'.

48. Robin Osborne (1991) 'Price and Prejudice, Sense and Subsistence: Exchange and Society in the Greek City', in John Rich and Andrew Wallace-Hadrill, eds, *City and Country in the Ancient World*, Routledge, pp. 119–45.

49. Dominic Rathbone and Sitta von Reden (2015) 'Mediterranean Grain Prices in Classical Antiquity', in R. J. Van der Spek, Jan Luiten van Zanden and Bas van Leeuwen, eds, *A History of Market Performance: From Ancient Babylonia to the Modern World*, Routledge, p. 156.

50. Van der Spek et al., *A History of Market Performance*; Karl Gunnar Persson (1999) *Grain Markets in Europe: Integration and Deregulation*, Cambridge University Press; David Jacks (2005) 'Intra- and International Commodity Market Integration in the Atlantic Economy, 1800–1913', *Explorations in Economic History* 42, pp. 381–413; Paul Erdkamp (2005) *The Grain Market in the Roman Empire*, Cambridge University Press.

51. Gary Reger (2007) 'Hellenistic Greece and Western Asia Minor', in Walter Scheidel, Ian Morris and Richard Saller, eds, *The Cambridge Economic History of the Greco-Roman World*, Cambridge University Press, p. 469.

52. Rathbone and Von Reden, 'Mediterranean Grain', pp. 169–70.

53. Reger, 'Hellenistic Greece', p. 469.

54. Van der Spek, quoted in Reger, 'Hellenistic Greece', p. 469.

55. Gary Reger (2002) 'The Price Histories of Some Imported Goods on Independent Delos', in Walter Scheidel and Sitta von Reden, eds, *The Ancient Economy*, Routledge, p. 145.

56. Léopold Migeotte (2009) *The Economy of the Greek Cities: From the Archaic Period to the Early Roman Empire*, University of California Press, pp. 136, 176–77.

57. Erdkamp, *Grain Market*, p. 204. On this point, primitivists see eye to eye with at least one modernist historian, Rostovtzeff. In the Roman Empire, in his understanding, 'every inland city tried to become self-sufficient and to produce on the spot the goods needed by the population'. In Saller, 'Framing the Debate', p. 226.

58. See for example Peter Temin (2001) 'A Market Economy in the Early Roman Empire', MIT Economics Working Paper 01-08; Peter Temin (2006) 'The Economy of the Early Roman Empire', *Journal of Economic Perspectives*, 20(1), pp. 133–51.

59. Willem Jongman (2013) 'Why Modern Economics Applies, Even to the Distant Past', *TRAC Proceedings 2013*.

60. Dale, *Karl Polanyi*, pp. 111–12.

61. Albeit often as mediated by the work of Moses Finley. See Bertram Schefold (2011) 'The Applicability of Modern Economics to Forms of Capitalism in Antiquity: Some Theoretical Considerations and Textual Evidence', *The Journal of Economic Asymmetries* 8(1), pp. 131–63; Mohammad Nafissi (2005) *Ancient Athens and Modern Ideology: Value, Theory and Evidence in Historical Sciences*, University of London; Todd Lowry (1979) 'Recent Literature on Ancient Greek Economic Thought', *Journal of Economic Literature* 17(1), pp. 65–86; Paul Cartledge, P. C. Millett and S. C. Todd (1990) *Nomos: Essays in Athenian Law, Politics and Society*, Cambridge University Press.

62. Alain Bresson (2015) *The Making of the Ancient Greek Economy: Institutions, Markets, and Growth in the City-States*, Princeton University Press, p. 27; see also Josiah Ober (2015) *The Rise and Fall of Classical Greece*, Princeton University Press.

63. James Acheson, ed. (1994) *Anthropology and Institutional Economics*, University Press of America; Jean Ensminger, ed. (2002) *Theory in Economic Anthropology*, Alta Mira Press.

64. Douglass North (1990) *Institutions, Institutional Change and Economic Performance*, Cambridge University Press; Douglass North (2005) *Understanding the Process of Economic Change*, Princeton University Press.

65. For example, Saller, 'Framing the Debate'; Neville Morley (2007) *Trade in Classical Antiquity*. Cambridge University Press; Walter Scheidel (2009) 'In Search of Roman Economic Growth', *Journal of Roman Archaeology*, 22, pp. 46–70.

66. Anastassios Karayiannis and Aristides Hatzis (2012) 'Morality, Social Norms and the Rule of Law as Transaction Cost-Saving Devices: The Case of Ancient Athens', *European Journal of Law and Economics*, 33(3), pp. 1–23; George Bitros and Anastassios Karayiannis (2011) 'Character, Knowledge and Skills in Ancient Greek Paideia: Some Lessons for Today's Policy Makers,' *Journal of Economic Asymmetries*, 8(1), pp. 196, 209.

67. George Bitros and Anastassios Karayiannis (2006) 'Morality, Institutions and Economic Growth: Lessons from Ancient Greece', MPRA Paper No. 994, http://mpra.ub.uni-muenchen.de/994/ pp.72, 75, 79; Karayiannis and Hatzis, 'Morality, Social Norms', pp. 621–43.

68. Other institutionalists do not emphasise the modernity of ancient Athens to the same degree. North, Wallis and Weingast, for example, describe Classical Athens as a 'mature natural state' 'on the doorstep of the transition' to an open access order. Douglass North, John Wallis and Barry Weingast (2009) *Violence and Social Orders:*

A Conceptual Framework for Interpreting Recorded Human History, Cambridge University Press, p. 150.

69. A further relevant factor in this period was the 'west' pulling away from the 'rest'.

70. Philip Mirowski (2002) *Machine Dreams: Economics Becomes a Cyborg Science*, Cambridge University Press, p. 21.

71. Herbert Spencer (1969 [1884/92]) *The Man Versus the State*, Penguin, p. 134.

72. Spencer, *Man Versus State*, p. 299.

73. North, Wallis, and Weingast, *Violence*, p. 41. North was not Hayek's disciple, and whereas Hayek draws a sharp opposition between *cosmos* and *taxis,* North sees all institutional orders as in some sense 'engineered'. However, he admired Hayek, calling him 'the greatest economist of the twentieth century, and by a long way'. Douglass North (2009) 'Interview by Karen Ilse Horn', in Karen Horn, ed., *Roads to Wisdom: Conversations with Ten Nobel Laureates in Economics*, Edward Elgar.

74. North, Wallis and Weingast, *Violence,* p. 3. Emphasis added.

75. It is unclear how this term, human exchange, is defined.

76. North, *Understanding*, pp. 1–2, 6, 53–56, 60, 163; North, Wallis and Weingast, *Violence*, pp. 50, 145.

77. Daniel Ankarloo and Giulio Palermo (2004) 'Anti-Williamson: a Marxian Critique of New Institutional Economics', *Cambridge Journal of Economics*, 28, p. 419.

78. Francesco Boldizzoni (2011) *The Poverty of Clio: Resurrecting Economic History*, Princeton University Press, pp. 18, 22.

79. Ankarloo and Palermo, 'Anti-Williamson', p. 417.

80. Daniel Ankarloo (2006) 'New Institutional Economics and Economic History', Historical Materialism conference paper, University of London.

81. Maucourant and Plociniczak, 'The Institution', p. 526.

82. North, *Understanding*.

83. On how such recontextualisations might proceed, see Daniel Hausman (2012) *Preference, Value, Choice and Welfare*, Cambridge University Press; Benedetto Gui and Robert Sugden (2010) *Economics and Social Interaction*, Cambridge University Press; Michael Bacharach (2006) *Beyond Individual Choice: Teams and Frames in Game Theory*, Princeton University Press.

84. Dimitris Milonakis and Ben Fine (2007) 'Douglass North's Remaking of Economic History: A Critical Appraisal', *Review of Radical Political Economics*, 39(1), pp. 27–57.

Index

Mills, Charles Wright, 142, 157, 230n21
Mises, Ludwig von, 8, 102–4, 116, 124, 215n73
Mitchell, Wesley, 207n12
money, 9, 26–7, 52–3, 96, 101, 105, 121, 124,
    131, 161–5, 168–9, 179, 187–90, 229n43
Morris, William, 62, 103
Murrow, Edward, 144–5, 231n34
Mussolini, Benito, 100, 111

Nafissi, Mohammad, 81
narodism, *see* populism
nationalisation of finance and industry, 60, 82,
    100, 103; *see also* planning
nationalism, 36, 80, 87, 91, 113, 126–7, 131,
    139; in Austro-Hungarian Empire 13, 30,
    126; in Germany, 24; in Hungary, 126; in
    Russia, 82; in USA, 1, 129, 153; national
    economies, 23, 57–8, 69, 97–103, 123, 125,
    131, 137; nation-state system, 11, 57–8, 87,
    97–102, 112, 123–31, 136–8; *see also*
    regionalism
NATO, 1–2, 142
Neale, Walter, 162
Needham, Joseph, 109, 118, 142
neoclassical economics, 7–8, 12, 171, 186, 198,
    200
neoconservatism, 1
neoliberalism, *see* capitalism: neoliberal
Neumann, Franz, 111
New Deal, 81, 91, 99, 111, 113, 127, 140–1, 159
New Institutional Economics, 35, 178–201
Nietzsche, Friedrich, 30
North, Douglass, 12, 161, 185, 191–3, 196–9
nuclear weapons, 213n34

objectivism, 19
oikos economies, 167
Oppenheim, Leo, 162, 165, 169
Oppenheimer, Franz, 16, 21, 43, 48
Orwell, George, 143, 145, 231n38
Österreichische *Volkswirt*, 100, 105, 111
Owen, Robert, 27, 58, 120
Owenism, 22

pacifism, 19, 144, 146
Parsons, Talcott, 11, 31, 100, 149, 151–3, 157,
    159, 171, 232n68
patriotism, *see* nationalism
Pikler, Gyula, 15, 31, 126
planning, 4, 82, 86, 91, 99–102, 104–11, 113,
    117–18, 125, 128, 141, 146, 178, 182–3, 196,
    223n54; in Soviet Union, 81–2, 85–6, 90–1,
    106; *see also* liberty: 'planning for freedom'
Polanyi, Laura, 213n38
Polanyi, Michael, 16, 108–9, 115, 140, 157,
    224n78, 233n86; and Congress for Cultural

Freedom, 158; and economic theory, 106–9;
    relations with Karl Polanyi, 89–90, 106, 116
poor laws, 226n137
Popper, Karl, 108, 224n74
populism, 2–4, 41, 150, 152–3, 155–6, 158
ports of trade, 183
positivism, 10, 14–16, 19–21, 30, 42–3, 108,
    118, 171
progress, 5, 10, 14–16, 30–1, 38–9, 41, 54, 60,
    62–4, 66, 126, 170, 176, 194, 196; *see also*
    Enlightenment
protectionism, 4–9, 28, 50, 68, 74–5, 98, 101,
    104–6, 114, 117, 119–22, 125, 133, 136; *see
    also* countermovement
Proudhon, Pierre-Joseph, 4, 21
Ptolemaic Egypt, 93, 182–3, 187

Quakers, 62, 144

racism, 1, 113, 141, 155, 177, 226n140; *see also*
    antisemitism
Radical Bourgeois Party, 39; *see also* bourgeois
    radical movement
reality of society, 16
reciprocity, 112, 116, 161, 174, 181–2, 185, 194,
    200
Red Scare, 11, 139–60, 176, 231n35, 231n38
redistribution, 94, 112, 116, 161–9, 171–2,
    174–5, 179–85, 191, 200, 236n61
refugees, 1, 125, 154
regionalism, 11, 91, 125–6, 128–9, 131, 137–8
reification, 208n40
Renner, Karl, 62
revolution 20, 42–3, 53–4, 65–6, 92;
    revolutionary left, 23, 35–7, 39, 62, 67, 83–7,
    124; Industrial Revolution, 8, 30, 54, 60, 100,
    114, 127; American Revolution, 59, 87–8;
    Austrian Revolution, 67, 215n73; English
    Revolution, 87–8; French Revolution; 87–8,
    100; Russian Revolution, 64, 81, 87–90; *see
    also* Hungary: 1918 revolution
Ricardo, David, 19, 43, 45, 48, 96–7, 117
Riesman, David, 149, 151, 153–4
Robbins, Lionel, 102–3
Robinson, Joan, 101
romanticism, 8, 13–14, 16, 24, 30, 62, 157, 171,
    178, 207n25
Roosevelt, Franklin Delano, 70, 99, 139, 155–7
Rousseau, Jean-Jacques, 35–6, 54, 62, 78
Ruskin, John, 22
Russell, Bertrand, 16, 111, 115n93
Russia, 1, 11, 37, 39, 41, 64, 80–94, 99, 106, 127,
    144, 152

Sahlins, Marshall, 174–6, 236n60, 236n61
Samuelson, Paul, 159